Illustrated History of the Civil War.

FRANK LESLIE'S
ILLUSTRATED HISTORY
OF THE
CIVIL WAR

THE

MOST IMPORTANT EVENTS OF THE CONFLICT BETWEEN THE STATES

GRAPHICALLY PICTURED.

STIRRING BATTLE SCENES AND GRAND NAVAL ENGAGEMENTS,

DRAWN BY SPECIAL ARTISTS ON THE SPOT.

PORTRAITS OF PRINCIPAL PARTICIPANTS, MILITARY AND CIVIL; FAMOUS FORTS:
PATHETIC EPISODES, ETC., ETC.

THE WHOLE FORMING

AN AUTHENTIC PICTORIAL HISTORY OF THE WAR,

BY SUCH WELL-KNOWN ARTISTS AS

BECKER, CRANE, BEARD, SCHELL, LUMLEY, FORBES, NEVILL, DAVIS, SIMONS, OSBORN, WILCOX, WEAVER, BOSSE, NEWTON, RAWSON, RUSSELL, SARTORIOUS, CHAMBERLAIN,

AND OTHERS.

A CONCISE HISTORY OF THE CIVIL WAR, BEING OFFICIAL DATA SECURED FROM THE WAR RECORDS.

EDITED BY

LOUIS SHEPHEARD MOAT.

WITH AN INTRODUCTION BY

JOSEPH B. CARR,

MAJOR-GENERAL.

THE FAIRFAX PRESS

Copyright © MCCMLXCV
Library of Congress Catalog Card Number : 77-82093
All rights reserved.
This edition is published by The Fairfax Press
a division of Barre Publishing Company, Inc., distributed by Crown Publishers, Inc.

a   b   c   d   e   f   g   h

The Fairfax Press 1977

PREFACE.

AS the years roll by, and the reverberating echoes of the great Civil War that shook our country from one end to the other slowly die away in the distance, the pictures of the stirring scenes of '61 to '65, drawn in the very midst of the strife, become not only interesting and attractive to the eye, but highly important and valuable as real, authentic representations of the way in which the events actually took place that no word description could possibly give.

To preserve in convenient and permanent form these valuable illustrations and to present to the public a grand panorama of the leading events of the war is the purpose of this book. The brave soldiers who, clad in the "Blue" or the "Gray," participated in the fierce struggles that marked the four years of war, will find here familiar scenes, and will be taken back, through the medium of excellent pictures, to the days they will never forget; those who remained at home will be reminded, in looking over these pages, of the exciting eagerness with which the appearance of each number of Frank Leslie's publications, with their famous war pictures, was awaited, and how every piece of news and illustration from the seat of battle was anxiously scanned; while those who were not born or were too young to remember now those stirring times will find much interest and instruction in studying the views of battles that became famous and have taken a prominent place in the nation's history.

The pictures in this work have been reproduced from the original cuts made by Frank Leslie's corps of war artists. They were taken from his publications because of their assured authenticity. They were drawn and engraved directly from sketches made on the scene of battle by the most famous artists of the time, and can therefore be relied upon as absolutely accurate. They are really the most authentic war illustrations that have ever been published.

The short, concise history of the war which appears at the end of this volume is intended to give the reader, in as few words as possible, a complete and accurate account of the great conflict from beginning to end; describing, in entertaining language, the circumstances that led to the struggle, the important battles both on land and sea, the men who participated in them, and the causes that brought about the downfall of the Confederacy. This description, with the graphic illustrations, will, it is hoped, bring about a better knowledge and a more correct idea of the Civil War than any yet presented to the public.

Neither trouble nor expense has been spared to make FRANK LESLIE'S ILLUSTRATED HISTORY OF THE CIVIL WAR perfectly reliable in every way. Editors of experience have gone over the whole work carefully and verified every date, so as to prevent the possibility of error.

To the Brave Soldiers who Fought the Battles herein Pictured

and to the Society of the Sons of Veterans,

THIS BOOK IS DEDICATED.

INTRODUCTION.

A GENERATION has passed away since the last battle of the Civil War was fought, and since the victorious armies of the Union passed in review, on the 22d and 23d of May, 1865, before the President of the United States in the City of Washington.

Upward of one million of men were on the rolls of the army when the work of mustering out officers and men began on the 1st of June, 1865, and by the middle of November upward of 800,000 of this vast host had returned to the pursuits of peace.

Altogether the whole number of men who had answered to their country's call during the war was 2,656,000. Out of this number 300,000 had sealed their patriotism with their blood.

As long as this nation lasts the memory of these defenders of the Union will be one of its holiest treasures. "Your marches," said General Grant in his farewell address, "your sieges and battles, in distance, duration, resolution and brilliancy of results, dim the lustre of the world's past military achievements, and will be the patriot's precedents in defense of liberty and right in all time to come.

Many of those to whom these words were addressed have already passed away, but the new generation still remembers with pride some relative to whose stories of battle and of march it has often listened. But as these veterans become fewer the tales of their deeds become less vivid; and it is to impress on the new age and to fix on posterity the memory of these heroes that this work is designed.

Nothing recalls the past so forcibly as pictures of the scenes taken at the time and on the very spot. A picture, too, is impartial. It cannot represent the success of the victors without representing the heroism of their opponents. It does justice to all sides, like Decoration Day, which North and South alike keep holy, and strengthens the bonds of sympathy between all true citizens.

This work will be a supplement to every written history, portraying as it does the striking incidents of battle, and giving the likenesses of the leaders whose names were on every lip in the days of strife.

Here the veterans will find the past recalled, and here the young may gain inspiration to emulate their patriotism and devotion.

Joseph B. Carr,
Major General,

INDEX TO ILLUSTRATIONS.

INDEX TO HISTORY.

OFFICIAL STATISTICS.
THE CIVIL WAR OF 1861–65.

NUMBER OF MEN IN THE UNION ARMY FURNISHED BY EACH STATE AND TERRITORY, FROM APRIL 15TH, 1861, TO CLOSE OF WAR.

STATES AND TERRITORIES.	NUMBER OF MEN FURNISHED.	AGGREGATE REDUCED TO A THREE YEARS' STANDING.	STATES AND TERRITORIES.	NUMBER OF MEN FURNISHED.	AGGREGATE REDUCED TO A THREE YEARS' STANDING.
Alabama	2,556	1,611	New York	448,850	392,270
Arkansas	8,289	7,836	North Carolina	3,156	3,156
California	15,725	15,725	Ohio	313,180	240,514
Colorado	4,903	3,697	Oregon	1,810	1,773
Connecticut	55,864	50,633	Pennsylvania	337,936	265,517
Delaware	12,284	10,322	Rhode Island	23,236	17,866
Florida	1,290	1,290	South Carolina		
Georgia			Tennessee	31,092	26,394
Illinois	259,092	214,133	Texas	1,965	1,632
Indiana	196,363	153,576	Vermont	33,288	29,068
Iowa	76,242	68,630	Virginia		
Kansas	20,149	18,706	West Virginia	32,068	27,714
Kentucky	75,760	70,832	Wisconsin	91,327	79,260
Louisiana	5,224	4,654	Dakota	206	206
Maine	70,107	56,776	District of Columbia	16,534	1,506
Maryland	46,638	41,275	Indian Territory	3,530	3,530
Massachusetts	146,730	124,104	Montana		
Michigan	87,364	80,111	New Mexico	6,561	4,432
Minnesota	24,020	19,693	Utah		
Mississippi	545	545	Washington	964	964
Missouri	109,111	86,530	U. S. Army		
Nebraska	3,157	2,175	U. S. Volunteers		
Nevada	1,080	1,080	U. S. Colored Troops	93,441	91,789
New Hampshire	33,937	30,849			
New Jersey	76,814	57,908	Total	2,778,304	2,326,168

The number of casualties in the volunteer and regular armies of the United States during the War of 1861–65, according to a statement prepared by the Adjutant General's Office, was as follows: Killed in battle, 67,058; died of wounds, 43,012; died of disease, 199,720; other causes, such as accidents, murder, Confederate prisons, etc.. 40,154; total died, 349,944; total deserted, 199,105. Number of soldiers in the Confederate service who died of wounds or disease (partial statement), 133,821. Deserted (partial statement), 104,428. Number of United States troops captured during the war, 212,608; Confederate troops captured, 476,169. Number of United States troops paroled on the field, 16,431; Confederate troops paroled on the field, 248,599. Number of United States troops who died while prisoners, 30,156; Confederate troops who died while prisoners, 30,152.

PRINCIPAL BATTLES OF THE LATE CIVIL WAR.

DATES.	NAMES AND PLACES OF BATTLES.	COMMANDERS. FEDERAL.	CONFEDERATE.	KILLED, WOUNDED, PRISONERS. FEDERAL.	CONFEDERATE.	REMARKS.
1861.						
April 12	Bombardment Fort Sumter	Major Anderson	General Beauregard	...no one hurt.	...5 w.	
April 19	Riot at Baltimore	Sixth Regiment Mass. Vols.		...3 k. 7 w.	...7 k. and 8 w.	
June 10	Big Bethel, Va.	Brigadier General Pierce	Major General Magruder	...16 k. 34 w. 6 m.	...no report	
July 5	Carthage, Mo.	Colonel Sigel*	Generals Price and Jackson	...13 k. 31 w.	...250 k. and w.	
July 12	Rich Mountain, W. Va.	General McClellan*	Colonel Pegram	...11 k. 35 w.	...140 k. 150 w.	150 p., loss of camp.
July 21	Bull Run, Va.	General Irwin McDowell	General Beauregard*	...4,500 k. w. p. 28 c. / ...481 k. 1,011 w. 700 p.	...1,852 k. and w.	{Beauregard's report. / {Federal report.
Aug. 10	Wilson's Creek, Mo.	General Lyon*	Generals Price and McCulloch	...223 k. 721 w. 292 m.	...421 k. 1,317 w. 3 m.	General Lyon killed.
Sept. 12-14	Cheat Mountain, W. Va.	General J. J. Reynolds	General R. E. Lee	...13 k. 20 w. 60 p.	...100 k. and w. 20 p.	
Sept. 20	Lexington, Mo.	Colonel Mulligan	General Price*	...42 k. 108 w. 1,624 p.	...25 k. 75 w.	
Sept. 21	Ball's Bluff, Va	Colonel E. D. Baker*	General Evans*	...220 k. 266 w. 500 p.	...36 k. 264 w. 2 p.	Colonel Baker killed.
Nov. 7	Belmont, Mo.	General Grant*		...84 k. 288 w. 285 m.	...261 k. 427 w. 278 m.	
Nov. 7	Port Royal, S. C.	{Commodore Dupont & / Gen. T. W. Sherman*	General Drayton	...8 k. 23 w. 250 p.	{k. and w. no report, / {2,500 p. 42 guns cap}	
Nov. 8	Piketon, Ky.	General Nelson*		...6 k. 24. w.	...400 k. and w. 2,000 p.	{70 wagons with stores / and equipage.
Dec. 18	Milford, Mo.	{Colonel J. C. Davis and / General Steele*		...2 k. 17 w.	...1,300 p.	
1862.						
Jan. 19	Mill Spring, Ky.	General Thomas*	General Zollicoffer	...39 k. 207 w.	...192 k. 140 p.	General Zollicoffer kill'd.
Feb. 8	Roanoke Island, N. C.	{Com. Goldsborough and / General Burnside*	General Wise	...50 k. 150 w.	...30 k. 50 w. 2,500 p.	
Feb. 8	Fort Henry, Tenn.	Surrendered to Com. Foote.	General Tilghman			
Feb. 16	Fort Donelson, Tenn.	{Commodore Foote and / General Grant*	General Buckner	...446 k. 1,735 w. 150 p.	231 k. 1,007 w. 15,000 p.	{6 forts, 65 guns, 17,500 / small arms captured.
March 8	Pea Ridge, Ark.	General Curtis*	Generals Van Dorn and Price	...1,351 k. w. and m.	1,100 k. 2,500 w. 1,600 p.	Generals McCulloch, McIntosh and Slack killed.
March 14	New Berne, N. C.	General Burnside*	General Branch	...91 k. 466 w.	...50 k. 200 w. 200 p.	
March 23	Winchester, Va.	General Shields*	General T. J. Jackson	...100 k. 400 w.	...600 k. and w. 300 p.	
April 6-7	Pittsburg Landing, Tenn.	Generals Grant and Buell*	Generals Johnston & Beauregard	...1,614 k. 7721 w. / ...3,963 m.	1,728 k. 8,012 w. 959 m.	
April 10	Island No. 10	{Cominodore Foote and / General Pope*	General Mackall		...17 k. 6,300 p.	{6 forts captured. / {Confederate report.
May 5	Williamsburg, Va.	{Generals Kearny and / Hooker*	General Longstreet	...2,073 k. and w. 623 p.	...700 k. 1,000 w. 300 p.	
May 25	Winchester, Va	General Banks	Generals Ewell & Johnson*			Federals retreated, 2,000 prisoners captured.
May 29	Hanover Courthouse, Va.	General Morell*	General Branch	...53 k. 526 m.	...400 k. and w. 600 p.	
May 30	Corinth, Miss.	General Halleck*	General Beauregard			
May 31	Fair Oaks, Va.	General McClellan	General J. E. Johnston*	890 k. 3,627 w. 1,222 p.	...2,800 k. 3897 w.	Federals were driven back.
June 1	Fair Oaks, Va.	General McClellan*	General J. E. Johnston	...5,739 k. and w.	...8,000 k. and w.	
June 8	Cross Keys. Va.	General Fremont.	General T. J. Jackson*	...125 k. 500 w.	...600 k. and w.	
June 9	Port Republic, Va.	General Shields	General T. J. Jackson*	...67 k. 361 w. 574 w.	...1,000 k. w. and m.	
June 26	Chickahominy, Va.	General McClellan*	General R. E. Lee	...80 k. 150 w.	...1,000 k. and w.	
June 27	Gaines's Mill, Va.	General Porter	General R. E. Lee*	...7,500 k. w. and m.	...About the same.	
July 1	Malvern Hill, Va.	General McClellan*	General R. E. Lee	...1,000 k. w. and m.	...Nearly 5,000	
August 5	Baton Rouge, La.	General Williams*	General J. C. Breckinridge	...250 k. w. and m.	...600 k. w. and m.	General Williams killed.
August 9	Cedar Mountain, Va.	General N. P. Banks*	General Jackson	...1,500 k. w. and m.	...1,000 k. 1,500 w.	Confederates repulsed.
August 22	Gallatin, Tenn.	General Johnson	General Morgan*	...64 k. 100 w. 200 p.	...110 k. and w.	General Johnson cap'd.
August 27	Kettle Run, Va.	General Hooker	General Ewell	...800 k. w. and w.	...800 k. and w. 1,000 p.	
August 29	Groveton, Va.	{Generals Hooker, Sigel, / Kearny, Reno*	Generals Jackson & Longstreet	...6,000 k. and w.	...12,000 k. w. and m.	
August 30	Bull Run 2d	General Pope	General Lee*	800 k. 4,000 w. 3,000 p.	...700 k. 3 000 w.	
Aug. 29-30	Richmond, Ky.	Generals Manson & Cruft.	General Kirby Smith*	...200 k. 700 w. 2,000 p.	...250 k. 500 w.	
Sept. 1	Chantilly, Va.	General Pope	General Lee*	...1,300 k. and w.	...800 k. and w.	Kearny and Stevens kd.
Sept. 14	South Mountain, Md.	Generals Hooker and Reno*	General Lee	...443 k. 1,806 w. 76 m.	500 k. 2,343 w. 1,500 p.	General Reno killed.
Sept. 15	Harper's Ferry, 3 days' siege	Colonel Miles	General A. P. Hill*	...80 k. 120 w. 11,583 p.	...1,500 k. and w.	Colonel Miles killed.
Sept. 17	Antietam, Md.	General McClellan*	General R. E. Lee.	...12,500 loss.	...15,000 loss.	
Sept. 19-20	Iuka, Miss.	General Rosecrans*	General Price	...135 k. 527 w.	...263 k. 400 w. 600 p.	
Oct. 3-5	Corinth, Miss.	{Generals Ord, Hurlbut / and Veatch*	{Generals Price, Van Dorn / and Lovell	...315 k. 1,812 w. 232 m.	1,423 k. 2.268 p. 5,692 w.	
Oct. 8	Perryville, Ky.	General Buell*	General Bragg	...3,200 k. w. and m.	1,300 k. 3,000 w. 200 p.	
Dec. 7	Prairie Grove, Ark.	Generals Blunt & Herron.	{Generals Hindman, Marma- / duke, Parsons and Frost.	...495 k. 600 w.	...1,500 k. and w.	
Dec. 13	Fredericksburg, Va.	General Burnside	General R. E. Lee*	1,512 k. 6,000 w. 2,078 p.	...1,800 k. and w.	
Dec. 27-29	Vicksburg, Miss.	General Sherman	General Johnston*	...191 k. 982 w. 756 m.	...no report.	
1863.						
Jan. 2	Stone River, Tenn.	General Rosecrans*	General Bragg	...1,533 k. 6,000 w.	9,000 k. and w. 1,000 p.	
Jan. 11	Fort Hindman, Ark.	{Admiral Porter & General McClernand*	General Churchill	...1,000 k. w. and m.	...550 k. w. 5,000 p.	
Feb. 3	Fort Donelson, Tenn.	Colonel Harding*	Generals Wheeler and Forrest.	...12 k. 20 w.	...100 k. 400 w. 300 p.	Confederates repulsed.
May 1	Suffolk, Va.	Colonel Nixon*		...130 k. 718 w. 5 m.	...1,500 k. w. and m.	
May 1	La Grange, Ark.	Captain DeHuff.		...2,000 k. w. and m.		
May 2	Fredericksburg, Va.	General Sedgwick.	General Longstreet*	...2,000 k. and w.		

* Indicates the victorious party.

PRINCIPAL BATTLES OF THE LATE CIVIL WAR—(Continued).

DATES.	NAMES AND PLACES OF BATTLES.	COMMANDERS.		KILLED, WOUNDED, PRISONERS.		REMARKS.
		FEDERAL.	CONFEDERATE.	FEDERAL.	CONFEDERATE.	
May 2-3	Chancellorsville, Va	General Hooker*	General R. E. Lee	15,000 k. & w. 17,000 p.	18,000 k. and w. 5,000 p.	
May 12	Jackson, Miss	General Grant*	General Johnston	40 k. 240 w. 6 m.	400 k. and w.	
May 14	Champion Hills, Miss	General Grant*	General Pemberton	426 k. 1,842 w.	400 k. w. and m.	29 cannon captured.
May 16	Big Black River, Miss	General Grant*	General Pemberton	29 k. 242 w.	2,600 k. w. and m.	17 cannon captured.
May 18-22	Vicksburg, Miss	General Grant, Admirals Porter and Farragut.	General Pemberton*	2,500 loss.	no report	
May 27	Port Hudson	General Banks	General Gardner*	900 k. w. and m.	600 k. w. and m.	
June 6	Milliken's Bend, La	General Thomas*	General McCulloch	127 k. 287 w. 157 m.	200 k. 500 w.	
June 9	Beverly Ford, Va	Generals Buford and Gregg*	Generals J. E. B. Stuart and Fitz Hugh Lee	380 k. w. and m.	750 k. w. and m.	Cavalry fight
June 14	Winchester, Va	General Milroy	General Ewell*	2,000 k. w. and m.	850 k. w. and m.	
June 26	Shelbyville, Tenn	General Rosecrans*	General Bragg	85 k. 468 w. 13m.	1,634 p. no report k. & w.	
July 1-2-3	Gettysburg, Pa	General Meade*	General R. E. Lee	total loss 23,198	total loss 37,000	
July 4	Vicksburg surrenders	General Grant*	General Pemberton	245 k. 3,688 w. 303 p.	9,000 k. and w. 30,000 p.	
July 4	Helena, Ark	General Prentiss*	Generals Price, Holmes and Marmaduke	250 k. w. and m.	500 k. and w. 1,000 p.	
July 5	Bolton, Miss	General Grant*	General Joseph E. Johnston		4,000 p.	Rear guard Johnston's army.
July 8	Port Hudson surrenders	General Banks*	General Gardner		5,500 p.	
July 18-19	Fort Wagner, S. C	General Gillmore	General Beauregard*	700 k. w. and m.	500 k. 331 w.	
Sept. 9	Cumberland Gap	General Burnside*	General Frazier		2,000 p.	
Sept. 19-20	Chickamauga	General Rosecrans	General Bragg*	1,644 k. 9,262 w. 4,945m.	17,000 k. w. and m.	
Sept. 14	Bristow Station, Va	General Warren*	General A. P. Hill	51 k. 329 w.	1,200 k. and w. 800 p.	
Dec. 4	Knoxville, Tenn	General Burnside*	General Longstreet	600 k. and w.	1,600 p.	
Dec. 23-25	Chattanooga	General Grant*	General Bragg	4,000 k. and w.	16,000 k. w. and m.	
Dec. 25	Missionary Ridge	General Hooker*	General Bragg			
Dec. 27	Ringgold, Ga	General Hooker*	General Hardee	800 k. w. and m.	300 p.	
Dec. 27-30	Locust Grove, Va	General Meade*	General Lee	1,000 k. w. and m.	2,500 k. w. and p.	
1864.						
March 5	Paducah, Ky	Colonel Hicks*	General Forrest	14 k. 46 w.	1,000 k. and w.	
April 8-9	Mansfield, La	General Banks*	General Kirby Smith	500 k. and w. 1,500 p.	2,000 p.	
April 17-20	Plymouth, N. C	General Wessells	General Hoke*	150 k. 1,700 p.	1,500 k. and w.	
May 5-7	Wilderness, Va	General Grant	General Lee	loss 30,000	loss 30,000	Longstreet wounded.
May 5-7	Spottsylvania, Va	General Grant	General Lee	loss 10,000	loss 10,000	
May 12	Spottsylvania, Va	General Grant	General Lee		4,000 p.	2 Confederate generals, 30 guns captured.
May 12-15	Fort Darling, Va	General Butler*	General Beauregard	5,000 k. w. and m.	no report	
May 13-15	Resaca, Ga	General Sherman*	General Joseph E. Johnston	700 k. 2,800 w.	no report	
May 25-28	Dallas, Ga	General Sherman*	General Longstreet	1,800 k. and w.	300 p. 4,000 k. and w.	
June 1	Cold Harbor, Va	General Grant	General Lee*	9,000 k. w. and m.	8,000 k. w. and m.	
June 15-18	Petersburg, Va	General Grant	General Lee*	loss 10,000	no report	
June 22	Weldon R. R., Va	General Meade	General Lee*	600 k. and w. 1,250 p.	no report	
June 27	Kenesaw Mountain, Ga	General Sherman*	General Johnston	1,000 k. and w.	no report	Johnston flanked.
July 9	Monocacy, Md	General Wallace	General Early*	1,000 k. and w.	no report	
July 20	Peach Tree Creek, Ga	General Sherman*	General Hood	1,713 k. w. and m.	5,000 k. and w. 1,000 p.	
July 22	Atlanta, Ga	General Sherman*	General Hood	3,521 k. and w.	10,000 k. and w.	McPherson killed.
July 27-30	Petersburg, Va	General Grant	General Lee*	5,000 k. w. and m.	1,200 k. w. and m.	
Aug. 5-20	Mobile Bay, Ala	Admiral Farragut and General Granger*	General Page and Admiral Buchanan	120 k. 88 w.	no report k. and w. 1,756 p.	150 guns captured.
Aug. 15-18	Deep Bottom, Va	General Grant	General Lee*	loss 4,000	loss 2,500	
Aug. 19	Six Mile Station, Va	General Warren*	General Pickett	3,000 k. and w.	1,500 p.	
Aug. 25	Weldon R. R., Va	General Grant	General Lee*	1,000 k. and w. 3,000 p.	1,500 k. and w.	
Aug. 31	Atlanta, Ga	General Sherman*	General Hood	50 k. 50 m. 439 w.	5,000 k. and w.	Confederates repulsed.
Sept. 19	Bunker Hill, Va	General Sheridan*	General Early	3,000 k. and w.	500 k. 4,000 w. 2,500 p.	Rhodes & Gordon killed.
Sept. 21	Fisher's Hill	General Sheridan*	General Early	600 k. and w.	400 k. and w. 1,100 p	Federals captured 16 pieces artillery.
Sept. 26	Ironton, Mo	General Ewing*	General Price	9 k. 60 w.	1,500 k. and w.	
Sept. 29-30	Petersburg, Va	General Grant	General Lee*	5,000 k. and w.	2,800 k. and w.	
Oct. 19	Cedar Creek, Va	General Sheridan*	General Early	4,000 k. and w. 1,300 p.	2,800 k. and w. 1,300 p.	
Oct. 26	Nim's Creek, Mo	General Pleasonton*	General Price	2,000 p. 1,000 k. and w.	900 k. 3,800 p.	Generals Marmaduke & Cabell captured.
Oct. 27	Hatcher's Run, Va	General Grant	General Lee*	400 k. 1,500 w. 150 m.	1,600 k. w. and m.	
Nov. 30	Franklin, Tenn	General Schofield*	General Hood	189 k. 1,033 w. 1,104 m.	1,750 k. 3,800 w. 702 p.	
Dec. 15	Nashville, Tenn	General Thomas*	General Hood	6,500 k. w. and m.	23,000 k. w. and m.	General Johnson captured and 47 guns.
1865.						
Jan. 15	Fort Fisher	General Terry*		110 k. 536 w.	440 k. and w. 2,500 p.	Fort and 72 guns captured.
Jan. 20-22	Wilmington, N. C	Admiral Porter & General Schofield*	General Bragg	250 k. and w.	1,072 p.	
Feb. 27	Waynesborough, Va	General Sheridan*	General Early	69 k. and w.	5 k. 1,352 p.	All of Early's guns.
Feb. 27	Kinston, N. C	General Schofield*	General Bragg	loss 1,000	1,200 k. and w. 2,400 p.	
Feb. 27	Averysborough, N. C	General Sherman	General Johnston	74 k. 774 w.	327 k. 373 p.	
March 19	Bentonville, N. C	General Sherman*	General Johnston	loss 1,646	167 k. 1,625 p.	
March 25-27	Petersburg, Va	Generals Grant and Meade*	General Lee	180 k. 1,240 w. 990 m.	2,200 k. and w. 2,800 p.	
April 1	Five Forks, Va	Generals Sheridan and Warren*	General Lee	loss 3,000	5,000 p.	All Lee's artillery capt'd.
April 2	Selma, Ala	General Wilson*	General Forrest		3,000 p.	Forrest, Rhoddy capt'd.
April 2-3	Petersburg & Richmond	General Grant*	General Lee	8,000 k. w. and m.	9,000 k. w. and m.	Richmond captured.
April 6	Farmville & Sailor's Creek	General Sheridan*	General Lee		6,000 p.	Gens. Ewell, Kershaw, Corse & Custis Lee capt.
April 9	Appomattox C. H	Surrendered to Gen. Grant*	General Lee		26,115 p.	
April 11	Fort Blakely, Mobile	Admiral Thatcher and General Canby	General Taylor	2,000 k. and w.	500 k. and w. 4,300 p.	32 guns captured.
April 12	Montgomery, Ala	Surrendered to Gen. Wilson.			2,700 p.	14 guns.
April 12	Salisbury, N. C	General Stoneman*	General Gardner		1,800 p.	
April 26	Surrender of J. E. Johnston	General Sherman*			27,500 p.	
May 1	Surrender of Gen. Morgan.	General Hobson*			1,200 p.	
May 4	Surrender of Gen. Taylor.	General Canby*			10,000 p.	
May 10	Tallahassee, Fla	Surrendered to Gen. McCook	Admiral Jones	70 k.	8,000 p.	
May 10	Palmetto Ranch, Tex	Colonel Barrett	General Slaughter	70 k.		This was the last engagement of the Civil War.
May 10	Capture of Jefferson Davis at Irwinsville, Ga					
May 26	Surrender of Gen. K. Smith				20,000 p.	

* Indicates the victorious party.

In addition to the battles given above, there were 421 battles, engagements and skirmishes.

TOTAL NUMBER OF TROOPS CALLED INTO SERVICE FROM THE NORTHERN STATES DURING THE CIVIL WAR.

DATE OF PRESIDENT'S PROCLAMATION.	NUMBER CALLED FOR.	PERIOD OF SERVICE.	NUMBER OBTAINED.
April 15th, 1861	75,000	3 months.	93,326
May 3d, 1861	82,748	3 years.	714,231
July 22d and 25th, 1861	500,000		
May and June, 1862	......	3 months.	15,007
July 2d, 1862	300,000	3 years.	431,958
August 4th, 1862	300,000	9 months.	87,588
June 15th, 1863	100,000	6 months.	16,361
October 17th, 1863	300,000	2 years.	374,807
February 1st, 1864	200,000		
March 14th, 1864	200,000	3 years.	284,021
April 23d, 1864	85,000	100 days.	83,652
July 18th, 1864	500,000	1, 2, 3 yrs.	384,882
December 19th, 1864	300,000	1, 2, 3 yrs.	204,568
Total	2,942,748		2,690,401

Not including the militia brought into service during the invasions of General Lee into Maryland and Pennsylvania.

PRINCIPAL NAVAL BATTLES OF THE CIVIL WAR.

1862, Feb. 6—Fort Henry, Tenn., captured by Commodore Foote.
Feb. 8—Roanoke Island, N. C., captured by Commodore Goldsborough and General Burnside.
Feb. 16—Fort Donelson, Tenn., combined forces of General Grant and Commodore Foote.
Mar. 8—Confederate ram *Merrimac* sinks United States frigates *Cumberland* and *Congress*, Hampton Roads, Va.
Mar. 9—Federal *Monitor* disables the *Merrimac*.
Apr. 6—Pittsburg Landing.
Apr. 8—Capture of Island No. 10.
Apr. 11—Fort Pulaski, Ga., captured by land and naval forces.
Apr. 24—Forts Jackson, St. Philip, and New Orleans.
May 13—Natchez, Miss., captured by Admiral Farragut.
July 1—Malvern Hill.
1863, Jan. 11—Fort Hindman, Ark., Admiral Porter.
Jan. 11—United States steamer *Hatteras* sunk by Confederate *Alabama*.
Jan. 17—Monitor *Weehawken* captures Confederate ram *Atlanta*.
May 18—Vicksburg, Miss., Admiral Porter.
July 8—Port Hudson, Miss., captured.
July 8—Natchez, Miss.
1864, June 19—United States steamer *Kearsarge* sinks the *Alabama* off Cherbourg, France.
Aug. 5—Mobile, Ala., Admiral Farragut.
1865, Jan. 15—Fort Fisher, N. C., captured by General Terry and Commodore Porter.

During the Civil War the Federal Navy was increased in two years to over 400 vessels, the greater part of which were used in blockading Southern ports.

From life by
F.B.Carpenter
1864.

Engᵈ by F. Halpin
N.Y.

Abraham Lincoln

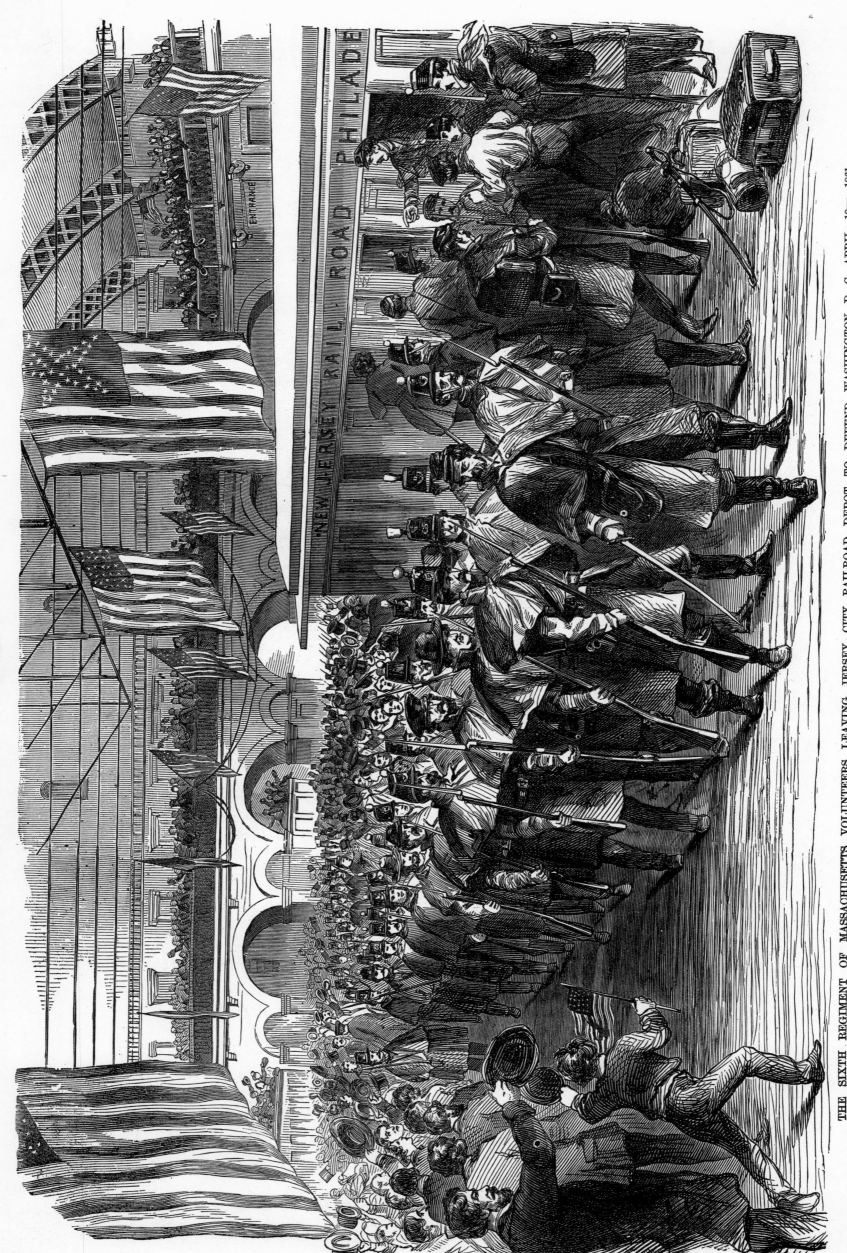

THE SIXTH REGIMENT OF MASSACHUSETTS VOLUNTEERS LEAVING JERSEY CITY RAILROAD DEPOT TO DEFEND WASHINGTON, D. C., APRIL 18TH, 1861.

Thousands of patriotic citizens filled every available space in the big railroad station in Jersey City when the Sixth Regiment of Massachusetts entered, on its way to defend the Capital, Washington, April 18th, 1861, after marching through the streets of New York. The people enthusiastically cheered the soldiers and wished them a safe journey as they boarded the waiting train. The regiment was composed of eight hundred men. This was the regiment which, upon its arrival in Baltimore, was stoned and shot at by a mob of Southern men who attempted to stop its progress to Washington.

THE SEVENTH REGIMENT, N. Y. S. M., PASSING DOWN CORTLANDT STREET ON THEIR WAY TO THE PENNSYLVANIA RAILROAD DEPOT, EN ROUTE FOR WASHINGTON, D. C., APRIL 19TH, 1861.

From the moment it became known that the pet regiment of New York, the gallant Seventh, was to be the first body of citizen soldiers to leave the city for the war the excitement among the people was intense. Early on the morning of April 19th, 1861, there was an extraordinary excitement in the city. Windows along the whole line of march were taken possession of, and groups of people accumulated on the stoops of houses and at the corners of every street. Deafening cheers greeted the soldiers everywhere. During a temporary halt a venerable man rushed in front of the staff, and cried out: "God bless you, boys! Do your duty—fight for your flag!"

THE GERMAN REGIMENT, STEUBEN VOLUNTEERS, COL. JOHN E. BENDIX COMMANDING, RECEIVING THE AMERICAN AND STEUBEN FLAGS IN FRONT OF THE CITY HALL, NEW YORK, FRIDAY, MAY 24TH, 1861.

The Seventh (Steuben) Regiment, commanded by Colonel Bendix, sailed for Fortress Monroe on May 25th, 1861. Previous to their departure they received a beautiful banner, the gift of some patriotic German ladies, and which was presented by Miss Bertha Kapff, daughter of the Lieutenant Colonel. Afterward they had another flag presented to them at the City Hall by Judge Daly, who made a forcible, brilliant and patriotic speech, which was enthusiastically received. The regiment was composed of 850 men. It was one of the most efficient regiments in the service.

20

TROOPS DRILLING IN THE GROUNDS ON THE NORTH SIDE OF THE CAPITOL, WASHINGTON, D. C.

The influx of Northern regiments of troops into Washington during the early days of the war rendered that city every hour in the day a scene of exciting and beautiful military display. The grounds north of the Capitol were used for brilliant dress parades and drills, which attracted throngs of visitors from all parts of the city and surrounding places. The various regiments had their cliques of admiring friends, who deemed the evolutions of their favorites entirely unapproachable. All the troops however, in their drill and bearing were considered worthy of warm praise, and called forth loud cheers from the spectators.

LIEUTENANT GENERAL WINFIELD SCOTT.

General Scott was born near Petersburg, Va., in 1786; was educated for a lawyer and admitted to the bar at the age of twenty. When the War of 1812 broke out he was appointed captain of artillery, thus beginning a military career unparalleled in brilliancy and success. Before long he became lieutenant colonel and was sent to the Niagara frontier. For his gallant services there he was promoted to the rank of major general, the highest then known in the American Army. His exploits in Mexico, in our war with that country, are too familiar to need repetition. His conduct of that war elicited from the veteran Wellington the declaration that that campaign was unsurpassed in military annals. Although born in the South, General Scott gave his services to the North in the Civil War, and was commander in chief of the army during the summer of 1861. After his resignation he spent his winters in New York and his summers at West Point. He died May 29th, 1866.

COLONEL ELMER E. ELLSWORTH.

THE MURDER OF COLONEL ELLSWORTH AT THE MARSHALL HOUSE, ALEXANDRIA, VA., MAY 24TH, 1861.

Colonel Ellsworth was passing the Marshall House in Alexandria, Va., when he saw a Confederate flag waving above it. On the spur of the moment he entered the hotel, and ascending to the roof with two or three friends, cut the halyards and took possession of the flag. As he descended the stairs he was fired at by James W. Jackson, proprietor of the hotel. Colonel Ellsworth fell to the ground mortally wounded.

FORT SUMTER, CHAR

CASTLE PINCKNEY, CHA

Fort Sumter, whose capture by the Confederate soldiers marked the real beginning of the Civil War, was built on an artificial island, immedi
brick masonry. The walls were fifty feet in height, and from eight to ten feet in thickness, and were pierced for three tiers of guns, besides nec
Castle Pinckney was a small fort on the southern extremity of Shute's Folly Island, in Charleston harbor, S. C. Though it was not in itself formid
the embrasures for which were about seven feet above low-water mark, and the upper being *en barbette.* The armament of the Castle consisted of

OUTH CAROLINA, 1861.

SOUTH CAROLINA, 1861.

h of Charleston Bay, S. C. It took ten years to build, and cost half a million of dollars. The fortification was of a pentagonal form, built of solid usketry, and designed for an armament of 140 pieces of ordnance of all calibres. It had two rows of guns, the lower being in bombproof casemates, es, 24- and 32-pounders, a few seacoast mortars and six columbiads.

LIEUTENANT TOMPKINS, AT THE HEAD OF B COMPANY, U. S. DRAGOONS, CHARGING INTO THE TOWN OF FAIRFAX COURTHOUSE, IN THE FACE OF 1,500 CONFEDERATE TROOPS, JUNE 1ST, 1861.

On June 1st, 1861, there was a smart skirmish between B Company, U. S. Dragoons, under Lieutenant Tompkins, and a body of 1,500 Confederates, at Fairfax Courthouse, Va. The Federal cavalry charged into the town, meeting with a brisk fire from houses on both sides of the street and from all quarters of the town. Lieutenant Tompkins's horse was shot under him, and falling beneath the animal, he sprained his ankle. After being completely inclosed by the Confederates for a short time Lieutenant Tompkins and his men fought their way out, taking with them seventeen prisoners.

28

CAMP CORCORAN, ON ARLINGTON HEIGHTS, VA., NEAR WASHINGTON.—THE SIXTY-NINTH REGIMENT, N. Y. S. M., DIGGING TRENCHES AND ERECTING BREASTWORKS.

Camp Corcoran was situated just beyond Arlington House, opposite Georgetown. It was occupied by the Sixty-ninth Regiment of New York. One of the first duties of these soldiers after enlisting for the war was the digging of trenches and erecting of breastworks around this camp. They worked unremittingly and with such success that their position became of immense strength. The result of their work was pronounced by military authorities to be perfect and admirable in every respect. The camp was named Corcoran in compliment to their colonel, who was greatly respected.

27

28

BATTLE AT GREAT BETHEL BETWEEN THE FEDERAL TROOPS UNDER GENERAL PIERCE AND THE CONFEDERATE TROOPS UNDER COLONEL MAGRUDER, JUNE 10TH, 1861.

The Federal troops, on arriving at Great Bethel, June 10th, 1861, found the Confederates in great force under Colonel Magruder, and posted behind batteries of heavy guns. The first intimation they had of the presence of the enemy was a heavy fire. After bravely standing their ground and succeeding in slacking the enemy's fire, they were ordered to retreat by General Pierce. A number of gallant officers were killed, among them Lieutenant Greble and Major Winthrop. The Federal troops retreated in splendid order. The cause of their defeat was explained by the incompetency of General Pierce.

GENERAL SCHENCK, WITH FOUR COMPANIES OF THE FIRST OHIO REGIMENT, SURPRISED AND FIRED INTO BY A CONFEDERATE MASKED BATTERY, NEAR VIENNA, VA., JUNE 17TH, 1861.

General Schenck and four companies of the First Ohio Regiment were approaching Vienna, Va., on June 17th, 1861, by railroad, when, on turning a curve, they were fired upon by masked batteries of three guns, with shells, round shot and grape, killing and wounding the men on the platform and in the cars before the train could be stopped. The engine then became damaged and could not draw the train out of the fire, so the soldiers left the cars and retired through the woods. They retreated slowly, bearing off the wounded about five miles away, where they made a stand, awaiting re-enforcements.

29

THE BATTLE OF BULL RUN, BETWEEN THE FEDERAL ARMY, COMMANDED BY MAJOR GENERAL McDOWELL, AND THE CONFEDERATE ARMY, UNDER GENERALS JOHNSTON AND BEAUREGARD, ON JULY 21st, 1861—ADVANCE OF THE FEDERAL TROOPS.

The first battle of Bull Run was fought on July 21st, 1861. It resulted in a loss on the Federal side of 481 killed, 1,011 wounded and 1,460 missing. The Confederate loss was estimated at nearly 2,000. The latter army, in action and reserve, numbered over 40,000 men, while the Federal force in action was about 35,000. Although the Confederates won a great victory, they were in no condition to pursue the advantage they had gained; had they done so they might have converted a repulse into a disastrous and total defeat. Our illustration shows the Federal troops advancing on the enemy's lines.

THE CHARGE OF THE FIRST IOWA REGIMENT, UNDER GENERAL LYON, AT THE BATTLE OF WILSON'S CREEK, NEAR SPRINGFIELD, MO., AUGUST 10TH, 1861.

The battle of Wilson's Creek, Mo., was fought August 10th, 1861. It was a bloody conflict between 5,200 Federals and 22,000 Confederates, and resulted in a victory for the latter. The First Iowa Regiment especially distinguished itself. Under the leadership of General Lyon the men made a gallant charge upon superior numbers. Although wounded in the head and leg and his horse killed, General Lyon quickly mounted another horse and dashed to the front of his regiment. He was among the first to be killed. At this battle the Union loss was 1,235 and the Confederate 1,095.

PASSAGE DOWN THE OHIO RIVER OF GENERAL NEGLEY'S PENNSYLVANIA BRIGADE (77TH, 78TH AND 79TH REGIMENTS, PENNSYLVANIA VOLUNTEERS), EN ROUTE FOR THE SEAT OF WAR IN KENTUCKY

One of the most striking and interesting scenes during the war was the passage down the Ohio River of General Negley's brigade, consisting of the following regiments, all of Pennsylvania; Seventy-seventh, under Colonel Hambright; Seventy-eighth, Colonel Stambrough; Seventy-ninth, Colonel Sewall. These regiments were dispatched in six river steamers for the purpose of re-enforcing the Federal army in Kentucky, as there was then great probability of the Confederate troops making that State a camping ground during the winter, if not driven out by the Federals.

32

MOVEMENT OF TROOPS FROM THE COLLINS LINE DOCK, CANAL STREET, NEW YORK

On April 6th, 1861, the neighborhood of Canal Street, New York, was a scene of great commotion, for three large ships, the *Atlantic*, *Baltic* and *Illinois*, were taking in, at the Collins Dock, troops and munitions of war to aid the Federal soldiers in the South. The number of soldiers shipped in the three vessels was 858. The accommodations on each of the ships were very poor.

UNITED STATES CAVALRY SCOUTING IN THE NEIGHBORHOOD OF FAIRFAX COURTHOUSE, VA.

The above picture represents a small party of Federal cavalry scouting in the vicinity of Falls Church, which was the scene just before of a short but unfortunate skirmish in which thirty Federal troops were either captured or slain. Hundreds of soldiers, at different times, were killed by thus venturing into dangerous places of this kind.

THE RETURN OF A FEDERAL FORAGING PARTY INTO CAMP NEAR ANNANDALE CHAPEL, VA.

The return of a foraging party was always an interesting and amusing incident of camp life. The one pictured here took place at Annandale Chapel, Va., a little village about seven miles from Alexandria and ten from Washington. The foragers in this case had great success, bringing back with them all kinds of provender, as can be seen from the illustration.

UNITED STATES ARSENAL AT CHARLESTON, S. C., SEIZED BY THE STATE AUTHORITIES, DECEMBER 28TH, 1860.

At the same time this picture was drawn the handsome arsenal of the government at Charleston was an object of great interest. An immense amount of ammunition was stored there, and raids upon it were expected at any moment. It was watched and guarded with great care by detachments of the Washington Light Infantry. It was afterward seized by the State authorities.

GENERAL McGOWEN ADDRESSING THE THIRTY-FIFTH ABBEVILLE (S. C.) VOLUNTEERS, IN FRONT OF THE CHARLESTON HOTEL.

The gallant band of Confederates known as the Abbeville Volunteers was composed of a hundred of the wealthiest citizens of the district. A number of them were accompanied by their negro servants, as the barons of old were by their armed vassals. General McGowen made a strong speech, and was loudly cheered.

GENERAL P. G. T. BEAUREGARD.

General Beauregard, who opened the Civil War by bombarding Fort Sumter, made a brilliant record during the conflict between the States. He won the battle of Bull Run; distinguished himself at Shiloh; held General Halleck in check for two months; defended Charleston; and commanding at Petersburg, aided General Lee in the long and gallant defense of Richmond.

MAJOR ROBERT ANDERSON.

Major Robert Anderson, the commander of Fort Sumter at the time of its fall, was born in Kentucky in the year 1805, and graduated at West Point in 1825. He was actively engaged through the Mexican War, and was severely wounded at Molino del Rev. In recognition of his services at Fort Sumter he was appointed brigadier general by President Lincoln. He was relieved from duty in October, 1861, on account of failing health. He died in France in 1871.

GENERAL WILLIAM TECUMSEH SHERMAN.

General Sherman was born in Ohio in 1818, was educated for the army at West Point, and received a commission as first lieutenant in 1841. At the breaking out of the war he was appointed colonel of infantry, and was in the battle of Bull Run. Raised to the rank of brigadier general, he succeeded General Anderson in the Department of Ohio, from which he was removed for declaring that it would require 200,000 men to hold Kentucky. After his famous march to the sea he moved north, capturing the most important Confederate positions, and by cutting off the resources of General Lee compelled the evacuation of Richmond and the surrender of Lee, April 9th, 1865. General Sherman died on February 14th, 1891.

THE BATTLE OF RICH MOUNTAIN, BEVERLY PIKE, VA., BETWEEN A DIVISION OF MAJOR GENERAL M⸱CLE

Upon the arrival of General McClellan's troops on the Beverly Pike, which runs along the summit of Rich Mountain, a heavy fire was c
advancing slowly. The enemy, mistaking this movement, rushed from their breastworks with a shout and approached the road. The Federals
The Confederates were soon driven up the hill, over their breastworks, and completely routed   The battle continued for an hour and a half from

LED BY GENERAL ROSECRANS, AND THE CONFEDERATE TROOPS UNDER COLONEL PEGRAM, JULY 11TH, 1861.

he Confederates firing shot, shell and grape, but so wildly that little damage was done. The Federal troops dropped flat, and deployed as skirmishers, rific and destructive volley, and rushed up the slope into the enemy's ranks with fixed bayonets. The fight now raged promiscuously all over the hill.

SCENE ON THE FLOATING BATTERY, CHARLESTON HARBOR, DURING THE BOMBARDMENT OF FORT SUMTER.

A very important factor in the bombardment of Fort Sumter was an immense floating battery, which did effective work in the silencing of the fort's guns. Major Anderson directed many of his shots at the floating battery; but while it was struck fifteen or eighteen times, not the slightest impression was made upon its iron-cased sides.

THE ATTACK UPON THE BATTERIES AT THE ENTRANCE OF ACQUIA CREEK, POTOMAC RIVER, BY THE UNITED STATES VESSELS "PAWNEE," "YANKEE," "THOMAS FREEBORN," "ANACOSTA" AND "RESOLUTE," JUNE 1st, 1861.

On May 31st Captain Ward, in command on board of the *Thomas Freeborn*, and assisted by two more of his gunboats, the *Resolute* and the *Anacosta*, began the attack on the Confederate batteries, and after a two hours' fight, succeeded in silencing the batteries at the landing; but, for want of long-range ammunition, could not effectually respond to the heavy fire from the heights, and so had to withdraw. The following day, however, with additional aid from the *Pawnee* and *Yankee*, the attack was resumed, and the batteries were at last silenced and the Confederates compelled to retreat.

BATTLE OF CARRICK'S FORD, BETWEEN THE TROOPS OF GENERAL McCLELLAN'S COMMAND, UNDER GENERAL MORRIS, AND THE CONFEDERATES UNDER GENERAL GARNETT, JULY 13TH, 1861.

After a long march through drenching rain, the Federal troops under General Morris reached Carrick's Ford, where they found the Confederates holding the cliff on the opposite bank of the river. Both sides began a heavy firing. Then the Seventh Indiana Regiment plunged into the river and scaled the cliff on the right of the enemy, while the others kept up the fight in front. As soon as the flanking party reached the top of the cliff the Confederates retreated, and were pursued for about two miles.

44

ENGAGEMENT AT BEALINGTON, VA., BETWEEN OHIO AND INDIANA REGIMENTS AND A DETACHMENT OF GEORGIA TROOPS.

On July 8th, 1861, from a high hill in the neighborhood of Bealington, two large bodies of troops were seen marching out of the Confederate camp. They advanced under cover of the wood, when the Federal skirmishers rushed at them. The Confederate cavalry then appeared, and the skirmishers retreated, when the Federal regiments threw a couple of shells into the midst of the cavalry, who at once retired. The Ohio troops then sent another volley and several shells into the wood, which did so much execution among the Confederates that the officers could not rally them.

45

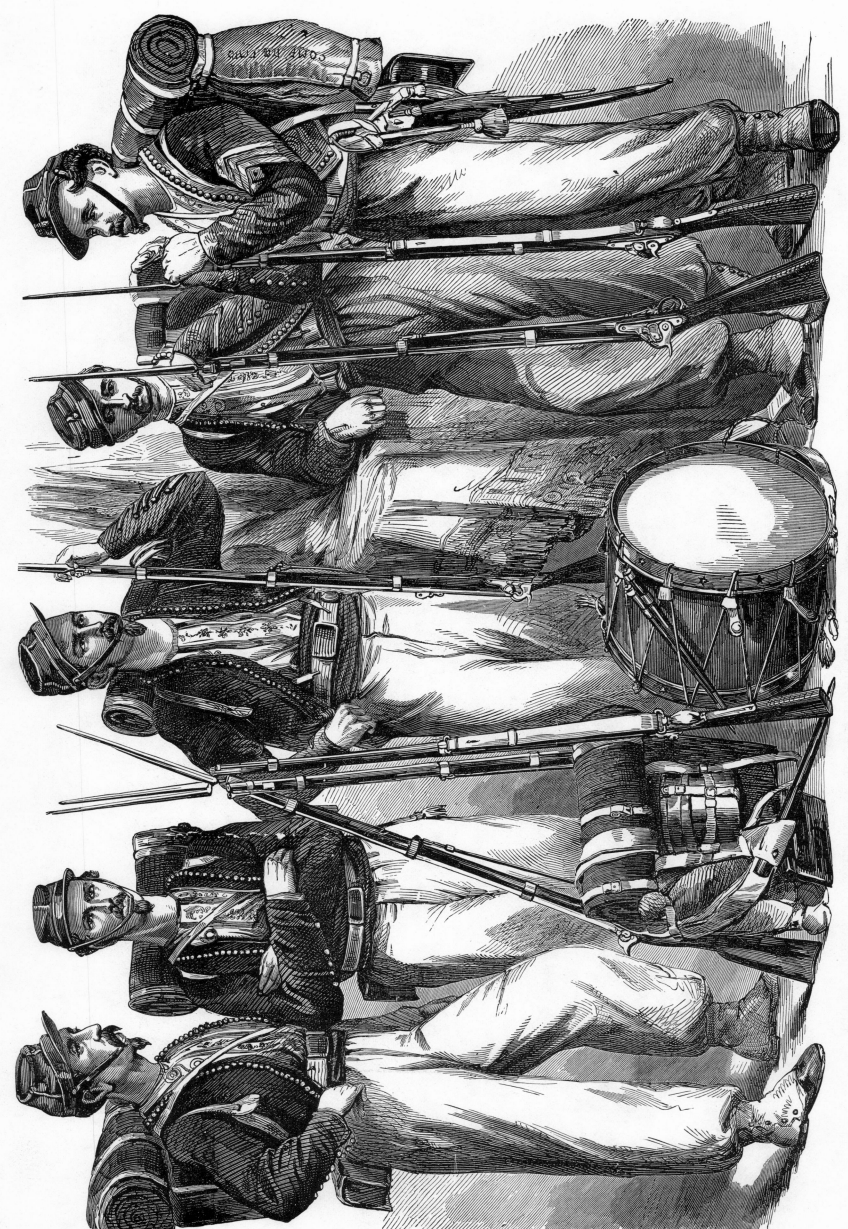

GROUP OF ELLSWORTH'S CHICAGO ZOUAVE CADETS.

No military organization during the war was more brilliant than the Chicago Zouave Cadets, with their striking and gay uniforms; their flowing red pants; their jaunty crimson caps; their peculiar drab gaiters and leggings, and the loose blue jackets, with rows of small, sparkling buttons, and the light-blue shirt beneath. In all their evolutions the Zouaves displayed great precision.

THE RAILROAD BATTERY PROTECTING WORKMEN ON THE PHILADELPHIA, WILMINGTON, AND BALTIMORE AND OHIO RAILROAD.

This remarkable railroad battery was built of half-inch boiler iron, and was proof against the best rifles at any distance. The sides had fifty rifle holes, and at one end was a 24-pounder cannon, which moved on a pivot, with a gun carriage complete. It accommodated sixty men. The car was built to assist workmen in rebuilding the bridges between Havre de Grace and Baltimore. At night it was used as a berth and guard car for the men.

47

RESCUE OF MAJOR REYNOLDS'S BATTALION OF MARINES FROM THE FOUNDERING STEAMER "GOVERNOR."

While being used as a transport, off Cape Hatteras, November 2d, 1861, the steamer *Governor*, Commander Phillips, foundered in the rough sea. Those on board, a battalion of marines under Major Reynolds, were transferred with great difficulty to the *Sabine*. The *Governor* was a sidewheel steamer of 650 tons burden. She was built in New York city in 1846, and was originally intended for river navigation.

EXPLOSION OF A SHELL IN THE CUTTER OF THE UNITED STATES STEAMER "NIAGARA," NOVEMBER 3D, 1861.

Few incidents in the war displayed more courage and coolness than the action of Fog Boatswain A. W. Pomeroy, of the United States frigate *Niagara*, in burning the Confederate brig *Nonsuch* near New Orleans. After setting the vessel on fire the Federal sailors were pulling back to the *Niagara*, when a shell struck the boat, throwing two of the officers in the water. The men were saved by a cutter dispatched from the *Niagara*.

GENERAL GEORGE B. McCLELLAN.

General George B. McClellan was born in Philadelphia in December, 1826. He was graduated from West Point in 1846, and joined the army as second lieutenant of engineers, to take an active part in the Mexican War, where he distinguished himself in the battles of Contreras, Churubusco, Molino del Rey and Chapultepec, and was promoted to a captaincy. At the breaking out of the Civil War he was appointed major general of Ohio militia, but soon afterward was made major general of the army. After a successful campaign in Western Virginia he was made commander in chief, and reorganized the Army of the Potomac. Being opposed to the extreme war party, he was superseded by General Burnside. In 1864 he was the Democratic candidate for the Presidency. He died in 1885.

BURNING OF THE UNITED STATES ARSENAL AT HARPER'S FERRY, VA., APRIL 18TH, 1861.

The arsenal at Harper's Ferry contained a large quantity of machinery and arms, and was garrisoned by a small detachment of United States Rifles, under the command of Lieutenant Roger Jones. Having been apprised of the approach of an overwhelming force of Confederates, under instructions from the Governor of Virginia to seize the arsenal, Lieutenant Jones, in order to prevent its falling into the hands of the enemy, set fire to the building, which was soon a mass of flames. Lieutenant Jones and his men then fled across the Potomac and reached Hagerstown about seven o'clock the next morning. The government highly commended the lieutenant for his judicious conduct, and promoted him to the rank of captain.

THE ("BILLY") WILSON ZOUAVES, AT TAMMANY HALL, TAKING THE OATH OF FIDELITY TO THE FLAG, APRIL 24TH, 1861.

WILSONS
UNION
SOUAVE
BATALLION
DEATH
TO
SECESSIONIST

Colonel Wilson was among the first to offer his services to the government on the breaking out of the war. He recruited a regiment of nearly twelve hundred men from the rowdy and criminal classes of New York city. The regiment was formally mustered in in the old Tammany Hall, and there, on April 24th, with the men arranged around the room, with the officers in the centre, the colonel, with a sword in one hand and the American flag in the other, led the men into swearing to "support the flag and never to flinch from its path through blood or death." The Zouaves, a few days afterward, left for the South.

THE FUNERAL CORTEGE, AT BOSTON, MASS., OF THE SIXTH MASSACHUSETTS SOLDIERS KILLED AT BALTIMORE.

The funeral of the four soldiers of the Sixth Massachusetts Regiment who were killed in Baltimore, April 19th, 1861, while en route to Washington, was held at Boston, May 1st. The bodies were received in the city by a military escort under Governor Andrew and Adjutant General Schouler, accompanied by a large concourse of citizens, and were temporarily deposited in the vaults of King's Chapel. The names of these "first martyrs" were Luther C. Ladd, Addison O. Whitney, Charles A. Taylor and Sumner H. Needham. The Legislature of Maryland, on March 5th, 1862, appropriated seven thousand dollars, to be dispensed, under the direction of the Governor of Massachusetts, for the relief of the families of those who were killed and injured.

52

THE FIGHT AT PHILIPPI, VA., JUNE 3D, 1861.—THE UNITED STATES TROOPS UNDER COMMAND OF COLONEL DUMONT, SUPPORTED BY COLONELS KELLEY AND LANDER, AND THE CONFEDERATES UNDER COLONEL PORTERFIELD.

Acting under instructions from Brigadier General Morris, the Federal troops were arranged in two columns, one commanded by Colonel B. F. Kelley and the other by Colonel E. Dumont. It was agreed that Colonel Kelley's command should proceed along the Beverly Turnpike, above Philippi, with the view of engaging Colonel Porterfield's rear, when Colonel Dumont's column would simultaneously open fire from the heights overlooking the village. Colonel Kelley being delayed by a treacherous guide, Colonel Dumont made a dash upon the Confederate pickets, carrying consternation in their ranks and capturing the barricaded bridge across the river. Colonel Kelley then arrived and pursued the fugitives through the streets of Philippi until he was badly wounded.

53

BRIGADIER GENERAL J. S. NEGLEY.

General Negley was born in East Liberty, Pa., December 26th, 1826. He enlisted as a private and served in the Mexican War. In April, 1861, he was commissioned brigadier general of volunteers; served in Alabama and Tennessee with the Army of the Ohio; and at the battle of Lavergne, October 7th, 1862, was in command, defeating the Confederates under Generals Anderson and Forrest. He was promoted major general for gallantry at Stone River, and at the battle of Chickamauga held Owen's Gap. He settled in Pittsburg after the war, and represented that city in Congress.

MAJOR GENERAL IRWIN McDOWELL.

Major General McDowell was born in Ohio, October 15th, 1818, graduated from West Point in 1838. He held several military positions until the breaking out of the war, when he was given command of the Army of the Potomac. On account of the loss of the battle of Bull Run, for which he was held responsible, he was superseded in the command by General McClellan, and given charge of the First Corps of the Army of the Potomac.

BRIGADIER GENERAL W. S. ROSECRANS.

Brigadier General Rosecrans was born in Ohio, September 6th, 1819, and was graduated from West Point in 1842. He received a commission as brigadier general in the regular army, May 16th, 1861, and took the field with command of a provisional brigade under General McClellan in Western Virginia. His first important action was that of Rich Mountain, which he won on July 11th, 1861.

MAJOR GENERAL DON CARLOS BUELL.

Major General Buell was born in Ohio, March 23d, 1818; graduated from West Point, 1841, as brevet second lieutenant of infantry; served in the Florida War, 1841–'42; on frontier duty, 1843–'45; made first lieutenant in June, 1846, and captain the following September. In 1861 he was made brigadier general and placed at the head of the Department of the Ohio, succeeding General Sherman. Upon assuming command of the Army of the Ohio he succeeded, with Grant, in gaining for the Federals the battle of Shiloh.

FORT PICKENS, ON SANTA ROSA ISLAND, PENSACOLA BAY, FLA.

Fort Pickens is a bastioned work of the first class. Its walls are forty-five feet in height by twelve in thickness. It is embrasured for two tiers of guns, which are placed under bombproof casemates, besides having one tier of guns *en barbette*. The guns from the work radiate to every point of the horizon, with flank and enfilading fire, at every angle of approach. The work was commenced in 1828, and finished in 1853 at a cost of nearly one million dollars. When on a war footing its garrison consists of 1,260 soldiers. The total armament of the work, when complete, consists of 210 guns, 63 of which are iron 42-pounders.

SPIKING THE GUNS OF FORT MOULTRIE BY MAJOR ANDERSON, BEFORE ITS EVACUATION, DECEMBER 26TH, 1860

Toward the middle of December it became evident, from the magnitude of military operations going on, and other indications, coupled with significant threats in the South Carolina Convention and out of it, that an occupation of Castle Pinckney and Fort Sumter was meditated. Major Anderson decided to anticipate the South Carolinians in their contemplated manœuvre. Accordingly, on the night of December 26th, at the very time the South Carolina Commissioners had arrived in Washington to demand the surrender of the forts, he evacuated Fort Moultrie, after spiking the guns and providing for the destruction of their carriages and other material by fire, and with the aid of three small vessels successfully transferred his little command to Fort Sumter.

BATTLE OF BULL RUN, VA., JULY 21st, 1861, BETWEEN THE FEDERAL ARMY, COMMANDED BY G

The battle of Bull Run, which the Confederates called the battle of Manassas, was the first really important action of the Civil War. The scene efforts to rally the troops were fruitless. In a short time the entire Federal line seemed to have broken in disorder, the force under General Sykes a confusion toward the passages leading to Centreville. By nine o'clock that evening the last of the fugitives had reached Centreville. The Confederate

LL, AND THE CONFEDERATE ARMY, COMMANDED BY GENERALS BEAUREGARD AND JOHNSTON.

rthwest of Manassas Junction, on the banks of Bull Run. It resulted, as everyone knows, in the complete routing of the Federals. The repeated
ng an effort to withstand the tide. But it was finally compelled to yield to the masses against it. The Federals then on all sides retreated in
be 378 killed, 1,489 wounded and 20 missing—total 1,887; that of the Federals, 481 killed, 1,011 wounded and 1,460 missing—total 2,952.

FIRST CHARGE OF FREMONT'S BODYGUARD, LED BY MAJOR ZAGONYI, ON THE CONFEDERATE GARRISON AT SPRINGFIELD, MO., OCTOBER 25TH, 1861.

While encamped at Pomme de Terre, Mo., Fremont learned that a Confederate force had just been established at Springfield. He at once ordered Major Zagonyi to take his cavalry on a reconnoissance, and to capture the camp if deemed practicable. When Zagonyi arrived near Springfield he learned that the Confederate force was nearly 2,000 strong, while he had but 150 men. Notwithstanding this disparity he made a gallant charge into the enemy's ranks in the face of a hailstorm of bullets. He succeeded in forcing the Confederates to break away in wild disorder, thus making the first charge of the bodyguard a great success.

SECOND CHARGE UPON THE CONFEDERATES BY GENERAL FREMONT'S BODYGUARD, UNDER MAJOR ZAGONYI, NEAR SPRINGFIELD, MO., ON OCTOBER 25TH, 1861.

After the first charge of Major Zagonyi, described on another page, Captain McNaughton reached the scene with fifty men. The order to follow the retreating Confederates was given, and all dashed ahead for a second charge through the woods. Many of the fugitives were overtaken there, as well as in the streets of Springfield and in the forest beyond the city. Only when further pursuit seemed useless did the Federals return. Zagonyi's brave followers suffered a loss of eighty-four dead and wounded in this engagement, which, for the boldness of its undertaking and the rapidity of its execution under the great disparity of numbers, certainly has but few parallels in any history.

THE SIXTEENTH REGIMENT, OHIO VOLUNTEERS, UNDER COLONEL IRWINE, CROSSING THE TRAY RUN VIADUCT, NEAR CHEAT RIVER, ON THE BALTIMORE AND OHIO RAILROAD.

On its way to Rowlesburg, Va., the Sixteenth Regiment of Ohio Volunteers crossed the Tray Run Viaduct, one of the most remarkable engineering works on the whole line of the Baltimore and Ohio Railroad. It spans a deep gorge in the mountains six hundred feet in width, and at a height of one hundred and sixty feet above the bed of the ravine. The roadway is supported on iron columns, secured and braced in a peculiar manner, and placed on a solid mass of masonry, which fills up the bottom of the run. The scenery at this point is equal to anything in the world, combining the choicest materials of mountain, forest and river.

RHODE ISLAND REGIMENTS EMBARKING AT PROVIDENCE FOR NEW YORK AND WASHINGTON.

Within five days after the President's call for troops the Rhode Island Marine Artillery, with 8 guns and 110 horses, commanded by Colonel Tompkins, passed through New York on their way to Washington, and the First Regiment of Infantry, 1,200 strong, under Colonel Ambrose E. Burnside, was ready to move. It was composed of many of the wealthier citizens of the State, and accompanied by the patriotic Governor, William Sprague, who had, from his private purse, armed and equipped the regiment, as well as contributed to the general war fund. The little State, on May 18th, 1861, appropriated $500,000 for equipping volunteers.

BATTLE OF BELMONT, MO., OPPOSITE COLUMBUS, KY., NOVEMBER 7TH, 1861.—FEDERAL FORCES COMMANDED BY U. S. GRANT; CONFEDERATE FORCES, BY LEONIDAS POLK.

EXPLANATION.—1. Brigadier General Grant and staff directing the movements of the troops. 2. Brigadier General McClernand leading the charge at the head of the Thirty-first Illinois. 3. Thirty-first Illinois, Colonel Logan. 4. Body of Lieutenant Colonel Wentz, Seventh Ohio. 5. Body of Captain Pulaski, aid-de-camp to McClernand, killed while leading the charge. 6. Caisson ordered to the field from the rear. 7. Twenty-seventh Illinois, Colonel Buford, taking the camp colors of the Confederates. 8. Thirtieth Illinois, Colonel Fonke. 8 A. Twenty-second Illinois, Colonel Dougherty. 9. Light artillery, Captain Taylor. 10. Seventh Ohio, Colonel Lamon. 11. Captain Schwartz, acting chief of artillery, taking the Confederate battery. 12. Watson's Louisiana field battery. 13. Confederate artillery horses. 14. Battery of heavy ordnance at Columbus. 15. Encampment near Columbus. 16. Confederate ferryboat. 17. Columbus.

LANDING OF UNITED STATES TROOPS AT FORT WALKER, AFTER THE BOMBARDMENT, NOVEMBER 7TH, 1861.

In order to establish a naval rendezvous where vessels on the way to or from blockading squadrons could coal and take refuge in case of need, it was decided by the Federal authorities to capture the entrance to Port Royal, South Carolina. A large expedition was fitted out, and after a heavy bombardment of about four hours, signal was given that the two forts, Walker and Beauregard, had been abandoned. When the Federal troops landed at Fort Walker they found numbers of dead and dying amidst dismounted guns in all directions, and the hospital building shot through and through in many places. The loss on the fleet was 8 killed and 23 wounded.

64

MORNING MUSTERING OF THE "CONTRABANDS" AT FORTRESS MONROE, ON THEIR WAY TO THEIR DAY'S WORK.

As a living illustration of one of the aspects of the Civil War, a sketch is given above of the contrabands, *née* "niggers," going to their daily work at Fortress Monroe. The variety of the Ethiopian countenance is capitally given, and while some remind us of the merry phiz of George Christy in his sable mood, others wear the ponderous gravity of a New Jersey justice. The colored men had a comparatively pleasant time under their state of contraband existence.

SCENE IN THE MILITARY MARKET AT BEAUFORT, S. C.

Our artist accompanied his sketch of the soldier's marketing by observing that at a bargain a contraband was as good as a gentleman of the Rothschild persuasion, and a great deal better, as the most liberal soldier could have no compunction in giving finally a quarter for what the darky originally asked fifteen dollars, since it was strongly suspected the contraband did not come honestly by the goods he sold. It was a source of considerable amusement to our soldiers to spend an hour in marketing. Sometimes a conversation like this took place: *Soldier* (after having paid for his chicken, which he firmly grasps)—"Sambo, where did you steal this?" *Truthful Contraband*—"From Marsa Drayton's farm. Dis chile will not lie; marsa, dis chile b'ong to de Baptist persuasion."

65

THE MORNING DETAIL OF THE FOURTH NEW HAMPSHIRE VOLUNTEERS GOING TO WORK ON THE HILTON HEAD FORTIFICATIONS.

The morning detail of a regiment going to work on the fortifications was rather a merry and a peculiar sight. Instead of rifles and cannon, the heroes were armed with shovels, hoes, spades, pickaxes and trowels, while their train of artillery was a battery of wheelbarrows. Above all the troubles, ravages and cares of a campaign rose that indomitable cheerfulness and willingness so characteristic of the American.

REVIEW OF THE CLINCH RIFLES BY CAPTAIN C. A. PLATT ON THE PARADE GROUND IN FRONT OF THE ARSENAL, AUGUSTA, GA.

The parade ground of the Augusta Arsenal is one of the finest in America, being nearly a mile square. It is well laid out, and overlooks the city and surrounding country. The view is splendid. The Clinch Rifles were famous for their efficiency, and were considered one of the best companies in the State, holding the right of the battalion volunteer companies. They were named after General Clinch. They were organized in 1861 by Captain S. C. Wilson, a veteran of the Florida War.

CAPTURE OF THE PROPELLER "FANNY" IN PAMLICO SOUND BY THREE CONFEDERATE STEAMERS WHILE CONVEYING MEN AND STORES TO THE TWENTIETH INDIANA REGIMENT.

On the 1st of October, 1861, Colonel Hawkins dispatched the propeller *Fanny*, with two cannon, ammunition, supplies and provisions, to the camp of the Twentieth Indiana Regiment, then stationed at Chicamacomico. While they were landing their stores into boats they were attacked, about five o'clock in the afternoon, by the Confederate steamer *Northampton* and two tugs, which came from the direction of Roanoke Island, and after a brief engagement the *Fanny* was surrendered to the enemy.

THE BOMBARDMENT OF FORT WALKER, PORT ROYAL HARBOR, S. C.—VIEW OF THE INTERIOR DURING THE BOMBARDMENT BY THE VESSELS OF THE FEDERAL FLEET, NOVEMBER 7TH, 1861.

Fort Walker was an irregular bastioned and curtained work, constructed on a bluff eight feet above high-water mark, and in a position commanding important points and channels in Port Royal harbor. The whole plan of attack had been admirably arranged by Commodore Dupont, and was at once daring, simple and original. It was for the ships to describe a circle following one another, each giving its fire on the fort as it steamed past. The firing on both sides was incessant, and about noon the Wabash, Bienville and Susquehanna approached within six hundred yards of the fort, and delivered their broadsides with a deliberation and effect which was terrible. This desperate combat lasted for three hours, principally with 10-second and then 5-second shells, when the firing ceased, the guns in the fort being completely silenced.

GENERAL LOUIS BLENKER.

General Blenker was born in Worms on the Rhine about 1815. In 1849 he came to the United States. When the rebellion broke out he was elected colonel of the First German Rifle Regiment, Eighth New York Volunteers, which was one of the first that went to the seat of war. After the battle of Bull Run, where Colonel Blenker acted as brigadier, he was promoted brigadier general. He died October 31st, 1863.

GENERAL WILLIAM S. HARNEY.

This daring and experienced soldier, whose promptness in Missouri stemmed the tide of secession, was born in Louisiana at the beginning of this century, and entered the army at a very early age, being appointed second lieutenant in the First Infantry in 1818. He continue in the service until his death, in 1889.

70

THE DURYEE ZOUAVES CARRYING THE BODY OF LIEUTENANT GREBLE FROM THE FIELD AT GREAT BETHEL.

The Federal troops, after having burnt Little Bethel, arrived at Great Bethel at ten o'clock in the morning. Here they found the Confederates in great force, under the command of Colonel Magruder, and strongly posted behind batteries of heavy guns. It was here that Lieutenant Greble was killed. The young hero fell dead by the side of his gun. His body was placed on a gun carriage and carried off the field by his sorrowing men.

THE DEATH OF GENERAL NATHANIEL LYON, AT THE BATTLE OF WILSON'S CREEK, NEAR SPRINGFIELD, MO.

General Lyon fell at the head of his little army of 5,500 men, in a desperate fight at Wilson's Creek, Mo., on the 10th of August, 1861, while leading a charge against the Confederate forces under Ben McCulloch, numbering 23,000 men. General Lyon was educated at the United States Military Academy at West Point, where he was graduated with distinction in 1841.

BATTLE AT WILSON'S CREEK, NEAR SPRINGFIELD, MO., BETWEEN 5,500 UNION TROOPS UNDER GEN

The attack was made by General Lyon, in command of the centre, supported by General Sigel and Major Sturgis, U. S. A., and notwithstanding th
however, was dearly purchased, General Lyon, the brave and able commander of the Union forces, was killed at the head of his troops, who suffered a

D SIGEL, AND 23,000 CONFEDERATES UNDER GENERALS McCULLOCH AND PRICE, AUGUST 10TH, 1861.

f numbers, the Confederates were driven from their position and their camp burned, with great loss in killed, wounded and prisoners. **The victory,** and between 600 and 700 wounded. There is every reason to believe that the Confederate loss was more than double these numbers.

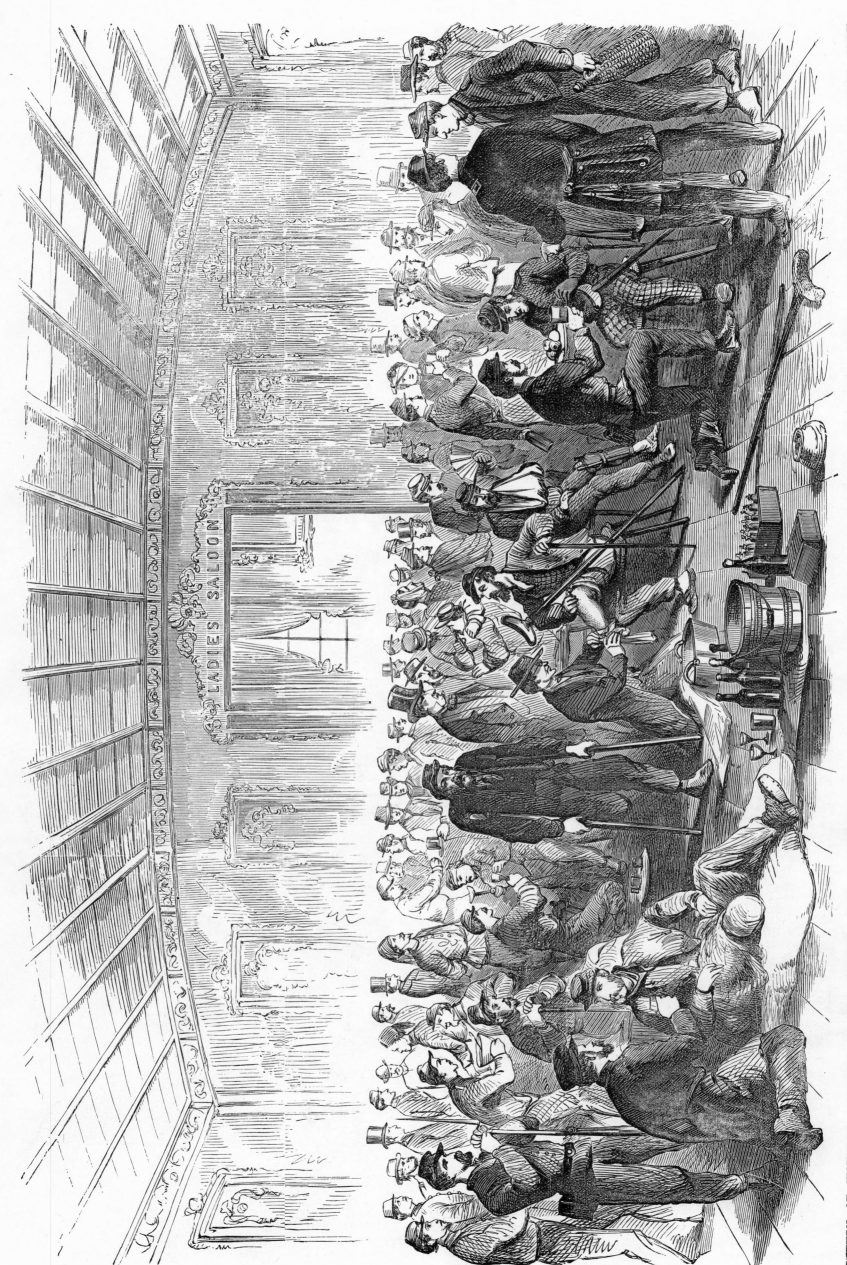

RETURN OF WOUNDED SOLDIERS OF THE FEDERAL ARMY CAPTURED AT BULL RUN—SCENE IN HAMPTON ROADS ON BOARD THE UNITED STATES STEAMER "LOUISIANA," TO WHICH THEY WERE TRANSFERRED, UNDER A FLAG OF TRUCE, OCTOBER 7TH, 1861.

The United States steamer *Express* met by agreement the Confederate steamer *Northumberland* with a flag of truce, about twelve miles above Newport News, and brought down fifty-seven wounded prisoners who had been captured at Bull Run and taken to Richmond. Their release was not due to the magnanimity of the Confederate authorities, but rather to their inability to supply their wants.

74

FORDING OF THE OSAGE RIVER AT WARSAW, MO., BY THE FREMONT HUSSARS, OCTOBER 18th, 1861.

The Confederate general Price, when retreating before General Fremont, rightly believed that if he could put the Osage River between him and the Federal commander, and destroy the bridge across it, he could so delay pursuit as to make an easy escape into Arkansas. But he did not rightly judge the resources or vigor of General Fremont. When Fremont approached the river at Warsaw he rode forward through mud and rain twenty-five miles, viewed the stream and gave prompt orders for bridging it; which were carried out so rapidly that within four days his entire force was able to cross and follow up the pursuit.

GENERAL FREMONT'S ARMY ON ITS MARCH FROM TIPTON TO WARSAW, OVER THE PRAIRIES TO HAW CREEK.

GENERAL STEVENS'S BRIGADE ENTERING BEAUFORT, S. C., ON THE EVENING OF DECEMBER 5TH, 1861.

General Stevens's brigade occupied Beaufort, S. C., on the evening of December 5th, 1861. It was a most brilliant and suggestive scene. The moon—just at the half—shone with splendor, reminding one of that beautiful passage in Homer which represents the orb of night rising merely to shed a glory upon the Grecian arms. At the end of the street the river flowed in silence and light. Here and there the streets were dotted with bivouac fires, around which arms were stacked and soldiers lounging.

ARRIVAL AND DEPARTURE OF FEDERAL TROOPS, ON THEIR WAY TO WASHINGTON, AT THE UNION VOLUNTEER REFRESHMENT SALOON, PHILADELPHIA, PA.

The want of proper refreshment for our troops while on their way to Washington was the cause of much complaint. Some special regiments were received by the municipal authorities and their officers royally feasted, but as a general rule our brave soldiers had to trust to chance and their knapsacks for sustenance on the road. This neglect was amply provided for by the organization of refreshment saloons in various parts of the city.

RECRUITING FOR HAWKINS'S NEW YORK ZOUAVES.

Recruiting for the New York Zouaves attracted a large body of athletic men to its ranks, which in 1861 numbered eight hundred gallant fellows who were desirous of emulating in the service of the Stars and Stripes the glory of their French prototypes. They were nearly of one height, and all under thirty years of age.

FORGING IRONWORK FOR GUN CARRIAGES AT THE WATERVLIET ARSENAL, WEST TROY, N. Y.

A more thorough and comprehensive establishment cannot be found. It embraces the whole scope of manufacture which properly belongs to an arsenal. The various departments are superintended by competent foremen, the whole governed by a commandant, assisted by ordnance officers.

THE ELEVENTH INDIANA ZOUAVES IN CAMP McGINNIS, RESTING, THE DAY AFTER THE BATTLE OF ROMNEY.

THE ORDNANCE ARMORY, CHARLESTON, S. C.—THE VOLUNTEER TROOPS TRYING THE ARMS.

The Confederate Ordnance Armory at Charleston, S. C., contained a splendid collection of arms, among which were specimens of all the arms known in modern warfare. Here were found the Minie, Warner and Colt's rifles, muskets of every possible make—breech, muzzle and chamber-loading pieces; also the terrible ten- and twelve-shooters known as Lindsay's repeaters. With this latter death-dealing weapon all the officers in the company were armed.

GENERAL ROBERT E. LEE.

General Robert E. Lee was born in Virginia in 1807; was admitted into West Point as a cadet in 1825; entered the United States Army in 1829. In 1845 he was appointed a member of the board of engineers, and in the following year chief engineer of the army in Mexico; was brevetted major, April 18th, 1846, for gallant conduct at Cerro Gordo; lieutenant colonel, August 20th, 1847, for bravery at Contreras and Churubusco, and colonel, September 13th, 1847, for gallant conduct at Chapultepec. In 1852 he was appointed superintendent of West Point Military Academy; on the 16th of March, 1861, he was appointed colonel of cavalry, and on the 25th of April in the same year he resigned his commission in the United States Army and offered his sword to Virginia, which State had just then seceded from the Union. He died October 12th, 1870.

JEFFERSON DAVIS.

Jefferson Davis, son of Samuel Davis, a Revolutionary soldier, was born in Todd County, Kentucky, in 1808; was graduated at West Point in 1828; served as lieutenant of infantry at Western posts, and on frontier service from 1828 to 1834; resigned in 1835, and became a cotton planter; chosen Presidential Elector from Mississippi in 1844; member of the United States House of Representatives, 1845–'46; colonel of the First Mississippi Rifle Volunteers in the Mexican War in 1846–'47; engaged at Monterey, and severely wounded at Buena Vista; member of the United States Senate, 1847–'51; Secretary of War, 1853–'57; Chairman of the Committee on Military Affairs from 1857 to 1861; President of the Southern Confederacy, February 18th, 1861; captured by the Federal troops May 10th, 1865, at Irwinville, Ga.; prisoner of war, 1865–'67, at Fortress Monroe, Va. Died December 6th, 1889.

81

NIGHT ATTACK ON THE FEDERAL FORCES UNDER MAJOR BOWEN, OCCUPYING SALEM, MO., BY THE CONFEDERATE FORCES UNDER COLONEL, FREEMAN, DECEMBER 8TH, 1861.

Sneaking upon an enemy at night is a very good policy if you succeed in catching him while he still sleeps; but if he should wake up in time he is generally in the maddest and most ferocious humor, and doubly dangerous. Colonel Freeman found this to be the fact. Company B pitched into his men like savages, slashing right and left, and pouring volleys of pistol and carbine shots into the crowd which blocked up the street and filled the yards around the houses in a thick, confused mass. Their superior numbers were only an impediment, and when another company, which was in an adjoining stable, broke loose upon them, and Company A commenced to get out of the house, while Company D, having mounted its horses, came clattering down the street with a wild war whoop, they had to seek safety in flight.

BATTLE OF DRANESVILLE, VA., DECEMBER 20TH, 1862, BETWEEN THE FEDERAL FORCES COMMANDED BY GENERALS McCALL AND ORD, AND THE CONFEDERATE GENERAL STEWART.

This battle, which lasted an hour, was one incessant firing. It commenced at 1 and ended at 2 P. M. The firing of the Confederates was very wild, most of the shot and shell going over the heads of our men. The enemy as suddenly abandoned their position as they had commenced the attack, and their superior knowledge of the locality and the dense woods made their escape easy. The Federal loss was eight killed and sixty wounded; the Confederate loss was much greater.

83

NORTH BATTERY OF THE CONFEDERATES AT SHIPPING POINT, ON THE VIRGINIA SIDE OF THE POTOMAC, LOOKING UP THE RIVER.

Shipping Point, at which the Confederates had erected a powerful battery, is on the eastern side of the entrance to Quantico or Dumfries Creek, on the Potomac River, the scene of Lieutenant Harwell's gallant exploit on the 11th of October. Shipping Point is thirty-three miles below Washington, and four miles above Acquia Creek, being immediately opposite Chicomoxon Creek in Maryland. The vessels whose smokestacks and masts are seen on the right are the *Martha Page* and *Fairfax*, safely ensconced in Quantico Creek.

84

CAPTURE OF FORT DONELSON.—CHARGE OF THE EIGHTH MISSOURI REGIMENT AND THE ELEVENTH INDIANA ZOUAVES, FEBRUARY 15TH, 1862.

Gen Lew Wallace, whose troops were comparatively fresh, made the assault. Cruft's brigade, headed by the Eighth Missouri and the Eleventh Indiana, from Colonel Smith's division, with two Ohio regiments in reserve, formed the assailing column. Across the valley, or extended ravine, in Wallace's front, was a ridge which had been yielded. Up this ridge a charge was made. Before them lay an ascent of one hundred and fifty yards; and a lively bushwhacking followed between them and the Confederate pickets. When less than fifty yards had been gained they received a volley from the hilltop. Smith ordered his men to lie down; and when the heavy firing was exhausted they arose and pushed on up the hill, at last reaching the top. The fight and pursuit lasted for nearly two hours, and by five o'clock the enemy had entirely disappeared from the field.

GENERAL J. K. F. MANSFIELD.

General Mansfield was born at New Haven, Conn., in 1803; was graduated from the United States Military Academy at West Point in 1822, and appointed brevet second lieutenant in the Corps of Engineers; first lieutenant in 1832; captain in 1838; chief engineer of the army commanded by General Taylor in the Mexican War, 1846–'47. In April, 1861, he was placed in command of the Department of Washington, receiving the appointment of brigadier general of volunteers. In 1862 he commanded a corps of the Army of the Potomac, at the head of which he received, at the battle of Antietam, the wounds from which he died on September 18th, 1862.

GENERAL NATHANIEL LYON.

General Lyon was born at Ashford, Conn., July 14th 1819; was graduated from the United States Military Academy at West Point, and entered the army July, 1841; took part in the Indian campaign in Florida; was sent to Mexico at the commencement of the war, and was wounded at the Belen Gate; was appointed captain in 1851, and remained in active frontier duty in Kansas until in April, 1861, he was placed in charge of the United States Arsenal at St. Louis, Mo., and afterward appointed commandant of the post. In May, 1861, he enrolled a large number of volunteers and surrounded Camp Jackson, compelling a prompt surrender. He was killed at the battle of Wilson's Creek.

GENERAL BEN McCULLOCH.

General McCulloch was born in Rutherford County, Tenn., in 1814. When the Mexican War broke out he took command of a band of Texans. He distinguished himself at the battles of Monterey and Buena Vista. At the breaking out of the Civil War, McCulloch raised a regiment of desperadoes and called them the Texan Rangers. He was fatally wounded while leading his division at the battle of Pea Ridge.

GENERAL FRANZ SIGEL.

General Sigel was born at Zinsheim, Bavaria, November 18th, 1824; entered the army of the Grand Duke of Baden, and in 1847 was appointed chief adjunct; emigrated to this country some years later, and in 1861 took command of the Germans in St. Louis who had tendered their services to the Federal Government, being made colonel of the Third Missouri Volunteers. He took part in many important engagements.

COLONEL E. D. BAKER.

DEATH OF COLONEL BAKER WHILE LEADING HIS REGIMENT AT THE BATTLE OF BALL'S BLUFF, VA., OCTOBER 21ST, 1861.

Colonel E. D. Baker, while commanding the First California Volunteers, which formed part of General Stone's brigade at the battle of Ball's Bluff, and who had just before he entered battle been notified of his appointment as brigadier general, was killed while at the head of his command, pierced by bullets in the head, body, arm and side. He died as a soldier would wish to die, amid the shock of battle, by voice and example animating his men to brave deeds.

GRAND REVIEW IN WASHINGTON OF EIGHT BATTERIES OF ARTILLERY AND THREE REGIMENTS

General McClellan held a grand review of cavalry and artillery, which went off with great *éclat*. The troops consisted of two full regiment These made up above two thousand men, and in addition there were eight batteries of United States regular flying artillery, comprising forty-eigh the Capitol, at about three o'clock P. M.

PRESIDENT LINCOLN, GENERAL McCLELLAN AND A PORTION OF THE CABINET. SEPTEMBER 24th, 1861.

fth Regulars and the Kentucky Volunteers—together with such portions of the Lincoln, Ira Harris and Cameron Guards as had their horses and sabres. witzer field pieces, with caissons, carriages, horses, riders and gunners in full quota. The review was held on a broad, level common one mile east of

FEDERAL TROOPS BUILDING A ROAD ACROSS LOW ISLAND, IN THE OHIO RIVER, OPPOSITE PADUCAH, KY.

BATTLE OF RICH MOUNTAIN, VA., JULY 12TH, 1861—THE THIRTEENTH INDIANA REGIMENT CAPTURING A GUN.

When the enemy were driven from their breastworks on the summit they attempted to run off one of their cannon. Captain Sayles and Lieutenant Atkinson, with about forty men of Company G of the Thirteenth Indiana, started in pursuit. The Indianians, on turning the road, found the enemy drawn up across in front, firing from a log cabin and from bushes on the side of the way. They fired, stormed the house, and charged bayonets down the road, driving the enemy from their position, taking several prisoners and capturing the cannon without losing a man.

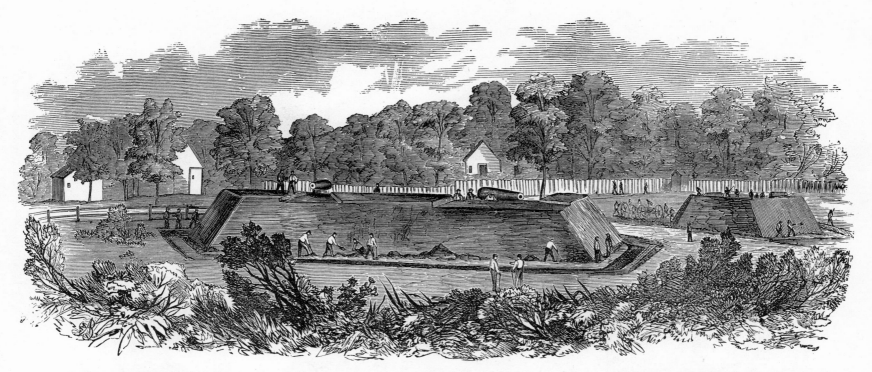

EARTHWORK BATTERIES SURROUNDING THE CITY OF PADUCAH, KY., BUILT BY THE FEDERAL TROOPS IN OCCUPATION.

DESTRUCTION OF GUNS AND GUN CARRIAGES AT THE ARSENAL, BEAUFORT, S. C., BY CAPTAIN AMMON OF THE UNITED STATES GUNBOAT "SENECA," NOVEMBER 14TH, 1861.

On November 14th, 1861, a party commanded by Captain Ammon landed at Beaufort, S. C., from the United States gunboat *Seneca*, visited the arsenal and destroyed the cannon they found there. Having burnt the gun carriages and knocked off the trunnions, they considered their work complete.

RECONNOISSANCE IN FORCE BY GENERAL GRANT TOWARD COLUMBUS, KY.—GENERAL GRANT'S BODYGUARD PASSING OVER MAYFIELD CREEK BRIDGE.

The scenery of the "Bottoms" is the most interesting in this part of Kentucky. During freshets they are from two to twelve feet under water. The soil is exceedingly rich and heavily timbered, and numberless creeks and bayous intersect the country in every direction. The few farms in this section of the State occupy the ridges, while the low ground is a primitive forest, unfit for cultivation on account of frequent overflows. The largest of the many streams which drain this swamp is Mayfield Creek.

94

GRAND REVIEW OF GENERAL THOMAS'S BRIGADE OF GENERAL BANKS'S DIVISION, WESTERN MARYLAND, BY MAJOR GENERAL BANKS AND STAFF.

The admirable manner in which General Thomas's brigade acquitted itself drew forth from General Banks the highest encomiums. It was a beautiful and striking scene—the thundering tramp of the artillery as it rattled past the general and his staff, while the Blue Ridge Mountains in the distance formed a background at once massive and grand.

93

FEDERAL TROOPS LANDING ON THE KENTUCKY SHORE, OPPOSITE CAIRO, FOR THE PURPOSE OF BUILDING FORT HOLT.

Fort Holt was situated on the Kentucky side of the Ohio River, and almost opposite Cairo. It was named in honor of that noble Kentuckian, Joseph Holt, who, during the time he held the War Department, after the defection of Floyd, endeavored to repair the damage done by his fraudulent predecessor.

RECEPTION BY THE PEOPLE OF NEW YORK OF THE SIXTY-NINTH REGIMENT, N.Y.S.M., ON THEIR RETURN FROM THE SEAT OF WAR, ESCORTED BY THE NEW YORK SEVENTH REGIMENT.

The return home of the gallant Sixty-ninth Regiment—composed entirely of Irish citizens—on Saturday, July 27th, 1861, was an ovation as warm and enthusiastic as their endurance and bravery deserved. Their service of three months had been of infinite value to their country and honor to themselves and their State. The Sixty-ninth had rendered good service at Arlington Heights, and especially distinguished itself at the battle of Bull Run. On the morning of their arrival the streets were crowded with people, and the gallant fellows were greeted with shouts of applause along the whole line of march.

HEADQUARTERS OF VINCENT COLLYER, SUPERINTENDENT OF THE POOR AT NEW BERNE, N. C.—DISTRIBUTION OF CAPTURED CONFEDERATE CLOTHING TO THE CONTRABANDS.

Never has Shakespeare's lines, "To what base uses may we not return," had a more fitting illustration than the picture we give of the distribution of the clothes of the captured Confederates among the contrabands. As one of the Southern chivalry said, "This is adding insult to injury. You first entice our property to run away, and then you clothe them in the glorious uniform of the South." It is needless to add that no insult was intended; it was simply the inevitable result of war.

REFUGEES FROM SOUTHERN MISSOURI, DRIVEN FROM THEIR HOMESTEADS BY THE CONFEDERATES, ENCAMPED NEAR GENERAL SIGEL'S DIVISION AT ROLLA.

This sketch of the Southern Missourians driven from their homes by the relentless barbarity of the Confederates is an appealing picture of the horrors of war—the misery and destitution of those unhappy people, of all ages, from the white-haired pioneer to the infant. In one short season men of substance have been stripped of all their hard earnings, their household goods trampled in the dust, their homesteads burnt, their sons murdered and their daughters outraged. The track of Southern chivalry was not told by its victories, but by its devastation. No Juggernaut ever rolled through a land with a more pitiless tread than that of an army which unfolded upon its lying banner that they were fighting for their altars and their homes.

97

THE UNITED STATES TRANSPORT "TERRY" PUSHING HER WAY THROUGH THE SWAMPS AND BAYOUS, BACK OF ISLAND NO. 10.
TO THE ASSISTANCE OF GENERAL POPE AT NEW MADRID.

The task of forcing vessels through the bayous to General Pope, at New Madrid, proved one of unusual difficulties. The United States transport *Terry*, in advance, drawing less water than any other, succeeded in forcing her way through to New Madrid, and opened a passage for steamers to General Pope's command below Island No. 10.

COLONEL LEWIS WALLACE, OF THE ELEVENTH INDIANA VOLUNTEERS (ZOUAVE REGIMENT), AND HIS STAFF, ON SERVICE IN WESTERN VIRGINIA.

This gallant officer, whose portrait, with those of his staff, we present to our readers, was the commander of the Eleventh Indiana Volunteers, and distinguished himself by his march upon Romney, where he surprised and defeated a large body of Confederates. The Eleventh Indiana Regiment distinguished itself most nobly under the gallant, daring, yet prudent leadership of Colonel Wallace. It rendered good service, acting offensively with gallantry and success, and maintaining itself, against all the efforts of the enemy, in a difficult and dangerous country.

NIGHT EXPEDITION TO ISLAND No. 10, IN THE MISSISSIPPI RIVER—SPIKING A CONFEDERATE BATTERY BY A DETACHMENT OF FEDERAL SOLDIERS AND SAILORS, APRIL 2D, 1862.

On the night of the 1st of April, 1862. Colonel Porter took advantage of a terrible storm to make a demonstration against the Confederates in Island No. 10. The night was very dark; there was a desperate gale raging, and the lightning was very frequent and blinding. The spray dashed over the banks of the river, and altogether it was emphatically a night of tempest. Such was the moment chosen by Colonel Porter to dash into the lion's mouth and spike some of his iron teeth. Selecting forty reliable men, and accompanied by six boats' crews of fifteen men each from the gunboats, they proceeded on their purpose, and after a most perilous passage they landed on the famous Island No. 10. The spot they reached was the upper fort, and under cover of the darkness they landed and spiked six guns they found mounted. The garrison fled at the approach of our men.

EMBARKING TROOPS AND GENERAL BUELL'S ARTILLERY AT BIRD'S POINT, MO, BY ORDER OF GENERAL FREMONT.

The threatening attitude which General Hardee, who commanded the Confederates near Cape Girardeau, on the Mississippi, assumed, after the battle of Wilson's Creek, toward Ironton, the terminus of the St. Louis and Iron Mountain Railroad, rendered some movement necessary. General Fremont, having no force to spare from St. Louis, in consequence of the singular apathy of the Minister of War, consequently ordered four regiments and a sufficient force of artillery from Bird's Point.

101

GENERAL SAMUEL D. STURGIS.

General Sturgis, born in Shippensburg, Pa., January 11th, 1822, was graduated from the United States Military Academy, 1846; served in the Mexican War; at the opening of the Civil War was appointed major of the Fourth Cavalry; served in Missouri under General Lyon, whom Sturgis succeeded in command after his death at the battle of Wilson's Creek; was made brigadier general of volunteers, August 10th, 1861; was at the battles of South Mountain, Antietam and Fredericksburg; brevetted major general, United States Army, March 13th, 1865.

GENERAL GEORGE F. SHEPLEY.

General Shepley, born in Saco, Me., January 1st, 1819, died in Portland, Me., July 20th, 1878. He was commissioned colonel of the Twelfth Maine Volunteers, and participated in General Butler's expedition against New Orleans. In 1862 he was appointed military governor of Louisiana. After the inauguration of a civil governor General Shepley was placed in command of the Military District of Eastern Virginia, and became chief of staff to General Weitzel. He continued with the Army of the James to the end of the war, and was appointed the first military governor of that city.

GENERAL DARIUS H. COUCH.

General Couch, born in Southeast, New York, July 23d, 1832, was graduated at the United States Military Academy in 1846. He served in the Mexican War, gaining the brevet of first lieutenant for gallant conduct at Buena Vista. In June, 1861, he became colonel of the Seventh Massachusetts Volunteers; was made brigadier general of volunteers in August, and assigned to a division in General Keyes's corps; was at Fair Oaks, Williamsburg and Malvern Hill; was promoted to major general on July 4th, 1862, and took part at Antietam, Fredericksburg and Chancellorsville.

GENERAL WILLIS A. GORMAN.

General Gorman, born near Flemingsburg, Ky., January 12th, 1814, died in St. Paul, Minn., May 20th, 1876. He served in the Mexican War, and was wounded at Buena Vista. In 1861 he was made colonel of the First Minnesota Regiment, and served in the battle of Bull Run. He was appointed brigadier general of volunteers on September 7th, 1861; was engaged at Fair Oaks, South Mountain and Antietam. He was at the head of the Second Division, Second Corps, till the reorganization of the army following McClellan's removal.

EFFECT OF THE GUNBOAT SHELLS ON THE CONFEDERATES IN THE WOODS, PORT ROYAL, S. C., JANUARY 1st, 1862.

DEATH OF THE CONFEDERATE GENERAL ZOLLICOFFER, IN THE BATTLE OF MILL SPRING, KY., JANUARY 19th, 1862.

While the Confederate waves were surging against the Federal breakers the opposed lines of battle were several times carried so close to each other. that portions of each were mixed up with the other, and hand-to-hand encounters were not unfrequent. Owing to the consequent confusion, the commanders of both sides at times unknowingly came in dangerous vicinity to foes. At one time two mounted officers came trotting along the right flank of the Fourth Kentucky, and noticing their firing upon Confederates near by, shouted to them, "Don't fire on your friends; they are Mississippians." Colonel Fry at this juncture came up the front of his regiment, and with a glance recognized in one of the officers General Zollicoffer. In a twinkling he had pulled out his revolver and fired at the Confederate chiftain, putting a bullet through his breast and causing his fall from the horse and instant death. The Confederate aid put spurs to his horse, and quickly spread the news among the Confederates of the fall of their general.

RETREAT OF THE CONFEDERATE GARRISON, COMMANDED BY GENERAL DRAYTON, FROM FORT WALKE

After gallantly enduring the fire of our invincible navy, under Commander Dupont, for about four hours, in the course of which the destroying
and a flight which eclipsed even that of Bull Run. The chivalry of South Carolina, which, according to Governor Pickens's account, is born inser
path of their flight was encumbered with accoutrements, arms of every description, knapsacks—in a word, everything that could facilitate a flying sol

DURING THE BOMBARDMENT BY THE FEDERAL FLEET, ON THE AFTERNOON OF NOVEMBER 7TH, 1861.

as getting nearer and nearer to the devoted forts, General Drayton gave orders for the retirement of his men. The retreat soon ripened into a flight,
g from Fort Walker to Scull Creek—which separates Hilton Head from the mainland, on which Bluffton stands—threw everything away. The exact
thrown away as worthless.

BATTLE OF PITTSBURG LANDING—BURNING THE DEAD HORSES NEAR THE PEACH ORCHARD.

GATHERING CONFEDERATE OATS—AN INCIDENT IN THE MARCH OF GENERAL PRENTISS'S DIVISION FROM IRONTON TO CAPE GIRARDEAU.

War has its comic as well as its tragic side, and among the former is the incident which we illustrate. A crop of oats, very carefully stowed away by some provident Confederate, came most opportunely to the aid of the loyal horses. That they were duly paid for by the Federal Government did not diminish the pleasure their possession gave to our troops.

LIEUTENANT TILLOTSON'S NAVAL BATTERY OF BOAT HOWITZERS AT THE BATTLE OF NEW BERNE, N. C.

"A CONFEDERATE TREED"—CAPTURE OF LIEUTENANT H. J. SEGAL, OF THE CONFEDERATE ARMY, NEAR FALLS CHURCH.

On Friday, the 4th of October, 1861, a scouting party of eighteen men, under Lieutenant Colonel Winslow and Captain Shattuck, of the Thirty-seventh Regiment, New York Volunteers, were out in the vicinity of Falls Church, Va. As they were proceeding cautiously through a dense wood they heard the tramp of horses and the jingle of sabre scabbards. The lieutenant colonel and the captain, ordering their men to halt, went to reconnoitre. In a short time one of them came upon an open space, where he saw four Confederates seated under a large chestnut tree, engaged in eating chestnuts. The Confederates saw him, and sprang upon their horses. The officer cried, in a loud voice, "Charge!" By the time the scouting party had got up the four gallant horsemen were beyond pursuit. Our men were about gathering up the spoils of victory, when they saw a horse tied to a tree by the roadside. A further search revealed its master, perched upon the lower limbs of a large chestnut. A dozen rifles pointed at his breast soon brought him to reason, and he surrendered.

VIEW OF THE CITY OF NEW BERNE, N. C., FROM THE OPPOSITE SIDE OF NEUSE RIVER.

New Berne was for a time the seat of the Federal Government in North Carolina. A pleasant town, beautifully situated at the confluence of the Neuse and Trent Rivers, midway on the Atlantic line of the State, admirably placed for a great inland water trade, and now over a century old. In 1862 it had only five thousand inhabitants. With its great advantages, had they been wielded by Northern energy, capital and skill, it would have had fifty thousand.

CONSTRUCTION OF FLOATING MORTAR BATTERIES, ETC, UPPER FERRY, ST. LOUIS, MO.

These boats were intended to carry one very heavy mortar each. They were flat boats, very strongly built, and were moved by six oars, two on each side and one at each end. They had breastworks of boiler iron about seven feet high, heavy enough to withstand the discharge of musketry and light field artillery. They were covered with strong awnings to protect the men and armament from the weather. They were painted black and numbered, and were altogether a very curious-looking fleet, evidently better adapted for hard work than for comfort.

BATTLE OF PITTSBURG LANDING—ENGAGEMENT ON THE LEFT WING, GENERAL HURLBUT'S DIVISION, APRIL 6TH, 1862—CHARGE AND REPULSE OF THE CONFEDERATES AT THE PEACH ORCHARD.

General Hurlbut ordered his troops to reserve their fire until the enemy had reached a little ridge near the middle of the field, when they opened a most destructive fire upon the Confederates with grape and musketry, which forced them to retreat precipitately, after losing between two and three hundred killed and wounded, which they left on the field. The Confederates then closed their ranks and retired in the same order as they advanced. The fight all along the left wing was the most bitter and severely contested of the day.

BATTLE OF PITTSBURG LANDING—RETREAT OF DRESSER'S BATTERY, CAPTAIN TIMONY, CENTRE OF FEDERAL POSITION, SUNDAY MORNING, APRIL 6TH, 1862.

Captain Timony was wounded early in the action and carried from the field; but his men fought like tigers. Horses and men dropped on all sides under the galling fire of the enemy, who nearly surrounded them. The Eleventh Iowa Regiment, which supported them, fought desperately; but the overwhelming masses of the enemy pressed closer and closer, and they had to fall back toward the left, leaving the unfortunate Dresser unsupported. The terrible character of this fight will be better understood from the fact that the engagement lasted only fifteen minutes, and that during this time Dresser's battery lost 48 horses and 30 men killed and wounded.

GENERAL PHILIP H. SHERIDAN.

General Philip H. Sheridan, born at Albany, N. Y., in 1831, died in Nonquitt, Mass., August 5th, 1888, was a graduate of United States Military Academy at West Point; served in the Civil War, 1861-'65; from army in Southwest Missouri was transferred to Army of the Cumberland; and for his successful operations at the battle of Murfreesborough was made major general of Volunteers; in the spring of 1864 took command of the cavalry corps of the Army of the Potomac; was in the battle of the Wilderness; and in the fall of 1864 was made major general; in the spring of 1865, through his successful operations at the battle of Five Forks, and others, the Confederates were compelled to abandon Petersburg and Richmond; present at the surrender of General Lee at Appomattox, April 9th, 1865. In 1869 he was made lieutenant general, and assigned to the command of the Missouri Division, with headquarters at Chicago.

GENERAL JOHN A DIX.

General Dix, born in Boscawen, N. H., July 24th., 1798, died in New York city, April 21st, 1879. In December, 1812, he was appointed cadet, and going to Baltimore, aided his father, Major Timothy Dix of the Fourteenth United States Infantry. He was made ensign in 1813, and accompanied his regiment, taking part in the operations on the Canadian frontier. Subsequently he served in the Twenty-first Infantry at Fort Constitution, N. H., where he became second lieutenant in March, 1814; was adjutant to Colonel John D. B. Walback, and in August was transferred to the Third Artillery. In 1819 he was appointed aid-de-camp to General Jacob Brown, then in command of the Northern Military Department, and stationed at Brownsville. At the beginning of the Civil War he took an active part in the formation of the Union Defense Committee, and was its first president. On the President's first call for troops he organized and sent to the field seventeen regiments, and was appointed one of the four major generals to command the New York State forces. In July, 1861, General Dix was sent to Baltimore to take command of the Department of Maryland, and it was through his energetic and judicious measures that the State and the city were prevented from going over to the Confederate cause. In 1863 he was transferred to New York as commander of the Department of the East, which place he held until the close of the war.

116

CAPE GIRARDEAU, MO., AN IMPORTANT STRAGETIC POSITION ON THE MISSISSIPPI BETWEEN CAIRO AND ST. LOUIS.

Cape Girardeau is about 45 miles northwest of Cairo and 160 miles southeast of St. Louis, 1,180 miles from New Orleans and 860 miles from St. Paul, Minn. It is also the terminus of a road which leads to Jackson, the capital of the county, and to Fredericktown, and from thence to Pilot Knob and Ironton. It thus formed the landing point where troops and supplies could be sent from Cairo to Central Missouri.

THE NAVAL BRIGADE, LIEUTENANT PERKINS COMMANDING, CONSTRUCTING THE MAIN BATTERY ON SHUTTER'S HILL TO GUARD ALEXANDRIA, VA., AND COMMAND THE FAIRFAX ROAD.

The New York Naval Brigade rendered good service in its department on many occasions. It was well organized and disciplined, and proved a most valuable arm of the service. In addition to its other duties, it was engaged in constructing a powerful marine battery at Shutter's Hill for the purpose of guarding Alexandria and commanding the approaches of the Fairfax Road. It was an important position, and the work was well planned, strongly constructed and armed with powerful and effective guns.

115

BATTLE OF PITTSBURG LANDING—RECAPTURE OF ARTILLERY BY THE FIRST OHIO AND OTHER REGIMENTS, UNDER GENERAL ROUSSEAU, APRIL 7TH, 1862.

The flight of the Fifty-third and Fifty-seventh Ohio Regiments left Waterhouse's battery, which was planted on a hill to the left of Shiloh Chapel, unprotected; but the Forty-third and Forty-ninth Illinois Regiments came to his aid, and supported it until Colonel Wreish of the Forty-third was killed, when they fell back in tolerable order. The Confederates now charged and took Waterhouse's battery, thus flanking General Sherman, who fell back to the Purdy Road in good order. Here the sudden death of Captain Behr, who was getting his battery in position on the left wing of the new line, created a panic in his company, which broke and left five guns. Not being supported by any other division, General Sherman was forced back to the right of McClernand, where he again formed and shared the fortunes of the day.

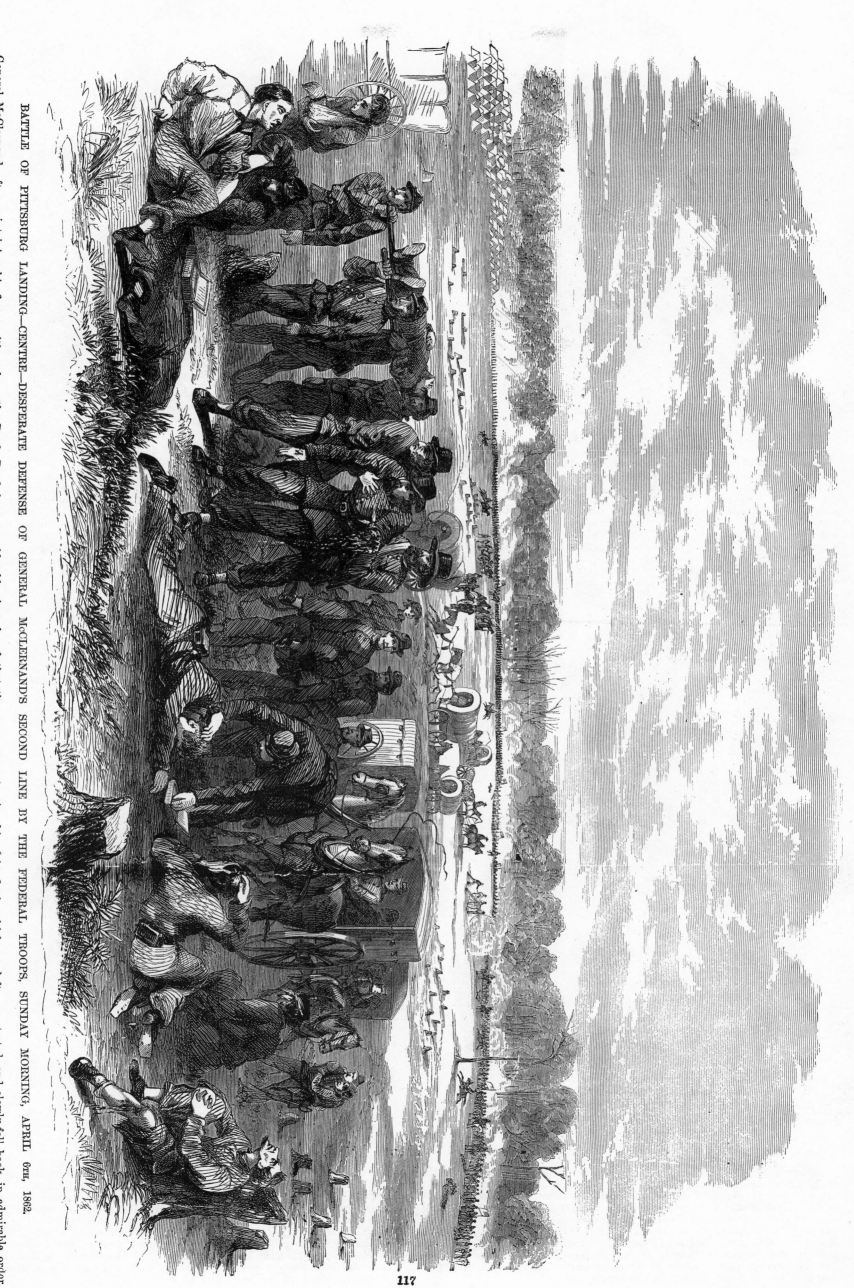

BATTLE OF PITTSBURG LANDING—CENTRE—DESPERATE DEFENSE OF GENERAL McCLERNAND'S SECOND LINE BY THE FEDERAL TROOPS, SUNDAY MORNING, APRIL 6TH, 1862.

General McClernand, after maintaining his first position along the Purdy Road for a considerable time, found that the enemy were turning his right flank, which was left unprotected, and slowly fell back, in admirable order, until he reached the large field occupied by General Oglesby's brigade, while the artillery and supporting regiments guarded his rear. He disposed his forces at right angles, forming in battle line along the edge of the timber fronting the Purdy Road, and toward the right, where the enemy were endeavoring to find an opening. The battle here was fought with extraordinary perseverance and success.

117

GENERAL JAMES SHIELDS.

General Shields, born in Dungannon, County Tyrone, Ireland, in 1810, died in Ottumwa, Ia., June 1st, 1879. He emigrated to the United States in 1826; studied law, and began practice at Kaskaskia, Ill., in 1832. When the Mexican War began he was appointed a brigadier general and was assigned to the command of the Illinois contingent. At Cerro Gordo he gained the brevet of major general, and was shot through the lung. He was mustered out on the 20th of July, 1848. In 1861, he was appointed a brigadier general of volunteers and assigned to the command of General Lander's brigade. After the latter's death, and on March 23d, 1862, at the head of a division of General Banks's army in the Shenandoah Valley, he opened the second campaign with the victory at Winchester, Va.; resigning his commission on the 28th of March, 1863.

COLONEL EVERETT PEABODY.

Colonel Peabody, born in Springfield, Mass., in 1831, died near Pittsburg Landing, Tenn., April 6th, 1862. Was graduated at Harvard in 1849; became a railway engineer. Was colonel of the Twenty-fifth Regiment, Missouri Volunteers, and was killed at Shiloh. Upon his joining the forces under General Grant the command of a brigade under General Prentiss was assigned him, and on the field at Pittsburg Landing he was acting brigadier on the exposed right of the army, nearest the enemy. To his alertness and bravery is in great part due the saving of our army on the field of Pittsburg.

GENERAL JOHN M. SCHOFIELD.

General Schofield, born in Chautauqua County, N. Y., September 29th, 1831, was graduated at the United States Military Academy in 1853. At the opening of the Civil War he entered the volunteer service as major of the First Missouri Volunteers April 26th, 1861, and was appointed chief of staff to General Nathaniel Lyon, with whom he served during his campaign in Missouri; was appointed brigadier general of volunteers November 21st, 1861, and major general November 29th, 1862. He took part in the battles of Resaca, Dallas, Kenesaw Mountain and Atlanta. For his services at the battle of Franklin he was made a brigadier general and brevet major general in the regular army.

GENERAL DANIEL E. SICKLES.

General Sickles was born in New York city, October 20th, 1823. At the beginning of the Civil War he raised the Excelsior Brigade of United States Volunteers in New York city, and was commissioned by the President as colonel of one of the five regiments on September 3d, 1861. The President nominated him brigadier general of volunteers. The Senate rejected his name in March, 1862, but confirmed a second nomination. He commanded a brigade under General Hooker, and gained distinction at Williamsburg, Fair Oaks and Malvern Hill. At Chancellorsville he displayed gallantry and energy, and at Gettysburg he lost a leg. He continued in active service until the beginning of 1865.

SHIP ISLAND, NEAR THE MOUTH OF THE MISSISSIPPI—UNITED STATES WAR STEAMER "MISSISSIPPI" FIRING ON A CONFEDERATE STEAMER.

GENERAL ASBOTH AND STAFF AT THE BATTLE OF PEA RIDGE, ARK., MARCH 6TH-8TH, 1862.

The gallantry displayed by General Asboth in the victory of Pea Ridge gives great interest to the spirited sketch of himself and staff which we present to our readers. Among the officers in the sketch were Acting Brigadier General Albert, Brigade Quartermaster McKay, the young commander of the Fremont Hussars, Major George E. Waring, Jr., from New York city, formerly major of the Garibaldi Guards, and the general's aids-de-camp, Gillen and Kroll, etc. Among General Asboth's most constant attendants was his favorite dog, York, a splendid specimen of the St. Bernard species.

BATTLE OF ROANOKE ISLAND, FEBRUARY 8TH, 1862—DECISIVE BAYONET CHARG

Our illustration was taken at the moment when the enemy, not waiting to receive the bayonet charge of the zouaves, who were then in the
that the Fifty-first New York Regiment, Colonel Ferrero, who had advanced on the battery by a flank movement on the left, planted the Stars an

NEW YORK VOLUNTEERS (HAWKINS'S ZOUAVES), ON THE THREE-GUN BATTERY.

over the parapets, fled in utter confusion, throwing away their arms and accoutrements to facilitate their escape. It was at this important moment over the ramparts.

THE BURNSIDE EXPEDITION—MELANCHOLY DEATHS OF COLONEL J. W. ALLEN, SURGEON WALLER AND THE SECOND MATE OF
THE "ANN E. THOMPSON," ON JANUARY 15TH, 1862, NEAR HATTERAS INLET.

LOSS OF THE "MONITOR"—GALLANT ATTEMPT OF THE OFFICERS AND CREW OF THE UNITED STATES STEAMER "RHODE ISDAND,"
TO RESCUE THE CREW OF THE "MONITOR," OFF CAPE HATTERAS, AT MIDNIGHT, DECEMBER 30TH, 1862.

The closing day of 1862 will always be a dark one in our history, for just on the threshold of its birth the pet monster of our ironclads went down
off Hatteras, with our flag flying on its tower, and in the midst of a furious storm. Its sudden and unlooked-for fate recalled to every mind that
memorable Sunday in March when it signalized its advent to war by driving back to its Norfolk retreat the terrible *Merrimac*.

SCOUTING PARTY OF THE NINTH INDIANA VOLUNTEERS, OR, AS THEY WERE CALLED, "THE TIGERS OF THE BLOODY NINTH."

DISCOVERY OF A CONFEDERATE BATTERY AT MESSECH'S POINT BY A SCOUTING PARTY OF THE TENTH REGIMENT
OF NEW YORK ZOUAVES.

The activity of the Confederates on the Potomac and the confluent rivers was almost incredible. In one night some point hitherto defenseless was made to bristle with cannon, and the first intimation of its locality was a leaden messenger winging its way on its mission of death. A party of the Tenth Regiment of New York Zouaves, while out scouting through a dense wood, came suddenly in sight of Messech's Point, and there beheld the Confederates at work upon an almost completed battery, which had sprung up with magical rapidity.

INTERIOR VIEW OF FORT BEAUREGARD, ON BAY POINT, OPPOSITE FORT WALKER, PORT ROYAL, S. C.

Fort Beauregard, at Bay Point, on the point opposite Fort Walker, was built of sand and palmetto logs on a sand spit on the extreme southerly end of Hunting Island. The work on the harbor or sea front was what is termed a lunette, and mounted twelve guns. To the right of this lunette was a small salient mounting three guns, and to the left, a small work, or redan, mounting two guns. In the work was a large magazine which, when captured by the Federal troops, contained one thousand five hundred rounds of fixed ammunition, and in the wet ditch were large quantities of loose powder, destroyed by the Confederates before they evacuated the fort.

124

VIEW OF THE CAMP OF THE TWENTIETH INDIANA REGIMENT; ALSO OF FORT HATTERAS AND THE ANCHORAGE AT HATTERAS INLET, N. C.

This camp, near Fort Hatteras, was formed when the Federal troops occupied the island. It first received Colonel Bendix and his German regiment. On their return to Newport News it was taken possession of by the Ninth Zouaves; who vacated it upon the arrival of the Twentieth Indiana Regiment, October 5th, 1861, the Ninth removing to Camp Wool.

125

EVACUATION OF CORINTH, MISS.—CONFEDERATE FORTIFICATIONS, FROM THE NORTHERN ANGLE, LOOKING SOUTH—PURSUIT OF THE RETREATING CONFEDERATES BY FEDERAL CAVALRY UNDER GENERAL SMITH.

The details of the evacuation of Corinth, by Beauregard, beyond those contained in the official reports of General Halleck, were that Beauregard's force did not exceed 60,000 men. Nobody was left in town except women and children and old men; everything was taken away except a few provisions, which were burned. They did not leave a single gun, and had been moving their stores for two weeks, and their troops for six days. Their fortifications were five miles long, extending from the Memphis and Charleston to the Mobile and Ohio Roads. But they were much weaker than supposed. They could have been carried by storm at any time.

BIVOUAC OF THE ELEVENTH INDIANA VOLUNTEER REGIMENT (ZOUAVES), COLONEL LEWIS WALLACE COMMANDING, AT CUMBERLAND, MD.

Our special artist who accompanied General McClellan's command sketched the gallant Eleventh Indiana Zouaves in their bivouac at Cumberland, Md. Great interest was attached to this regiment after its brilliant attack at Romney.

EVACUATION OF CORINTH, MISS.—BURNING OF STATIONS, WAREHOUSES AND SUPPLIES—ENTRY OF FEDERAL TROOPS.

Corinth was not demolished, but it was very much deteriorated—about as bad as the Corinth of old. In the town the scene was dismal indeed; nothing was occupied, all was vacant. In the fields north of the town, where the Confederate camps had been, there were the common evidences of their late presence, but nothing uncommon. Arms were picked up in all parts of the field, and a few hundred prisoners were taken.

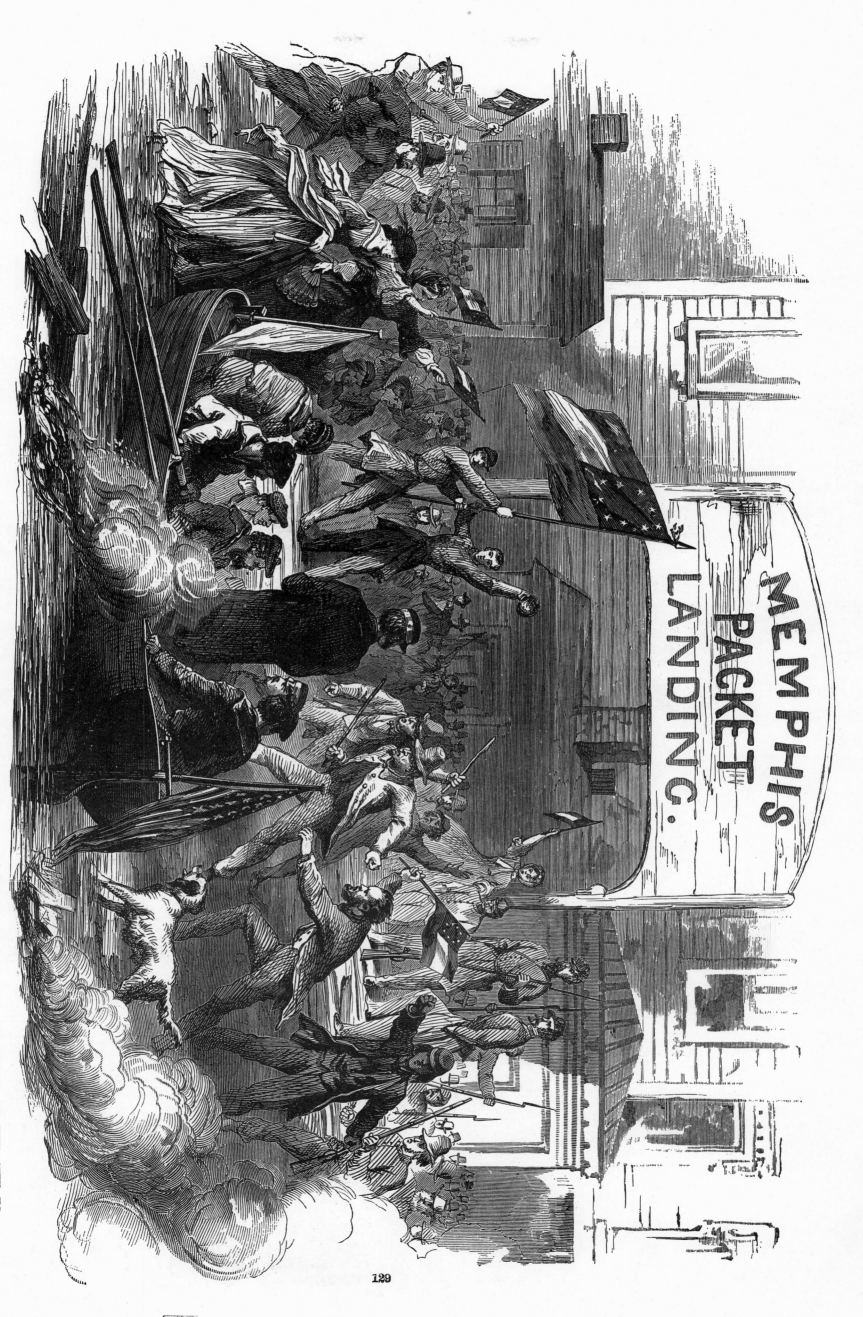

LANDING OF CAPTAIN BAILEY AND LIEUTENANT PERKINS ON THE LEVEE, NEW ORLEANS, WITH A FLAG OF TRUCE, TO DEMAND THE SURRENDER OF THE CITY TO THE FEDERAL GOVERNMENT.

Captain Bailey, bearing a flag of truce, put off in a boat, accompanied by Lieutenant George H. Perkins, with a demand for the surrender of the city, as well as for the immediate substitution of the Federal for the Confederate ensign. They stepped ashore and made their way to the City Hall through a motley crowd, which kept cheering for the South and Jefferson Davis, and uttering groans and hisses for President Lincoln and the "Yankee" fleet. General Lovell returned an unqualified refusal, besides advising Mayor Monroe of New Orleans not to surrender the city.

129

ADVANCE OF THE FEDERAL ARMY UNDER GENERAL McCLELLAN TOWARD YORKTOWN, VA.—SCENE ON THE ROAD BETWEEN BIG BETHEL AND YORKTOWN, APRIL 5TH, 1862.

When General McClellan reached Locust Hill, on April 2d, 1862, he found fifty-eight thousand men and much of his artillery already there. The following day he moved his whole army toward Yorktown, in order to prevent, if possible, Johnston's re-enforcement of General Magruder, expecting to receive in time the co-operation of the naval force in Hampton Roads, which he thought would reduce the Confederate batteries both on the James and York Rivers.

ARRIVAL OF GENERAL McCLELLAN, APRIL 5TH, 1862, TO TAKE PERSONAL COMMAND OF THE FEDERAL ARMY IN ITS ADVANCE ON YORKTOWN—ENTHUSIASTIC RECEPTION BY THE TROOPS.

On the 11th of March, 1862, the President issued an order relieving General McClellan of part of the responsibility heretofore devolving upon him. The order stated that "General McClellan, having personally taken the field at the head of the Army of the Potomac, until otherwise ordered, he is relieved from the command of the other military departments he retaining the command of the Department of the Potomac." Our illustration represents his arrival, and enthusiastic reception by the troops.

THE GREAT NAVAL BATTLE ON THE MISSISSIPPI—FIRST DAY'S BOMBARDMENT—FEDERAL SCHOONERS OFF FORTS JACKSON AND ST. PHILIP, COMMANDING THE PASSAGE OF THE RIVER.

The Federal offensive force consisted of six sloops of war, sixteen gunboats and twenty-one mortar vessels. These were accompanied by a large number of storeships, tenders, etc. On the 18th of April they anchored three miles below Forts Jackson and St. Philip, and prepared for active operations. Captain Porter, commanding the mortar flotilla, wishing to ascertain their range before his actual attack, stationed the *Arietta, John Griffiths* and *Orvetta* about two and a half miles from the forts. The *Arietta* fired the first shot, to which Fort Jackson replied. The Confederate shots fell short more than fifty yards every time, while the effect of our shells on the fort was such that after two explosions the enemy retired from their barbette guns, and afterward only used those in the casemates.

132

THE GREAT NAVAL BATTLE ON THE MISSISSIPPI—PASSAGE OF THE SECOND DIVISION OF THE FEDERAL SQUADRON PAST FORT ST. PHILIP, APRIL 24th, 1862.

On April 24th, at three o'clock in the morning, the greater part of Commodore Farragut's squadron passed the forts through one of the most terrible fires ever known. It consisted of five sloops of war and nine gunboats. The mortar flotilla and eight war steamers remained below, thus putting the forts between two fires, and cutting off all communication with New Orleans. General Duncan surrendered the forts unconditionally to Captain Porter, on Monday, April 28th. There were found about seven hundred men in each fort.

133

GENERAL JOHN FULTON REYNOLDS.

General Reynolds, born in Lancaster, Pa., September 20th, 1820, died near Gettysburg, Pa., July 1st, 1863, was graduated at the United States Military Academy in 1843; served in the Mexican War and was brevetted major for services at Buena Vista. He was appointed military governor of Fredericksburg, Va., in May, 1862, and was engaged at the battles of Mechanicsville, Gaines's Mill and Glendale, where he was taken prisoner. He rejoined the army on his exchange, August 8th, 1862, was engaged in the campaign of Northern Virginia, and commanded his division at the second battle of Bull Run. He was commissioned major general of volunteers, November 29th, 1862; succeeded General Hooker in command of the First Corps of the Army of the Potomac; was engaged at Fredericksburg, and at Gettysburg he was struck by a rifle ball and killed.

GENERAL GEORGE C. STRONG.

General Strong, born in Stockbridge, Vt., October 16th, 1832, died in New York city, July 30th, 1863, was graduated at the United States Military Academy in 1857; assigned to the ordnance, and in 1859 became assistant at Watervliet Arsenal, of which he took command in May, 1861. He was ordnance officer on General McDowell's staff at Bull Run, and was then attached successively to the staffs of General McClellan and General Butler, whose chief of staff he became in May, 1862. He commanded the expedition from Ship Island to Biloxi, Miss., in April, 1862, and that to Ponchatoula in September. He was made brigadier general of volunteers, November 29th, 1862; was on sick leave in New York from the following December till June, 1863, and then commanded a brigade in the operations against Charleston, S. C. At the assault on Fort Wagner, July 18th, he was mortally wounded. He was at once removed to New York city.

GENERAL GODFREY WEITZEL.

General Weitzel, born in Cincinnati, O., November 1st, 1835, died in Philadelphia, Pa., March 19th, 1884, was graduated from the United States Military Academy in 1855; became first lieutenant of engineers in 1860, and was attached to the staff of General Butler as chief engineer of the Department of the Gulf. After the capture of New Orleans he became assistant military commander and acting mayor of the city. He was commissioned brigadier general of volunteers, August 29th, 1862; captain of engineers, March 3d, 1863; on July 8th, 1863, he was brevetted lieutenant colonel, United States Army, for gallant services at the siege of Port Hudson. He joined the Western Louisiana campaign, and from May till September, 1864, was chief engineer of the Army of the James. In August, 1864, he was brevetted major general of volunteers.

GENERAL JOHN SEDGWICK.

General Sedgwick, born in Cornwall, Conn., September 13th, 1813, died near Spottsylvania Courthouse, Va., May 9th, 1864, was graduated at the United States Military Academy in 1837; served in the Florida and Mexican Wars, and was successively brevetted captain and major for gallant conduct at Contreras, Churubusco and Chapultepec. At the beginning of the Civil War he was lieutenant colonel of the Second Cavalry; on April 25th, 1861, he was promoted to the colonelcy of the Fourth Cavalry; and on August 31st was commissioned a brigadier general of volunteers. He took part in the siege of Yorktown, and rendered good service at the battle of Fair Oaks. While directing the placing of some pieces of artillery in position in front of Spottsylvania Courthouse he was struck in the head by a bullet from a sharpshooter and killed.

FIRST DIVISION OF PENNSYLVANIA VOLUNTEERS, UNDER BREVET MAJOR GENERAL CADWALADER, ENTERING BALTIMORE HARBOR FOR THE OCCUPATION OF BALTIMORE, MAY 15TH, 1861.

On Wednesday, May 15th, 1861, the steamers and propellers containing General Cadwalader's division, were seen entering the harbor of Baltimore. The troops consisted of the First Division of Pennsylvania Volunteers, under the command of General Cadwalader, intended for the occupation of Baltimore. The fleet of boats was cordially greeted on its way up the harbor, the large ships and the small bungies displaying the American flag.

SKIRMISH NEAR BEAUFORT, S. C., BETWEEN CONFEDERATE CAVALRY AND THE FEDERAL PICKETS, DECEMBER 5TH, 1861.

On December 5th, 1861, about eight o'clock in the evening, the first skirmish on land took place between the Federal troops and a party of South Carolinians. The pickets which had been thrown out on the shell road—the main and only avenue to the village—had been stationed in their position but a few moments before a body of Confederate cavalry, numbering twenty or thirty men, came upon them, unexpectedly to both sides. The Confederates discharged their revolvers, and hit one of the Federals in the neck, inflicting a painful but not dangerous wound. The fire was returned, but, as it was dark, with what effect could not be ascertained. After this the pickets were not disturbed. The spot where this skirmish took place is about a mile and a half to the southwest of Beaufort, on the main road.

GALLANT CHARGE OF THE SEVENTEENTH, FORTY-EIGHTH AND FORTY-NINTH REGIMENTS OF IL

The first charge on the Confederate works of Fort Donelson was made Thursday afternoon. The surroundings of this intrenchment were of th
had a spectral look, from the few dead leaves which hung to their branches. Beyond this was a very steep hillside, on which the intrenchment was
Seventeenth, Forty-eighth and Forty-ninth Regiments rushed headlong on the foe; but the nature of the ground was too much for them, and after
good order, after losing forty men killed and two hundred wounded.

, LED BY COLONEL MORRISON, ON THE OUTWORKS OF FORT DONELSON, FEBRUARY 13TH, 1862.

cter for our troops. In front of the intrenchment was a quantity of fallen timber, and the ground was full of underbrush and oak scrub. These efended by a long line of rifle pits. About two o'clock in the afternoon General McClernand gave the order to charge, and at the word the te conflict, in which many fell without seeing their foe, Colonel Morrison, who had led them like a hero, ordered them *to* retire. This was done in

THE THIRD RHODE ISLAND VOLUNTEERS DRIVING THE CONFEDERATE SHARPSHOOTERS FROM THE WOODS ON JAMES ISLAND, SOUTH CAROLINA, BY A BAYONET CHARGE, JUNE 16TH, 1862.

A DETACHMENT OF THE NEW YORK RIFLES FIRING UPON COMPANY B OF THE SAME REGIMENT, NEAR WILLETT'S POINT, SEPTEMBER 9TH, 1861.

A sad affair occurred near Willett's Point, on Monday night, September 9th, 1861, in which two soldiers were shot dead and several wounded. A company of men, ostensibly recruited for the New York Rifles, Colonel Legendre, were offered by Captain Cresto, who commanded them, to Colonel Fardella, who was also raising a regiment, and Monday night was fixed on for the desertion to take place. At Captain Cresto's request his company, B, was placed on guard, and pickets were stationed near Roe's tavern; but before the time appointed Colonel Legendre heard of the plot, and ordered Captain Gossamer and Lieutenant Georgeo to take charge of the camp. Patrols were sent out, who ordered every man back to his quarters. Captain Cresto demanded the authority for such a proceeding, and while they were parleying a pistol was accidentally discharged by one of the intended deserters. The detachment sent to stop their desertion, fancying they were attacked, immediately fired, and killed privates Markoe and Sassi, besides wounding several others. Captain Cresto escaped, but was subsequently captured near Flushing.

CAMP LILLIE, HEADQUARTERS OF GENERAL FREMONT, JEFFERSON CITY, MO., OCTOBER 1st, 1861.

Jefferson City is on the Missouri River, 142 miles from its mouth, and 125 miles from St. Louis. It is on the direct route of the Pacific Railroad. The location of Jefferson City is very striking. On the towering hill which frowns over the Missouri stands the Capitol, built of magnesium limestone. The town site is seamed with sharp ridges and deep hollows running parallel with the river. These had been eagerly taken advantage of in constructing the fortifications. About a mile to the south of the city was the headquarters of General Fremont, situated upon a beautiful slope, commanding a fine military prospect. It was called Camp Lillie, after his eldest daughter, Lillie Benton Fremont.

COOKING IN CAMP—THE KITCHEN OF THE FREMONT DRAGOONS AT TIPTON, MO.

Tipton, which is 38 miles from Jefferson City, 26 from Sedalia and 13 from California City, is situated on the Pacific Railway, which passes through Jefferson City, and has its terminus at Sedalia. At all these cities large bodies of troops were placed by General Fremont, so as to enable him to concentrate, at a very short time, an overwhelming force to bear upon the Confederates. Our sketch of the kitchen was made when the army of cooks were in full preparation for the daily dinner.

FORT PULASKI, AT THE ENTRANCE OF THE SAVANNAH RIVER, GA., IN 1861.

Fort Pulaski, on Cockspur Island, was built by the United States Government in 1829–'31, for the defense of Tybee Roads and the Savannah River approach to the city of Savannah, Ga. In January, 1861, it was seized and occupied by the military authorities of the State of Georgia, and held by them until transferred to the Confederate Government, by whom it was strongly armed and garrisoned.

THE BOMBARDMENT OF FORT PULASKI—SECOND DAY, FRIDAY, APRIL 11TH, 1862.

General Quincy A. Gillmore took personal command of Tybee Island on the 20th of February, 1862, and at once began the construction of earthworks. On the 9th of April everything was in readiness for the bombardment, and early on the following morning a summons for the surrender of Fort Pulaski was sent, through Lieutenant J. H. Wilson, to its commander, Colonel Charles H. Olmstead, by General David Hunter. The surrender having been refused, order was given to immediately open fire. This was done at about eight o'clock on the morning of the 10th, from the two 13-inch mortars in charge of Captain Sanford. The remaining two batteries joined in, and their united fire thundered all day, and was steadily responded to from the fort. The bombardment of the fort was kept up until the next morning, and at daybreak of the 11th the firing again commenced on both sides. The Federal fire was mainly directed against the southeastern portion of the fort, and by two o'clock in the afternoon the breach had become so wide that the arches of the casemate were laid bare. This was followed by the hoisting of a white flag, when firing ceased. The immediate and unconditional surrender of the fort was agreed on.

141

WHITE HOUSE LANDING, PAMUNKEY RIVER, VA., THE GRAND DEPOT OF THE COMMISSARIAT AND ORDNANCE DEPARTMENT OF THE ARMY BEFORE RICHMOND.

White House Landing, on the Pamunkey River, was the grand depot of General McClellan's army, and from it there was a constant communication with Fortress Monroe and Washington. It derived its name from the house in the centre of the sketch, the residence of Mrs. Custis before she became the wife of George Washington.

BATTLE OF WILLIAMSBURG, VA., ON THE PENINSULA BETWEEN YORK AND JAMES RIVERS, MAY 6TH, 1862.

General Hancock's sudden charge decided the battle, for it left the rear ker of the position in Federal hands. With the re-enforcements which McClellan had caused to be sent him immediately upon reaching the scene, late in the afternoon, Hancock took possession of all the ground he had previously occupied, and night closed upon what proved to be a dearly bought victory for the Federals. They had, in fact, gained it after sustaining a loss of 2,228 in killed and wounded, the Confederate loss being only about half that number. Early on the 6th of May Williamsburg was occupied by the Federals, while Johnston's army was again beyond the Chickahominy.

143

ADMIRAL DAVID D. PORTER.

Admiral Porter, born in Chester, Delaware County, Pa., June 8th, 1813, entered the United States Navy as midshipman on February 2d, 1829 cruised in the Mediterranean, and then served on the Coast Survey until he was promoted to lieutenant, February 27th, 1841. He was in the Mediterranean and Brazilian waters until 1845, when he was appointed to the Naval Observatory in Washington; and in 1846 he was sent by the government on a secret mission to Hayti, and reported on the condition of affairs there. He served during the entire Mexican War, had charge of the naval rendezvous in New Orleans, and was engaged in every action on the coast, first as lieutenant, and afterward as commanding officer of the *Spitfire*. At the beginning of the Civil War he was ordered to command the steam frigate *Powhatan*, which was dispatched to join the Gulf Blockading Squadron at Pensacola, and to aid in re-enforcing Fort Pickens. On April 22d, 1861, he was appointed commodore, and subsequently he was placed in command of the mortar fleet; joined Farragut's fleet in March, 1862, and bombarded Fort Jackson and Fort St. Philip, below New Orleans, from the 18th to the 24th of April, 1862, during which engagement twenty thousand bombs were exploded in the Confederate works. In July Admiral Porter was ordered with his mortar flotilla to Fort Monroe, where he resigned charge of it, and was ordered to command the Mississippi Squadron as acting rear admiral in September, 1862. For his services at Vicksburg Porter received the thanks of Congress and the commission of rear admiral, dated July 4th, 1863. Soon afterward he ran past the batteries of Vicksburg, and captured the Confederate forts at Grand Gulf. On August 1st, 1863, he arrived at New Orleans in his flagship *Black Hawk*, accompanied by the gunboat *Tuscumbia*. In the Spring of 1864 he co-operated with General Banks in the unsuccessful Red River expedition. In October, 1864, he was transferred to the North Atlantic Squadron. He appeared at Fort Fisher on December 24th, 1864, and began to bombard the forts at the mouth of the Cape Fear River. The works were captured January 15th, 1865, by a combined body of soldiers, sailors and marines, after seven hours of desperate fighting. Admiral Porter received a vote of thanks from Congress, which was the fourth that he received during the war. He was promoted vice admiral July 25th, 1865, and admiral of the navy August 15th, 1870. Died in Washington, D. C., February 13th, 1891.

GENERAL WINFIELD SCOTT HANCOCK.

General Hancock, born in Montgomery Square, Montgomery County, Pa., February 14th, 1824, died on Governor's Island, New York harbor, February 9th, 1886, was graduated at the United States Military Academy, July 1st, 1844. He was at once brevetted second lieutenant in the Sixth Infantry, and assigned to duty at Fort Towson, Indian Territory. Served in the Mexican War, and was brevetted first lieutenant for gallant and meritorious conduct at Contreras and Churubusco. From 1848 till 1855 he served as regimental quartermaster and adjutant, being most of the time stationed at St. Louis. On November 7th, 1855, he was appointed assistant quartermaster, with the rank of captain, and ordered to Fort Myers, Fla., where General Harney was in command of the military forces operating against the Seminoles. He served under this officer during the troubles in Kansas in 1857–'58, and afterward accompanied his expedition to Utah. He was commissioned a brigadier general of volunteers by President Lincoln, September 23d, 1861, and at once bent all his energies to aid in the organization of the Army of the Potomac. During the Peninsula campaign under General McClellan he was especially conspicuous at the battles of Williamsburg and Frazier's Farm. He took an active part in the subsequent campaign in Maryland, at the battles of South Mountain and Antietam, and was assigned to the command of the First Division of the Second Army Corps on the battlefield during the second day's fight at Antietam, September 17th, 1862. He was soon afterward made a major general of volunteers, and commanded the same division in the attempt to storm Marye's Heights at the battle of Fredericksburg, December 13th, 1862. In the three days' fight at Chancellorsville, in May, 1863, Hancock's division took a prominent part. At Gettysburg he commanded on the left centre, which was the main point assailed by the Confederates, and was shot from his horse. Though dangerously wounded, he remained on the field till he saw that the enemy's assault was broken. Disabled by his wound, he was not again employed on active duty until March, 1864. On March 12th, 1864, he was appointed a brigadier general in the Regular Army for gallant and distinguished services in the battles of the Wilderness, Spottsylvania and Cold Harbor, and in all the operations of the army in Virginia under Lieutenant General Grant. In the movement against the Southside Railroad, which began October 26th, General Hancock took a leading part, and, although the expedition failed, his share of it was brilliant and successful. This was his last action. On July 26th, 1866, he was appointed a major general in the Regular Army, and was assigned to the command of the Department of the Missouri. He was relieved at his own request, March 28th, 1868, and given the command of the Division of the Atlantic, with headquarters in New York city.

145

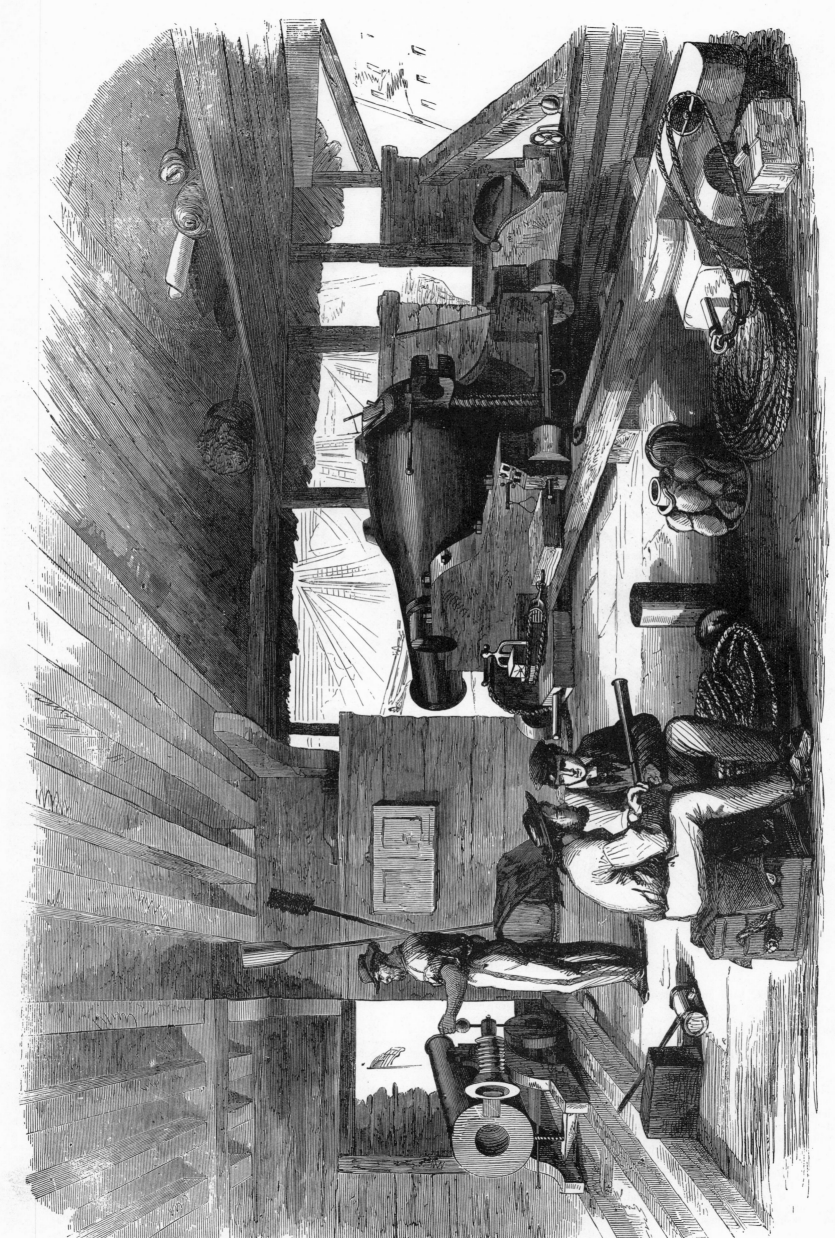

NAVAL PRACTICE BATTERY, NAVY YARD, WASHINGTON, D. C.

We present to our readers a sketch of what was called the Naval Practice Battery, where our young gunners rehearsed before they got into the terrible ordeal of battle. Simple as the loading and firing of a gun may sound, it is an operation which tries the nerves, and requires the utmost nicety of adjustment. It is really and truly as much an act of science, if properly done, as the most delicate surgical operation.

TERRIBLE EFFECT OF A DISCHARGE OF GRAPE FROM FORT JACKSON ON THE FEDERAL GUNBOAT "IROQUOIS," CAPTAIN DE CAMP, APRIL 24TH, 1862, WHICH KILLED EIGHT AND WOUNDED SEVEN SEAMEN, OUT OF A DAHLGREN GUN'S CREW OF TWENTY-FIVE MEN, UNDER LIEUTENANT McNAIR.

One of the most terrible events of this desperate battle was the slaughter on board the gunboat Iroquois. In the midst of the engagement of the 24th of April, 1862, a discharge of grape from Fort Jackson killed eight and wounded seven, out of a gun's crew of twenty-five men, at the same minute. A spectator of the horrible scene told our artist it was one of the most appalling things he had ever seen, but it only nerved the survivors to renewed exertions. Lieutenant McNair fought his gun with great gallantry, and was one of those who escaped.

147

FRONT ROYAL, MANASSAS GAP RAILROAD, BLUE RIDGE MOUNTAINS IN THE DISTANCE—THE FEDERAL ARMY ENTERING THE TOWN.

Front Royal is situated on the Manassas Gap Railroad, on the banks of the Shenandoah, is ten miles from Strasburg and fifty-one miles from Manassas Junction. General Banks, at the head of his troops, dashed down the mountain and through the romantic village of Front Royal, which resounded with the rumble of wagons and clatter of hoofs, mingled with the music of the church bells calling to morning service. Hastening on toward the scene of conflict, to his surprise he brought up against his own pickets, and found that, instead of his own column, Fremont was upon the enemy.

148

GENERAL BANKS'S DIVISION RECROSSING THE POTOMAC FROM WILLIAMSPORT, MD, TO ATTACK THE CONFEDERATE ARMY UNDER GENERAL JACKSON—THE BAND OF THE FORTY-SIXTH PENNSYLVANIA VOLUNTEERS PLAYING THE NATIONAL AIRS ON THE VIRGINIA SHORE.

The retreat of General Banks was, under the circumstances of the case, a great military necessity, and admirably conducted; but, directly the pressure was removed, he returned to the Valley to drive out the invader. Our illustration is of the impressive scene of recrossing the Potomac on the mission of vengeance and patriotism.

GENERAL GEORGE G. MEADE.

General Meade, born in Cadiz, Spain, December 31st, 1815, died in Philadelphia, Pa., November 6th, 1872, was graduated from the United States Military Academy in 1835, and began active service in the Seminole War in the same year, as second lieutenant; upon the call to arms in 1861, he was made brigadier general; fought valiantly at Mechanicsville, Gaines's Mill and at Cross Roads, Va., where he was wounded; at Antietam he took charge of General Hooker's corps upon the latter being wounded. In 1862, he was made major general, and on June 28th, 1862, a message from Washington arrived on the field with orders for Meade to relieve Hooker as commander of the Army of the Potomac. On July 1st he met Lee at Gettysburg, where the greatest battle of the war was fought.

GENERAL JOHN A. LOGAN.

General Logan, born in Jackson County, Ill., February 9th, 1826, died in Washington, D. C., December 26th, 1886. In July, 1861, he fought in the ranks of Colonel Richardson's regiment in the battle of Bull Run. In August he organized the Thirty-first Illinois Infantry, and was appointed its colonel, September 13th. He led his regiment in the attack on Fort Henry and at Fort Donelson, where he received a wound that incapacitated him for active service for some time. He was made brigadier general of volunteers, March 5th, 1862; during Grant's Northern Mississsippi campaign General Logan commanded the Third Division of the Seventeenth Army Corps under General McPherson, and was promoted major general of volunteers.

GENERAL JAMES B. McPHERSON.

General McPherson, born in Sandusky, Ohio, November 14th, 1828, died near Atlanta, Ga., July 22d, 1864, was graduated at the United States Military Academy in 1853. At the beginning of the Civil War he applied for active duty with the army in the field, where his promotion was very rapid. When active operations began in the spring of 1862 he was transferred to the staff of General Grant, with whom he served as chief engineer at Fort Henry, Fort Donelson, Shiloh and the siege of Corinth. He repulsed the Confederates at Canton, Miss.; second in command to General Sherman in the expedition to Meridian in 1864; and commanded the Seventeenth Army Corps in the great four months' campaign of 1864 that ended in the capture of Atlanta, near where he was killed.

GENERAL GEORGE H. THOMAS.

General Thomas, born in Southampton County, Va., July 31st, 1816, died in San Francisco, Cal., March 28th, 1870, was graduated from the United States Military Academy, July 1st, 1840, and commissioned second lieutenant in the Third Artillery; served in the Florida War, 1840–'42; Mexican War 1846–'48; War against the Seminoles 1849–'50. He was appointed brigadier general of volunteers, August 17th, 1861, and assigned to duty on the Department of the Cumberland. On 25th of April, 1862, he was made major general. General Thomas served with distinction to the close of the War and was rewarded by receiving a vote of thanks from Congress.

BATTLE OF SHILOH, OR PITTSBURG LANDING—COLONEL JOHNSON ENDEAVORING TO CAPTURE A CONFEDERATE OFFICER,
BUT GETS ONLY A WIG.

Colonel A. K. Johnson of the Twenty-eighth Illinois Regiment has, during the late war, shared in the dangers of many a daring adventure. On the last day of the action at Shiloh, or Pittsburg Landing, and while the Confederates were flying in confusion from their works, three of the officers in their flight passed very near the place where Colonel Johnson was stationed. The colonel instantly started in pursuit. Coming within pistol range, he fired at the nearest of his flying foes. This brought the Confederate officer down on his horse's neck. Colonel Johnson, believing this to be a feint to avoid a second shot, determined to drag him from his saddle by main force. Riding up to his side for this purpose, he seized him by the hair of his head, but to his astonishment and disgust he only brought off the Confederate major's wig. Instantly recovering his headway, he again started for the delinquent, but his pistol had done its work, and before the colonel reached him his lifeless body had fallen from the saddle.

SUCCESSFUL CHARGE OF COMPANY H, FIRST MASSACHUSETTS REGIMENT (CAPTAIN CARRUTH), ON A CONFEDERATE REDAN
BEFORE YORKTOWN, APRIL 26TH, 1862.

On the morning of Saturday, April 26th, 1862, Company H of the First Massachusetts Volunteers, led by Captain Carruth, made a most brilliant charge on a Confederate redoubt, and took it at the point of the bayonet. It was defended by a company of the First Virginia Regiment, who fought with that Old Dominion valor which, to use a phrase probably heard before, "was worthy of a better cause." The Federals were exposed to a most galling fire from the instant they left the shelter of the woods until they reached the brink of the deep ditch fronting the parapet.

BOMBARDMENT OF FORT HENRY—INT

The fleet of gunboats commanded by Commodore Foote steamed up the channel, and reached the head of the island soon after 12 o'clock. At 12: The boats kept steadily on, slowly but constantly in motion, and the firing was kept up deliberately and with regularity. The shots, some of them, we in the fort stuck well to their guns, and fired with great coolness and accuracy of aim, many of their shots striking the boats. They lost the use of their missiles into the fort. Soon one of the Confederate guns was dismantled, and then the fire from the fort perceptibly slackened. The fleet kept sand. One shell burst directly over one of the guns, and killed or wounded every Confederate at it. Commodore Foote was still getting nearer and

...TING OF A RIFLED 42-POUNDER GUN.

...ened with an 80-pounder shell which screamed over the water, dropped squarely into the fort, and produced a great commotion among the Confederates.
...to the camp, and smashed the barracks about, making kindling wood of the log huts, and sending terror and dismay to the soldiers. The artillerists
...nder, it bursting on the fourth fire. Still onward moved the boats—straight on—their bows puffing out immense volumes of white smoke and sending
... in their shells slowly but surely. The shells tore through the embankment, knocked the gabions and sandbags about, and smothered the garrison with
... three hundred yards distant when the Confederate flag came down.

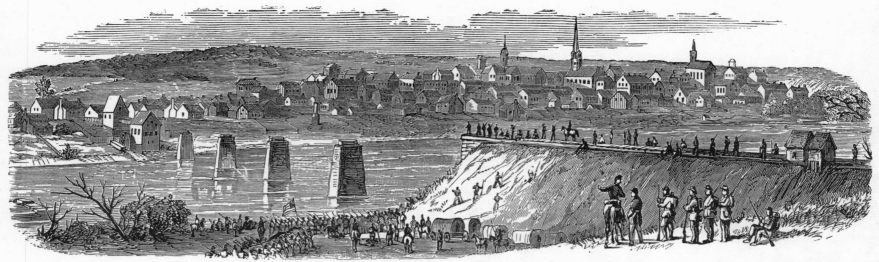

THE CITY OF FREDERICKSBURG, VA., FROM THE NORTH SIDE OF THE RAPPAHANNOCK.—FROM A SKETCH BY OUR SPECIAL ARTIST WITH GENERAL McDOWELL'S DIVISION IN 1862.

ADVANCE OF GENERAL ROSECRANS'S DIVISION THROUGH THE FORESTS OF LAUREL HILL TO ATTACK THE CONFEDERATE INTRENCHMENTS AT RICH MOUNTAIN.

General McClellan's plan for attacking the Confederates under General Garnett in Western Virginia and driving them beyond the Alleghanies involved the surprise of a large body strongly intrenched at Rich Mountain, in a position commanding the turnpike over Laurel Hill. He detailed General Rosecrans to surprise them. This in turn involved a circuitous march through the dense forests of Laurel Hill, over a wild and broken country. General Rosecrans's column of 1,600 men was guided by a woodsman named David L. Hart, who described the march as follows: "We started at daylight, and I led, accompanied by Colonel Lander, through a pathless wood, obstructed by bushes, laurels, fallen timber and rocks, followed by the whole division in perfect silence. Our circuit was about five miles; rain fell, the bushes wet us through, and it was very cold. At noon we came upon the Confederate pickets, and after drawing the dampened charges from our guns immediately opened action." The result of the battle is well known. It ended in the utter rout and final capture of the Confederates under Colonel Pegram, with a loss of 150 killed and 300 wounded.

SHILOH LOG CHAPEL, WHERE THE BATTLE OF SHILOH COMMENCED. APRIL 6TH, 1862.

GALLANT CHARGE OF THE SIXTH REGIMENT, UNITED STATES REGULAR CAVALRY, UPON THE CONFEDERATE STUART'S CAVALRY— THE CONFEDERATES SCATTERED IN CONFUSION AND SOUGHT SAFETY IN THE WOODS, MAY 9TH, 1862.

At three o'clock P. M. on May 9th, 1862, eighty men of the Sixth Regular Cavalry had advanced to Slatersville, when a considerable force of the enemy was observed directly in front. The Sixth charged upon the Confederates, and obliged them to retreat precipitately. The charge made by the Federal cavalry at the commencement of the skirmish was splendidly executed, and elicited the praise of the general in command of the troops. The Confederate cavalry was advancing toward the Federals when they formed in line and waited the approach of the enemy. When he had arrived sufficiently near they made dash upon him, cutting their way through the line and causing the utmost confusion to prevail, after which they returned to quarters by a road leading through the woods on the right of the enemy.

GENERAL ROSECRANS, COMMANDING THE DEPARTMENT OF WESTERN VIRGINIA, SURROUNDED BY HIS STAFF, AT THEIR HEADQUARTERS, CLARKSBURG, VA.

We present to our readers a most interesting and valuable sketch of General Rosecrans and his staff—a sketch rendered all the more interesting by the brilliant triumph he gained over the Mercury of the Confederates, Floyd. We enumerate the names of the gallant men who so efficiently carried out the plans of their chief: Joseph Derr, Jr., private secretary; Captain C. Kingsbury, Jr., aid-de-camp; Captain N. P. Richmond, adjutant; and Captain Charles Leib, quartermaster.

MANASSASAS JUNCTION, SHOWING THE EVACUATED CONFEDERATE FORTIFICATIONS, ABANDONED CAMPS AND WAGONS, AND THE RUINS OF THE RAILWAY DEPOT AND OTHER BUILDINGS BURNT BY THE CONFEDERATES.

The sight here cannot be portrayed. The large machine shops, the station houses, the commissary and quartermaster store houses, all in ashes. On the track stood the wreck of a locomotive, and not far down the remains of four freight cars which had been burned; to the right 500 barrels of flour had been stored, and 200 barrels of vinegar and molasses had been allowed to try experiments in chemical combinations; some 50 barrels of pork and beef had been scattered around in the mud, and a few hundred yards down the track a dense cloud of smoke was arising from the remains of a factory which had been used for rendering tallow and boiling bones.

157

RECEPTION OF WOUNDED SOLDIERS BY THE FEDERAL AUTHORITIES AT FORTRESS MONROE, VA.—THE CARS CONVEYING THEM TO THE HOSPITAL—SURGEONS DRESSING THEIR WOUNDS.

One of the most terrible features of war is the fact that the proportion of those who die by agonizing inches is four times greater than those who fall in battle. Our sketch speaks for itself; it is a truthful picture of the solemn cost of the gigantic effort to save the Union. When the poor fellows—some Confederates and some Federals—arrived at the wharf they were landed with as much tenderness as possible, and when the weather admitted their wounds were examined and dressed. Then they were placed in the long cars and taken to the hospital.

THE BATTLE OF CROSS KEYS—OPENING OF THE FIGHT—THE FEDERAL TROOPS, UNDER GENERAL FREMONT, ADVANCING TO ATTACK THE CONFEDERATE ARMY UNDER GENERAL JACKSON, JUNE 8TH, 1862.

By one of those singular chances which have made the conventional day of rest the day of famous battles, on the morning of Sunday, June 8th, 1862, the advance of General Fremont's army came up with the Confederate forces at Cross Keys, about six miles to the south of Harrisonburg. The enemy were posted among woods, and their position was much strengthened by the uneven surface of the ground. Before the Federals was spread an open amphitheatre, not of level ground, but of rolling hills skirted by forests, which completely shielded the enemy. General Stahl, who, with his brigade, had the left, advanced, driving the enemy's outposts through a thick belt of timber, and over an open wheat field into quite a thick wood. It was while crossing this wheat field in pursuit that his own Eighth New York Regiment suffered much loss. The enemy, ambushed in the wheat on the edge of the field, behind the fence, and in the woods, suddenly revealed themselves by a terrible fire that cut down nearly the whole of the two companies in advance. In accordance with their usual tactics they then gave way, and Stahl drove them back at the point of the bayonet until he found his brigade with its batteries nearly surrounded. They pressed around the guns, but the pelting storm of grape and canister, with the rifles of the brave Bucktails, who were detailed to the support of the batteries, held them at bay. Stahl's command then fell back, at first in some confusion, but finally in good order, and took position on the open ground, expecting the enemy to follow; but they preferred the woods, and made no pursuit.

159

THE ARMY OF GENERAL FREMONT ON ITS MARCH UP THE SHENANDOAH VALLEY—WOUNDED AND RAGGED SOLDIERS.

Fremont crossed the mountains with as little delay as was practicable, and through heavy roads reached Strasburg just after Jackson had passed through it. There he was joined the following morning by General Bayard, who brought with him the vanguard of Shields's cavalry, and, without waiting either for re-enforcements or to afford the fatigued troops their much-needed rest, they immediately started in pursuit of Jackson. They shortly after overtook his rear, with which they had a slight skirmish, and followed close upon the retreating force, until their advance was checked by the burning of the Mount Jackson bridge.

NEGRO DRIVERS OF THE BAGGAGE TRAIN ATTACHED TO GENERAL PLEASONTON'S CAVALRY BRIGADE WATERING THEIR MULES IN THE RAPPAHANNOCK.

General Pleasonton's cavalry was attended by a very efficient forage brigade, consisting of mules and colored riders. Our sketch represents their drivers taking them to water at the river. The hard work these animals will endure is something wonderful, and justifies the high estimation in which they are held in the army.

"TRAVELING IN STATE"—GENERAL BURNSIDE ON THE ROAD FROM NEW BERNE TO BEAUFORT, N. C.

BURNING OF THE AMERICAN MERCHANTMAN "HARVEY BIRCH," OF NEW YORK, CAPTAIN NELSON, IN THE BRITISH CH
BY THE CONFEDERATE STEAMER "NASHVILLE," CAPTAIN PEAGRIM, NOVEMBER 17TH, 1861.

On the 17th of November, 1861, the *Harvey Birch*, a splendid New York vessel of 1,480 tons and valued at $150,000, was on her way f
to New York in ballast, commanded by Captain Nelson, with officers and crew, all told, twenty-nine men. In latitude 49.6 north, longitude
she was brought to by the Confederate steamer *Nashville*, and boarded by an officer and boat's crew, who took the crew of the *Birch* on
Nashville, robbed the vessel of everything valuable, and then set fire to it, the commander, Peagrim, watching her destruction from his own

DESPERATE ENGAGEMENT, APRIL 24TH, 1862, BETWEEN THE UNITED STATES GUNBOAT "VARUNA," COMMANDER BOGGS, AND THE CONFEDERATE STEAM RAM "J. C. BRECKINRIDGE" AND THE GUNBOAT "GOVERNOR MOORE."

Captain Boggs of the *Varuna*, finding that the Confederate ram *J. C. Breckinridge* was about to run into him, put the vessel in such a position that in being damaged he could repay it with interest. On came the ram, all clad with iron about the bow, and hit the *Varuna* in the port waist, cutting and crushing in her side. She dropped alongside, and cleared out to butt again. She hit the *Varuna* a second time, and while in a sinking condition the *Varuna* poured her 8-inch shells into her so fast that the Confederate was set on fire and driven on shore.

INFERNAL MACHINE DESIGNED BY THE CONFEDERATES TO DESTROY THE FEDERAL FLOTILLA IN THE POTOMAC DISCOVERED BY CAPTAIN BUDD OF THE STEAMER "RESOLUTE."

An infernal machine designed by the Confederates to blow up the *Pawnee* and the vessels of the Potomac flotilla, which was set adrift near Aquia Creek, was picked up on the 7th of July, 1861, floating toward the *Pawnee*. The following description of the article was sent to the Navy Department: "Two large eighty-gallon oil casks, perfectly watertight, acting as buoys, connected by twenty-five fathoms of three-and-a-half-inch rope, buoyed with large squares of cork, every two feet secured to casks by iron handles. A heavy bomb of boiler iron, fitted with a brass tap and filled with powder, was suspended to the casks six feet under water. On top of the cask was a wooden box, with fuse in a gutta-percha tube. In the centre of the cork was a platform with a great length of fuse coiled away, occupying the middle of the cask."

GENERAL W. W. AVERILL.

General Averill, born in Cameron, Steuben County, N. Y., November 5th, 1832, was graduated at the United States Military Academy in June, 1855, and assigned to the mounted riflemen. He was promoted to be first lieutenant of the mounted riflemen, May 14th, 1861, and was on staff duty in the neighborhood of Washington, participating in the battle of Bull Run and other engagements, until August 23d, 1861, when he was appointed colonel of the Third Pennsylvania Cavalry. He was engaged with the Army of the Potomac in its most important campaigns. In March, 1863, he began the series of cavalry raids in Western Virginia that made his name famous. His services were continuous up to May, 1865, when he resigned, having been brevetted major general in the meantime.

GENERAL GORDON GRANGER.

General Granger, born in New York in 1821, died in Santa Fé, N. M., January 10th, 1876, was graduated at the United States Military Academy in 1845; took part in the principal battles of the Mexican War. When the Civil War began he served on the staff of General McClellan in Ohio; then in Missouri; was brevetted major for gallant services at Wilson's Creek; and on September 2d, 1861, became colonel of the Second Michigan Cavalry; on March 26th, 1862, he was made a brigadier general, and commanded the cavalry in the operations that led to the fall of Corinth. He became a major general of volunteers on September 17th, 1862. He distinguished himself in the battles of Chickamauga and Missionary Ridge. On January 15th, 1866, he was mustered out of the volunteer service.

GENERAL JUDSON KILPATRICK.

General Kilpatrick, born near Deckertown, N. J., January 14th, 1836, died in Valparaiso, Chili, December 4th, 1881, was graduated from the United States Military Academy in 1861; was appointed a captain of volunteers, May 9th; promoted first lieutenant of artillery in the Regular Army, May 14th, 1861; was wounded at Big Bethel and disabled for several months; was engaged in various skirmishes in the Western Virginia campaign and at the second battle of Bull Run; took part in the battle of Gettysburg, earning there the brevet of lieutenant colonel in the United States Army; was brevetted colonel for bravery at Resaca, and promoted major general of volunteers, June 18th, 1865. He resigned his volunteer commission on January 1st, 1886.

COLONEL E. E. CROSS.

Colonel Cross, born in Lancaster, N. H., April 22d, 1832, died near Gettysburg, Pa., July 2d, 1863. In 1860 he held a lieutenant colonel's commission in the Mexican Army, but when the news of the attack on Fort Sumter reached him he at once resigned and offered his services to the Governor of New Hampshire; organized the Fifth New Hampshire Regiment and was commissioned as its colonel; distinguished himself in many important engagements. He was mortally wounded at Gettysburg while leading the First Division of the Second Army Corps.

DESPERATE SKIRMISH AT OLD CHURCH, NEAR TUNSTALL'S STATION, VA., BETWEEN A SQUADRON OF THE FIFTH UNITED STATES CAVALRY AND STUART'S CONFEDERATE CAVALRY, JUNE 13TH, 1862—DEATH OF THE CONFEDERATE CAPTAIN LATANE.

The Confederate cavalry raid was first to Old Church, where they had a skirmish with a squadron of the Fifth United States Cavalry, who gallantly cut their way through the greatly superior numbers of the enemy, killing a Confederate captain. The Confederates then proceeded to Garlick's Landing, on the Pamunkey River, and only four miles from the White House; thence to Tunstall's Station; thence to Baltimore Crossroads, near New Kent Courthouse, on their way to Richmond, which they reached by crossing the Chickahominy, between Bottom's Bridge and James River.

BATTLE OF SHILOH, OR PITTSBURG LANDING—LEFT WING—THE WOODS ON FIRE DURING THE ENGAGEMENT OF SUNDAY, APRIL 6TH, 1862—FORTY-FOURTH INDIANA VOLUNTEERS ENGAGED.

The right wing of General Hurlbut's division stopped the advance of the Confederates by a determined defense along a side road leading through the woods on the right of the field. The Twenty-fifth and Seventeenth Kentucky and Forty-fourth and Thirty-first Indiana Regiments were engaged. By some means the dry leaves and thick underbrush which covered this locality took fire, filling the woods with volumes of smoke, and only discovering the position of the opposing forces to each other by the unceasing rattle of musketry and the whizzing of the bullets.

"FIRE-RAFT SENT DOWN FROM FORT JACKSON" TO DESTROY THE FEDERAL FLEET BELOW THE FORT—THE BOATS OF THE SQUADRON, WITH GRAPNELS, BUCKETS, ETC, AND THE FERRYBOAT "WESTFIELD," TOWING IT AWAY FROM THE FEDERAL VESSELS.

On April 17th, 1862, as the fire raft came on, the ferryboat *Westfield* ran into it, and then rapidly backing, poured a tremendous stream of water from a hose at the burning mass as it slowly floated down the river. The *Westfield* was assisted by numerous boats from the fleet, who used their buckets and boathooks to guide it safely away from the vessels at anchor. After a long and desperate conflict with the floating and fiery mass the **brave** Federal tars triumphed, the fire was extinguished, and only a mass of blackened and half-burned timber remained.

THE GREAT BAKERY FOR THE UNITED STATES ARMY AT THE CAPITOL, WASHINGTON, D. C.

STORMING OF FORT DONELSON—DECISIVE BAYONET CHARGE OF THE IOWA SECOND REGIMENT ON THE CONFEDERATE

"The Iowa Second Regiment led the charge, followed by the rest in their order. The sight was sublime. Onward they sped, heedless of the bulle this gap they were bound to go. Right up they went, climbing upon all fours, their line of dark-blue clothing advancing regularly forward, the whit over the works—they fall—they are lost! Another group, and still another and another, close up the gap. All is covered in smoke. The lodgr 10-pounders was tugging up the hill, the horses plunging, the riders whipping. Upward they go, where never vehicle went before—up the precipitou the Parrott guns at the flying enemy. The day was gained, cheers upon cheers rent the air, and in a few minutes all was hushed."

AT FORT DONELSON, FEBRUARY 15TH, 1862, RESULTING IN THE CAPTURE OF THE WORKS ON THE FOLLOWING MORNING.

nemy above. The hill was so steep, the timber cleared, that the Confederates left a gap in their lines of rifle pits on this crest of hill. Through the top of the works opposed by a line of the Federal troops. "They reach the top. Numbers fall. The surprise was breathless. See, they climb oops swarm up the hillside, their bright bayonets glittering in the sun. The firing slackens. Close behind the brigade Captain Stone's battery of rifled f the hill. No sooner on the crest than the guns were unlimbered, the men at their posts. Percussion shells and canister were shot spitefully from

SHELLING CONFEDERATE CAVALRY ACROSS THE POTOMAC RIVER FROM THE HEIGHTS OF GREAT FALLS, BY MAJOR WEST, OF CAMPBELL'S PENNSYLVANIA ARTILLERY, OCTOBER 4TH, 1861.

On Friday, October 4th, 1861, Major West, of Campbell's Pennsylvania Artillery, was ordered to shell a barn, in which there was every reason to conclude a large quantity of Confederate provisions and supplies was stored. The major, therefore, placed a Parrott gun on the heights of Great Falls, and threw a few shells across the Potomac. Several of them fell into the barn, which had the effect of unhousing a number of Confederate cavalry, who rode with all speed for the neighboring woods.

SKIRMISHING BETWEEN THE PICKETS OF THE TWO ARMIES NEAR MUNSON'S HILL—THE HILL IN THE DISTANCE.

Munson's Hill is about five miles from the Chain Bridge, on the northern side of the Leesburg Turnpike, about one mile from Bailey's Crossroads, where our pickets were stationed, and about three miles this side of Falls Church, which was in full possession of the enemy. In this neighborhood they had strong pickets, which frequently came into collision with those sent out upon the Federal side from Ball's Roads.

MARTIN'S MASSACHUSETTS BATTERY C OPENING FIRE ON THE CONFEDERATE FORTIFICATIONS COMMANDING THE APPROACHES TO YORKTOWN, APRIL 5TH, 1862.

BURNSIDE EXPEDITION—THE FLEET AND TRANSPORTS OFF HATTERAS DURING THE STORM—THE GENERAL GIVING ORDERS.

Never had any expedition in the history of the world to pass through a severer ordeal; everything seemed to conspire against it—nature with her storms, and human nature with her villainy. In addition to the warring elements there was the subtle treachery of Northern traitors who deliberately periled the lives of thousands for the sake of gain. Compared to such men as the New York contractors whom the gallant Burnside anathematized in the bitterness of his heart even Judas Iscariot becomes human. Our correspondent wrote that one of the most exciting scenes during this trying crisis was when, off Hatteras, General Burnside sprang up the rigging of the vessel to give his directions.

THE FEDERAL KITCHEN ON THE MARCH TO FREDERICKSBURG WITH THREE DAYS' RATIONS.

CAPTAIN MULLER'S BATTERY COMPANY OF THE SEVENTY-SEVENTH PENNSYLVANIA REGIMENT MAKING FASCINES AND GABIONS FOR BREASTWORKS.

Fascines have long been employed in temporary defenses, the word being derived from *facis*, the Latin for *bundle*. In fortification, fascines stand for a fagot, a bundle of rods or small sticks of wood, bound at both ends and in the middle, used in raising batteries, in filling ditches and making parapets. Sometimes they are dipped in melted pitch or tar, and made use of to set fire to the enemy's works or lodgments. A gabion in fortification is a hollow cylinder of wickerwork, resembling a basket but having no bottom. This is filled with earth, and so serves to shelter the men from the enemy's fire. During the preparatory work of concentrating and organizing the army in Kentucky opportunities were afforded for perfecting the men in a knowledge of this practical part of war and erecting fortifications. Captain Muller, who was in command of the battery attached to Colonel Stambaugh's Seventy-seventh Pennsylvania Regiment, was an accomplished officer, having served with much distinction in the Prussian Army. Our illustration represents the men cutting down the oak saplings, using the trunks, branches and twigs in fastening the gabions, the pointed stakes of which are ranged in a continuous line, forming a complete breastwork.

CAPTAIN KNAPP'S BATTERY ENGAGING THE CONFEDERATES AT THE BATTLE OF CEDAR MOUNTAIN, AUGUST 9TH, 1862—THIS BATTERY FIRED THE FIRST AND LAST SHOT.

Captain Knapp's battery deserved great credit ; it's firing was admirable ; and although the first to fire a shot, it was also the last. Several times did this skillful soldier and his well-trained men check the advance of the enemy, and finally compelled him to retire. The skill with which Captain Knapp chose his position was very conspicuous, and was much commended by General Banks.

ESCORTING MAJOR TAYLOR, OF NEW ORLEANS, THE BEARER OF A FLAG OF TRUCE, BLINDFOLDED, TO THE CONFEDERATE LINES, AFTER HIS UNSUCCESSFUL MISSION.

On the 8th of July, 1861, the pickets of the Eighth New York Regiment, Colonel Lyons, observed a small party of Confederate soldiers approaching with a flag of truce. This proved to be from Manassas Junction, and protected Major Taylor, of New Orleans, who bore letters from Jefferson Davis and General Beauregard to President Lincoln and General Scott. Colonel Lyons telegraphed to Washington, and in reply received orders to send the dispatches on. A council was held, when the dispatches from the eminent Confederates were read. It is sufficient to say that no answer was given, and Major Taylor was conducted to the Confederate lines in the manner portrayed in our sketch.

FIRST AND LAST REVIEW OF THE FIRST REGIMENT, SOUTH CAROLINA NEGRO VOLUNTEERS, ON HILTON HEAD, S. C., UNDER COLONEL FESSENDEN, U. S. A., JUNE 25TH, 1862.

Our correspondent at Hilton Head wrote us: "I witnessed the parade entire, as well as the company drills in the manual of arms, etc., afterward, and I must acknowledge my complete surprise at the discipline and even vim evinced by the sable crowd. Dressed in the regulation uniform of the United States Army, tall and strong men generally speaking, they, considering that the regiment had not been fully armed but about ten days, spoke well for officers and men."

GORDON'S AND CRAWFORD'S BRIGADES DRIVING THE CONFEDERATE FORCES FROM THE WOODS AT THE BATTLE OF CEDAR MOUNTAIN, AUGUST 9TH, 1862.

As soon as the order to advance was given the brigade moved forward, until it came to the open field, in perfect silence. As soon as it was clear from the woods, with a cheer that could have been heard all over the battle ground, it took the double-quick, and though at every step its ranks grew thinner from the murderous fire through which it passed, yet there was no faltering, no hesitancy; onward, across the field, up the slope and into and through the woods it went, until it met the second line of the enemy's overpowering forces. Forced at last to yield to overwhelming odds, it retired over the ground gained at such a frightful cost until it reached the cover from which it started. Here what remained held their position until the third brigade could come to its support. When exhausted, cut to pieces, its officers all gone, with no one to direct it, those who survived returned as fast as they could, and in the morning all that was left of that brigade was less than seven hundred men.

175

GENERAL ULYSSES SIMPSON GRANT.

General Grant, eighteenth President of the United States, born at Point Pleasant, Clermont County, O., April 27th, 1822, died on Mount McGregor, near Saratoga, N. Y., July 23d, 1885, was graduated from the United States Military Academy in 1843, and commissioned brevet second lieutenant in the Fourth Infantry; captain; adjutant general of Illinois; colonel of the Twenty-first Illinois Volunteers; brigadier general, lieutenant general and general of the United States armies; Republican in politics; famous for his successes in the Civil War, 1861–'65; captured Fort Henry, on the Tennessee River, and Fort Donelson, on the Cumberland, in 1862; defeated at Shiloh Church, near Pittsburg Landing, by General Albert Sidney Johnston, where the latter was mortally wounded, but, being re-enforced by General Buell, drove the Confederate army back to Corinth, which was afterward evacuated by the Confederates, May 29th, 1862; this involved the fall of Fort Pillow and Memphis, Tenn.; defeated Pemberton at Champion Hills and at the Big Black, and forced the Confederates to surrender Vicksburg, Miss., with 30,000 men, July 4th, 1863; Port Hudson surrendered to General Banks, and the Mississippi River was thus wrested from the Confederates. Grant's victories in the West and Lee's defeat at Gettysburg, Pa., were decisive. Defeated Lee's Confederate army at Five Forks, Va., April 1st, 1864; Lee evacuated Richmond and Petersburg on the night of April 2d, and surrendered his army to Grant at Appomattox Courthouse on the 9th; Johnston's army surrendered, 26th of the same month, 1864; and so the greatest Civil War of modern times was ended. General Grant made a tour around the world, passing through the great countries of the globe, and arrived back at San Francisco, Cal., September 20th, 1879.

MORTAR PRACTICE—PUTTING IN THE SHELL.

**SIEGE OF ISLAND NO. 10, ON THE MISSISSIPPI RIVER—NIGHT BOMBARDMENT BY THE FEDERAL MORTAR BOATS,
TEN O'CLOCK P. M., MARCH 18TH, 1862.**

On the 16th of March, 1862, the mortar fleet and the gunboats, consisting of the *Cincinnati, Pittsburg, St. Louis, Silver Wave, Carondelet, Mound City, Conestoga, Louisville, Rob Roy, Alps, Wilson, Lake Erie, Great Western* and *Torrence*, and nine mortar boats, arrived near the Point. These were accompanied by several tugboats. On the 18th they opened fire, which, after some hours' delay, was returned by the Confederate batteries. This continued for several days, with very little loss to the Federal troops, owing to the iron casing of the vessels. The study of mortar firing is very interesting. Our sketch represents the manner in which the smoke rolls, and a small column frequently splits out when the shell passes. The shell itself can be seen at night during its entire flight, the fuse having the appearance of a star, which appears and disappears as the shell rolls through the air, very like the twinkling of the celestial orbs. The explosion of the shell at night is a magnificent and fearful sight, sending a glow of surpassing brightness around it as though some world of combustible light had burst.

TRANSFER OF THE RELEASED FEDERAL PRISONERS FROM THE STEAMER "PILOT BOY" TO THE "COSSACK," IN PAMLICO RIVER, NEAR WASHINGTON, N. C.

BOMBARDMENT OF ISLAND NO. 10 AND THE FORTIFICATIONS OPPOSITE, ON THE KENTUCKY SHORE, BY THE FEDERAL MORTAR BOATS AND GUNBOATS, MARCH 17TH, 1862.

BLOWING UP THE CONFEDERATE FORTS ON CRANEY ISLAND BY COMMODORE GOLDSBOROUGH, JUNE 2D, 1862.

THE CONFEDERATE BATTERIES SHELLING THE FEDERAL POSITION ON THE NIGHT OF THE BATTLE OF CEDAR MOUNTAIN, AUGUST 9TH, 1862.—WOUNDED MEN LYING ON THE GROUND, McDOWELL'S DIVISION MARCHING ON THE FIELD.

The scene at night was very striking. It was past ten o'clock, and there was a bright moonlight and a clear blue sky. The Federal troops were on a rising ground, while the enemy's batteries were shelling from the woods, the Federal batteries replying, and one by one driving them further back. The hospital was near the Federal position, and wounded men were lying on the ground, waiting their turn to receive surgical attention. Near them were groups of stragglers, ambulances, ammunition wagons, etc.

BATTLE OF WINCHESTER, VA., MARCH 23D, 1862—DECISIVE BAYONET CHARGE OF THE FEDERAL TROOPS, LED BY GENERAL TYLER.

The contest raged furiously till three o'clock in the afternoon, the fighting being done chiefly by the artillery and musketry, at a range of not more than three or four hundred yards, and often much less. The Confederate infantry opposite the right now debouched from the woods, and attempted to capture Doan's battery by a charge. The first effort was nearly successful, but the heavy discharge of grape compelled them to retire in confusion. A second and weaker attempt likewise failed, and the enemy fell back, with heavy loss, behind the stone parapet. General Tyler then ordered his brigade to charge the enemy's batteries on the left, and a most

GENERAL GEORGE A. CUSTER.

General Custer, born in New Rumley, Harrison County, Ohio, December 5th, 1839, died in Montana, June 25th, 1876, was graduated at the United States Military Academy in June 1861, and reported for duty at Washington; was assigned to duty as lieutenant in the Fifth Cavalry, and participated, on the day of his arrival at the front, in the first battle of Bull Run. For daring gallantry in a skirmish at Aldie, and in the action at Brandy Station, as well as in the closing operations of the Rappahannock campaign, he was appointed brigadier general of volunteers. General Custer, with his entire command, was slain by the Sioux Indians in the battle of Little Big Horn, in Montana, June 25th, 1876.

COLONEL ULRIC DAHLGREN.

Colonel Dahlgren, born in Bucks County, Pa., in 1842, died near King and Queen's Courthouse, Va., March 4th, 1864. At the beginning of the Civil War he was sent by his father to plan and take charge of a naval battery on Maryland Heights. He then became aid to General Sigel, and served through Fremont's and Pope's campaigns, acting as Sigel's chief of artillery at the second battle of Bull Run; served on General Hooker's staff, distinguishing himself at Chancellorsville, and as aid to General Meade at Gettysburg rendering important service. He lost his life in a raid planned by him, in concert with General Kilpatrick, to release the Federal prisoners at Libby Prison and Belle Isle.

GENERAL J. T. SPRAGUE.

General Sprague, born in Newburyport, Mass., July 3d, 1810, died in New York city, September 6th, 1878. In 1834 he became second lieutenant in the Marine Corps, and served in the Florida War, being twice promoted for meritorious conduct, and brevetted captain on March 15th, 1842. He was given the full rank in 1846, and brevetted major, May 30th, 1848. He was made major of the First Infantry, May 14th, 1861, and when stationed with his regiment in Texas was taken prisoner by General Twiggs, but was released on parole, and became mustering and disbursing officer at Albany, N. Y. He retired from the army, July 15th, 1870.

GENERAL LORENZO THOMAS.

General Thomas, born in Newcastle, Del., October 26th, 1804, died in Washington, D. C., March 2d, 1875, was graduated from the United States Military Academy in 1823; served in the Florida and Mexican Wars, and received the brevet of lieutenant colonel for gallantry at Monterey. On the 7th of May, 1861, he was brevetted brigadier general, and made adjutant general of the army on August 3d, with the full rank of brigadier general. He served until 1863, when he was intrusted for two years with the organization of colored troops in the Southern States. He was brevetted major general, United States Army, on March 13th, 1865. He was retired in 1869.

INCIDENT IN THE MARCH OF GENERAL BANKS'S DIVISION DURING A STORM IN WESTERN MARYLAND.

THE HUMORS OF A PRISON—SCENE IN A STATION-HOUSE CELL, WASHINGTON, D. C., AFTER THE APPOINTMENT OF THE PROVOST MARSHAL, GENERAL PORTER, OCTOBER, 1861.

After the appointment of General Porter as provost marshal there was a marked improvement in the public thoroughfares of Washington. Till then too many officers imbibed at Willard's and other fashionable bars, while their men drank at the lower grogshops. The result was a saturnalia of drunkenness and military insurbordination which culminated at Bull Run. Our sketch represents the incongruous elements found one early morning in the cell of a station house.

GALLANT ATTACK BY 150 OF THE PENNSYLVANIA BUCKTAILS, LED BY COLONEL KANE, UPON A PORTION

We illustrate one of the most heroic actions of the war, the attack of the famous Bucktails, under their gallant leader, Colonel Kane
Harrisonburg, on the road to Port Republic, toward which place the Confederates were in full retreat, closely but warily pursued by Gene
ambuscade, where his regiment was fearfully cut up, and himself wounded and taken prisoner. It will be seen that the humanity of Col
of Pennsylvania Bucktails. But the Sixtieth Ohio had already beaten back the bold Confederates. The evening was waxing late; Gene
remonstrated brave Colonel Kane of the Bucktails. "Let me at 'em, general, with my Bucktails." "Just forty minutes I'll give you, co
in the pines; they were soon surrounded by a cordon of fire flashing from the muzzles of more than a thousand muskets; but not a sign,
Bucktails were forced to retreat across the fields of waving green, firing as they did so—but not the 150 that went in. The rest lie unde

NEWALL JACKSON'S CONFEDERATE ARMY, STRONGLY POSTED IN THE WOODS, NEAR HARRISONBURG, FRIDAY, JUNE 6TH, 1862.

a of Stonewall Jackson's army, consisting of infantry, cavalry and artillery. The spot where this deadly conflict took place was about a mile and a half beyond
elds. On Friday, June 6th, Colonel Sir Percy Wyndham, of the First New Jersey Cavalry, having been sent by General Bayard to reconnoitre, was led into an
to a similar trap. News of what had occurred was rapidly transmitted to headquarters, and General Bayard was ordered out with fresh cavalry and a battalion
vish to bring on a general engagement at this hour, and the troops were ordered back. "But do not leave poor Wyndham on the field, and all the wounded,"
ayard, pulling out his watch. "Peep through the woods on our left, see what is in there, and out again when the time is up." In go the 150 at an opening
gn, of yielding. Their fire met the enemy's straight and unyielding as the blade of a matador. Oh for re-enforcements! But none came. The brave
the treacherous forest.

GENERAL FREMONT'S DIVISION CROSSING THE PONTOON BRIDGE OVER THE SHENANDOAH RIVER IN PURSUIT OF
THE CONFEDERATE GENERAL JACKSON AND HIS ARMY.

SCENE IN ADAMS EXPRESS OFFICE, AT FORTRESS MONROE, VA., IN 1861—VOLUNTEERS RECEIVING LETTERS AND PACKAGES
FROM HOME.

It is only those who had relatives in camp that could tell the feverish anxiety of the troops to hear from those they had left at home. We need hardly describe a scene which so thoroughly explains itself. The name of Adams Express was a household one, both to the donor and receiver of good things sent to the absent soldier.

BIVOUAC OF THE FIELD AND STAFF OFFICERS OF THE TWELFTH MASSACHUSETTS REGIMENT DURING A STORMY NIGHT, ON THEIR MARCH FROM HYATTSTOWN, MD.

GROUP OF CONFEDERATE PRISONERS CAPTURED AT FORT DONELSON, ON THE MORNING AFTER THE SURRENDER, CLOTHED IN BED BLANKETS, PIECES OF CARPETING, ETC.

The Confederate prisoners who lounged around the fort the day after its surrender presented a state of haggard misery which took all the romance out of rebellion and made it seem the horrible thing it was. The prisoners had the double aspect of wretchedness—that of the countenance and of the garb.

THE NEW JERSEY TROOPS CROSSING THE CHESAPEAKE BAY, IN SIXTEEN PROPELLERS, ON THEIR WAY TO WASHINGTON, MAY 4TH, 1861.

FIRST NAVAL BATTLE IN HAMPTON ROADS BETWEEN THE CONFEDERATE IRON-PLATED STEAMERS "MERRIMAC," "YORKTOWN" AND "JAMESTOWN," AND THE FEDERAL WOODEN SAILING FRIGATES "CUMBERLAND" AND "CONGRESS."—SINKING OF THE "CUMBERLAND" BY A BLOW FROM THE "MERRIMAC," SATURDAY, MARCH 8TH, 1862.

SECOND NAVAL BATTLE IN HAMPTON ROADS—FIGHT BETWEEN THE FEDERAL IRONCLAD "MONITOR," OF TWO GUNS, AND THE CONFEDERATE IRON-PLATED STEAMERS "MERRIMAC," "YORKTOWN" AND "JAMESTOWN," CARRYING TWENTY-FOUR GUNS—THE "MERRIMAC" CRIPPLED AND THE FRIGATE "MINNESOTA" RESCUED, SUNDAY, MARCH 9TH, 1862.

NAVAL HOSPITAL AND BATTERY AT PORTSMOUTH, VA.

GENERAL VIEW OF FORTS HATTERAS AND CLARK, N. C., CAPTURED ON THE 29TH OF AUGUST, 1861, BY THE FEDERAL NAVAL AND MILITARY FORCES, UNDER COMMAND OF COMMODORE STRINGHAM AND MAJOR GENERAL BUTLER.

Articles of stipulation were signed on the flagship by Commodore Stringham and General Butler on the part of the United States, and by Commodore Barron, Colonel Martin and Major Andrews on the Confederate side, and the swords of the latter delivered up. The two forts remained in possession of the Federal troops, Fort Hatteras under command of Colonel Weber, and Fort Clark under that of Colonel Hawkins. The enemy's loss in killed was 15, and wounded 42; on the Federal side not a single man was either killed or wounded.

CAMP PRINCETON, VA. THE HEADQUARTERS OF GENERAL RUNYON'S NEW JERSEY BRIGADE.

Sketch of the New Jersey Camp at Arlington, Va., designated as Camp Princeton in honor of one of the Revolutionary battle grounds of New Jersey: At the head is a portrait of the brigadier general, Theodore Runyon, of Newark, N. J. At his right stands his aid-de-camp, Captain James B. Mulligan, of Elizabeth, N. J. At the left is a representation of the officers' tents of the Jersey City Zouave Company, acting as guard of honor to General Runyon. Below is a general representation of the camp, taken from the intrenchments constructed by the brigade at the junction of the Alexandria and Columbia Roads.

VALLEY OF THE CHICKAHOMINY, LOOKING SOUTHEAST FROM THE VICINITY OF MECHANICSVILLE, THE SCENE OF THE BATTLES BETWEEN THE FEDERAL FORCES COMMANDED BY
GENERAL McCLELLAN AND THE CONFEDERATE ARMIES LED BY GENERALS LEE, JACKSON, MAGRUDER AND LONGSTREET.

About two o'clock in the afternoon, June 26th, 1862, the Confederates were seen advancing in large force across the Chickahominy, near the railroad, close to Mechanicsville, where General McCall's division was encamped.
Placing their batteries in the rear of the Federals, the Confederates commenced a steady fire. The Federal batteries replied, and very soon the roar of the artillery was deafening. For three hours the fight raged with great
fierceness, the enemy attempting a flank movement, which was defeated. Toward six o'clock in the evening General Morell's division arrived on the ground, and marched straight on the enemy, in spite of the shower of shot
and shell rained upon them.

BURNING OF THE WHITE HOUSE—THE FEDERAL TROOPS, BY COMMAND OF GENERAL McCLELLAN, ABANDONING THEIR POSITION AT THE WHITE HOUSE, AND BREAKING UP THE COMMISSARIAT DEPOT ON THE PAMUNKEY RIVER—DEPARTURE OF THE UNION FLOTILLA FOR THE JAMES RIVER, JUNE 26TH, 1862.

The Confederate raid of Stuart's cavalry at Garlick's Landing and Tunstall's Station had struck the occupants of the White House Landing with a deep sense of insecurity; and, consequently, when they received orders on Wednesday, June 25th, to prepare for the hasty removal of all the government stores, they set to work with great activity, and by Thursday the greater portion of the heavy stores were embarked on board the numerous transports lying in the river. Unfortunately, through some accident the White House took fire, and the house of Washington's wife was soon destroyed.

193

BURNING OF THE CONFEDERATE GUNBOATS, RAMS, ETC., AT NEW ORLEANS AND ALGIERS, ON THE APPROACH OF THE FEDERAL FLEET.

CAMP DENNISON, SIXTEEN MILES ABOVE CINCINNATI, ON THE BANKS OF THE MIAMI RIVER, GENERAL COX COMMANDING.—THE CLEVELAND, CINCINNATI AND COLUMBUS RAILROAD PASSED

ENGAGEMENT BETWEEN THE FEDERAL TROOPS AND THE CONFEDERATES ON THE VIRGINIA SIDE OF THE POTOMAC, OPPOSITE EDWARD'S FERRY, ON OCTOBER 22D, 1861.—BATTERY OF PARROTT GUNS ON MARYLAND SHORE.

OLD FORT NORFOLK, BUILT BY THE FEDERAL GOVERNMENT, BUT ALTERED AND STRENGTHENED BY THE CONFEDERATES.

ENGAGEMENT AT ROMNEY, VA., TWENTY MILES FROM NEW CREEK, TUESDAY, JUNE 11TH, 1861—THE ELEVENTH INDIANA ZOUAVES CROSSING THE BRIDGE OVER THE POTOMAC, AT DOUBLE QUICK TIME, TO ATTACK THE CONFEDERATE FORCES.

On Tuesday, June 11th, 1861, Colonel Lewis Wallace, in command of the Eleventh Regiment, Indiana Volunteer Zouaves, stationed at Cumberland, Md., received orders to attack the Confederates assembled at Romney, the capital of Hampshire County, Va. He took six hundred men and left the same evening, reaching New Creek Bridge, twenty-eight miles by rail from Cumberland, at eleven o'clock P. M. Colonel Wallace reached the neighborhood of Romney about eight o'clock A. M., and was not surprised to find that the enemy had got the alarm, there having been time enough for horsemen to give warning. Picket guards had been placed on the heights commanding the road, at a distance of about one mile and a half from the town. These fired their pieces at the advance of the Zouaves, and as the fire was promptly and effectually returned, they immediately withdrew. The Zouaves entered Romney at half-past eight o'clock A. M., in time to partake of the breakfast which had been prepared for the "evacuates."

BATTLE OF PEA RIDGE, ARK., FOUGHT MARCH 6TH, 7TH AND 8TH, 1862, BETWEEN THE FEDERAL FORCES, 13,000 STRONG, UNDER GENERALS CURTIS, SIGEL AND ASBOTH, AND THE COMBINED CONFEDERATE ARMY OF THE SOUTHWEST, 25,000 STRONG, UNDER GENERALS VAN DORN, PRICE AND McCULLOCH—TOTAL DEFEAT OF THE CONFEDERATES.

The official report of this battle by General Curtis is as follows: "On Thursday, March 6th, the enemy commenced an attack on my right wing, assailing and following the rear guard of a detachment under General Sigel to my main lines on Sugar Creek Hollow, but ceased firing when he met my re-enforcements about 4 P. M. Early on the 7th I ordered an immediate advance of the cavalry and light artillery, under Colonel Osterhaus, with orders to attack and break what I supposed would be the re-enforced line of the enemy. This movement was in progress when the enemy commenced an attack on my right. The fight continued mainly at these points during the day, the enemy having gained the point held by the command of Colonel Carr at Cross Timber Hollow, but was entirely repulsed, with the fall of the commander, McCulloch. At sunrise on the 8th my right and centre renewed the firing, which was immediately answered by the enemy with renewed energy. I immediately ordered the centre and right wing forward, the right turning the left of the enemy and cross firing on his centre. This final position of the enemy was in the arc of a circle. A charge of infantry extending throughout the whole line completely routed the entire Confederate force, which retired in great confusion, but rather safely, through the deep, impassable defiles of cross timber."

197

GENERAL EDWARD FERRERO.

GENERAL MICHAEL CORCORAN.

General Ferrero was born in Granada, Spain, January 18th, 1831. His parents were Italian, and he was brought to the United States when an infant. At the beginning of the war he was lieutenant colonel of the Eleventh New York Militia Regiment. In 1861 he raised the Fifty-first New York Regiment, called the "Shepard Rifles," and led a brigade in Burnside's expedition to Roanoke Island, where his regiment took the first fortified redoubt captured in the war. He was in the battles of South Mountain and Antietam, and for his bravery in the latter engagement was appointed brigadier general, September 19th, 1862. He served with distinction at Fredericksburg, Vicksburg and the siege of Petersburg. He was brevetted a major general, December 2d, 1864, and mustered out in 1865.

General Corcoran, born in Carrowkeel, County Sligo, Ireland, September 21st, 1827, died near Fairfax Courthouse, Va., December 22d, 1863. Upon the first call of the President for troops in 1861 Colonel Corcoran led the Sixty-ninth Regiment to the seat of war. It was ordered into Virginia, built Fort Corcoran, on Arlington Heights, and fought with impetuous valor at the battle of Bull Run. The colonel was wounded and taken prisoner. He was offered his liberty on condition of not again taking up arms against the South, but refused to accept on such terms. An exchange being finally effected, August 15th, 1862, he was released, and commissioned brigadier general, dating from July 21st, 1861. He next organized the Corcoran Legion, which took part in the battles of the Nansemond River and Suffolk during April, 1863. General Corcoran was killed by the falling of his horse upon him.

GENERAL LEWIS WALLACE.

GENERAL GEORGE SYKES.

General Wallace, born in Brookville, Franklin County, Ind., April 10th, 1827, served in the Mexican War as first lieutenant of Company H, First Indiana Infantry. At the beginning of the Civil War he was appointed adjutant general of Indiana, soon afterward becoming colonel of the Eleventh Indiana Volunteers, with which he served in Western Virginia. He became brigadier general of volunteers, September 3d, 1861; led a division at the capture of Fort Donelson, and displayed such ability that his commission of major general of volunteers followed on March 2d, 1862. In 1863 he prepared the defenses of Cincinnati, and was subsequently assigned to the command of the Eighth Army Corps. With 5,800 men he intercepted the march of General Early, with 28,000 men, on Washington, D. C.; and on July 9th, 1864, he fought the battle of the Monocacy. General Wallace was mustered out of the volunteer service in 1865.

General Sykes, born in Dover, Del., October 9th, 1822, died in Brownsville, Texas, February 9th, 1880, was graduated from the United States Military Academy in 1842, and assigned to the Third Infantry; served in the Florida and Mexican Wars, and was brevetted captain for gallantry at Contreras, Churubusco and the capture of the city of Mexico. He became major of the Fourteenth Infantry, May 14th, 1861; was at the battle of Bull Run, and then commanded the regular infantry at Washington till March, 1862. He took part in the Peninsula campaign, receiving the brevet of colonel for gallantry at Gaines's Mill and in the succeeding operations of the Army of the Potomac. At the close of the war he was brevetted major general for gallant services in the field.

THE MILITARY AUTHORITIES AT WASHINGTON, D. C., EXAMINING PASSES IN 1861.

This scene was of frequent occurrence. A gallant volunteer wishes to take a short furlough in order to show his *fiancée* the wonders of the capital city. The provost marshal is scrutinizing the document with considerable interest, as though he has some latent doubts of its genuineness.

TAKING AWAY THE COLORS OF THE SEVENTY-NINTH NEW YORK REGIMENT FOR INSUBORDINATION AND MUTINY, WASHINGTON, D. C., AUGUST 14TH, 1861.

The scene during the reading of the order of General McClellan was exceedingly impressive. The sun was just going down, and in the hazy mountain twilight the features and forms of officers and men could scarcely be distinguished. Immediately behind his aid was General Porter, firm and self-possessed. Colonel Stevens was in front of the regiment, endeavoring to quiet his rather nervous horse. In the rear of the regulars, and a little distance apart, General Sickles sat carelessly on horseback, coolly smoking a cigar and conversing with some friends. At one time during the reading a murmur passed through the lines of the mutineers; and when the portion of the order directing the regiment to surrender its colors was read a private in one of the rear lines cried out, in broad Scotch tones, "Let's keep the colors, boys!" No response was made by the remainder of the regiment. Major Sykes at once rode up the line to where the voice was heard. It would have been more than the soldier's life was worth had he been discovered at the moment in pistol range by any of the officers.

BATTLE OF MILL SPRING, ON THE CUMBERLAND RIVER, NEAR JAMESTOWN, BETWEEN A CONFEDERATE FORCE, 8,000 S
JANUARY 19TH, 1862—

One of the most dashing, desperate and decisive battles of the war took place on Sunday, January 19th, 1862, when a Confederate army of 8,0
o'clock in the morning, and the engagement soon became general. Zollicoffer found, however, that instead of surprising General Thomas, that able a
result was doubtful till near the conclusion of the conflict. The death of Colonel Peyton, who fell gallantly at the head of his regiment, had mate
hour, as the Fourth Kentucky Regiment was deploying on the flank of the Confederate army, Zollicoffer, attended by several of his aids, mistook h
being discovered one of the Confederate officers fired at Fry and shot his horse. Almost at the same instant Colonel Fry drew his revolver and sh
Somerset. The news spread like wildfire through the Confederate army, which fled with precipitation, and at half-past three not a Confederate stoo

ENERAL ZOLLICOFFER, AND THE FEDERAL TROOPS, 4,000 STRONG, COMMANDED BY GENERAL THOMAS, FOUGHT SUNDAY,
CONFEDERATE ARMY.

rals Zollicoffer and Crittenden; were totally routed by General Thomas, at the head of about 4,000 Federal troops. The cannonading began at four
as ready for him. The Confederates fought gallantly throughont that dismal Sabbath day, and owing to their decided superiority in numbers the
irits of the Confederates, but the fall of thei. commander, Zollicoffer, abont ten minutes past three in the afternoon, completed their rout. At that
ood, and suddenly emerged before Colonel Fry, who was also with several officers. At first they mistook each other for friends, but upon the mistake
through the heart. His aids, seeing their commander slain, deserted the body, which was taken charge of by the Federal troops, and carried to

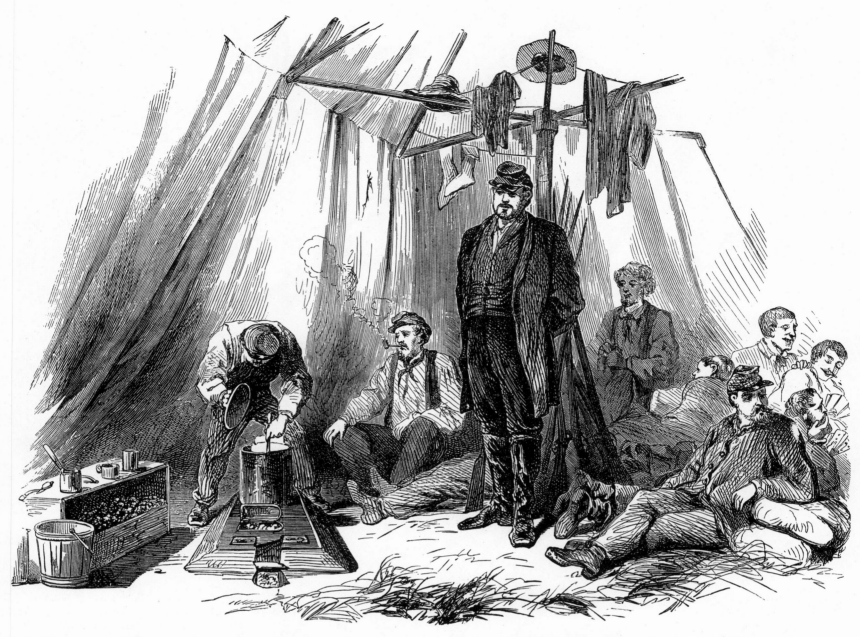

SCENE IN CAMP LIFE—COMPANY MESS OF THE THIRTEENTH ILLINOIS VOLUNTEERS IN THEIR CAMP BEFORE CORINTH, MISS.

FORT BUILT AROUND THE OFFICERS' QUARTERS OF THE FIRST MINNESOTA REGIMENT, COLONEL SULLY, NEAR FAIR OAKS, VA.

The First Minnesota Regiment, Colonel A. Sully, little dreaming how soon they would have to abandon their handiwork to the enemy, erected a fort around the commodious farmhouse, near Fair Oaks, which, after the battle of Seven Pines May 31st, 1862, had been given to their captains and lieutenants for their quarters. The appearance was so strange that an officer of General McClellan's staff made a sketch and sent it to us.

BATTLE OF CHARLES CITY ROAD—CHARGE OF THE JERSEY BRIGADE—THE FIRST NEW JERSEY BRIGADE, GENERAL TAYLER, DE-TACHING ITSELF FROM GENERAL SLOCUM'S DIVISION AND RUSHING TO THE SUPPORT OF GENERAL KEARNY'S DIVISION, WHICH HAD BEEN DRIVEN BACK, THUS TURNING THE FORTUNES OF THE DAY, JUNE 30TH, 1862, SIX O'CLOCK P. M.

COLONEL PILSON'S BATTERY SHELLING THE REAR GUARD OF THE CONFEDERATE GENERAL JACKSON'S ARMY, AT THE CROSSING OF THE SHENANDOAH RIVER, TUESDAY, JUNE 3D, 1862.

As soon as Colonel Pilson could bring up his guns they were unlimbered on either side of the road and opened on the Confederate batteries. Beyond the river stretched a broad plain, the further end of which sloped gradually up into an irregular eminence, along which the enemy had placed its artillery on its further side, and in the neighboring woods its troops were quietly encamped, out of range, and with the Shenandoah River in their rear were safe for the night, as they supposed. It was soon found that the distance was too great for the guns. Colonel Albert, chief of staff, was in advance, and reconnoitring the position, with a soldier's eye saw that the river bent suddenly half a mile beyond the bridge, and sent Schirmer's battery to a hill on this side, which flanked the Confederate camp, and at once forced them to withdraw to a more secure position.

STUART'S CONFEDERATE CAVALRY, AFTER THEIR SUCCESSFUL RAID INTO PENNSYLVANIA, ESCAPING WITH THEIR STOLEN HORSES INTO VIRGINIA BY THE LOWER FORDS OF THE POTOMAC, SUNDAY, OCTOBER 12TH, 1862.

ENCAMPMENT OF COLONEL ELLSWORTH'S NEW YORK FIRE ZOUAVES ON THE HEIGHTS OPPOSITE THE NAVY YARD, WASHINGTON, D. C.

VIEW OF GRAFTON, WESTERN VIRGINIA, OCCUPIED BY THE FEDERAL TROOPS UNDER THE COMMAND OF GENERAL McCLELLAN IN 1861.

ADVANCE OF THE FEDERAL TROOPS, NEAR HOWARD'S BRIDGE AND MILL, FOUR MILES FROM BIG BETHEL, ON THE ROAD TO YORKTOWN.

BATTLE AT WILLIS CHURCH, MONDAY, JUNE 30TH, 1862.—THE FEDERAL FORCES, UNDER GENERAL HEINTZELMAN, ENGAGED WITH THE ENEMY.

This desperate battle between the Confederates on one hand and the divisions of General Heintzelman and Franklin on the other was fought on the morning of Monday, June 30th, 1862, at Willis Church, a place midway between the White Oak Swamp Bridge and Turkey Bend, where, later in the day, another fierce fight raged, the week of combat being closed next day by the deadly but drawn battle of Malvern Hill. Our sketch represents the position of part of the Federal army at ten o'clock in the morning, just as the battle was commencing, and the enemy is advancing upon the Federal lines, and covering the advance with a heavy shower of shells. Willis Church is on the left of the illustration, being what most of the Southern places of worship were, mere wooden barns.

208

BATTLE OF GAINES'S MILL, FRIDAY, JUNE 27TH, 1862.

At eleven o'clock each division, brigade, regiment and gun was in place. Some were in the broad, open field and others under the cover of the woods. The day was intensely warm, and many of the men, worn out with their previous day's fighting, lack of sleep and toilsome march, had already thrown themselves upon the ground and were indulging in a short slumber, when a sharp volley and then the roar of artillery announced that the Confederates had opened the fight. Their shells burst in front of the farmhouse which General Morell had made his headquarters. The Federal batteries, after some little delay, replied, and for an hour this artillery duel and shelling the woods continued. It was not till near three o'clock in the afternoon that the engagement became general, and then the battle raged for four hours with unexampled fury. As though by common consent, there was a pause now; but it did not last long, for the enemy had evidently received large re-enforcements, as the whole Federal line was attacked with a vigor which showed that those who made it were fresh men. To prevent defeat, General Porter sent for re-enforcements, for under the additional pressure the Federal troops were giving way. Fortunately, General Slocum's division came to the rescue, and with it Generals Palmer, French and Meagher with their brigades and two bodies of cavalry. This changed the character of the struggle. Meagher's gallant fellows, coats off and sleeves rolled up, charged the enemy and drove them back. General Palmer's men and Duryee's Zouaves also went in with valor, and finally the Confederates rolled back like a retreating wave. This was the close of the day's fight. Toward the end the Federals had fifty-four regiments on the field, numbering about 36,000 men.

SHATTERED APPEARANCE OF A 9-INCH DAHLGREN GUN IN THE PRINCIPAL CASEMATE OF FORT HINDMAN. ARKANSAS POST

THE BOUQUET BATTERY, COMMANDING THE VIADUCT OVER THE PATAPSCO RIVER, ON THE BALTIMORE AND OHIO RAILROAD, NEAR THE RELAY HOUSE, IN 1861.

The Relay House was a small railroad station about seven miles from Baltimore, on the Northern Central Railroad. It was of small population and trade, but its position elevated it into considerable importance. Immediately after the troubles in Baltimore this position was seized upon, and General Butler made it his headquarters, and by so doing not only held the control of the railroad to Harper's Ferry and the Baltimore and Ohio Railroad and Patapsco River, but threatened the city of Baltimore with a strong military force. The Relay House was romantically situated in a country of exquisite natural beauty. Our sketch shows the battery stationed to command the viaduct, with the Relay House in the distance.

HEROIC CONDUCT OF LIEUTENANT COLONEL MORRISON, SEVENTY-NINTH NEW YORK HIGHLANDERS, ON THE PARAPET OF THE TOWER BATTERY. JAMES ISLAND, S. C.

A SUTLER'S STORE, HARPER'S FERRY, VA.—FROM A SKETCH BY OUR SPECIAL ARTIST WITH GENERAL GEARY'S DIVISION IN 1862.

The sutler's store at Harper's Ferry represents one of those apparently inevitable evils which attend even the best-arranged armies. The negligence and delay of the government in settling with the troops rendered the sutler's a necessary evil, which a more regular course would have obviated. As a study of human life, a sutler's store is full of the most sorrowful reflections, and demands the most earnest care of the superior officers. A little pure stimulant, when administered with the rations, is capable of warding off many ills which flesh is heir to, more especially when under the prostration of fatigue or privation.

OCCUPATION OF NORFOLK, VA., BY THE FEDERAL TROOPS—VIEW OF THE CITY—FEDERAL VESSELS AT ANCHOR.

PANORAMIC VIEW OF THE FEDERAL FLEET PASSING THE FORTS OF THE MISSISSIPPI, ON ITS WAY TO NEW ORLEANS. APRIL 19TH, 1862.

RECONNOISSANCE OF THE CONFEDERATE POSITION AT STRASBURG, VA., BY A DETACHMENT OF CAVALRY UNDER GENERAL BAYARD, PREVIOUS TO ITS OCCUPATION BY GENERAL FREMONT.

REBUILDING THE RAILROAD BRIDGE OVER THE RAPPAHANNOCK TO FREDERICKSBURG, BURNT BY THE CONFEDERATES IN THEIR RETREAT FROM FALMOUTH, APRIL 19TH, 1862.

THE DEPARTURE OF COLONEL ELLSWORTH'S ZOUAVES FROM NEW YORK, ESCORTED BY THE FIRE DEPARTMENT—THE REGIMENT AND ESCORT PASSING THE CORNER OF BROADWAY AND CANAL STREET, APRIL 29TH, 1861.

The Fire Zouaves, under command of Colonel Ellsworth, mustering over eleven hundred strong, embarked on board the *Baltic*, on Monday, April 29th, 1861, amid a most enthusiastic ovation. Chosen from so popular a corps as the firemen of New York, they could not fail to arouse public sympathy to a large extent. As it was generally known that three separate stands of colors would be presented to them—one at their barracks, another by Mrs. Astor, and the third at the Astor House by Mr. Stetson—an immense crowd attended every movement of this gallant regiment. The first flag was presented by Mr. Wickham, on behalf of the Fire Department and Common Council. The Hon. J. A. Dix then, in behalf of Mrs. Augusta Astor, presented them with another stand of colors, with a very handsome letter from the fair donor. The regiment then marched through Bond Street, the Bowery and Chatham Street to the Astor House, where Mr. Stetson presented them with a third flag in the name of the ladies of the house. After a short soldierly response from the colonel, the regiment with their noble escort, marched to the foot of Canal Street, where they embarked on board the *Baltic*, which steamed down the river on her way to Annapolis.

SUCCESSFUL RETREAT OF THE FEDERAL TROOPS FROM THE VIRGINIA SHORE ACROSS A CANAL-BOAT BRIDGE AT EDWARD'S FERRY, ON THE NIGHT OF OCTOBER 23D, 1861.

Of the 1,900 Federals who crossed the river in the morning but a sad remnant reached the island and opposite shore on that awful night. Upward of 500 were taken prisoners; more than 100 were drowned; nearly the same number were killed on the field or shot in the retreat, and upward of 200 were wounded. We shrink from detailing all the incidents of horror which marked this most disastrous action and retreat. It was a fearful blunder from beginning to end. Our illustration represents the successful retreat to the Maryland shore on the night of Wednesday, October 23d, by moonlight, during a high, cold windstorm.

GENERAL GEORGE CROOK.

General Crook, born near Dayton, O., September 8th, 1828, died in Chicago, Ill., March 21st, 1890, was graduated at the United States Military Academy in 1852, and was on duty with the Fourth Infantry in California in 1852-'61. He had risen to a captaincy, when, at the beginning of the Civil War, he returned to the East and became colonel of the Thirty-sixth Ohio Infantry. He afterward served in the Western Virginia campaign, in command of the Third Provisional Brigade, from May 1st to August 15th, 1862, and was wounded in the action at Lewisburg. He served in Tennessee in 1863, and on July 1st he was transferred to the command of the Second Cavalry Division. After various actions, ending in the battle of Chickamauga, he pursued Wheeler's Confederate cavalry and defeated it. He entered upon the command of the Kanawha District, in Western Virginia, in February, 1864; made constant raids and was in numerous actions. He took part in Sheridan's Shenandoah campaign, and received the brevet of brigadier general and major general in the United States Army, March 13th, 1865. General Crook had command of the cavalry of the Army of the Potomac from March 26th to April 9th, during which time he was engaged at Dinwiddie Courthouse, Sailor's Creek and Farmville, till the surrender at Appomattox.

GENERAL BENJAMIN F. BUTLER.

General Butler was born in Deerfield, N. H., November 6th, 1818. At the time of President Lincoln's call for troops in April, 1861, he held the commission of brigadier general of militia. On the 17th of that month he marched to Annapolis with the Eighth Massachusetts Regiment, and was placed in command of the District of Annapolis, in which the city of Baltimore was included. On May 13th, 1861, he entered Baltimore at the head of 900 men, occupied the city without opposition, and on May 16th was made a major general and assigned to the command of Fortress Monroe and the Department of Eastern Virginia. In August he captured Forts Hatteras and Clark. He then returned to Massachusetts to recruit an expedition for the Gulf of Mexico and the Mississippi. On March 23d, 1862, the expedition reached Ship Island, and on April 17th went up the Mississippi. The fleet under Farragut having passed the forts, April 24th, and virtually captured New Orleans, General Butler took possession of the city on May 1st. Near the close of 1863 he was placed in command of the Army of the James. In December, 1864, he conducted an ineffectual expedition against Fort Fisher, and soon afterward was removed from command by General Grant. He died in Washington, D. C., January 11th, 1893.

GENERAL RICHARD J. OGLESBY.

General Oglesby, born in Oldham County, Ky., July 25th, 1824, served in the Mexican War; was present at the siege of Vera Cruz and the battle of Cerro Gordo. In 1860 he was elected to the State Senate, but resigned to accept the colonelcy of the Eighth Illinois Volunteers. He commanded a brigade at the capture of Fort Henry and Fort Donelson, and was promoted, for gallantry, brigadier general of volunteers, March 21st, 1862. He added to his reputation at Corinth, where he was severely wounded and disabled from duty until April, 1863. In the meantime he had been made major general of volunteers, and assigned to the command of the Sixteenth Army Corps. This commission he resigned in May, 1864.

GENERAL JOSEPH G. TOTTEN.

General Totten, born in New Haven, Conn., August 23d, 1788, died in Washington, D. C., April 23d, 1864, was graduated from the United States Military Academy in 1805, and promoted second lieutenant in the corps of engineers. After the beginning of the Civil War he had charge of the engineer bureau in Washington. When the corps of engineers and that of topographical engineers were consolidated, in 1863, he was made brigadier general on March 3d; and for his long, faithful and eminent services was brevetted major general, April 21st, 1864.

IN THE SHENANDOAH VALLEY—GENERAL FREMONT'S DIVISION MARCHING THROUGH THE WOODS TO ATTACK THE CONFEDERATES.

This exciting pursuit commenced on Saturday, May 31st, 1862, when the first collision occurred between the hostile armies in the lower valley, near Strasburg, to which place Jackson had fallen back from the Potomac upon hearing that Fremont was on the march to intercept him. In this retreat the indomitable and daring Ashby, the "Murat of the Confederates," occupied the post of danger, dashing against the Federal troops whenever they pressed the retreating enemy too closely. At ten o'clock on the 31st the First Jersey Cavalry, led by the gallant Wyndham, and Ashby's men had a desperate skirmish, in which the Confederates were driven back with some loss. Jackson rested his Confederate troops in Strasburg this night, and next morning resumed his retreat, when the Ashby cavalry and the First Jersey had another and heavier conflict, in which artillery was used. That night the enemy occupied Woodstock, having made fourteen miles in their retreat this day. So close was the Federal advance on the Confederates that General Bayard's cavalry, when they entered Strasburg, captured the Confederate provost marshal and two hundred men. At the village of Edinburgh, five miles from Woodstock, the Confederate General Ashby, by Jackson's orders, after seeing the rear guard safely across the bridge over Stony Creek, fired the wooden structure, and it was soon enveloped in flames.

CAMP OF THE NINTH MASSACHUSETTS REGIMENT IN THE WOODS, ONE MILE FROM THE CONFEDERATE FORTIFICATIONS, YORKTOWN, VA., APRIL 10TH, 1862.

ADVANCE OF FEDERAL TROOPS ON CORINTH—THE CARNIVAL OF MUD—SCENE AT LICK CREEK BOTTOM, BETWEE
THEIR

Our illustration cannot fail to fasten the grand fact of mud firmly on the reader's mind. It was carefully sketched on the spot at Lick Cree
pull through the cannon and wagon train, but the mud was too deep, and the result was that in a few hours the bottom was filled with wagons a

...DING AND MONTEREY, FOUR MILES FROM CORINTH, MONDAY, MAY 5TH, 1862—GENERAL HURLBUT'S DIVISION FORCING

...HE MUD.

...al Hurlbut's division of Halleck's grand army was advancing from Pittsburg Landing to Monterey. On Monday, May 5th, an attempt was made to

...ired, and waiting for dry weather to be dug out.

MORTAR PRACTICE—13-INCH SHELL MORTAR, AS USED BY THE FEDERAL GOVERNMENT—WEIGHT OF MORTAR 17,000 POUNDS.

MORTAR PRACTICE—REAR VIEW OF 13-INCH MORTAR, WITH ITS USUAL COMPLEMENT OF SEVEN GUNNERS.

The mortar is one of the most ancient forms of cannon, being used as early as 1495 by Charles VIII. at the siege of Naples. In 1478 the first attempt was made to project hollow shot filled with powder ; but owing to their clumsy make the accidents were so frequent as to cause their discontinuance. In 1634 a French mechanic overcame the difficulty, and mortars were revived in the French service. Our illustrations represent a 13-inch mortar, the largest in general practice, weight 17,000 pounds, exclusive of the carriage. The number of men required to work one of these guns is seven, for all of whom there is distinct and adequate occupation. Mortars are not used in hand to-hand encounters, their value consisting in pitching shells into camps and towns, or shelling fortifications erected on elevations, against which cannons are of no avail.

THE VICTORY AT **BLUE RIDGE** PASS, SUNDAY, SEPTEMBER 14TH, 1862—INFANTRY CHARGE, AND ROUT OF THE CONFEDERATES.

On Sunday, September 14th, 1862, having previously evacuated Frederick City, the rear of the Confederate army had reached the Blue Ridge Pass, on the line of the Federal road leading from Frederick City to Hagerstown and the fords of the Upper Potomac. Here it was overtaken by the Federal advance under Generals Hooker and Reno. The position was a strong one, and strongly guarded, but was carried after a severe action by the Federal forces, the Confederates falling back in disorder. In this engagement General Reno was killed on the Federal side, and General Garland on that of the Confederates.

A STREET IN HARPER'S FERRY, VA., DURING THE PASSAGE OF THE POTOMAC BY THE FEDERAL TROOPS FROM MARYLAND, OCTOBER 24TH, 1862.

We give a specimen of the grotesque in war. Experience proves that where there is much excitement there is always a rollicking gayety in proportion to the excitement. The terrible stimulus of war constantly produced scenes which almost approached those of a carnival. Among the younger of the Federal soldiers this was very apparent, more especially among some of the zouave regiments.

IN THE SHENANDOAH VALLEY—MOUNT JACKSON, THE HEADQUARTERS OF GENERAL FREMONT IN HIS ADVANCE TO HARRISONBURG.

EXPEDITION TO PORT ROYAL—GOVERNMENT BUILDINGS ERECTED ON HILTON HEAD, S. C., BY THE FEDERAL FORCES UNDER GENERAL SHERMAN, 1861-2—SIGNAL STATION, POST OFFICE, ETC.

EXPEDITION TO PORT ROYAL—GOVERNMENT BUILDINGS ERECTED ON HILTON HEAD, S. C., BY THE FEDERAL FORCES UNDER GENERAL SHERMAN, 1861-'2—COMMISSARY'S QUARTERS, CAMPS OF THE EIGHTH MAINE, THIRD NEW HAMPSHIRE, FORTY-SEVENTH AND FORTY-EIGHTH NEW YORK REGIMENTS, ETC.

A DETACHMENT OF THE FIRST SOUTH CAROLINA (COLORED) FEDERAL VOLUNTEERS, UNDER THE COMMAND OF COLONEL BEARD, REPELLING THE ATTACK OF CONFEDERATE TROOPS IN THE VICINITY OF DOBOY RIVER, GA.

VIEW OF NEW BERNE, N. C., FROM THE INTERIOR OF FORT THOMPSON AFTER ITS CAPTURE BY THE FEDERAL FORCES—BURNING OF ROSIN WORKS, RAILWAY BRIDGE AND NAVAL STORES, AND SHOWING VESSELS SUNK IN THE CHANNEL OF THE NEUSE RIVER, TO PREVENT THE APPROACH OF FEDERAL GUNBOATS.

Captain Rowan, in his account of the doings of his gunboats, after modestly narrating the important services he rendered General Burnside the day previous in the debarkation of the land forces, thus recounts his own separate share of the expedition to New Berne: "At 6:30 A. M. on Friday, April 14th, 1862, the fleet steadily moved up and gradually closed in toward the batteries. The lower fortification was discovered to have been abandoned by the enemy. A boat was dispatched to it, and the Stars and Stripes planted on the ramparts. As we advanced the upper batteries opened fire upon us. The fire was returned with effect, the magazine of one exploding. Having proceeded in an extended line as far as the obstructions in the river would permit, the signal was made to follow the movements of the flagship, and the whole fleet advanced in order, concentrating our fire on Fort Thompson, mounting 13 guns, on which rested the enemy's land defenses. The army having with great gallantry driven them ont of these defenses, the fort was abandoned."

BATTLE OF SECESSIONVILLE, JAMES ISLAND, S. C.—BAYONET CHARGE OF FEDERAL TROOPS, COMMANDED BY GENERAL STEVENS, UPON THE CONFEDERATE BATTERIES ON JAMES ISLAND, JUNE 16TH, 1862.

Our sketch represents the desperate bayonet charge of the Federal troops which drove back the Confederates; but the Federals were so exhausted with their victory that the reconnoissance for the next day was postponed, and some heavy guns having arrived, it was proposed to put them in battery in advance of General Stevens's camp and try their effect upon the Confederate fort before renewing the project of an assault. The battery produced no effect upon the Confederate fort; and as its shells and shot commanded the Federal position and rendered its camp insecure, it became necessary to recur again to the old plan of the reconnoissance, and to attempt to reduce it by assault. The Federals were met by a murderous fire of grape and canister. Two regiments only reached the front, much cut up—the Eighth Michigan and the Seventy-ninth New York "Highlander." The Twenty-eighth Massachusetts broke and scattered, while the Forty-sixth New York did little better. The first two drove the gunners from their guns; some mounted the parapet, and some even penetrated the fort; but the other regiments, there being two besides those named, not rushing up to their support, they were obliged to retire after having really held it for nearly twenty minutes.

DESPERATE NAVAL COMBAT BETWEEN THE CONFEDERATE IRON-PLATED RAM "ARKANSAS" AND THE FEDERAL GUNBOAT "CARONDELET," AT THE MOUTH OF THE YAZOO RIVER, TUESDAY, JULY 15TH, 1862.

Next to the ever-memorable combat between the *Merrimac* and the *Monitor*, that of the *Carondelet* and the *Arkansas* was the most exciting. Like the former engagement, it ended in a drawn battle. On July 14th, 1862, the gunboats *Carondelet* and *Tyler* were sent by Commodore Farragut to survey the Yazoo River and ascertain the exact condition of the Confederate iron-plated ram *Arkansas*, about which there were various reports. They arrived at the mouth of the Yazoo, fifteen miles above Vicksburg, at seven o'clock in the evening, and anchored for the night. Next morning, at daylight they tipped anchor and slowly steamed up the Yazoo, the *Tyler* considerably in advance. About two miles up the river smoke was seen across a little point of land, which, as Captain Gwin of the *Tyler* surmised, proceeded from the Confederate ram, now rapidly steaming toward the *Tyler*. In another moment a heavy report was heard from the enigmatical gunboat, and a huge round shot went howling over the deck of the *Tyler*. Captain Walke of the *Carondelet* ordered the *Tyler* to proceed with all speed to alarm the fleet and advise it to prepare for her approach while he engaged the Confederate monster. In ten minutes afterward the *Carondelet* and *Arkansas* were alongside each other, and the conflict commenced in earnest. The *Carondelet* commenced with her bow guns, striking her opponent with a rapidity and precision which the enormous strength of the iron plating alone prevented taking immediate effect. The *Arkansas* used in return her rifled and smooth-bore guns with terrible effect, some of the shots going right through the *Carondelet*. Seeing her inability to cope with her antagonist, Captain Walke ran the *Carondelet* alongside the *Arkansas* and grappled her. The order "Boarders away!" was instantly passed, and the crew of the Federal gunboat speedily mounted the deck of its adversary. When there they found no foe to engage. The crew of the *Arkansas* had retired below, and the iron hatches were closed, so that it was utterly impossible to go down and continue the action.

224

INTERIOR OF THE OUTBUILDING ATTACHED TO MARSHAL KANE'S POLICE HEADQUARTERS, HOLLIDAY STREET BALTIMORE—DISCOVERY OF CANNON, MUSKETS AND AMMUNITION INTENDED FOR THE SERVICE OF THE SECESSIONISTS.

General Banks promptly arrested Marshal Kane as the most active Secessionist in Maryland, and incarcerated him in Fort McHenry. He supplied his place by Colonel Kenley a tried and trustworthy officer. Provost Marshal Kenley actively pursued his search after concealed arms. He took possession of the late marshal's office, the entrance of which was guarded by a cannon planted in the hall and officers with drawn swords, a precautionary measure rendered necessary by the disturbed state of the city. The search after arms was eminently successful. In an old back building of the City Hall, used by Marshal Kane, were found two 6-pounder and two 4-pounder guns, half a ton of assorted shot, four hundredweight of ball, eight hundred rifle-ball cartridges, gun carriages, etc. In the office and under the marshal's office, in the floors and in the ceiling, arms and ammunition were found, among them a case of splendid pistols, two hundred and fifty muskets and rifles, twenty-five of which were Minié, besides several muskets which were supposed to belong to the Massachusetts soldiers dis-

225

BURNING OF THE GUNPOWDER CREEK RAILROAD BRIDGE, ON THE PHILADELPHIA AND BALTIMORE RAILROAD, BY THE MARYLAND SECESSIONISTS.

BATTLE OF SAVAGE'S STATION—BRIGADIER GENERAL SMITH'S DIVISION HOTLY ENGAGED WITH THE ENEMY, AT NOON, JUNE 28TH, 1862.

SHELLING OF THE BATTERIES AT GALVESTON BY THE UNITED STATES WAR STEAMER "SOUTH CAROLINA," ON MONDAY AFTERNOON, AUGUST 5TH, 1861.

BATTLE OF CEDAR MOUNTAIN, FOUGHT SATURDAY, AUGUST 9TH, 1862, BETWEEN THE FEDERAL TROOPS COMMANDED BY GENERAL BANKS AND THE CONFEDERATE ARMY LED BY GENERALS JACKSON, EWELL, WINDER, ETC.—FINAL REPULSE OF THE CONFEDERATES.

General Pope's report of the battle is as follows: "On Saturday, August 9th, 1862, the enemy advanced rapidly to Cedar Mountain, the sides of which they occupied in heavy force. General Banks was instructed to take up his position on the ground occupied by Crawford's brigade, of his command, which had been thrown out the day previous to observe the enemy's movements. He was directed not to advance beyond that point, and if attacked by the enemy to defend his position and send back timely notice. The artillery of the enemy was opened early in the afternoon, but he made no advance until nearly five o'clock, at which time a few skirmishers were thrown forward on each side under cover of the heavy wood in which his force was concealed. The enemy pushed forward a strong force in the rear of his skirmishers, and General Banks advanced to the attack. The engagement did not fairly open until after six o'clock, and for an hour and a half was furious and unceasing. I arrived personally on the field at 7 P. M., and found the action raging furiously. The infantry fire was incessant and severe. I found General Banks holding the position he took up early in the morning. His losses were heavy. Ricketts's division was immediately pushed forward and occupied the right of General Banks, the brigades of Crawford and Gordon being directed to change their position from the right and mass themselves in the centre. Before this change could be effected it was quite dark, though the artillery fire continued at short range without intermission. The artillery fire, at night, by the Second and Fifth Maine batteries which had been advanced against it. Our troops rested on their arms during the night in line of battle, the heavy shelling being kept up on both sides men and horses and broken gun carriages of the enemy's batteries which had been advanced against it. Our troops rested on their arms during the night in line of battle, the heavy shelling being kept up on both sides until midnight. At daylight the next morning the enemy fell back two miles from our front, and still higher up the mountain."

228

BELLAIRE, O.—STEAMBOATS CONVEYING TROOPS AND MUNITIONS OF WAR FOR THE FEDERAL FORCES ON THE GREAT KANAWHA.

Bellaire is a town situated on the Ohio River, three miles below Wheeling, Va. It is the eastern terminus of the Central Ohio Railroad, and the point for crossing the river connecting the Baltimore and Ohio with the above-named railroad. The place contained a population of fifteen hundred or two thousand inhabitants in 1861. Its importance was owing to its eligible position for the rapid concentration of troops. The sketch represents a fleet of boats lying in the river, awaiting their quota of troops and munitions for the prosecution of the war on the Great Kanawha.

GENERAL DAVID HUNTER.

General Hunter, born in Washington, D. C., July 21st, 1802, died there, February 2d, 1886, was graduated at the United States Military Academy in 1822; appointed second lieutenant in the Fifth Infantry; promoted first lieutenant in 1828, and became a captain in the First Dragoons in 1833. He resigned his commission in 1836, and engaged in business in Chicago. He re-entered the military service as a paymaster, with the rank of major, in March, 1842. On May 14th, 1861, he was appointed colonel of the Sixth United States Cavalry, and three days later was commissioned brigadier general of volunteers. He commanded the main column of McDowell's army in the Manassas campaign, and was severely wounded at Bull Run, July 21st, 1861. He was made a major general of volunteers, August 13th, 1861; served under General Fremont in Missouri, and on November 2d succeeded him in the command of the Western Department. In March, 1862, General Hunter was transferred to the Department of the South, with headquarters at Port Royal, S. C. In May, 1864, he was placed in command of the Department of West Virginia. He defeated a considerable force at Piedmont on June 5th. He was brevetted major general United States Army, March 13th, 1865, and mustered out of the volunteer service in January, 1866.

GENERAL ALFRED PLEASONTON.

General Pleasonton, born in Washington, D. C., June 7th, 1824, was graduated at the United States Military Academy in 1844; served in the Mexican War, and was brevetted first lieutenant for gallant and meritorious conduct in the battles of Palo Alto and Resaca de la Palma; was commissioned first lieutenant in 1849, and captain in 1855; commanded his regiment in its march from Utah to Washington in 1861; was commissioned major of the Second Cavalry in 1862; served through the Virginia Peninsula campaign; became brigadier general of volunteers in July of that year, and commanded the division of cavalry of the Army of the Potomac that followed Lee's invading army into Maryland. He was engaged at Boonesborough, South Mountain, Antietam and the subsequent pursuit; engaged the enemy at Fredericksburg, and staid the further advance of the enemy at Chancellorsville. He received the brevet of lieutenant colonel for Antietam in 1862; was promoted major general of volunteers in June, 1863, participating in the numerous actions that preceded the battle of Gettysburg. In March, 1865, he was made major general, United States Army, for services throughout the Civil War.

GENERAL T. E. RANSOM.

General Ransom, born in Norwich, Vt., November 29th, 1834, died near Rome, Ga., October 29th, 1864, was educated at Norwich University; learned civil engineering, and in 1851 removed to Illinois, where he engaged in business. He was elected major, and then lieutenant colonel, of the Eleventh Illinois, and was wounded while leading a charge at Charlestown, Mo., August 20th, 1861. He participated in the capture of Fort Henry, and led his regiment in the assault upon Fort Donelson, where he was severely wounded. He was promoted colonel for his bravery. In 1863 he was made a brigadier general, his commission dating from November 29th, 1862. In the battle of Sabine Crossroads he received a wound in the knee, from which he never recovered. He was brevetted major general, September 1st, 1864.

GENERAL ALEXANDER S. WEBB.

General Webb, born in New York city, February 15th, 1835, was graduated from the United States Military Academy in 1855, and assigned to the artillery. He served in Florida, Minnesota, and for three years as assistant professor at West Point. He was present at Bull Run and in the defenses of Washington until 1862, when he participated in the battles of the Peninsula campaign of the Army of the Potomac, and as chief of staff of the Fifth Corps during the Maryland and Rappahannock campaigns till June 23d, 1863. He was then commissioned brigadier general of volunteers, and placed in command of a brigade of the Second Corps, serving with great credit at the battle of Gettysburg. He was made major general, United States Army, for gallant and meritorious services in the campaign terminating with the surrender of the insurgent army under General Lee.

THE CONFEDERATE RAID INTO KENTUCKY—THE FIGHT AT THE LICKING BRIDGE, CYNTHIANA, BETWEEN THE FEDERAL TROOPS AND THE MORGAN CONFEDERATE GUERRILLAS.

Cynthiana, the scene of the fight between the Cincinnati Volunteers and Morgan's Confederate cavalry, is the capital of Harrison County, Ky. When Morgan with his guerrillas arrived on the south side of the Licking River, on Thursday, July 17th, 1862, he found Lieutenant Colonel Landrum, of the Eighteenth Kentucky Regiment, with a hastily gathered force, ready to oppose him. The splendidly mounted Confederates were, however, too much for him, and after making a gallant defense the Confederates forced their way over the bridge, killed a number of the Federals and captured one cannon. Landrum and about forty of his troops made good their retreat to Lexington, which was in a perfect panic at the proximity of the Confederate chief.

THE CONFEDERATE RAID INTO KENTUCKY—EXCITEMENT AT COVINGTON—GATHERING OF ARMED FEDERAL CITIZENS AT THE RAILROAD AND TELEGRAPH OFFICE, ON HEARING OF THE CAPTURE OF CYNTHIANA BY THE CONFEDERATE MORGAN.

The dash of Morgan from his mountain haunts in Tennessee through Kentucky caused considerable alarm throughout the State, for it was well planned and boldly executed. It is said to have been an inspiration from Jeff. Davis himself, intended to produce a general uprising in Kentucky against the Federal Government. The people, however, soon recovered from their momentary terror; and it was then seen how much stronger the Federal sentiment was in Kentucky than that of Secession.

BATTLE OF MALVERN HILL, NEAR TURKE

The battle of Malvern Hill commenced with the advance of a large body of Confederates, extending quite across the country, with cavalry on e
Federal column was formed with General Couch, of General Keyes's corps, on the extreme left; Franklin and Heintzelman took up the centre, and
Owen, and being gallantly seconded by Dana's, Meagher's and French's brigades, they dashed within fifty yards of the enemy and opened a splen
pouring volleys into him all the time. After fighting two hours, with a loss of about 400, the night fell, and having moved across Turkey Island C

IVER, VA., FOUGHT TUESDAY, JULY 1st, 1862.

erals at once jumped up wearily, and waited their approach, while all the signal officers, on their several stations, waved their cabalistic muslin. The
he remnants of Porter and Sumner. Burns's brigade, being ordered to charge, advanced with the Sixty-ninth Pennsylvania Regiment (Irish), Colonel
The left of the line was now advanced, and the troops of General Couch really behaved wonderfully, facing the enemy wherever he appeared, and
the bridge, and soon the whole army closed up at and near Harrison's Bar, twenty-seven miles from Richmond.

REMOVING SUNKEN SCHOONERS FROM CORE SOUND, N. C., PLACED TO OBSTRUCT THE PASSAGE OF THE FEDERAL GUNBOATS, UNDER THE SUPERINTENDENCE OF CAPTAIN HAYDEN, OF THE NEW YORK SUBMARINE ENGINEERING COMPANY.

The perverse ingenuity which the Confederates showed in obstructing the channels which led to their strongholds was only exceeded by the persistent ingenuity with which the Federal officers removed them. The Confederates obstructed the channel of Core Sound by sinking schooners; but under the superintendence of Captain Hayden, of the New York Submarine Engineering Company, they were removed by blasting. The shock was perceptibly felt a considerable distance, and it was some time before the water resumed its usual appearance.

DESTRUCTION OF THE CONFEDERATE IRONCLAD STEAMER "MERRIMAC," BLOWN UP BY ITS COMMANDER, ON THE MORNING OF MAY 11th, 1862.

The abandonment of Norfolk compelled the evacuation of the Confederate positions at Sewell's Point and at Craney Island, and on May 11th, 1862, the Merrimac was blown up to prevent her falling into the hands of the Federals.

FEDERAL TROOPS MARCHING THROUGH SECOND STREET, NEW FERNANDINA, FLA.

Our sketch of New Fernandina in 1862 shows the principal business street in the city, called Second Street. There seemed to be quite a joke in numbering streets where there were not half a dozen in the place; but the spirit of imitation was strong, and as Philadelphia and New York, with their thousands of blocks, are simplified and rendered more easily findable by the aid of arithmetic, so must be the villages of the South.

REVIEW OF CONFEDERATE TROOPS ON THEIR MARCH TO VIRGINIA, IN FRONT OF THE PULASKI MONUMENT, MONUMENT SQUARE, SAVANNAH, GA., AUGUST 7TH, 1861.

The Pulaski Monument is situated in Johnson or Monument Square. It is a fine Doric obelisk of marble, 53 feet in height. The base of the pedestal is 10 feet 4 inches by 6 feet 8 inches, and its elevation is about 12 feet. The corner stone was laid by Lafayette during his visit to the United States in 1825. The needle which surmounts the pedestal is 37 feet high. Another and very elegant structure has also been erected to the memory of this gallant foreigner in Chippewa Square. Pulaski was killed in the attack made by the allied American and French armies in 1779, when the British held possession of Savannah.

PRESIDENT LINCOLN, ATTENDED BY GENERAL McCLELLAN AND STAFF, REVIEWING THE FEDERAL ARMY, ON TUESDAY, JULY 8TH, 1862, NEAR HARRISON'S LANDING, VA.

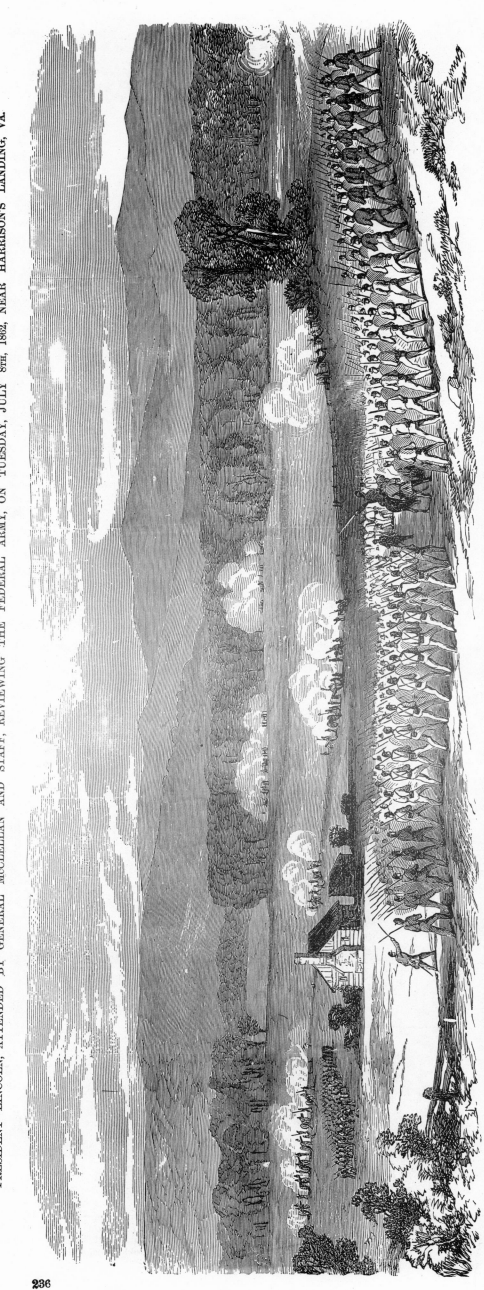

BATTLE OF CROSS KEYS, SUNDAY, JUNE 8TH, 1862—CENTRE AND FRONT OF THE FEDERAL ARMY IN THE ENGAGEMENT.

236

THE CONFEDERATE FORCES UNDER GENERAL JACKSON ADVANCING UPON THE RAPPAHANNOCK STATION AT THE RIVER—FEDERAL BATTERIES REPLYING TO THE CONFEDERATE ARTILLERY, AUGUST 23D, 1862, BEING THE COMMENCEMENT OF THE BATTLES BETWEEN GENERALS POPE AND LEE AND JACKSON, ENDING AT BULL RUN, AUGUST 30TH.

HEADQUARTERS OF GENERAL BUTTERFIELD, NEAR HARRISON'S LANDING, JAMES RIVER, VA.

LANDING OF FEDERAL TROOPS AT PARKERSBURG, WESTERN VIRGINIA.

Parkersburg, Va., in 1861 was a thriving post village on the Ohio River, situated at the mouth of the Little Kanawha River, and altogether presented a most picturesque appearance, the houses being very neatly built and well placed. It is about one hundred miles from Wheeling and two hundred and fifty-eight miles from Richmond in a direct W.N.W. line. It contained a courthouse, churches of several denominations, a bank, a printing office and several steam mills. Its population was nearly four thousand. It has excellent turnpike roads to Staunton and Winchester, and the Northwestern branch of the Baltimore and Ohio Railroad terminates here. Our view represents the arrival of Federal troops previous to the total clearance of the Kanawha Valley from the presence of Wise and his Confederate troops.

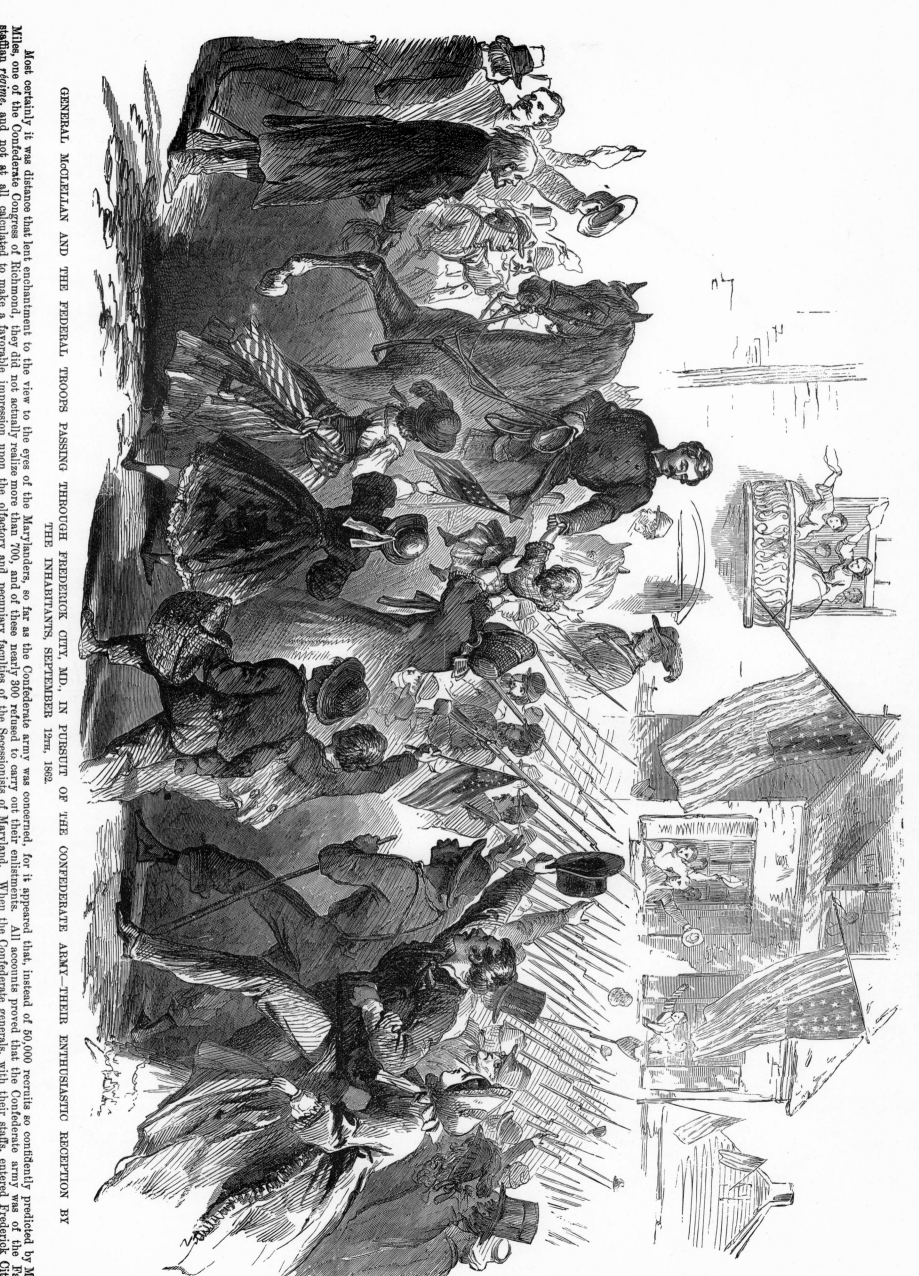

GENERAL McCLELLAN AND THE FEDERAL TROOPS PASSING THROUGH FREDERICK CITY, MD, IN PURSUIT OF THE CONFEDERATE ARMY—THEIR ENTHUSIASTIC RECEPTION BY THE INHABITANTS, SEPTEMBER 12TH, 1862.

Most certainly it was distance that lent enchantment to the view to the eyes of the Marylanders, so far as the Confederate army was concerned, for it appeared that, instead of 50,000 recruits so confidently predicted by Mr. Miles, one of the Confederate Congress of Richmond, they did not actually realize more than 700, and of these nearly 300 refused to carry out their enlistments. All accounts proved that the Confederate army was of the Falstaffian *régime*, and not at all calculated to make a favorable impression upon the olfactory and pecuniary faculties of the Secessionists of Maryland. When the Confederate generals, with their staffs, entered Frederick City, they were at first welcomed, but when the ragged regiments made their appearance a change came over the spirit of their dream, and the inhabitants woke from their delusion. Our sketch represents the rapturous reception given to General McClellan. It was a perfect ovation. Flowers were showered down upon the shoes of the inhabitants, committed the inspiring scene

GENERAL RUTHERFORD B. HAYES.

General Hayes, nineteenth President of the United States, born in Delaware, O., October 4th, 1822, was graduated at Kenyon College in 1842. In 1845 he was admitted to the bar at Marietta, O., and soon afterward entered into practice at Fremont and Cincinnati. On June 7th, 1861, the Governor of Ohio appointed Mr. Hayes a major of the Twenty-third Regiment of Ohio Volunteer Infantry, and in July the regiment was ordered into West Virginia. On September 19th, 1861, Major Hayes was appointed by General Rosecrans judge advocate of the Department of Ohio, the duties of which office he performed for about two months. On October 24th, 1861, he was promoted to the rank of lieutenant colonel. On September 14th, 1862, in the battle of South Mountain, he distinguished himself by gallant conduct in leading a charge and in holding his position at the head of his men, after being severely wounded in his left arm, until he was carried from the field. On October 4th, 1862, he was appointed colonel of the same regiment. In July, 1863, he took part in the operations of the national army in Southwestern Virginia. In the spring of 1864 Colonel Hayes commanded a brigade in General Crook's expedition to cut the principal lines of communication between Richmond and the Southwest. He took a creditable part in the engagement at Berryville, and at the second battle of Winchester, September 19th, 1864, where he performed a feat of extraordinary bravery. At the battle of Cedar Creek, October 19th, 1864, the conduct of Colonel Hayes attracted so much attention that his commander, General Crook, on the battlefield took him by the hand, saying: "Colonel, from this day you will be a brigadier general." The commission arrived a few days afterward; and on March 13th, 1865, he received the rank of brevet major general for gallant and distinguished services during the campaign of 1864 in West Virginia, and particularly at the battles of Fisher's Hill and Cedar Creek, Va. He died January 17th, 1893.

GENERAL JAMES A. GARFIELD.

General Garfield, twentieth President of the United States, born in Orange, Cuyahoga County, O., November 19th, 1831, died in Elberon, N. J., September 19th, 1881, was graduated from Williams College with the highest honors in the class of 1856. In the next six years he was a college president, a State Senator, a major general in the national army and a Representative-elect in the national Congress. American annals reveal no other promotion so rapid and so varied. In August, 1861, Governor Dennison commissioned him lieutenant colonel in the Forty-second Regiment of Ohio Volunteers. The men were his old pupils at Hiram College, whom he had persuaded to enlist. Promoted to the command of this regiment, he drilled it into military efficiency while waiting orders to the front, and in December, 1861, reported to General Buell, in Louisville, Ky. General Buell was so impressed by the soldierly condition of the regiment that he gave Colonel Garfield a brigade, and assigned him to the task of driving the Confederate general Humphrey Marshall from Eastern Kentucky. The undertaking itself was difficult; General Marshall had 5,000 men, while Garfield had but half that number, and must march through a State where the majority of the people were bitterly hostile to attack an enemy strongly intrenched in a mountainous country. Garfield, nothing daunted, concentrated his little force, and moved it with such rapidity, sometimes here and sometimes there, that General Marshall, deceived by those feints, and still more by false reports which were skillfully prepared for him, abandoned his position and many supplies at Paintville, and was caught in retreat by Garfield, who charged the full force of the enemy, and maintained a hand-to-hand fight with it for four hours. The enemy had 5,000 men and 12 cannon; Garfield had no artillery, and but 1,100 men. But he held his own until re-enforced by Generals Graner and Sheldon, when Marshall gave way, leaving Garfield the victor at Middle Creek, January 10th, 1862, one of the most important of the minor battles of the war. In recognition of these services President Lincoln made the young colonel a brigadier general, dating his commission from the battle of Middle Creek. He took part in the second day's fight at Shiloh, and was engaged in all the operations in front of Corinth; and in June, 1862, rebuilt the bridges on the Memphis and Charleston Railroad, and exhibited noticeable engineering skill in repairing the fortifications of Huntsville. In February, 1863, General Rosecrans made him his chief of staff. At the battle of Chickamauga, January 24th, 1863, Garfield volunteered to take the news of the defeat on the right to General Thomas, who held the left of the line. It was a bold ride, under constant fire, but he reached Thomas and gave the information that saved the Army of the Cumberland. For this action he was made a major general, September 19th, 1863. At the request of President Lincoln he resigned his commission, December 3d, 1863, and hastened to Washington to sit in Congress, to which he had been chosen, fifteen months before, as the successor of Joshua R. Giddings. General Garfield was inaugurated President of the United States in 1881, and was shot by a disappointed office seeker (Guiteau), July 2d, the same year.

VIEW OF ROLLA, MO., TAKEN FROM THE FORT.

ENCAMPMENT OF THE FEDERAL ARMY NEAR ROLLA. MO.

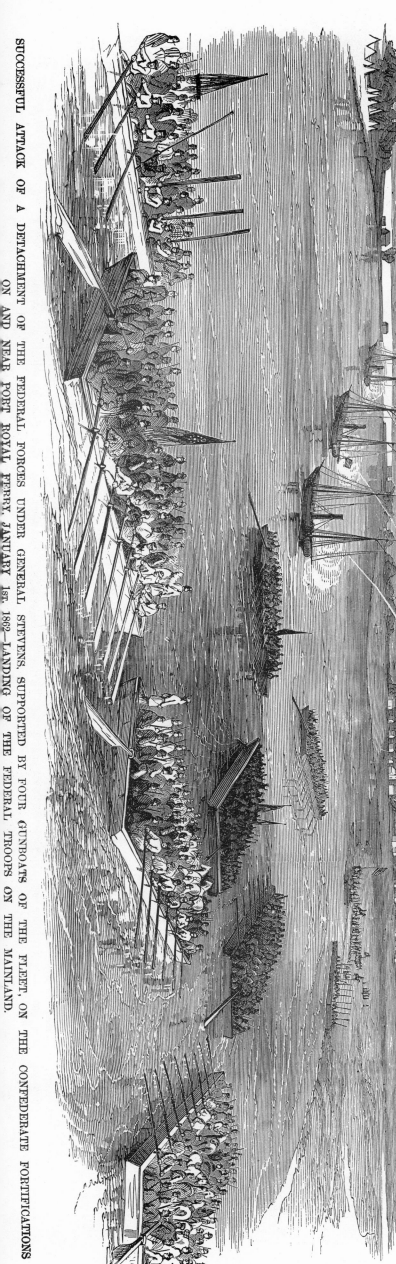

SUCCESSFUL ATTACK OF A DETACHMENT OF THE FEDERAL FORCES UNDER GENERAL STEVENS, SUPPORTED BY FOUR GUNBOATS OF THE FLEET, ON THE CONFEDERATE FORTIFICATIONS ON AND NEAR PORT ROYAL FERRY, JANUARY 1ST, 1862.—LANDING OF THE FEDERAL TROOPS ON THE MAINLAND.

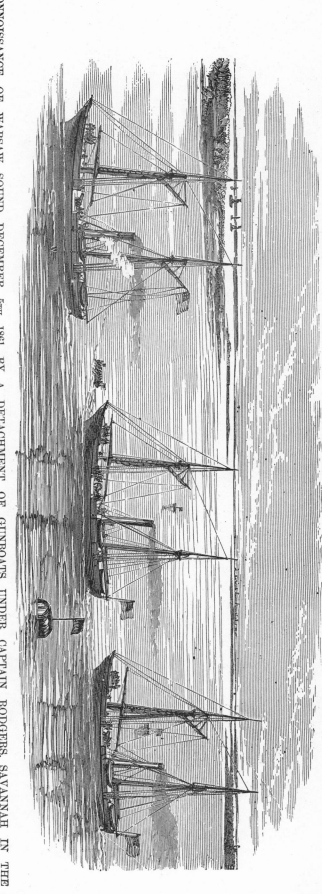

RECONNOISSANCE OF WARSAW SOUND, DECEMBER 5TH, 1861, BY A DETACHMENT OF GUNBOATS UNDER CAPTAIN RODGERS, SAVANNAH IN THE DISTANCE.

CAMP ZAGONYI—ENCAMPMENT OF FREMONT'S ARMY ON THE PRAIRIE, NEAR WHEATLAND, MO., OCTOBER 14TH, 1861.

This spot, where Fremont's army rested after their their first day's march from Tipton, is on the vast prairies of Missouri, about fifteen miles from Tipton and two miles from Wheatland. The Grand Army of the West here pitched their tents on the afternoon of the 14th of October, 1861. A brilliant sunset fell over the whole, which looked more like a monster picnic than the advanced corps of an army bent on the destruction of traitorous brothers. The rapidity with which the evening's meal for a marching regiment is prepared has something of the marvelous in it. Appetite quickens practice, and the air is soon filled with the savory aromas of culinary processes. Then comes the hearty enjoyment of food which at another time would be passed by, but which now, under the appetizing provocative of hunger, is thankfully received. Not the least of a soldier's trials is the inroad a long march and privation makes upon that fastidiousness which plenty to eat engenders in the human diaphragm. The camp was called after the colonel of General Fremont's bodyguard, whose gallant achievements at Springfield on the 25th of October we have recorded.

VILLAGE OF CLARKSBURG, WESTERN VIRGINIA, HEADQUARTERS OF GENERAL ROSECRANS.

Clarksburg, a post village, capital of Harrison County, is situated on the west fork of the Monongahela River, at the mouth of Elk Creek, about two hundred and twenty miles northwest of Richmond. It is built on a high tableland environed by hills. It had in 1861 several churches, academies, two printing offices and many fine stores. Stove coal abounded in its vicinity. The Northwestern Railroad, a branch of the Baltimore and Ohio, passed through it. It had about two thousand inhabitants. For a short time Clarksburg was the headquarters of General Rosecrans. The situation was briefly this: The Cheat Mountain Gaps, the key to the whole country, were held by a strong force, a portion of General Reynolds's brigade, the remainder of which was stationed at Beverly, Huttonsville, and in that vicinity. Other portions of General Rosecrans's command were scattered over almost the whole northwestern part of Virginia, guarding the railroad lines from Wheeling and Parkersburg down to Grafton, and then eastward through the Cheat River country, Oakland, Altamont, and almost to Cumberland, occupying the Kanawha Valley by General Cox's brigade, and holding towns like Weston, Buckhannon, Summerville, Philippi and Bealington.

245

GENERAL FITZJOHN PORTER.

GENERAL JOHN M. BRANNAN.

General Porter, born at Portsmouth, N. H., June 13th, 1822, was graduated from the United States Military Academy in 1845, and assigned to the Fourth Artillery, in which he became second lieutenant, June 18th, 1846. He served in the Mexican War, was commissioned first lieutenant on May 29th, and received the brevet of captain, September 8th, 1847, for services at Molino del Rey, and that of major for Chapultepec. On May 14th, 1861, he became colonel of the Fifteenth Infantry, and on May 17th, 1861, he was made brigadier general of volunteers, and assigned to duty in Washington. In 1862 he participated in the Virginia Peninsula campaign, at Yorktown, Gaines's Mill and Malvern Hill, and received the brevet of brigadier general in the regular army for gallant conduct at the battle of Chickahominy, Va., June 27th, 1862. On November 27th, 1862, General Porter was arraigned before a court-martial in Washington, charged with disobeying orders at the second battle of Bull Run, and on January 21st, 1863, he was cashiered. A bill for his relief was signed by President Cleveland, and he was restored to the United States Army as colonel, August 7th, 1886.

General Brannan, born in the District of Columbia in 1819, was graduated from the United States Military Academy in 1841, and stationed at Plattsburg, N. Y., in 1841-'42. During the Mexican War he was first lieutenant in the First Artillery. He took part in the battles of Vera Cruz, Cerro Gordo, La Hoya, Contreras and Churubusco, and for gallant and meritorious conduct was brevetted captain on August 28th, 1847. During the next fourteen years he performed much arduous service on the frontier, and from 1856 till 1858 took a gallant part in the campaign against the Seminoles. On September 28th, 1861, he was promoted to be brigadier general of volunteers, serving in the far South until January 24th, 1863. On October 10th, 1863, he became chief of artillery of the Department of the Cumberland, and held that position till June 25th, 1865. On March 13th, 1865, he was brevetted brigadier general in the regular army for his part in the capture of Atlanta, and major general for gallant and meritorious services during the war.

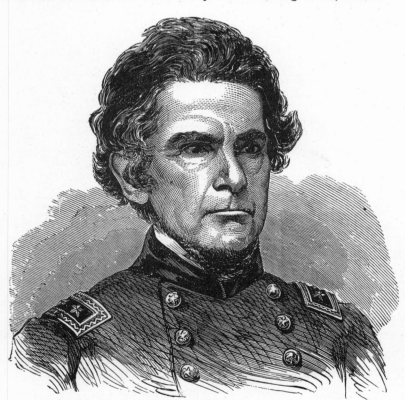

GENERAL ORMSBY MacKNIGHT MITCHEL

GENERAL JESSE L. RENO.

General Mitchel, born at Morganfield, Union County, Ky., August 28th, 1809, died at Hilton Head, S. C., October 30th, 1862, was graduated from the United States Military Academy in 1829. Immediately after his graduation he was made assistant professor of mathematics at the Military Academy, which position he held for two years, when he was assigned to duty at Fort Marion, St. Augustine, Fla. He soon resigned and moved to Cincinnati, where he commenced the study of law and was admitted to the bar. In 1861 he entered the Civil War in the cause of the Union, and was placed in command of a division of General Buell's army. He served with the Army of the Ohio during the campaigns of Tennessee and Northern Alabama, and reached the brevet title of major general of volunteers, April 11th, 1862. Afterward he was placed in command of the Department of the South at Hilton Head, S. C., where he was fatally stricken with yellow fever in the prime of his career.

General Reno, born in Wheeling, W. Va., June 20th, 1823, died on South Mountain, Md., September 14th, 1862, was graduated from the United States Military Academy in 1846, and at once promoted brevet second lieutenant of ordnance. He served in the Mexican War, taking part in the battles of Cerro Gordo, Contreras, Churubusco and Chapultepec, and in the siege of Vera Cruz he was commissioned second lieutenant, March 3d, 1847; brevetted first lieutenant, April 18th, for gallant conduct in the first-named engagement, and captain, September 13th, for bravery at Chapultepec, where he was severely wounded. In the Civil War he was commissioned brigadier general, November 12th, 1861, and major general of volunteers, July 18th, 1862; led a brigade under General Burnside in the taking of Roanoke Island, N. C., February 8th, 1862; was engaged under General Pope at Manassas and Chantilly, Va. At Turner's Gap in South Mountain, Md., he repelled the Confederates under Lee, and after being in action all day he was killed in the evening of September 14th, 1862.

SHELLING OF A CONFEDERATE CAMP ON THE POTOMAC BY LIEUTENANT TOMPKINS, OF THE FIRST RHODE ISLAND BATTERY.

Lieutenant Tompkins, of the First Rhode Island Artillery, observing on the other side of the Potomac a Confederate camp, fixed one of his guns, and after one or two trials got the range so perfectly that they fled in the greatest confusion.

BATTLE OF CARRICK'S FORD, WESTERN VIRGINIA—DISCOVERY OF THE BODY OF GENERAL GARNETT, BY MAJOR GORDON
AND COLONEL DUMONT, AFTER THE BATTLE.

After the Confederates had crossed the fourth ford General Garnett again endeavored to rally his men, standing waving his hand on an exposed point near the river bank, by his side only one young man (Chaplet), wearing the uniform of the Georgia Sharpshooters. Three of Dumont's men fired at the same time, and Garnett and his companion fell at the first round. The men rushed across, and on turning the body discovered that the Confederate leader of Western Virginia had paid the penalty; he was shot through the heart. Major Gordon, U. S. A, closed his eyes reverently, and Colonel Dumont. coming up, had him carried into a grove close by, where they laid him down, taking care of his sword and watch, to be sent with his body to his family.

BATTLE OF WHITE OAK SWAMP BRIDGE, MONDAY, JUNE 30TH, 1862—AYRE

After the battle of Savage's Station the Federals continued on their retreat, and by eight o'clock on the morning of June 30th, 1862, they had crossed crossing White Oak Creek the Federals had quickly formed a new line of battle at Willis Church, General Hancock's forces being on the extreme he reached the creek, at about noon, he found the approaches well defended by artillery. Jackson opened upon Hancock's troops, and made re Federal force at a place two miles away, called Frazier's Farm. Here stood Sumner and Hooker, on the extreme right. McCall somewhat in advan o'clock when he commenced the attack. McCall's left was first assailed by Kemper's brigade, which was met by the Pennsylvania Reserves under enabled the Confederates to drive back the Federals, who in turn lost heavily. Longstreet and Hill now pressed on, and the conflict became a severe one open field upon McCall's left, directly against Randall's battery, which centred upon the Confederates a most galling fire. Nothing daunted, they mov A charge was then ordered for the recapture of the guns. The Confederates bravely met the severe attacks that followed. A still more desperate ha remained on that portion of the field which they had lost earlier in the action. The Federal loss was about 1,800 killed and wounded, whilst that o

RANDALL'S BATTERIES CHECKING THE ADVANCE OF THE CONFEDERATES.

nd Creek, after destroying the bridge over the latter and warding off the repeated attacks to which they were subjected throughout the night. After
occupied the left, and Heintzelman's and Sumner's the intervening space. Jackson's advance was checked by the destruction of the bridge, and when
ild the bridge under cover of his heavy artillery, but he was every time repulsed. While this was going on Longstreet and Hill had come upon a
and Kearny on the extreme left. When Longstreet found this force arrayed against him he waited for re-enforcements to come up, and it was four
, after a bitter conflict, drove the Confederates into the woods with a loss of 250 killed and wounded and about 200 prisoners. Fresh troops then
. One point, then another, was vainly tried in the determined effort to break the Federal line. At length Wilcox's Alabama Brigade rushed across an
aging in a desperate hand-to-hand fight, first captured Cooper's battery, and afterward Randall's battery, which had been doing such terrible execution.
ook place for the possession of the lost batteries, which were finally recaptured. By dark the Confederates had retired into the woods, and the Federals
as over 2,000. Colonel Simmons and General Meade were both severely wounded, while General McCall was a made prisoner.

SECTION OF FORT RUNYON, VA., GUARDING THE ROAD TO ALEXANDRIA, OCCUPIED BY THE TWENTY-FIRST REGIMENT, NEW YORK VOLUNTEERS, AUGUST, 1861.

Fort Runyon, named after the commander of the New Jersey regiments which were formerly stationed there, entirely commanded the road to Alexandria. Our sketch shows the battery erected on this important point. The spot was a most picturesque one, commanding a splendid view all around, the background being the Potomac and Washington.

PRACTICING WITH THE CELEBRATED SAWYER GUN ON THE CONFEDERATE BATTERIES AT SEWELL'S POINT, NEAR NORFOLK, VA., FROM FORT CALHOUN, ON THE RIPRAPS, IN FRONT OF FORTRESS MONROE.

The Ripraps, on which Fort Calhoun was erected, was in advance of Fortress Monroe, being between it and Sewell's Point, and was an important position, as with guns of a proper calibre it could completely command and destroy the enemy's batteries at Sewell's Point. General Butler gave special attention to this point, and various kinds of ordnances were experimented with, the Sawyer rifled cannon and the Hotchkiss shell having been proved the most complete and effective.

LANDING STATE PRISONERS AT FORT LAFAYETTE, NEW YORK HARBOR, IN 1861.

Fort Lafayette, New York harbor, the state prison of the republic during the Civil War, is built upon a shoal about four hundred yards from Long Island, and is entirely surrounded by water. In shape it is quadrangular, with the angles pointing to the sea and shore diamondwise; hence it was formerly called Fort Diamond.

A RECONNOITRING DETACHMENT OF GENERAL BANKS'S CAVALRY, HYATTSTOWN, MD., IN THE DISTANCE.

There are few sights more picturesque than a detachment of cavalry winding along the road to some quiet little village. Nature and man seem then so little in harmony that the contradiction becomes strikingly attractive. Our illustration represents a scene of this kind—a detachment of Federal cavalry, sent by order of General Banks, reconnoitring in the neighborhood of Hyattstown, a post village of Montgomery County, Md., and situated on Bennett's Creek, about thirty-six miles to the northwest of Washington.

THE UNITED STATES GUNBOAT "MOHAWK" CHASING THE CONFEDERATE STEAMER "SPRAY" INTO THE ST. MARK'S RIVER.

BOMBARDMENT OF FORT HENRY, TENNESSEE RIVER, TENN., BY THE MISSISSIPPI FLOTILLA, FLAG OFFICER FOOTE, FEBRUARY 6TH, 1862.

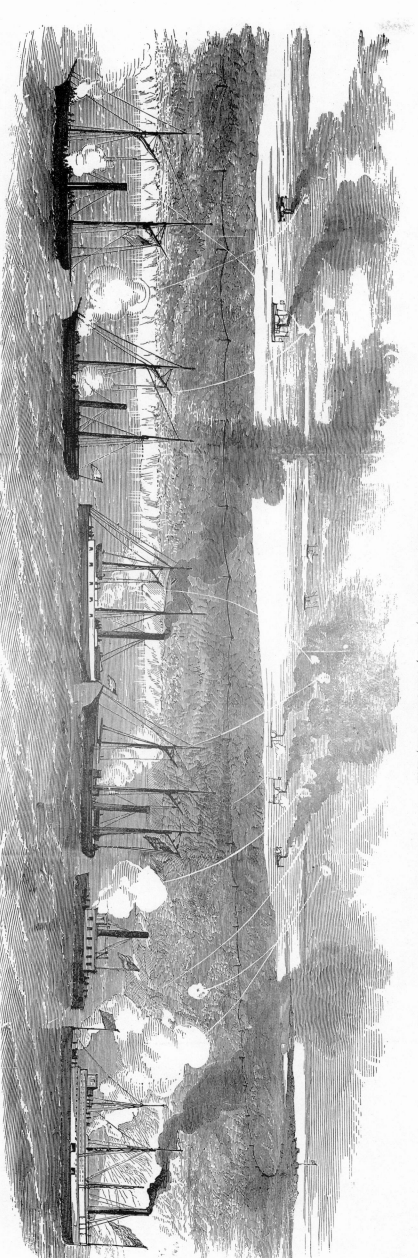

A DETACHMENT OF UNITED STATES SAILORS FROM THE GUNBOATS "ALBATROSS" AND "GEMSBOK" BURNING THE CONTRABAND VESSEL "YORK," MOUTH OF ROGUE'S INLET, NEAR BEAUFORT, N. C., JANUARY 23D, 1862.

ENGAGEMENT BETWEEN UNITED STATES GUNBOATS COMMANDED BY COMMODORE DAVIS AND THE CONFEDERATE MOSQUITO FLEET UNDER COMMODORE TATNALL NEAR FORT PULASKI, SAVANNAH RIVER, JANUARY 28TH, 1862.

VIEW OF THE TOWN OF STRASBURG, VALLEY OF THE SHENANDOAH, OCCUPIED BY THE FEDERAL FORCES UNDER GENERAL BANKS, MARCH 25TH, 1862.

Towns which had hitherto remained buried in obscurity and pleasant foliage were suddenly converted into places of national importance. Strasburg, through whose rural streets the resounding tramp of two hostile armies had passed, was a post village of Shenandoah County, Va., on the north fork of Shenandoah River and on the Manassas Gap Railroad, eighteen miles southwest of Winchester. It had three churches and a population of about eight hundred persons. It was occupied by General Banks's division of the Federal army immediately after the battle of Winchester.

CAMP OF THE GARIBALDI GUARDS, COLONEL D'UTASSY, NEAR ROCHE'S MILLS, VA., POTOMAC RIVER IN THE DISTANCE.

The fine body of men called the Garibaldi Guards were remarkable for the number of trained men in its ranks, at least one-half having fought in European battlefields. It comprised Frenchmen, Italians, Hungarians, Germans, Swiss, Irish, Scotch, and a few English who had served in the Crimean War. When reviewed by the President, on their arrival at Washington, they were highly commended. They formed a part of Blenker's brigade, and were stationed near Roche's Mills, in a most picturesque spot, rendered more so by the foreign tastes of some of the Garibaldians.

CAMP LIFE IN THE WEST.

During one of the pauses in the active part of the Missouri campaign our special artist sent us some sketches which belong more to the romance of war than its struggle. We have formed some of these into this page, which cannot fail to interest our readers. Among them is a most characteristic scene in which two phases of civilization meet. We allude to the sketch where the Indian warriors are giving a war dance by firelight in the presence of the officers and soldiers of General Asboth's division. Sad and suggestive spectacle! Pagans and Christians traveling as companions on the same war path. The companion sketches of sunrise and midnight outside the tent are also equally thought provoking; while, as though to show the folly and vanity of the whole gigantic struggle, the dead horse, the vultures, and the last two of the army cavalcade as it travels over that magnificent solitude, the Hundred Mile Prairie of Missouri, close the melancholy series.

DELAWARE INDIANS ACTING AS SCOUTS FOR THE FEDERAL ARMY IN THE WEST.

General Fremont, on taking command in the West in 1861, while he shrank from employing the Indians as soldiers, saw the advantage of using them as scouts, and for this purpose organized a band of them, selecting only the most reliable, robust and best-charactered. They soon made their value known by the early intelligence they brought of the enemy's movements. Some of them were also employed by General Grant.

GATHERING OF FREMONT'S TROOPS ON THE PRAIRIE, NEAR TIPTON, MO, ON THE EVE OF ITS DEPARTURE IN PURSUIT OF GENERAL PRICE.

JEFFERSON CITY, CAPITAL OF MISSOURI—THE ARRIVAL OF GENERAL FREMONT'S DIVISION, SEPTEMBER 26TH, 1861.

CAMP WOOL, TWO MILES FROM FORT CLARK, HATTERAS ISLAND, OCCUPIED BY HAWKINS'S ZOUAVES, NINTH REGIMENT, N.Y., IN OCTOBER, 1861.

GENERAL BANKS'S HEADQUARTERS NEAR EDWARD'S FERRY, MD.

BATTLE AT DAM NO. 4, POTOMAC RIVER, BETWEEN BUTTERFIELD'S BRIGADE AND A LARGE CONFEDERATE FORCE.

A desperate and disastrous action occurred on the banks of the Potomac, at Dam No. 4. General Butterfield's brigade, consisting of the Forty-fourth New York, Seventeenth New York, Eighteenth Massachusetts and One Hundred and Eighteenth Pennsylvania, were ordered to make a reconnoissance on the Virginia side. Crossing over at Dam No. 4, which is about six miles northwest in a straight line from Sharpsburg, and eight south from Williamsport, they had hardly landed when a most murderous fire was opened upon them from an entire division of the Confederate army, every volley of which told, as they had the Federals completely under range. The Federals made a desperate resistance, but they were compelled to retire before superior numbers, and retreated in moderate order across the river.

BATTLE OF MUNFORDVILLE, KY., SUNDAY, SEPTEMBER 14th, 1862.—THE CONFEDERATES CHARGING THROUGH THE ABATIS IN FRONT OF THE FORTIFICATIONS NEAR GREEN RIVER.

Our correspondent reports of this battle: "At five o'clock the Confederates were seen forming in front of our rifle pits, and soon, from the cover of the woods and abatis, began the engagement by a rapid fire of musketry. It was plainly seen that a disposition of our men was being made by Colonel Wilder to repel the attack anticipated on the left, and, thinking it a favorable hour, the Confederate force made a desperate assault on our right. This was made by a Mississippi and a Georgia regiment. The assault was led by the colonel of the Mississippi regiment, and he died for his daring. The major of the same regiment was wounded and taken prisoner. The newly formed Confederate right marched from the woods in splendid order, with ranks apparently full. When they appeared over the brow of the hill it was at a double-quick; all pushed on with desperate courage, to meet resistance not the less desperate. With grape from the artillery and a shower of balls from the musketry they were met and mowed down; but they never faltered; and it was only when they sprang on the breastworks and were met with the bayonet that they fell back, leaving the field strewn with their dead and dying. After a momentary struggle on the whole Confederate force broke into disorder and fled from the field.

GENERAL ROBERT H. MILROY.

GENERAL HIRAM G. BERRY.

General Milroy, born in Washington County, Ind., June 11th, 1816, was graduated at Norwich University, Vt., in 1843, and served in the Mexican War as captain in the First Indiana Volunteers. He studied law, was admitted to the bar in 1849, and in 1850 was graduated at the law department of Indiana University. At the beginning of the Civil War he issued a call for volunteers, and was made a captain, becoming colonel of the Ninth Indiana Volunteers, April 26th, 1861. He served in Western Virginia under McClellan and Rosecrans, receiving a commission as brigadier general on February 6th, 1862, and thereafter continued in various commands in Virginia, under Fremont and Sigel, until March 11th, 1863, when he was made major general of volunteers. In this capacity he had charge of the Second Division of the Eighth Army Corps, and was stationed at Winchester, Va. Here, on June 15th, 1863, he was attacked by nearly the whole of Lee's army, which was marching toward Pennsylvania. General Milroy resisted this superior force for three days, and then cut his way out by night, losing a large portion of his forces. He resigned from the army in 1865.

General Berry, born in Thomaston (now Rockland), Me., August 27th, 1824, died at Chancellorsville, Va., May 2d, 1863. He originated and commanded for several years the Rockland Guard, a volunteer company, which attained a very high reputation for drill and discipline. At the beginning of the Civil War he entered the service as colonel of the Fourth Maine Infantry. He took part in the battle of Bull Run and the siege of Yorktown, was made a brigadier general, April 4th, 1862, and was given command of the Third Brigade of the Third Division of Heintzelman's Third Army Corps. He was present at the battles of Williamsburg and Fair Oaks, bore a conspicuous part in the Seven Days' fight, and was in the second Bull Run campaign and Chantilly. In January, 1863, he was nominated by the President as major general of volunteers, with rank dating from November 29th, 1862, confirmed by the Senate on March 9th, 1863, and placed in command of the Second Division of the Third Army Corps, succeeding General Sickles. At the battle of Chancellorsville he headed one of his brigades in several successful bayonet charges, and in one of them was killed by a shot from the enemy.

GENERAL GEORGE D. BAYARD.

GENERAL CHRISTOPHER C. AUGUR.

General Bayard, born in Seneca Falls, N. Y., December 18th, 1835, died December 14th, 1862, was graduated from the United States Military Academy in 1856. He was assigned to the First Cavalry. Four years were passed in frontier and garrison duty. He was severely wounded in a fight with the Kiowa Indians. In 1861 he was cavalry instructor at West Point, and on March 16th of that year was promoted to first lieutenant in Third Cavalry; captain, Fourth Cavalry, August 20th; and was granted leave of absence to become colonel of the First Pennsylvania Cavalry Volunteers, September 14th, 1861. He became brigadier general of volunteers, April 28th, 1862, and served in the arduous campaigns of the Shenandoah, Northern Virginia, and on the Rappahannock, distinguishing himself by the dash and bravery of his reconnoissances. He was mortally wounded at Fredericksburg, December 13th, 1862, and died the following day. He was buried with military honors at Princeton, N. J.

General Augur, born in New York in 1821, was graduated from the United States Military Academy in 1843. During the Mexican War he served as aid-de-camp to General Hopping, and after his death to General Caleb Cushing. He was promoted captain, August 1st, 1852, and served with distinction in a campaign against the Indians in Oregon in 1856. On May 14th, 1861, he was appointed major in the Thirteenth Infantry, and was for a time commandant of cadets at West Point. In November of that year he was commissioned a brigadier general of volunteers, and joined McDowell's corps. In July, 1862, he was assigned to a division under Banks, and in the battle of Cedar Mountain was severely wounded. He was promoted major general of volunteers, August 9th, 1862, and in November joined his corps and took part in the Louisiana campaign. He was brevetted brigadier general in the United States Army, March 13th, 1865, receiving on the same date the brevet of major general for services in the field during the rebellion.

CONRAD'S FERRY, MD., ABOVE HARRISON'S ISLAND, ON THE POTOMAC RIVER, THE PLACE OF PASSAGE OF COLONEL BAKER'S REGIMENT, OCTOBER 21ST, 1861.

Conrad's Ferry is situated on the Maryland side of the Upper Potomac, about five miles above Edward's Ferry. It was in possession of the Federal troops. It commands a view of Harrison's Island, the scene of so much disaster at the battle of Ball's Bluff, and is immediately opposite to Leesburg Heights, the town of Leesburg being about five miles from the Ferry, on the south side of the Potomac.

"FRESH BREAD!"—IMPROMPTU OVEN BUILT BY THE NINETEENTH REGIMENT, NEW YORK VOLUNTEERS, IN GENERAL BANKS'S DIVISION, WESTERN MARYLAND.

The impromptu oven which we illustrate testified to the Federal cleverness, and ministered to the wants of the brave defenders of the Union. The regiment undoubtedly contained men whose means gave them every epicurean indulgence; but we question if any French bread, fresh butter, with all the appliances of Delmonico, ever tasted so sweet as the newly baked bread they got from the primitive oven.

MAJOR GENERAL BURNSIDE ASSUMING COMMAND OF

"HEADQUARTERS ARMY OF THE POTOMAC, November 10th, 1862.—In accordance with General Orders, No. 182, issued by the President of the United hearty co-operation of its officers and men, will, I hope, under the blessing of God, insure its success. Having been a sharer of the privations, and a v McClellan, entertained through a long and most friendly association with him, I feel that it is not as a stranger I assume command. To the Ninth Ar unswerving loyalty and determination of the gallant army now intrusted to my care, I accept its control, with the steadfast assurance that the just cause

HE POTOMAC—ISSUING ORDERS TO HIS STAFF.

he command of the Army of the Potomac. Patriotism, and the exercise of my every energy in the direction of this army, aided by the full and of the old Army of the Potomac in the Maryland campaign, and fully identified with them in their feelings of respect and esteem for General intimately associated with me, I need say nothing: our histories are identical. With diffidence for myself, but with a proud confidence in the URNSIDE, Major General Commanding." Our illustration represents the general issuing orders to his staff immediately after assuming command.

SURRENDER OF FORT MACON, GA., APRIL 26TH, 1862—EXTERIOR ON SIDE FACING THE FEDERAL BATTERIES, SHOWING EFFECT OF SHOT ON THE GLACIS AND WALLS.

BATTLE OF ANTIETAM, MD.—BURNSIDE'S DIVISION CARRYING THE BRIDGE OVER THE ANTIETAM CREEK AND STORMING THE CONFEDERATE POSITION, AFTER A DESPERATE CONFLICT OF FOUR HOURS, WEDNESDAY, SEPTEMBER 17TH, 1862.

On the left, during the afternoon, Burnside carried the bridge, after an obstinate contest of four hours' duration and a loss of about five hundred killed and wounded. Hawkins's Zouaves then crossed, and finding the enemy ready drawn up under cover of the hills, advanced in line of battle on their new position, about half a mile distant. The ground over which they advanced was open clover and plowed fields, the latter very difficult and fatiguing to march in, owing to the softness of the ground. The enemy's guns, fourteen in number, kept up a terrible fire on the advancing line, which never wavered, but slowly toiled along, receiving shelter, however, when they were in the hollows. They were halted a few moments to rest in the hollow nearest the enemy's position, and then were ordered to charge with a yell. As they came up the hill in front of the enemy's batteries they received a heavy volley from a large force of infantry behind a stone wall about two hundred feet in front of the enemy's batteries. The Federals, though terribly decimated, gave them a volley in return, and then went on with the bayonet. The enemy did not stay to contest the ground, and although two to one, broke and ran, leaving their guns.

SURRENDER OF FORT MACON, GA., APRIL 26TH, 1862—LOWERING THE CONFEDERATE FLAG.

KILLING'S CAVE, ON THE BANKS OF THE POTOMAC, NEAR SHARPSBURG, THE PLACE OF REFUGE OF MANY CITIZENS
DURING THE BATTLE OF ANTIETAM.

A glance at the map of the battle of Antietam will enable our readers to perceive how terribly exposed the little town of Sharpsburg was during the conflict, situated as it was almost between two fires; for, however anxious the Federal generals might be to spare the town, it was impossible to prevent many of the shot and shell from falling into its midst. In the cellar of the Kretzer mansion were congregated men, women and children, all spellbound as they listened to the terrible thunder of the battle. They could tell by the whiz and the awful explosions every now and then how near to them was the work of destruction; and their terror rose to perfect agony when a shell exploded before one of the openings which gave them a dim light and was the chief means of ventilation in this chamber of horrors. Of a similar character is our sketch of the cave of refuge near Sharpsburg, and situated on the banks of the Potomac.

VIEW OF THE FORTIFICATIONS ERECTED BY THE FEDERAL TROOPS AT BIRD'S POINT, MO., OPPOSITE CAIRO, ILL.

ADVANCE OF THE ARMY OF THE POTOMAC—OCCUPATION OF WINCHESTER, VA., AND THE ABANDONED, CONTESTED OR FORTIFIED ARMYS, BY DEPARTMENT OF GENERAL, BY GENERAL BANKS'S DIVISION

CONFEDERATES IN AMBUSH FIRING ON A RECONNOITRING EXPEDITION TO OYSTER CREEK, ROANOKE ISLAND, N. C.

BOMBARDMENT AND CAPTURE OF FORT THOMPSON, THIRTEEN GUNS, NEAR NEW BERNE, ON THE NEUSE RIVER, BY THE FEDERAL GUNBOATS OF GENERAL BURNSIDE'S EXPEDITION, COMMANDED BY COMMANDER S. C. ROWAN, U. S. N., MARCH 14TH, 1862.

DESTRUCTION OF RAILROAD TRACK BY FEDERAL TROOPS

ATTACK ON ENEMY'S TRAIN by 48TH VOL. R.C.

THE FEDERAL TROOPS UNDER GENERALS BRANNAN AND TERRY DRIVING THE CONFEDERATES UNDER BEAUREGARD ACROSS THE POCOTALIGO BRIDGE, NEAR THE CHARLESTON AND SAVANNAH RAILROAD. OCTOBER 22D, 1862.

PASSAGE OF THE RAPPAHANNOCK BY THE GRAND ARMY OF THE POTOMAC AT FREDERICKSBURG, VA., WEDNESDAY, MIDNIGHT, DECEMBER 10TH, 1862.

The crossing over of the Federal army, on December 10th, 1862, was a most striking scene. "Although a slight mist shrouded the lower part of the scene, floating a few feet above the river, the moonlight was resplendent. The shore was crowded with troops, while the glimmer of the bayonets and the camp fires made a picture never to be forgotten."

FEDERAL BAGGAGE TRAIN ON ITS WAY TO THE ARMY AT FALMOUTH, VA., DECEMBER, 1862.

REAR ADMIRAL SILAS H. STRINGHAM.

Rear Admiral Stringham, born in Middletown, Orange County, N. Y., November 7th, 1798; died in Brooklyn, N. Y., February 7th, 1876. He entered the Navy as a midshipman, November 15th, 1809, and was in continuous service up to the breaking out of the Civil War in 1861, when he was summoned to Washington to advise upon the preparations for war. He took command of the North Atlantic Blockading Fleet, and planned the expedition to Hatteras Inlet. General Butler accompanied him with 900 men. The squadron bombarded the forts, sailing in an ellipse, by which means it concentrated its fire on the forts, and manœuvred so skillfully that none of the fleet were hit. Both forts surrendered, and the troops were landed to garrison them on August 29th, 1861. Not one of the Federal troops was injured. This was the first naval victory of any importance. Stringham declined further active ....ccount of his age, and was retired as a commodore, December 21st, 1861. He was promoted to rear admiral on the retired list, July 16th, 1862.

ATTACK UPON THE UNITED STATES SLOOP OF WAR "SEMINOLE," FROM THE CONFEDERATE BATTERIES, EVANSPORT, POTOMAC RIVER, OCTOBER 15TH, 1861.

THE MASQUERADE OF WAR—INGENIOUS METHOD OF DISGUISING THE MASTS AND HULLS OF COMMODORE PORTER'S MORTAR FLOTILLA WITH BOUGHS OF TREES, ETC., TO DECEIVE THE CONFEDERATE ARTILLERISTS.

GENERAL VIEW OF COLUMBUS, KY., AND ITS FORTIFICATIONS, LOOKING DOWN THE RIVER, SHOWING THE "IRON BLUFFS" CROWNED WITH BATTERIES, THE WATER BATTERIES, AND THE ARRIVAL OF THE FEDERAL GUNBOATS, MARCH 4TH, 1862.

WHARF BOAT AT CARROLLTON, ILL. OPPOSITE HAWESVILLE, KY.

VIEW OF THE TOWN OF PADUCAH, KY., AT THE CONFLUENCE OF THE RIVERS OHIO AND TENNESSEE, THE NORTHERN TERMINUS OF THE MOBILE AND OHIO RAILROAD.

This flourishing city, the capital of McCracken County, is situated at the confluence of the Ohio and Tennessee Rivers, and is connected with Mobile by railroad. It had a fine range of warehouses fronting the river, contained five churches, two banks and two newspaper offices; it had also a marine hospital. Its position had given it many commercial advantages, which were fast operating to make it one of the most progressive cities of the West. When, however, the Confederates took possession of Columbus and Hickman, two important points in Kentucky on the Mississippi, it became necessary to hold them in check and to prevent their flanking the Federal stronghold of Cairo; and, with his usual sagacity and promptitude, General Grant immediately occupied Paducah. This step, although an apparent invasion of the sacred soil of Kentucky, received the entire approval of that loyal and gallant State as expressed through her Legislature; and Paducah was of course retained while the necessity for its occupation existed. Paducah contained about 8,000 inhabitants, very few of whom were tainted with the secession treason. It is named after a famous Indian chief who formerly lived in its vicinity.

HEADQUARTERS OF THE FEDERAL ARMY COMMANDED BY GENERAL GRANT, ON THE BANKS OF THE MISSISSIPPI, NEAR VICKSBURG.

Our artist's sketch needs no description—it explains itself. A more perfect picture of the Slough of Despond was never painted. General Grant established himself on board the *Magnolia*, where he superintended the entire operations. One of his aids wrote: "As for mud, it beats Broadway, and considerable fun is got out of the wallowings undergone by the commissariat wagons and their drivers. Frequently the men place logs at certain intervals, and crowds amuse themselves by seeing how often the log disappears, leaving the man who trusted to it up to his middle in that magnificent mud and slush, which throws even Virginia into the shade." The second boat to the right of the *Magnolia* is the hospital ship.

GENERAL JOHN BUFORD.

General Buford, born in Kentucky in 1825, died in Washington, D. C., December 16th, 1863, was graduated at the United States Military Academy in 1848; was appointed brevet second lieutenant in the First Dragoons, and served on the plains until the Civil War began. He was made a major in the inspector general's corps on November 12th, 1861. On June 6th, 1862, he was attached to the staff of General Pope in the Army of Virginia; and on July 27th he was made a brigadier general, and assigned to the command of a brigade of cavalry under General Hooker in the Northern Virginia campaign. He engaged in the skirmish at Madison Courthouse; the passage of the Rapidan in pursuit of Jackson's force; Kelly's Ford, Thoroughfare Gap, and Manassas, where he was wounded. He commanded the cavalry division of the Army of the Potomac in the Pennsylvania campaign, and at Gettysburg he began the attack on the enemy before the arrival of Reynolds, on July 1st, 1863. His last sickness was the result of toil and exposure. His commission as major general reached him on the day of his death.

GENERAL THOMAS L. CRITTENDEN.

General Crittenden, born in Russellville, Ky., May 15th, 1815, studied law under his father, was admitted to the bar, and became Commonwealth's Attorney in Kentucky in 1842. He served in the Mexican War as lieutenant colonel of Kentucky infantry, and was volunteer aid to General Taylor at the battle of Buena Vista. At the beginning of the Civil War he espoused the national cause, and on October 27th, 1861, was appointed brigadier general of volunteers. He commanded a division at the battle of Shiloh, and was promoted major general, July 17th, 1862, for gallant service on that occasion, and assigned to the command of a division in the Army of the Tennessee. He served under Rosecrans in the battle of Stone River, and at Chickamauga commanded one of the two corps that were routed. In the Virginia campaign of 1864 he commanded a division of the Ninth Corps. He resigned December 13th, 1864, but entered the regular army as colonel of the Thirty-second Infantry on July 28th, 1866. He was retired on May 19th, 1881.

GENERAL GEORGE W. MORGAN.

General Morgan, born in Washington County, Pa., September 20th, 1820, died at Old Point Comfort, Va., July 26th, 1893. At the beginning of the War with Mexico he was made colonel of the Second Ohio Volunteers, and he was subsequently appointed colonel of the Fifteenth United States Infantry, which he led with ability under General Scott, receiving for his gallantry at Contreras and Churubusco, where he was severely wounded, the thanks of the Ohio Legislature and the brevet of brigadier general. On November 21st, 1861, he was made brigadier general of volunteers. In March, 1862, he assumed the command of the Seventh Division of the Army of the Ohio, with which he was ordered to occupy Cumberland Gap, in Southern Kentucky, then held by the Confederates. He forced the enemy to retire on June 18th, 1862. He also served in the Valley of the Kanawha and at Vicksburgh, and was afterward assigned to the Thirteenth Army Corps, and commanded at the capture of Fort Hindman, Ark. Owing to failing health he resigned in June, 1863.

GENERAL JOHN G. FOSTER.

General Foster, born in Whitefield, N. H., May 27th, 1823, died in Nashua, H. H., September 2d, 1874, was graduated at the United States Military Academy in 1846, assigned to the Engineer Corps, and served in the Mexican War under General Scott. He received the brevets of first lieutenant and captain for gallantry. At the beginning of the Civil War he was stationed at Charleston, S. C., and safely removed the garrison of Fort Moultrie to Fort Sumter during the night, December 26th–27th, 1860. He was made brigadier general of volunteers October 23d, 1861, commanded a brigade in Burnside's North Carolina expedition, and received the brevet of lieutenant colonel for his services at Roanoke Island. While in command of the Department of North Carolina, in 1862–'3, he conducted several important expeditions. In 1865 he was brevetted brigadier general in the regular army for gallant services in the capture of Savannah, Ga., and major general for services in the field during the rebellion.

RECONNOISSANCE BY COLONEL MAX WEBER'S TURNER RIFLES IN THE VICINITY OF NEWMARKET BRIDGE, ON THE ROAD
TO YORKTOWN, VA.

FEDERAL ARTILLERY TAKING UP POSITION AT THE BATTLE OF SOUTH MOUNTAIN.

The Federal movement was admirably executed in face of the well-directed fire from the Confederates, who had the advantage of position and could contest almost every inch of the steep, wooded and rocky approach. By four o'clock (September 14th, 1862) the engagement became general, and the entire ground was vigorously contested until the crest was reached and darkness put an end to the fight. In this engagement the total loss on both sides in killed, wounded and missing was nearly 3,000. General Jesse L. Reno was killed while at the head of his command, and was replaced by General Cox, General Hatch and Colonel Wainwright being severely wounded.

"THE FORLORN HOPE"—VOLUNTEER STORMING PARTY, CONSISTING OF PORTIONS OF THE SEVENTH MICHIGAN AND NIN[...]
WHO WERE FIRING UPON THE

We illustrate one of those numerous acts of daring which have raised the character of the Federal soldier to the highest position in the mil[...]
General Burnside called for 100 volunteers to cross and dislodge, at the bayonet's point, the concealed sharpshooters. Thousands sprang forward, bu[...]
lant "forlorn hope" sprang into the boats, and, on reaching the other side, drove the Confederates from their posts at the point of the bayonet, capt[...]

USETTS, CROSSING THE RAPPAHANNOCK IN ADVANCE OF THE GRAND ARMY, TO DRIVE OFF THE CONFEDERATE RIFLEMEN
NIERS, WEDNESDAY, DECEMBER 10TH, 1862.

he fire of the enemy from the rifle pits on the south side of the Rappahannock became so deadly that the pontoniers could not carry on their work
quired was chosen. These consisted of men from the Seventh Michigan and Nineteenth Massachusetts Regiments. With the utmost alacrity this gal-
Only one man was killed and five wounded in this desperate duty. The bridge was soon finished, and a sufficient force passed over to hold the town.

NAVAL ACTION BETWEEN THE UNITED STATES WAR STEAMER "MISSISSIPPI" AND THE CONFEDERATE IRON-CASED FLOATING BATTERY RAM AND OTHER STEAMERS, OFF THE MOUTH OF THE PASS A L'OUTRE, NEW ORLEANS, JANUARY 1ST, 1862.

BIRD'S-EYE VIEW OF THE BURNING OF A CONFEDERATE SCHOONER IN QUANTICO OR DUMFRIES CREEK, POTOMAC RIVER, ON THE NIGHT OF OCTOBER 11TH, 1861, BY LIEUTENANT A. D. HARRELL AND A DETACHMENT FROM THE POTOMAC FLOTILLA.

On the 10th of October, 1861, Lieutenant Harrell, commanding the steamer *Union*, of the Potomac Flotilla, stationed at the mouth of Aquia Creek, learning that the Confederates had fitted out a large schooner in Quantico or Dumfries Creek, and had collected a considerable body of troops there, with the intention of crossing the Potomac, determined that the vessel should be destroyed. He accordingly organized an expedition, and with one boat and two launches entered the mouth of the creek about half-past two o'clock on the morning of the 11th. The schooner was discovered some distance up, in charge of a single sentry, who fled and gave the alarm. She was immediately boarded and set on fire; and when her destruction was rendered certain Lieutenant Harrell's men returned to their boats and pulled again for the steamer. Their position was fully revealed by the light of the burning schooner, and they were fired upon continuously from both banks of the narrow stream; but not one of them was injured, though their clothing in many instances was perforated with bullets. The success of the enterprise was complete.

ENCAMPMENT OF COLONEL MAX WEBER'S GERMAN TURNER RIFLE REGIMENT, TWENTIETH NEW YORK VOLUNTEERS, AT HAMPTON CREEK, VA.—OFFICERS' QUARTERS AT THE SUMMER RESIDENCE OF EX-PRESIDENT TYLER.

THOROUGHFARE GAP, VA., A PASS IN THE MOUNTAINS ON THE MANASSAS GAP RAILROAD, NEAR STRASBURG, HELD BY GENERAL GEARY.

This famous natural break in that part of the mountain ridge called Bull Run Mountain is about nine miles northeast of Warrenton, forty-seven miles southwest of Washington, and one hundred and twenty-four miles from Richmond. The western side is of granite, covered with soil, on which trees grow up to the summit. On the east side is the Gap, which has been called the Virginia Thermopylæ, since a few determined men might hold it against thousands. This splendid defense caught the eye of General Geary, and had there been a necessity to act on the defensive he had resolved there to make his stand. The rocks lie scattered around in such wild confusion as to suggest the idea of being the result of some convulsion of nature. Near the Gap is a spring, issuing from under an immense rock, of the purest and coldest water, which is neither increased nor diminished in any season. It stands on the roadside, and is called by travelers 'The Diamond Spring in Palestine.'

THE CAMPAIGN IN KENTUCKY—FEDERAL TROOPS UNDER GENERAL JOHNSTON, ADVANCING ON THE LOUISVILLE AND NASHVILLE TURNPIKE, OVERTAKEN BY THE EQUIPAGE AND BAGGAGE TRAIN ON THE LOUISVILLE AND NASHVILLE RAILROAD.

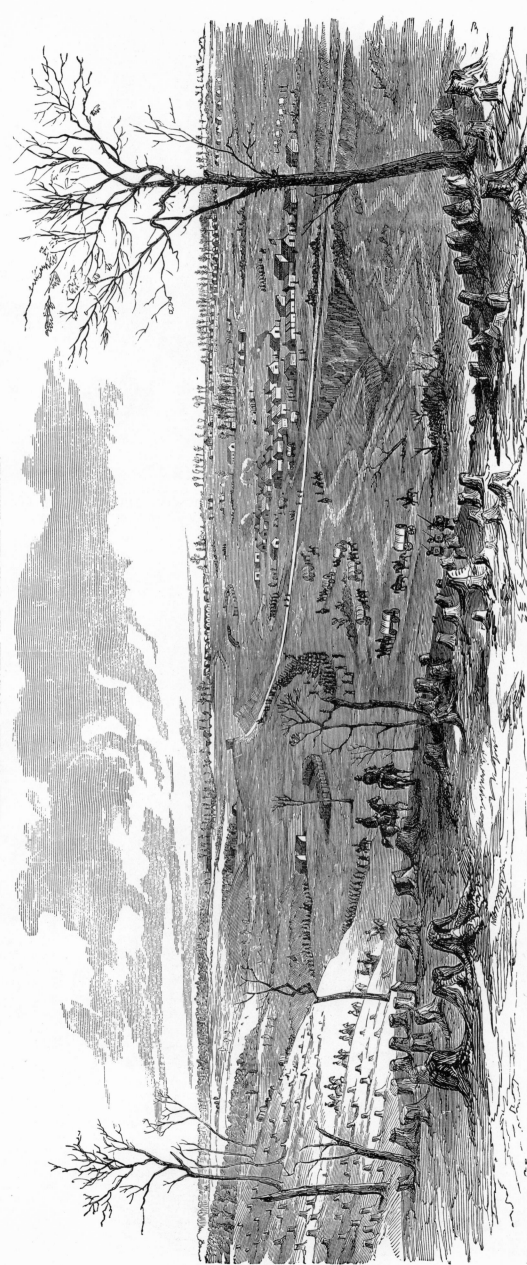

CONFEDERATE POSITION NEAR CENTREVILLE, VA., AT THE CROSSING OF THE ORANGE AND ALEXANDRIA RAILWAY OVER BULL RUN SHOWING CONFEDERATE ENCAMPMENT, FORTIFICATIONS, ETC.

INTERIOR OF THE PRINCIPAL CONFEDERATE FORTIFICATIONS NEAR NEW BERNE, N. C. AFTER THEIR CAPTURE BY THE FEDERAL FORCES UNDER GENERAL BURNSIDE, MARCH 14TH, 1862.

ERECTING STOCKADES AT NEWPORT NEWS, VA., BY THE FEDERAL TROOPS, JUNE, 1861.

DESTRUCTION OF THE FAMOUS CONFEDERATE PRIVATEER "NASHVILLE," IN THE OGEECHEE RIVER, GA., BY THE FEDERAL IRONCLAD "MONTAUK," CAPTAIN WORDEN, FEBRUARY 28TH, 1863.

Captain Worden's report: "The enemy's steamer *Nashville* was observed by me in motion above the battery known as Fort McAllister. A reconnoissance immediately made proved that in moving up the river she had grounded in that part known as Seven' Miles Reach. Believing that I could, by approaching close to the battery, reach and destroy her, I moved up at daylight this morning, accompanied by the blockading fleet in these waters. By moving up close to the obstructions I was enabled, although under a very heavy fire from the battery, to approach the *Nashville*, still aground, within the distance of twelve hundred yards. A few well-directed shells determined the range, and I soon succeeded in striking her with 11-inch and 15-inch shells. I soon had the satisfaction of observing that the *Nashville* had caught fire from the shells exploding in her in several places, and at amidships. At 9:20 A. M. a large pivot gun mounted abaft her foremast exploded from the heat; at 9:40 her smoke chimney went by the board, and at 9:55 her magazine exploded with terrific violence, shattering her in smoking ruins. Nothing remains of her.

286

THE CONFEDERATE PRIVATEER STEAMER "ALABAMA" ("290"), CAPTAIN RAPHAEL SEMMES.

Our illustration of the *Alabama* was taken from a photograph while she was at Liverpool, where she was facetiously termed the Emperor of China's yacht. The *Alabama* was built at Birkenhead; she was about 1,200 tons burden, with draught of about 14 feet; her engines built by Laird & Sons, of Birkenhead, 1862. She was a wooden vessel propelled by a screw, copper bottom, about 210 feet long, rather narrow, painted black outside and drab inside; had a round stern, billethead, very little sheer, flushed deck fore and aft; a bridge forward of the smokestack; carried two large black boats on cranes amidships forward of the main rigging; two black quarter boats between the main and mizzen masts, one small black boat over the stern on cranes; the square spars on a gallows between the bridge and foremast showed above the rail. She carried three long 32-pounders on a side, and was pierced for two more amidships; had a 100-pound rifled pivot gun forward of the bridge, and a 68-pound pivot on the main track; had tracks laid forward for a pivot bow gun, and tracks aft for a pivot stern chaser; her guns were of the Blakely pattern, and were manufactured by Wesley & Preston, Liverpool, 1862. She took her armament and crew and most of her officers on board near Terceira, Western Islands, from an English vessel. Her

287

EXTEMPORE MUSICAL AND TERPSICHOREAN ENTERTAINMENT AT THE UNITED STATES ARSENAL, BATON ROUGE, LA., UNDER THE PATRONAGE OF THE FORTY-FIRST MASSACHUSETTS, THE ONE HUNDRED AND THIRTY-FIRST NEW YORK AND THE TWENTY-FIFTH CONNECTICUT VOLUNTEERS—CONTRABAND CHILDREN DANCING THE BREAKDOWN.

If anything were necessary to show the sensuous nature of music, it would be found in the eagerness with which the contraband race pursued it. The Federals, with that love of fun which ever distinguishes the brave soldier off duty, got up, a few evenings after their arrival at Baton Rouge, an extempore musical and terpsichorean entertainment, in which the darky element was largely and loudly represented. The hall was one of the extensive rooms in the United States Arsenal building, and prominent among the promoters were the Forty-first Massachusetts, One Hundred and Thirty-first New York and the Twenty-fifth Connecticut Volunteers. One of the features was a breakdown, which was danced, or rather jumped, with great vigor by a couple of contraband juveniles.

RETURN OF A FORAGING PARTY OF THE TWENTY-FOURTH REGIMENT, CONNECTICUT VOLUNTEERS, WITH THEIR SPOILS, TO BATON ROUGE, HAVING CAPTURED HORSES, CARTS, WAGONS, MULES, CONTRABANDS, PROVISIONS, ETC.

On January 29th, 1863, General Grover, who commanded at Baton Rouge, having received intelligence that a large quantity of supplies had been gathered at a place some miles away, sent a foraging party, consisting of the Twenty-fourth Connecticut Regiment, to capture them. This was happily accomplished without losing a man, the Confederate guard flying at the first sight of the Federal party. The spoils were several horses, carts, wagons, mules, corn and potatoes, saying nothing of a few "contrabands" who came to enjoy "Massa Linkum's" proclamation.

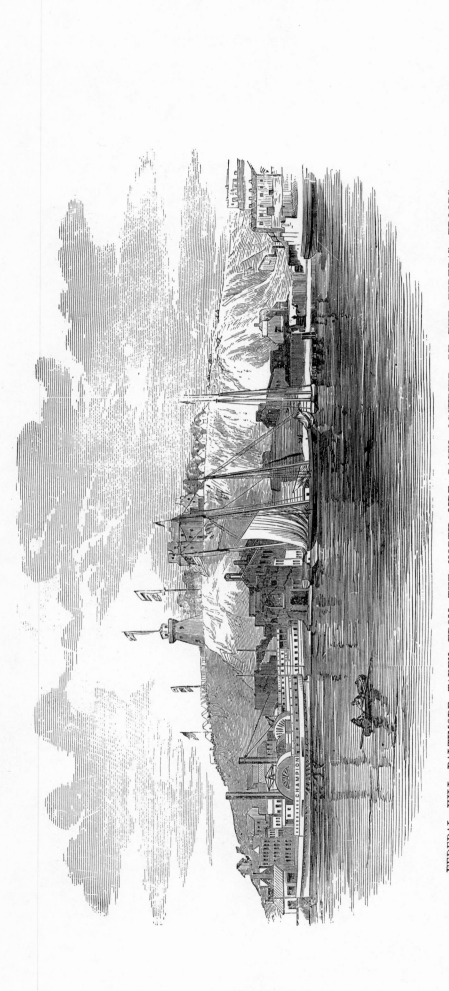

FEDERAL HILL, BALTIMORE, TAKEN FROM THE NORTH SIDE BASIN, OCCUPIED BY THE FEDERAL TROOPS.

EXTERIOR VIEW OF FORT CLINCH, ON AMELIA ISLAND, FLA., COMMANDING THE HARBOR OF FERNANDINA, CAPTURED BY THE FEDERAL LAND AND NAVAL FORCES UNDER COMMODORE DUPONT AND GENERAL WRIGHT, MARCH 4TH, 1862.

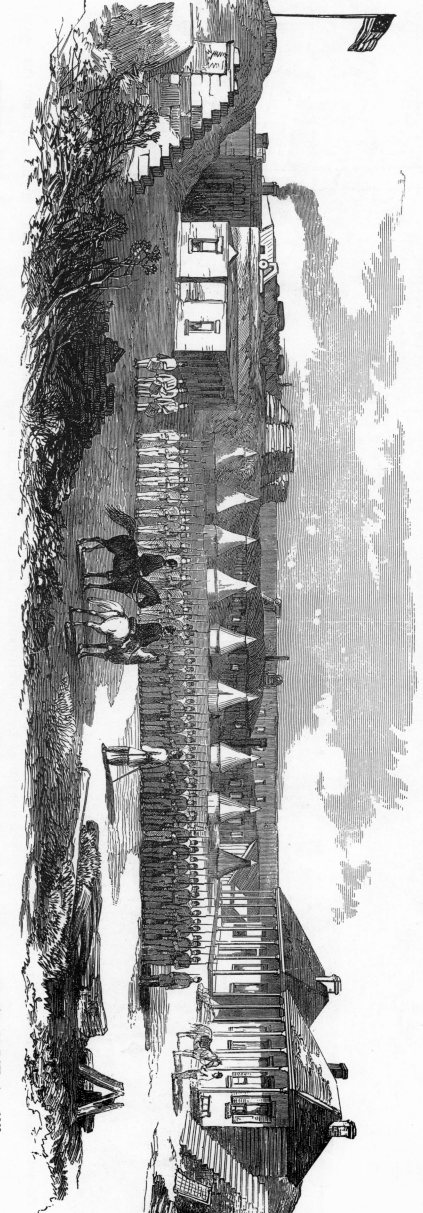

INTERIOR VIEW OF FORT CLINCH, ON AMELIA ISLAND, FLA., COMMANDING THE HARBOR OF FERNANDINA, CAPTURED BY THE FEDERAL FORCES, MARCH 4TH, 1862.

ENCAMPMENT OF THE FIRST VERMONT REGIMENT, COLONEL PHELPS, AT NEWPORT NEWS, VA.

FEDERAL VOLUNTEERS CROSSING FROM CINCINNATI TO COVINGTON ON A BRIDGE OF COAL BOATS, CONSTRUCTED FOR THE OCCASION, ON THEIR WAY TO DEFEND KENTUCKY FROM THE CONFEDERATES UNDER GENERAL KIRBY SMITH, SEPTEMBER 5TH, 1862.

The Confederate army under command of General Kirby Smith was variously estimated from 15,000 to 30,000 men. They were poorly clad, but well armed, and considering their organization were tolerably well disciplined. Their officers were bitter desperadoes, and they united in their expressed determination to pillage Cincinnati, against which city they pretended to have some terrible grudge to settle. General Kirby Smith, the Confederate commander, was much trusted by his troops, and was a cool and daring leader. Our sketch represents the Federal volunteers crossing from Cincinnati to Covington to defend Kentucky.

BATTLE OF ANTIETAM—BURNSIDE'S DIVISION, LEFT WING—BRILLIANT AND DECISIVE BAYONET CHARGE OF HAWKINS'S ZOUAVES, COLONEL KIMBALL, ON THE CONFEDERATE BATTERY ON THE HILL, RIGHT BANK OF ANTIETAM CREEK, NEAR SHARPSBURG, ON THE AFTERNOON OF SEPTEMBER 17TH, 1862—UTTER ROUT OF THE CONFEDERATES.

(See Description in Part 17.)

GENERAL EDWARD O. C. ORD.

General Ord, born in Cumberland, Md., October 18th, 1818, died in Havana, Cuba, July 22d, 1883, was graduated from the United States military Academy in 1839, and assigned to the Third Artillery. He served with distinction in the Florida and Mexican Wars and during the War for the Union. The battle of Dranesville, in 1861, was won under his leadership, and he was severely wounded at the battle of Hatchie and at the assault on Fort Harrison. Having been several times promoted for gallant and meritorious conduct, he became commander of the Department of Virginia and North Carolina in 1865, and led the Army of the James in the victorious engagements that ended the war. In March, 1865, he received the brevet of major general in the regular army, and he subsequently held successive command of the Departments of Arkansas, California, Texas and the Platte.

GENERAL FRANCIS C. BARLOW.

GENERAL GEORGE H. SHARPE

General Barlow, born in Brooklyn, N. Y., October 19th, 1834, was graduated at Harvard in 1855. In 1861 he enlisted as a private in the Twelfth Regiment, New York State National Guard, and went to the front on the first call for troops to defend the capital. At the end of the three months' term of service he had been promoted lieutenant. He at once re-entered the service as lieutenant colonel of the Sixty-first New York Volunteers, was promoted colonel during the siege of Yorktown, and distinguished himself at the battle of Fair Oaks, May 31st and June 1st, 1862, for which he was afterward promoted brigadier general. At the battle of Gettysburg he was severely wounded and taken prisoner; but he was exchanged, and recovered in time to take the field again the following spring. He also participated in the final campaigns of the Potomac Army under General Grant.

General Sharpe, born in Kingston, N. Y., February 26th, 1828, was graduated at Rutgers in 1847; studied law at Yale College; was admitted to the bar in 1854, and practiced until he entered the army in 1861 as captain in the Twentieth New York Infantry. He became colonel of the One Hundred and Twentieth New York Infantry in 1862, and took part in all the battles of the Army of the Potomac. He served upon the staffs of Generals Hooker, Meade and Grant, and was brevetted brigadier general in 1864 and major general in 1865. He was attached to the United States Legation at Vienna in 1851, and was a special agent of the State Department in Europe in 1867. In 1870-'73 he was United States Marshal for the Southern District of New York, and took the census that demonstrated the great election frauds of 1868 in New York city, which led to the enforcement of the Federal election laws for the first time in 1871.

BATTLE OF ANTIETAM—THE OPENING OF THE FIGHT—HOOKER'S DIVISION FORDING THE GREAT ANTIETAM CREEK TO ATTACK THE CONFEDERATE ARMY UNDER GENERAL LEE, TEN O'CLOCK A. M., SEPTEMBER 17TH, 1862.

CONFEDERATE CAVALRY DRIVING STRAGGLERS AND SKULKERS BACK TO THEIR DUTY AT THE BATTLE OF ANTIETAM.

One of the greatest evils in a volunteer army is the practice of straggling. This decreases under the elevating process of discipline; but all our artists agree in declaring that they have seen nearly one-fourth of a regiment, including officers, dropping off one by one at convenient opportunities. In some cases this may have proceeded from sheer exhaustion, but generally it was for the purpose of cooking their rations, taking a nap, or for shirking a battle. Federal discipline was very lax in this respect, and more stringent regulations were imperatively demanded. The Confederate generals, whom no consideration of humanity ever restrained from making the most cruel examples, treated stragglers without mercy, and hundreds of these miserable men were cut down or shot by their own officers in their attempts to evade the stern necessity of battle. The result was that the Confederate troops very often fought with a desperation unknown in modern warfare. Our artist, who from a hill at Antietam had a capital view of the field of battle, saw many instances in which some mounted Confederate officers rode amid a body of stragglers and drove them back into the conflict. Our sketch illustrates this peculiar mode of Southern drilling.

BOMBARDMENT OF FREDERICKSBURG, VA., BY THE ARMY OF TH

Our correspondent reports of this event: "At ten o'clock General Burnside gives the order, 'Concentrate the fire of all your guns on the cit right centre, eleven batteries; Colonel Tyler, left centre, seven batteries; Captain De Russy, left, nine batteries. In a few moments these thirty-five circle formed by the bend of the river and land opposite Fredericksburg, opened on the doomed city. The effect was, of course, terrific, and, regar intermission, of the very loudest thunder peals. It lasted thus for upward of an hour, fifty rounds being fired from each gun, and I know not ho tantalizing was, that though a great deal could be heard, nothing could be seen, the city being still enveloped in fog and mist. Only a denser pill presently saw that at least a dozen houses must be on fire. Toward noon the curtain rolled up, and we saw that it was indeed so. Fredericksburg was found by our gunners almost impossible to obtain a sufficient depression of their pieces to shell the front part of the city, and the Confederate s

!' You may believe they were not loath to obey. The artillery of the right—eight batteries—was commanded by Colonel Hays; Colonel Tompkins,
…otal of one hundred and seventy-nine guns, ranging from 10-pounder Parrotts to 4½-inch siege guns, posted along the convex side of the arc of the
…omenon, was among the most awfully grand conceivable. Perhaps what will give you the liveliest idea of its effect is a succession, absolutely without
…of iron were thrown into the town. The congregated generals were transfixed; mingled satisfaction and awe was upon every face. But what was
…itself on the background of the fog indicated where the town had been fired by our shells. Another and another column showed itself, and we
…Tremendous though this firing had been, and terrific though its effect obviously was on the town, it had not accomplished the object intended. It
…comparatively safe behind the thick stone walls of the houses."

LAND PRACTICE OF SAILORS WITH THE DAHLGREN HOWITZER BOAT GUN—SPONGING OUT THE GUN.

ARTILLERY PRACTICE WITH THE DAHLGREN HOWITZER BOAT GUN—LOADING.

ARTILLERY PRACTICE WITH THE DAHLGREN HOWITZER BOAT GUN—OFFICER GIVING THE WORD OF COMMAND TO FIRE.

"THE PIRATE'S DECOY"—CAPTAIN SEMMES, OF THE CONFEDERATE PRIVATEER "ALABAMA," DECOYING SHIPS TOWARD HIM
BY BURNING A PRIZE VESSEL.

The plan that Captain Semmes adopted to bring fish to his net was as follows : Whenever he captured a ship, after taking from her all that he and his officers wanted, he lay by her until dark, and then set her on fire. The light of the burning ship could be seen many miles, and every other ship within seeing distance stood toward the light, thinking to rescue a number of poor fellows from destruction. The pirate kept in the immediate vicinity, awaiting the prey that was sure to come, and the next morning the poor fellows who to serve the cause of humanity had gone many miles out of their course found themselves under the guns of the *Alabama*, with the certainty that before another twenty-four hours they would share the fate of the ship they went to serve.

THE "QUAKER CITY," ONE OF THE POTOMAC FLOTILLA, ENGAGING CONFEDERATE DRAGOONS IN LYNN HAVEN BAY,
NEAR CAPE HENRY VA.

The *Quaker City*, Commander Carr, one of the United States Flotilla of the Potomac, while cruising in Lynn Haven Bay, near Cape Henry, picked up a man named Lynch, a refugee from Norfolk, who represented that the master plumber of the Norfolk Navy Yard was ashore and wished to be taken off. An armed boat which was sent for the purpose was fired upon when near the shore, mortally wounding James Lloyd, a seaman of Charlestown, Mass. A few 32-pound shells dispersed the Confederates.

THE HARBOR OF CHARLESTON, S. C.—FORT MOULTRIE, ON SULLIVAN'S ISLAND.

EXTERIOR VIEW OF FORTIFICATIONS ERECTED BY THE FEDERAL TROOPS AT HILTON HEAD, PORT ROYAL, S. C.

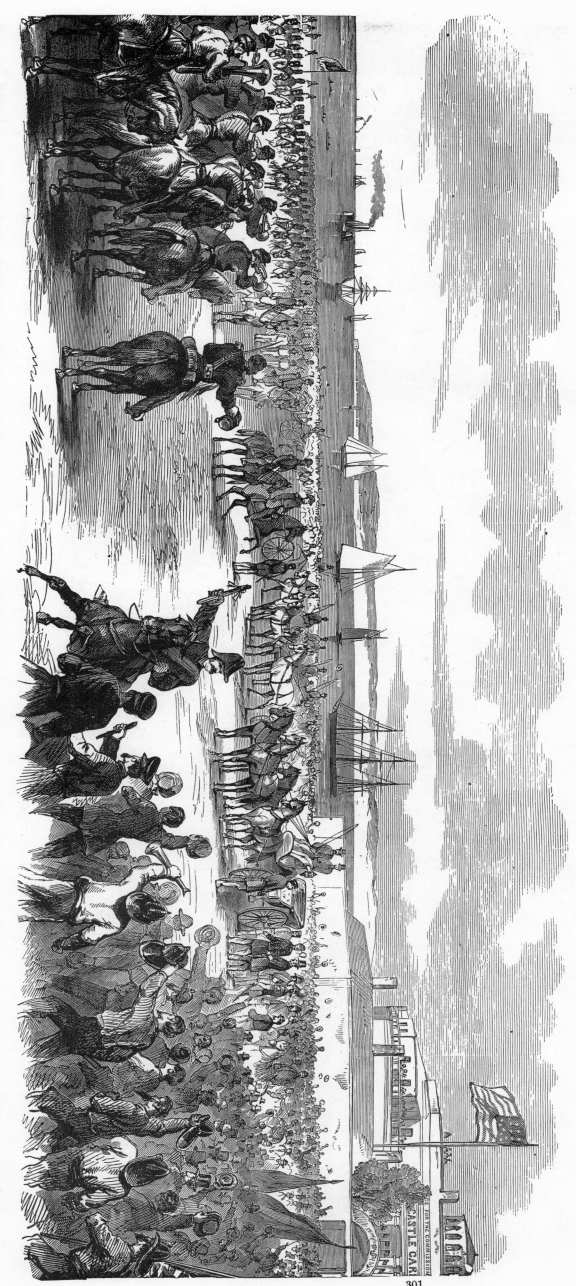

RECEPTION OF BRIGADIER GENERAL CORCORAN BY MAYOR OPDYKE AND THE CITIZENS OF NEW YORK, AT CASTLE GARDEN, AUGUST 22D, 1862.—MAYOR OPDYKE ESCORTING THE GENERAL TO HIS CARRIAGE.

THE HARBOR OF CHARLESTON, S. C.—FORT PINCKNEY.

THE "GRAND SKEDADDLE" OF THE INHABITANTS FROM CHARLESTON, S. C., WHEN THREATENED BY AN ATTACK FROM THE FEDERAL TROOPS.

When General Brannan made his daring and successful dash upon the railroad between Pocotaligo and Coosawhatchie the terror both in Savannah and Charleston was very great. Despite the fact that General Beauregard with thirty thousand troops was stationed midway between the cities a restless desire for flight took possession of thousands, and for three days the roads to the interior were crowded with as miscellaneous a group as that which marched into Noah's ark. Lieutenant Kirby, of the Forty-seventh Massachusetts Regiment, being then a prisoner, had an excellent opportunity of sketching this motley stream of humanity. But our sketch renders all further description unnecessary.

BATTLE OF BAKER'S CREEK, MAY 16TH, 1863—DEFEAT OF THE CONFEDERATES UNDER PEMBERTON BY GENERAL GRANT.

On May 16th General Grant met Pemberton, with the whole garrison of Vicksburg, at Baker's Creek, and defeated him, driving him back toward Vicksburg, with a loss of 29 pieces of artillery and 4,000 men, and cutting him off from all hopes of relief. Pressing rapidly on, Grant, on the 17th, overtook Pemberton at Big Black River Bridge, and again defeated him, with a loss of 2,600 men and 17 guns. Pemberton then retired into the city.

GENERAL CHESTER A. ARTHUR.

General Arthur, twenty-first President of the United States, was born in Fairfield, Franklin County, Vt., October 5th, 1830; died in New York city, November 18th, 1886. In 1841 he entered the law office of Erastus D. Culver as a student, was admitted to the bar during the same year, and at once became a member of the firm of Culver, Parker & Arthur. On January 1st, 1861, Governor Morgan, who on that date entered upon his second term, and between whom and Mr. Arthur a warm friendship had grown up, appointed him on his staff as engineer in chief, with the rank of brigadier general. In April, 1861, his active services were required by Governor Morgan, and he became acting quartermaster general, and as such began in New York city the work of preparing and forwarding the State's quota of troops. On February 10th, 1862, he was appointed inspector general, with the rank of brigadier general, and in May he inspected the New York troops at Fredericksburg and on the Chickahominy. In June, 1862, Governor Morgan ordered his return from the Army of the Potomac, and he acted as secretary of the meeting of the governors of the loyal States which was held at the Astor House, New York city, June 28th. The governors advised President Lincoln to call for more troops; and on July 1st he called for 300,000 volunteers. At Governor Morgan's request General Arthur resumed his former work, resigned as inspector general, and July 10th, was appointed quartermaster general. He went out of office on December 31st, 1862, when Horatio Seymour succeeded Governor Morgan. General Arthur was elected Vice President of the United States, and took the oath of office March 4th, 1881. President Garfield died September 19th. His cabinet announced his death to the Vice President, then in New York, and at their suggestion he took the oath as President on the 20th, at his residence, 123 Lexington Avenue, before Judge John R. Brady, of the New York Supreme Court. On the 22d the oath was formally administered again in the Vice President's room in the Capitol, Washington, by Chief Justice Waite.

GENERAL JOSEPH HOOKER.

General Hooker, born in Hadley, Mass., November 13th, 1814, died in Garden City, N. Y., October 31st, 1879, was graduated from the United State Military Academy in 1837, and appointed a second lieutenant in the First Artillery, serving in the Florida and Mexican wars with distinction. He resigned from the army, February 21st, 1853, and from that time until 1861 lived a precarious and not very successful life. At the beginning of the Civil War he promptly offered his services, which the government made haste to accept, and he was appointed a brigadier general of volunteers, May 17th, 1861. He saw the battle of Bull Run without participating in it. He was employed in the defenses of Washington, August 12th, 1861, and then on the eastern shore of the Lower Potomac; and was appointed, in April, 1862, to the command of the Second Division in the Third Corps, Army of the Potomac, under Heintzelman, and fought in that capacity during the Peninsular campaign. He was distinguished at the siege of Yorktown, and was appointed a major general of volunteers on the day after the evacuation, May 5th. In the battle of Williamsburg his single division held the whole Confederate army in check and lost 2,228 men, killed or wounded, while 30,000 national troops looked on and gave no assistance until, when all his men had been engaged and he was obliged to retire, Kearny and Hancock came to his relief. He was also distinguished at the battle of Fair Oaks, Frazier's Farm, Glendale and Malvern Hill. At the close of the campaign Hooker was employed, still as a division commander, in the new movement under General Pope against Lee's Army of Northern Virginia, and fought with skill and valor at Bristoe Station, Manassas and Chantilly, where he held the enemy in check with the gallant Kearny, who was killed there. He took a prominent part in the Maryland campaign, and was engaged in the battle of South Mountain, September 14th, 1862, where he carried the mountain side on the right of Turner's Gap. At the battle of Antietam, September 17th, he again did more than his share of the fighting. He was shot through the foot and carried from the field. His wound only kept him out of the field until November 10th, when he rejoined the army for the campaign on the Rappahannock, with Fredericksburg as the objective point. He was appointed to the command of the Army of the Potomac, January 25th, 1863, and reorganized it. Perceiving the inferiority of his army, Hooker demanded that the 11,000 troops under French at Harper's Ferry should be added to his force. This was refused, and for this reason ostensibly Hooker sent in his resignation of the command. The President issued an order, under date of June 27th, 1863, relieving General Hooker, and conferring the command of the Army of the Potomac upon General Meade, who conducted it to Gettysburg. On September 24th Hooker was assigned to the command of the Twentieth Army Corps. With these troops he was sent to the South for the relief of Chattanooga, first under Rosecrans and afterward under Grant. He distinguished himself at Lookout Mountain and Missionary Ridge. When Sherman organized his army for the invasion of Georgia Hooker was retained in command of the Twentieth Corps, and gained new laurels at Mill Creek Gap, Resaca, Dallas and Pine Mountain. He was relieved of his command at his own request, July 30th, 1864. For the part he took in the movements under Grant and Sherman he was brevetted a major general in the regular army under date of March 13th, 1865. He was at his own request placed on the retired list, October 15th, 1868, with the full rank of a major general.

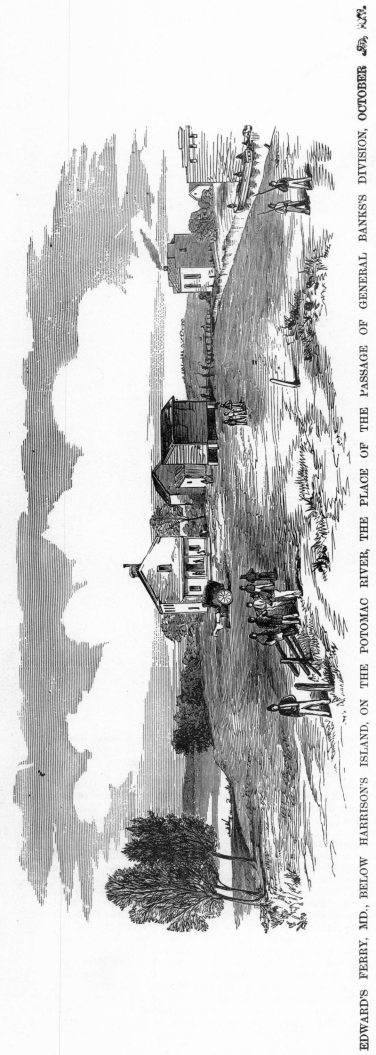

EDWARD'S FERRY, MD., BELOW HARRISON'S ISLAND, ON THE POTOMAC RIVER, THE PLACE OF THE PASSAGE OF GENERAL BANKS'S DIVISION, OCTOBER 22.

BIRD'S-EYE VIEW OF CAMP DOUGLAS, CHICAGO, ILL., USED FOR THE DETENTION OF CONFEDERATE PRISONERS IN 1862.

TYBEE ISLAND, SAVANNAH RIVER, GA.—VIEW OF THE LIGHTHOUSE AND BARRACKS—DESTRUCTION OF THE LIGHTHOUSE BY THE CONFEDERATES.

FIRING ON THE SCHOONER "SHANNON," LADEN WITH ICE, FROM THE BATTERY ON MORRIS ISLAND, CHARLESTON HARBOR, S. C., APRIL 3D, 1861.

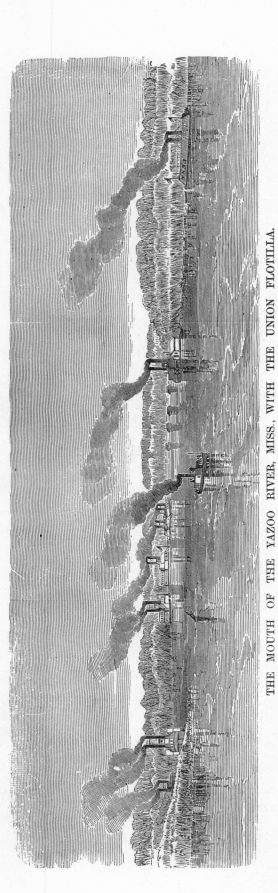

THE MOUTH OF THE YAZOO RIVER, MISS., WITH THE UNION FLOTILLA.

INTERIOR OF THE MORTAR BATTERY STANTON, TYBEE ISLAND, GA., SHOWING THE OPERATION OF 13-INCH MORTARS DURING THE BOMBARDMENT OF FORT PULASKI, APRIL 10TH, 1862.

UNITED STATES GENERAL HOSPITAL, HILTON HEAD, S. C.—EXTERIOR AND INTERIOR.

The United States General Hospital at Hilton Head, S. C., was built very strongly of wood, and really had somewhat of an architectural appearance. It was about four hundred feet long, and had excellent accommodation for about five hundred patients. On the right hand of the hospital is the chief doctor's residence. We also publish a view of one of the wards, taken shortly after the battle of James Island, where so many Federals fell, either killed or wounded.

THE NEW GENERAL HOSPITAL HILTON HEAD S.C.

GENERAL GOUVERNEUR K. WARREN.

General Warren, born in Cold Spring, N. Y., January 8th, 1830, died in Newport, R. I., August 8th, 1882, was graduated from the United States Military Academy in 1850, and assigned to the Topographical Engineers as brevet second lieutenant. At the beginning of the Civil War he entered active service as lieutenant colonel of the Fifth New York Volunteers, of which regiment he became colonel on August 31st, 1861. His regiment was ordered to Fortress Monroe, and he took part in the battle of Big Bethel. During the remainder of the year he was stationed at Baltimore, where he constructed the fort on Federal Hill. In the spring of 1862 he joined the Army of the Potomac, serving in the Peninsular campaign and at Yorktown. He was given a brigade in the Fifth Army Corps in May, with which he covered the extreme right of the army and took part in the capture of Hanover Courthouse, the pursuit of Confederate cavalry under Stuart, the battle of Gaines's Mill, the affair at Malvern Hill and subsequent battle, and the skirmish at Harrison's Landing. His brigade was then sent to re-enforce General Pope, and he participated in the battle of Manassas, was engaged at Antietam and the battle of Fredericksburg. On September 26th, 1862, he was appointed brigadier general of volunteers for his services at Gaines's Mill. On March 3d, 1863, he was appointed chief of engineers of the Army of the Potomac, and during the Chancellorsville campaign he took part in the action on Orange Pike, the storming of Marye's Heights and the battle of Salem. He continued as chief of engineers under Meade, and was engaged at Gettysburg, where he seized Little Round Top. On August 11th, 1863, he was made major general of volunteers. He participated in the battles of the Wilderness campaign and those around Petersburg. He received the successive brevets in the United States Army up to major general.

GENERAL JOHN JAMES PECK.

General Peck, born at Manlius, N. Y., January 4th, 1821, died at Syracuse, N. Y., April 28th, 1878, was graduated from the United States Military Academy in 1843, and commissioned a brevet second lieutenant of artillery. Served in the Mexican War, and distinguished himself at the battles of Palo Alto, Resaca de la Palma, Contreras and Churubusco. On August 9th, 1861, he was made a brigadier general, and at the time of the Virginia Peninsula campaign, in April and May, 1862, was given the command of a brigade in the Fourth Corps under General Couch. He was appointed a major general in July, 1862, and afterward commanded at Suffolk, Va. He stormed Hill's Point, capturing it, and thus ending the siege. Here he was severely wounded. He was mustered out of the service August 24th, 1865.

GENERAL GEORGE W. CULLUM.

General Cullum, born in New York city, February 25th, 1809, died in New York city, February 28th, 1892, was graduated from the United States Military Academy in 1833, and brevetted a second lieutenant in the Engineer Corps. During the Mexican War he rendered valuable services as superintending engineer for devising and constructing sapper, miner and pontoon trains. In 1861 he was appointed chief engineer of the Department of the Missouri, with the rank of brigadier general of volunteers, and made chief of staff to General Halleck. The latter position he continued to hold after Halleck was made general in chief, and accompanied him in his Southwestern campaigns, and afterward to headquarters in Washington, D. C., until 1864, when he became superintendent of the United States Military Academy.

BATTLE OF NEW BERNE—LIEUTENANT HAMMOND CAPTURING COLONEL AVERY, OF SOUTH CAROLINA, WHILE HE WAS
ENDEAVORING TO RALLY THE FLYING CONFEDERATES.

Our illustration represents the moment when Lieutenant Hammond, of the gunboat *Hetzel*, who served one of the guns of McCook's naval battery at the battle of New Berne, hearing that a Confederate colonel was, flag in hand, endeavoring to rally a South Carolina regiment, resolved to capture him. Riding up to the Confederate, the gallant Hammond, pointing his pistol at his head, demanded his surrender. A glance at the flying Confederates convinced the colonel that the day was lost, and he gave up his sword to the lieutenant. Two flags were also taken—one made of blue and white silk, elegantly fringed, with this inscription, "Then conquer we must, for our cause is just," with "Victory or death" in the centre. The other flag was of black bunting, with the simple inscription, "Victory or death." The name of the Confederate officer taken was Colonel Avery; three hundred of his regiment were also captured at the same time.

FEDERAL CAVALRY LEADERS—GENERALS PLEASONTON, BAYARD AND COLONEL PERCY WYNDHAM MAKING A RECONNOISSANCE
NEAR FREDERICKSBURG, VA.

BATTLE OF STONE RIVER, TENN THE DECISIVE CHARGE OF GENERA

We question if a more spirited sketch was ever published than our double page engraving representing the final charge of General Negley's divisio
critical moment has arrived, gave orders for General Negley to cross the river and drive the enemy from his position. This was done in a manner
behind. Our artist reported: "The scene was grand in the extreme. It was indeed a momentous battle on a miniature scale. Nothing could resi
when they broke and fled, ever and anon rallying to check our too hasty pursuit. Night fell on the scene, and the victors and vanquished rested fr

SION ACROSS THE RIVER—THE CONFEDERATES FLYING IN CONFUSION.

f Friday, January 2d, 1863, at the battle of Murfreesborough, or Stone River. About four o'clock in the afternoon General Rosecrans, seeing that the disciplined troops in the world. The Eighteenth Ohio Regiment dashed into the river, the Nineteenth Illinois and Twenty-first Ohio following close on they rushed; the Confederates met the shock, then wavered, and then were driven back at the bayonet's point, step by step, for some half-mile; as was won the great battle of Stone River, in which, if ever men met foemen worthy of their steel, they met them then."

ARMY OF THE POTOMAC RECROSSING THE RAPPAHANNOCK FROM FREDERICKSBURG TO FALMOUTH, ON THE NIGHT OF MONDAY, DECEMBER 15TH, 1862

THE RAID IN KENTUCKY—THE CONFEDERATE MORGAN WITH HIS GUERRILLAS BIVOUACKING IN COURTHOUSE SQUARE, PARIS, BOURBON COUNTY, AFTER LEVYING CONTRIBUTIONS ON THE INHABITANTS.

The Confederate Morgan reached Paris and Cynthiana, both of which places he occupied, levying large contributions on its unfortunate inhabitants. Our artist reported that it was a most animated and interesting sight to see the blank dismay of the "Parisians" when Morgan and his men dismounted and bivouacked in their fine square. Beyond some robberies there were no outrages committed. The Courthouse is a very imposing building, and, standing on the highest spot in the town, is visible for miles around.

LAKE PROVIDENCE, LA., HEADQUARTERS OF GENERAL McPHERSON AND THE FEDERAL DIVISION UNDER HIS COMMAND.

Our artist wrote: "The Seventeenth Army Corps, under General McPherson, have been exceedingly fortunate in being ordered to Lake Providence, La. Their tents are pitched in pleasant places. I have not seen a position anywhere along the Mississippi River, or anywhere else, which offers such inducements for an army 'to stay awhile' as the banks of this beautiful lake. There is a little town on the landing, which is only fit for, and therefore only occupied by, negro quarters and sutler shops. The lake is immediately back of the village, and not more than a quarter of a mile from the river. Immense cotton fields stretch away on both sides of it, and beautiful residences, surrounded by elaborate gardens full of Southern shrubbery, adorn its banks."

THE ADVANCE ON PORT HUDSON—THE BAGGAGE TRAIN OF GENERAL AUGUR'S DIVISION CROSSING THE BAYOU MONTECINO, MARCH 13TH, 1863.

Our sketch represents a baggage train belonging to General Augur's division crossing a little creek, or bayou, about four miles from Baton Rouge. It will be remembered that General Banks made a feigned advance against Port Hudson on March 13th, in order to facilitate Commodore Farragut's movements past the batteries.

WINTER QUARTERS ON THE RAPPAHANNOCK—ARMY HUTS OF THE ONE HUNDRED AND NINETEENTH REGIMENT, PENNSYLVANIA VOLUNTEERS, NEAR FALMOUTH, VA,

BATTLE OF ANTIETAM—THE CENTRE AND RIGHT WING OF GENERAL McCLELLAN'S ARMY, COMMANDED BY GENERALS HOOKER, SUMNER AND FRANKLIN, ENGAGED WITH THE CONFEDERATE ARMY, LED BY GENERALS LONGSTREET, JACKSON AND LEE, WEDNESDAY, SEPTEMBER 17th, 1862.

BATTLE OF STONE RIVER, TENN.—DECISIVE CHARGE AND CAPTURE OF BYRNE'S CONFEDERATE BATTERY BY THE SEVENTY-EIGHTH PENNSYLVANIA AND TWENTY-FIRST OHIO VOLUNTEERS, FRIDAY EVENING, JANUARY 2D, 1863.

Our correspondent's report: "The capture of Byrne's Confederate battery was a most gallant achievement, and worthy of the finest troops in the world. This battery consisted of two 12-pound Napoleons, two howitzers and one 6-pound rifled cannon. These were admirably served, and did considerable execution. Over it floated the colors of the Twenty-sixth Tennessee and the standard of the Fourth Florida Regiment. It was situated on a rising ground in a cornfield, while a forest at the back afforded an excellent retreat. After our troops, under Negley and others, had succeeded in crossing Stone River on Friday afternoon and driven the enemy before them, a general rush was made to storm this battery, which still maintained its fire. The first regiments to reach this were the Seventy-eighth Pennsylvania and Twenty-first Ohio Volunteers, under lead of Colonel Miller, who, though wounded, still kept the field, and acted throughout with a valor worthy the days of Washington. Up went our brave boys, bayonet in hand, to the very muzzles of the guns, which still belched death to the advancing line. The guns once reached, the gunners were driven from them by our men, and the battery was our own. The colors of the Twenty-sixth Tennessee Regiment were captured after a desperate resistance, the Confederate color bearer fighting for them till a bayonet thrust through his arm compelled him to drop them."

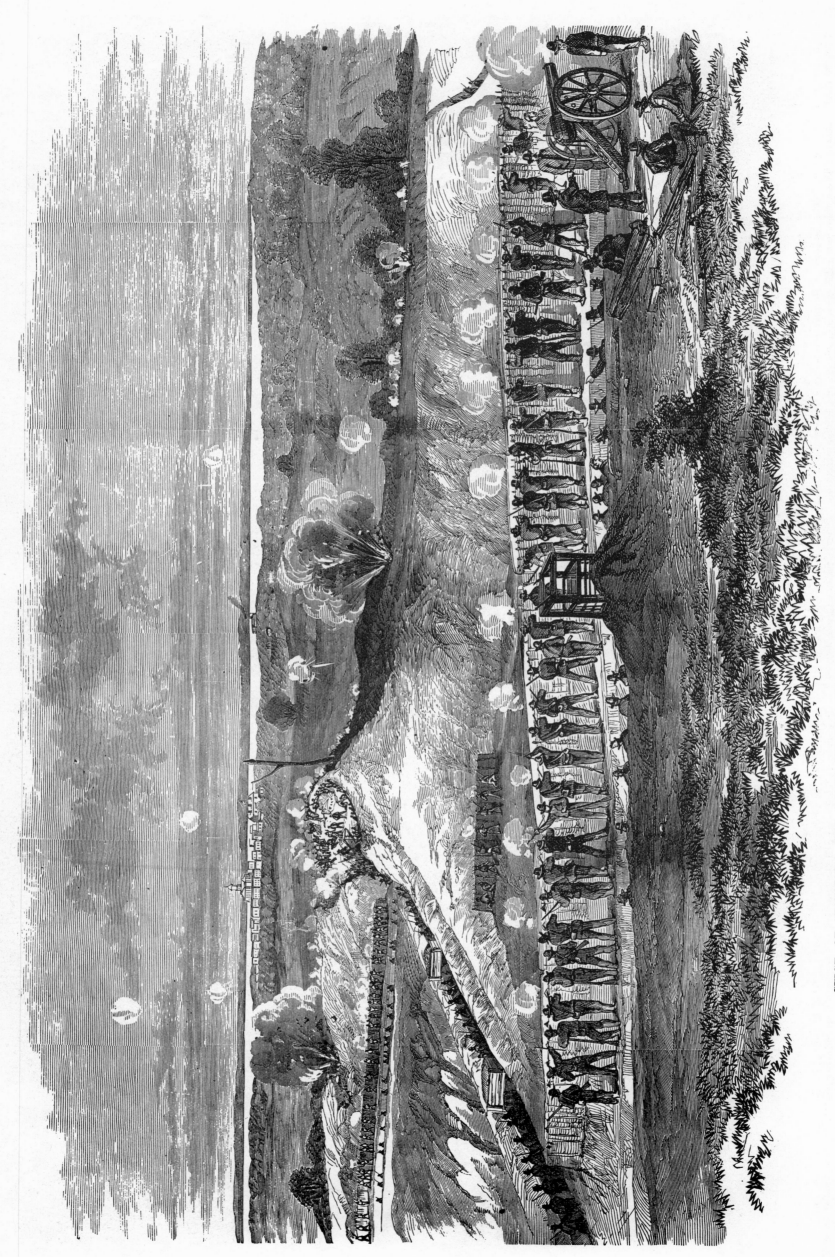

SIEGE OF VICKSBURG—THE FIGHT IN THE CRATER OF FORT HILL AFTER THE EXPLOSION, JUNE 27TH, 1863.

Our sketch shows the crater in its relative position to the surrounding works, and the city of Vicksburg in the distance. The entire crest, with the exception of this point, was held by the Confederates, although unable to use artillery on it in consequence of the bearing of the Federal guns upon it, as shown by the effect of two shots to right and left of the crater. The sharpshooters were protected by gabions filled with earth, on top of which were placed heavy logs, with small portholes, through which they kept up a continuous fire. The key of the Confederate works had been carried, and Pemberton, after a fruitless endeavor to obtain terms, surrendered on the 4th of July.

BATTLE OF GETTYSBURG—CEMETERY HILL DURING THE ATTACK OF THE CONFEDERATES, THURSDAY EVENING, JULY 2d, 1863.

Emmittsburg, Md. Gen. Meade's Army pursuing Gen. Lee.

No attack was made until about half-past three o'clock, when Lee ordered a simultaneous advance against each flank of the Federal army while demonstrations were being kept up against the centre. The attacks were **not**, however, made simultaneously, as Lee had intended. Longstreet began by sending Hood's force against Sickles's extreme left, then held by General Ward, of Birney's division, whose three brigades extended their line from the Round Top across the Emmittsburg Road, along the Peach Orchard. Ward's force was driven back after a bitter contest, and before De Trobriand, who stood next in line, could give him **any** assistance. Upon turning Ward's left Hood fell upon De Trobriand's flank and rear, leading part of his force between that portion of the field and the Round Top, while McLaws, with Anderson's support, was assaulting De Trobriand's centre. The attack was made with such vigor that Sickles called for re-enforcements, and Burling's brigade of Humphrey's division, as well as the two brigades of Barnes's division, under Tilton and Sweitzer, **were** therefore sent him. A terrible struggle followed, and the ground was contested bitterly at all points.

HURDLE SACK RACE.   CATCHING THE PIG

BURLESQUE   DRESS PARADE

THANKSGIVING BALL.   INTERIOR OF A CASEMATE.

WHEELBARROW RACE.   MEAL FEAT FOR NEGROES   CLIMBING THE GREASED POLE.

THANKSGIVING FESTIVITIES AT FORT PULASKI, GA., THURSDAY, NOVEMBER 27TH, 1862.

While the loyal citizens of the North were eating their turkeys the Federal soldiers in the South were also celebrating their Thanksgiving. We illustrate the amusement indulged in at Fort Pulaski, Ga. The grand attraction of the day, however, was the *fête* given by the officers of the Forty-eighth Regiment, New York Volunteers, Colonel Barton, and Company G, Third Rhode Island Regiment.

ADMIRAL DAVID G. FARRAGUT.

Admiral Farragut, born at Campbell's Station, near Knoxville, Tenn., July 5th, 1801, died in Portsmouth, N. H., August 14th, 1870. He was appointed to the navy from his native State, and as a midshipman saw active service as early as 1810. In the *Essex*, under Commodore Porter, he took part, in 1812–'13, in her famous cruise against the English commerce in the Pacific. After the capture of the *Essex* he served on board the line-of-battle ship *Independence*, and afterward as lieutenant on the *Brandywine*. In 1847 he was given command of the *Saratoga*, and in her took part in the naval operations of the Mexican War. When the Civil War broke out Farragut was given command of the Gulf Squadron. The Mississippi River below New Orleans was defended with forts, chains stretched across the stream, fire ships, torpedoes, and every kind of appliance. Before commencing actively the attack a council of war was held in the cabin of the admiral's ship, at which all the commanders of the various vessels in the fleet were present. With the exception of two the opinions were unanimously in favor of making the attack; and then was inaugurated the series of naval triumphs which surpassed anything of the kind ever before attempted. The capture of New Orleans was thus secured on April 28th, 1862. The next year Admiral Farragut commanded the attack on Mobile, and in this engagement went into action lashed to the rigging of his ship. He served in the navy more than fifty years, and of this time spent only eleven unemployed on the sea.

CONFEDERATE IRONCLAD RAM "GEORGIA" LYING OFF FORT JACKSON, SAVANNAH RIVER, GA., DECEMBER, 1862.

FORT TAYLOR, KEY WEST, FLA.

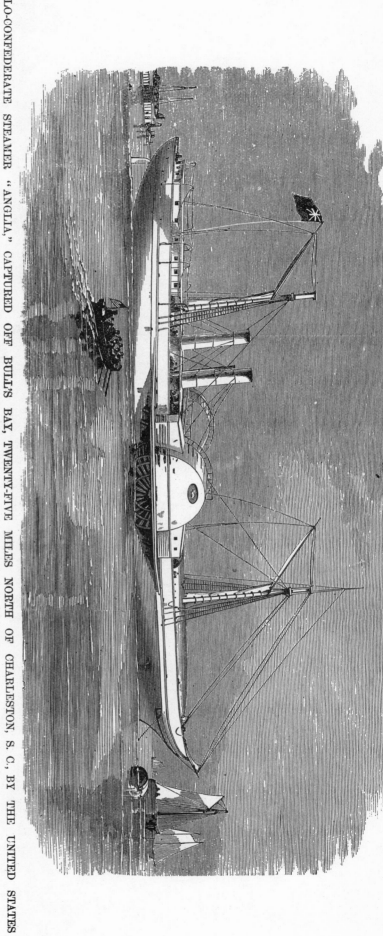

THE ANGLO-CONFEDERATE STEAMER "ANGLIA," CAPTURED OFF BULL'S BAY, TWENTY-FIVE MILES NORTH OF CHARLESTON, S. C., BY THE UNITED STATES GUNBOATS "RESTLESS" AND "FLAG," SUNDAY, OCTOBER 19TH, 1862.

HARRISON'S LANDING, JAMES RIVER, VA. THE COMMISSARIAT DEPOT AND BASE OF OPERATIONS OF GENERAL McCLELLAN, OCCUPIED BY THE FEDERAL ARMY, JULY 1ST, 1862.

BATTLE OF CHANCELLORSVILLE, VA., FRIDAY, MAY 1ST, 1863.

We give a fine sketch of the point where the memorable battle of Chancellorsville began. It was at the junction of the Gordonsville Plank Road, the Old Turnpike, and the road from Ely's and United States or s. The first fighting took place here, on Friday, May 1st, and on Saturday the Eleventh Corps was routed, and the enemy repulsed by consummate generalship and the most resolute bravery of the Federal troops. Here, too, en Sunday the enemy made an attack with such overwhelming force as to force the Federal army back to the second line. Few spots possess greater interest than this scene of fearful battle.

BATTLE OF CHANCELLORSVILLE, VA.—ATTACK ON GENERAL SEDGWICK'S CORPS, ON MONDAY, MAY 4TH, 1863, AT 5 P. M., AS SEEN FROM FALMOUTH HEIGHTS.

After General Sedgwick had carried the fortifications on Sunday, May 3d, he pushed along the Gordonsville Plank Road in pursuit till night stopped his advance. Before morning the enemy threw a heavy force in his rear, cutting him off from his small force at Fredericksburg on the rear, and began to mass troops on his front and left flank. About half-past five o'clock in the afternoon they began the attack, and columns poured from be- hind the breastworks and marched down the hill to the plain above the town and opposite Falmouth, receiving, as they came in range, a brisk fire from the Federal artillery beyond the river. Unchecked by this, however, they rushed on Sedgwick's line, which repeatedly repulsed them, gradually to Banks's Ford, which they crossed in the morning on pontoons. In the sketch the breastworks captured on Sunday are seen, with the Confederates passing between them and the river in columns to attack Sedgwick's troops, which are the continuous line in the distance.

GEN. HOOKER'S HEAD QUARTERS CHANCELLORVILLE MAY 1ST.

325

REAR ADMIRAL CHARLES WILKES.

Rear Admiral Wilkes, born in New York city, April 3d, 1798, died in Washington, D. C., February 8th, 1877   He entered the navy as a midshipman, January 1st, 1818, and was promoted to lieutenant, April 28th, 1826.   He served several years in the Mediterranean Sea and the Pacific Ocean.   In 1843 Wilkes was on coast survey duty, being commissioned commander, July 13th, 1843 ; captain, September 14th, 1855 ; and placed in command of the sloop of war *San Jacinto* in 1861, on the outbreak of the Civil War. His first duty was the pursuit of the Confederate war vessel *Sumter*.   On November 8th the *San Jacinto* encountered the English mail steamer *Trent*, which was on its way from Havana to St. Thomas, West Indies, having on board the Confederate Commissioners to France and Great Britain—John Slidell, of Louisiana, and James M. Mason, of Virginia—with their secretaries.   On overtaking the *Trent* Wilkes ordered Lieutenant Fairfax to bring them off.   The officials were removed to the *San Jacinto*, in which they were taken to Fort Warren, in Boston harbor.   In 1862 Wilkes commanded the James River Flotilla, and shelled City Point.   He was promoted to commodore on July 16th, 1862, and took charge of a special squadron in the West Indies.   He was placed on the retired list, because of age, June 25th, 1864, and promoted to rear admiral on the retired list, July 25th, 1866.

GENERAL ROBERT PATTERSON.

General Patterson, born in Cappagh, County Tyrone, Ireland, January 12th, 1792, died in Philadelphia, Pa., August 7th, 1881.   He was commissioned first lieutenant of infantry in the War of 1812, and afterward served on General Joseph Bloomfield's staff.   He became major general of volunteers at the beginning of the Mexican War, and served with distinction at Cerro Gordo and Jalapa.   At the beginning of the Civil War he was mustered into the service as major general of volunteers.   He crossed the Potomac on June 15th at Williamsport.   When General McDowell advanced into Virgina General Patterson was instructed to watch the troops under General Johnston at Winchester, Va.   He claimed that the failure of General Scott to send him orders, for which he had been directed to wait, caused his failure to co-operate with McDowell in the movements that resulted in the battle of Bull Run.   He was mustered out of service on the expiration of his commission, July 27th, 1861.

GENERAL GEORGE STONEMAN.

General Stoneman, born in Busti, Chautauqua County, N. Y., August 8th, 1822, was graduated from the United States Military Academy in 1846, and entered the First Dragoons.   In February, 1861, while in command of Fort Brown, Texas, he refused to obey the order of his superior, General Twiggs, for the surrender of the government property to the Secessionists, evacuated the fort and went to New York by steamer.   He became major of the First Cavalry, May 9th, 1861, and served in Western Virginia till August 13th, when he was appointed brigadier general of volunteers and chief of cavalry of the Army of the Potomac.   He served during the Virginia Peninsular campaign of 1862.   He was appointed major general, November 29th, 1862.   He was engaged in the Atlanta campaign from May to July, 1864 ; was captured at Clinton, Ga., July 31st, and held a captive till October 27th.   He became colonel of the Twenty-first Infantry, July 28th, 1866, and was brevetted colonel, brigadier and major general for gallant conduct.

EXPLOSION OF 3,000 MUSKET CARTRIDGES IN A TENT AT FORT TOTTEN, NEW BERNE, N. C., THE HEADQUARTERS OF THE THIRD NEW YORK ARTILLERY.

Our correspondent wrote: "There is a great carelessness in the handling of munitions of war, of which we have just had a proof in our camp. Thinking to blow the flies from the tent by flashing powder—a common practice—a spark caught a box of three thousand musket cartridges, thereby causing a tremendous explosion, which wounded four men (two dangerously) and blew the tent to atoms."

SKIRMISHING IN THE WOODS, ON THE ADVANCE TO VICKSBURG.

Our artist presents a most beautiful scene. could we but forget the deadly nature of it. A party of skirmishers. thrown out in front in the almost impenetrable forest, came suddenly upon a similar party of the enemy, and the woods soon rang with the sharp report of the rifle, sending death to each other, and announcing to the main bodies that the struggle had begun.

DARING AND DESPERATE ATTACK—SURPRISE AND CAPTURE OF THE UNITED STATES GUNBOAT "HARRIET LANE" BY THE C

About two o'clock in the morning of January 1st, 1863, the Federal gunboats were attacked by five Confederate steamers, protected by double r
Wainwright and Lieutenant Commander Lee, and a crew of 130, all told, had been killed by musketry from the Confederate steamers. The gunboats
into the hands of the Confederates. The *Westfield* (flagship, Commodore Renshaw) was not engaged, being ashore in another channel. Her crew
explosion took place before a boat containing Commodore Renshaw, First Lieutenant Zimmerman and the boat's crew got away, and they were blown
Burrui, ot Massachusetts, did not exceed 300, the residue not having disembarked at the time of the fight. The Federal loss was 160 killed and 2

DER GENERAL MAGRUDER, AND DESTRUCTION OF THE FLAGSHIP "WESTFIELD," IN GALVESTON HARBOR, TEX., JANUARY 1st, 1863.

n, and loaded with troops armed with rifles, muskets, etc. The *Harriet Lane* was captured by boarding, after about all her officers, including Captain were engaged and escaped, the former losing no men and but 1 wounded. The *Owasco* lost 1 killed and 15 wounded. Two barks, loaded with coal, fell ansports, and Commodore Renshaw, fearing she would fall into the hands of the Confederates, blew her up. By some mismanagement or accident the The Confederate force was estimated at 5,000, under the command of General Magruder. The Federal land force, under the command of Colonel The navy suffered the most. The Confederate loss was much greater, as the Federal guns were firing grape and canister continually in their midst.

CAPTURE OF THE UNITED STATES MAIL STEAMER "ARIEL," CAPTAIN JONES, OFF THE EAST END OF CUBA BY THE
PIRATE "ALABAMA" ("290"), CAPTAIN SEMMES, DECEMBER 7TH, 1862.

Report of the first officer of the *Ariel:* "On the 7th of December, at 1:30 P. M., when rounding Cape Maysi, the eastern point of Cuba, we saw a vessel about four miles to the westward, close under the high land, bark-rigged and under canvas. As there was nothing in her appearance indicating her to be a steamer, her smokepipe being down, no suspicions were aroused until in a short time we saw she had furled her sails, raised her smokestack, and was rapidly nearing us under steam, the American flag flying at her peak. Such was her speed in comparison to ours that in about half an hour she had come up within half a mile of us, when she fired a lee gun, hauled down the American ensign and ran up the Confederate flag. No attention was paid to the summons, and the *Ariel* was pushed to her utmost speed. She then sailed across our wake, took a position on our port quarter, about four hundred yards distant, and fired two guns almost simultaneously, one shot passing over the hurricane deck, and the other hitting the foremast and cutting it half away. A body of United States marines, consisting of 126 men, passengers on board the *Ariel*, had been drawn up and armed, but the officers in command deemed it worse than folly to resist, as we could plainly see they were training a full broadside to bear upon us, and Captain Jones gave orders to stop the ship and haul down the ensign."

THE BANKS EXPEDITION—SCENE ON THE HURRICANE DECK OF THE UNITED STATES TRANSPORT "NORTH STAR"—THE SOLDIERS
OF THE FORTY-FIRST MASSACHUSETTS REGIMENT WRITING HOME TO THEIR FRIENDS, UPON THEIR ARRIVAL AT SHIP
ISLAND, GULF OF MEXICO.

We publish a sketch taken on the evening of the arrival of the Forty-first Massachusetts Regiment at Ship Island. The thoughts of the dear ones at home were uppermost in every soldier's mind, and in a very short time the hurricane deck of the steamer *North Star* was occupied by a regiment of letter-writers, all hard at work in the service of Cadmus. It is only those separated from all they hold dear who can realize the luxury of that invention which wafts a sigh from Indus to the Pole.

FEDERAL SOLDIERS SHOOTING CATTLE FOR THE SUPPLY OF THE ARMY

BUTCHERING AND DRESSING CATTLE FOR DISTRIBUTION TO THE FEDERAL ARMY.

The romance and reality of life were never so strikingly displayed as in the Civil War. Fact and fiction never seemed more apart than the soldier waving his sword when leading the forlorn hope and when sitting before his tent cooking rations; for, despite all the commissariat arrangements, there was much room for improvement in these particulars. We give a couple of sketches which will enable our readers to see how matter-of-fact and mechanically base were some of the soldiers' employments when in camp. Men who would shrink from turning butcher in New York, Boston or Philadelphia were forced by the resistless tide of circumstances to lend a hand to the killing a beeve and afterward to the dressing and cooking it.

FEDERAL TROOPS MARCHING BACK INTO FALMOUTH AFTER THE BATTLE OF CHANCELLORSVILLE.

BATTLE OF BLUE RIDGE PASS, SUNDAY SEPTEMBER 14th, 1862.—THE FIRST FEDERAL VICTORY IN MARYLAND.

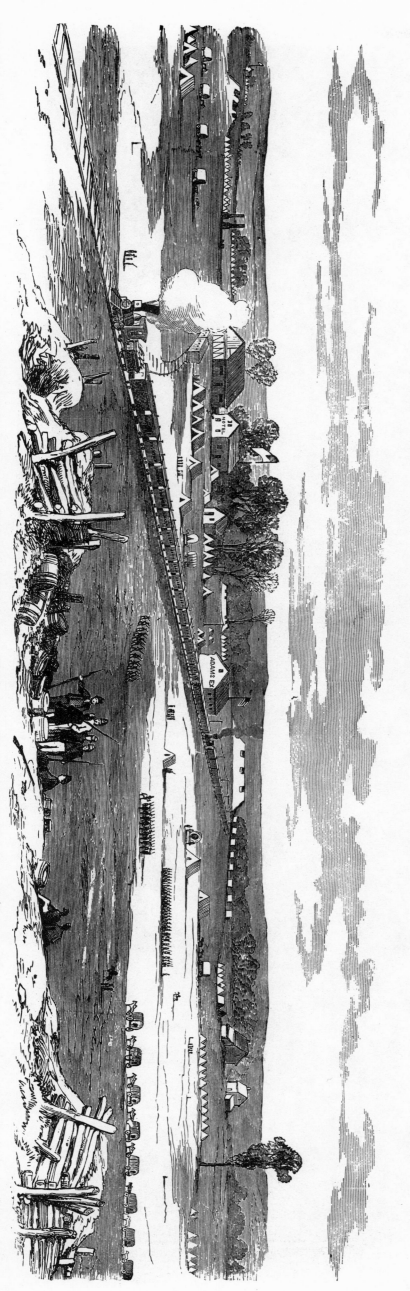

COMMISSARIAT DEPOT OF THE UNITED STATES ARMY OF THE RAPPAHANNOCK AT MANASSAS, VA

CAPTURE OF THE BRITISH STEAMER "ANNE," LADEN WITH ARMS AND MUNITIONS OF WAR FOR THE CONFEDERATES, BY THE UNITED STATES GUNBOAT "KANAWHA," ACTING MASTER PARTRIDGE, FROM UNDER THE GUNS OF FORT MORGAN, MOBILE, JUNE 29TH, 1862.

SIEGE OF VICKSBURG—LIFE IN THE TRENCHES—BIVOUAC OF LEGGETT'S BRIGADE, McPHERSON'S CORPS, AT THE WHITE HOUSE.

Our illustration shows the life led by the besieging troops. The deep ravine is studded with the rude huts, or quarters, burrowed in the earth. Here, at the White House, well riddled with Confederate shell, **were** bivouacked Leggett's brigade of McPherson's Seventeenth Army Corps. To the left of the house an opening in the bank shows the entrance to the covered way by which the Confederate works were approached.

BATTLE OF GETTYSBURG—CHARGE OF THE CONFEDERATES ON CEMETERY HILL, THURSDAY EVENING, JULY 2b, 1863.

The odds against the Federals were great, but in face of heavy losses they fought with a bravery rarely equaled. The Confederates were at last beaten back from the face of the hill, but, passing along the ravines they penetrated between both the Round Tops, thus flanking the Federals. The conflict was renewed more bitterly than before. The Federal ammunition again gave out, but the bayonet was once more made to play such an effective part, that at nightfall the Confederates had entirely withdrawn from Little Round Top. What Warren justly deemed to be, and what really was, at that juncture, the most important position in the field, had thus been successfully maintained, though at a frightful cost of life. While Johnson was operating against Culp's Hill, Early made an attempt to carry Cemetery Hill, after opening upon it with his artillery from Brenner's Hill. He was beaten back and compelled to seek his original position before darkness had fairly set in.

335

THE PLANTATION POLICE, OR HOME GUARD, EXAMINING NEGRO PASSES ON THE LEVEE ROAD, BELOW NEW ORLEANS, LA.

The Plantation Police, or Patrol, was an institution peculiar to the Slave States. It was a semi-military organization, raised and supported by the planter, but recognized by the old State authorities. Their principal duty was to visit the various plantations and patrol the roads at night, arresting all negroes and others not having proper passes. The war, the President's proclamation, and the actual possession of most of the State of Louisiana by the Federal authorities, rendered these patrols doubly rigorous. Some of the negroes submitted reluctantly. The colored man in the foreground is a specimen of this class. He seems to yield to the superior force of a tottering power, satisfied that his day is at hand ; others show the obsequious, submissive stamp—the negro satisfied with his lot if he is clothed and fed.

A NEW YEAR'S DAY CONTRABAND BALL AT VICKSBURG, MISS.

The negroes preserve all their African fondness for music and dancing, and in the modified form which they have assumed here have given rise to negro dancing and melodies in our theatres, a form of amusement which has enriched many. But the colored people should be seen in one of their own balls to enjoy the reality. The character of the music and the dance; the strange gradation of colors, from the snow black or the pure breed to those creatures, fair and beautiful, whose position among their darker brethren shows the brutal cruelty of their male ancestors for generations, who begot them to degrade them, and who had thus for years been putting white blood into slavery. There is in these negro balls one thing which cannot fail to impress any observer. Coming as they all do from a degraded and oppressed class, the negroes assume nevertheless, in their intercourse with each other, as far as they can, the manners and language of the best classes in society. There is often a grotesque exaggeration, indeed; but there is an appreciation of refinement and an endeavor to attain it which we seldom see in the same class of whites.

337

PARIS, CAPITAL OF BOURBON COUNTY, SITUATED ON STONER CREEK, KY., OCCUPIED BY MORGAN'S GUERRILLAS IN 1862.

THE FEDERAL ARMY, UNDER GENERAL POPE, LANDING ON THE KENTUCKY SHORE, OPPOSITE NEW MADRID, APRIL 1st, 1862.

A DETACHMENT OF THE FIRST SOUTH CAROLINA "COLORED" FEDERAL VOLUNTEERS, UNDER COMMAND OF COLONEL BEARD, IN THE UNITED STATES TRANSPORT STEAMER "DARLINGTON," PICKING OFF CONFEDERATE SHARPSHOOTERS CONCEALED IN THE TREES ON THE BANKS OF THE SAPELO RIVER, GA.

FORT VULCAN, JONESS'S ISLAND, SAVANNAH RIVER, GA., ONE OF THE FEDERAL BATTERIES CUTTING OFF COMMUNICATION BETWEEN FORT PULASKI AND SAVANNAH.

THE INVESTMENT OF FORT HINDMAN, ARKANSAS POST, ARK., BY THE FEDERAL TROOPS UNDER GENERAL McCLERNAND, AND ITS BOMBARDMENT BY THE FEDERAL GUNBOATS COMMANDED BY REAR ADMIRAL D. D. PORTER, JANUARY 11TH, 1863.

Fort Hindman was what is known in military parlance as a star fort, with four angles—two on the river and two extending nearly to the morass in the rear. In front of the southwestern angle was a cluster of small houses, into which the enemy had thrown their sharpshooters, and from which a most galling fire was poured upon Burbridge's brigade, which stormed them and carried them by assault. At the given signal on went the splendid brigade with a shout and a yell, now floundering like bemired horses in the morass, then pausing to dress their lines as if on parade, and anon charging again, regardless of the storm of grape and shell, shot and canister that pelted pitilessly around them. For three long hours they fought ere the houses were carried and made to screen the Federal troops. All that while sharpshooters were picking off, from their secure hiding places, officers and men; 10-pound Parrotts were sending their hissing messengers of death through the lines of the devoted brigade, crushing its bones, spattering its brains, and strewing its path with mangled corpses and dying men. At last the houses were gained and occupied by the Eighty-third Ohio, the Ninety-sixth Ohio, the Sixteenth, the Sixtieth and Sixty-seventh Indiana and the Twenty-third Wisconsin, had fought for them so gallantly.

340

GOING INTO CAMP AT STAFFORD'S STORE, VA.—THIRD BRIGADE, THIRD DIVISION, SIXTH CORPS, CARRYING OFF RAILS AND GATHERING PERSIMMONS.

Stafford's store is on the road from New Baltimore to Falmouth, and had attached to it a meadow of about an acre, entirely surrounded with a rail fence, which was somewhat unusual in Virginia. When the Third Brigade of the Third Division and Sixth Army Corps approached it they found that they had come upon a place where the supplies were more abundant than in other districts; there were heard the cackling of hens, the crowing of roosters, the bleating of sheep, and all those pleasant sounds so suggestive of a good larder. Our artist significantly added that those sounds would be heard no more, plainly intimating that our hungry soldiers made their originators go the way of all flesh. It was a curious sight to see the Federal soldiers each pull up a rail and shoulder it. Before long, therefore, the fence had disappeared, leaving the field without the palisades.

341

GENERAL OLIVER O. HOWARD.

General Howard, born in Leeds, Me., November 8th, 1830, was graduated at Bowdoin in 1850, and at the United States Military Academy in 1854; became first lieutenant and instructor in mathematics in 1854, and resigned in 1861 to take command of the Third Maine Regiment. He commanded a brigade at the first battle of Bull Run, and for gallantry in that engagement was made brigadier general of volunteers, September 3d, 1861. He was twice wounded at the battle of Fair Oaks, losing his right arm on June 1st, 1862. In November, 1862, he became major general of volunteers. He commanded the Eleventh Corps during General Hooker's operations in the vicinity of Fredericksburg; served at Gettysburg, Lookout Valley and Missionary Ridge, and was on the expedition for the relief of Knoxville in December, 1863. He was in occupation of Chattanooga from this time till July, 1864, when he was assigned to the the Army of the Tennessee in the invasion of Georgia; was at the surrender of Atlanta, and joined in pursuit of the Confederates in Alabama, under Hood, from October 4th till December 13th, 1864. In the march to the sea he commanded the right wing of General Sherman's army. He was in command of the Army of the Tennessee, and engaged in all the important battles from January 4th till April 26th, 1865.

GENERAL JOHN POPE.

REAR ADMIRAL JOHN A. WINSLOW.

General Pope, born in Louisville, Ky., March 16th, 1822, was graduated from the United States Military Academy in 1842, and made brevet second lieutenant of engineers. He served in Florida in 1842-'44, and took part in the Mexican War, being brevetted first lieutenant for gallantry at Monterey, and captain for his services in the battle of Buena Vista. In May, 1861, he was made brigadier general and assigned to command in Missouri. When General Curtis was sent in pursuit of Price General Pope was dispatched to Commerce, Mo., where he organized rapidly an army of 12,000 men, and by his vigorous movements in March, 1862, captured New Madrid and Island No. 10, with thousands of prisoners. He was then promoted to be major general of volunteers and brigadier general in the regular army. He went to Washington, where he took command of the Army of Virginia, with which he fought the battle of Cedar Mountain and the second battle of Bull Run. He died September 23d, 1892.

Rear Admiral Winslow, born in Wilmington, N. C., November 19th, 1811, died in Boston, Mass., September 29th, 1873. He entered the navy as a midshipman, February 1st, 1827, and was made a lieutenant, February 9th, 1839. He was commissioned captain, July 16th, 1862, and commanded the steamer *Kearsarge* on special service in 1863-'64 in pursuit of the *Alabama*. Captain Winslow arrived off Cherbourg, June 14th, 1864, where he found the *Alabama*, and blockaded her in the harbor. The *Alabama* made preparations for fight, and Captain Raphael Semmes caused Winslow to be informed of this intention through the United States Consul. On Sunday, June 19th, 1864, he was lying three miles off the eastern entrance of the harbor when the *Alabama* came out. Winslow steamed off seven miles from the shore so as to be beyond the neutral ground, and then steamed toward the *Alabama*. The engagement lasted one hour and twenty minutes. After the last shot was fired the *Alabama* sank out of sight.

DISTRIBUTING RATIONS AND APPOINTING A KNAPSACK GUARD BEFORE A RECONNOISSANCE NEAR WARRENTON, VA.

Our sketch represents the Federal soldiers receiving their rations and the appointment of a guard for their knapsacks. Thanks to our illustration the exempts, whether sneaks, aliens, valetudinarians, or members of that peace society, the Home Guards, could get a pretty accurate idea of a soldier's life, and be present in spirit with their noble brothers on whom they had devolved the sacred duty of battle.

THE PONTOON BRIDGE "ON THE MARCH"—THE PONTOON WAGONS ON THEIR WAY FROM AQUIA CREEK
TO THE RAPPAHANNOCK.

SIEGE OF VICKSBURG—ATTACK

Our sketch represents the terrible but fruitless assault made on Pemberton's last line of defense around the city of Vicksburg. On May 22d, 18
yards apart, connected by deep intrenchments and extending for seven miles. Lawler's brigade rushed up amid a cross fire, and with heavy loss
faltered. McClernand ordered up Benton and Burbridge on the right. Sherman and McPherson also advanced, and at point after point the old flag
display the bravery of the men. Covered by the ravines which intersected the ground the Federal troops would get near the works and make a galla
that the Federals, even when in the fort, were almost as far from victory as before. In one case a party of twelve Iowans, led by a youth named G
had discharged their pieces, and brought them off. The Confederates used for almost the first time hand grenades, which they rolled down the s
earnest. No army could stand such losses Closer were the lines drawn around the enemy Siege guns were mounted. The mines began their wor

ERATE WORKS, MAY 22D, 1863.

ult was made on the grass-covered fortifications held by the Confederate army. These works consisted of a chain of forts about eight hundred
Stripes on the edge of a parapet; but the enemy gathered there, and the Federals were overpowered. Landrum's brigade came to the relief, but
on the works. On the extreme right Steele's division, with Blair on his left, advanced as Pemberton fell back, and, like the others, could only
the parapet, yet when the edge of the fort was gained the interior was swept by a line of rifle pits in the rear and a partition breastwork, so
a fort, but all finally fell under the fire of their assailants except Griffiths, who, with musket and revolver, captured fourteen Confederates who
the assaulting party in the ditch or clinging to the side. This dreadful day swept away thousands of gallant Federals. The siege now began in
ns were assailed from beneath.

SIEGE OF VICKSBURG—THE TWENTY-THIRD INDIANA AND FORTY-FIFTH ILLINOIS REGIMENTS, LEGGETT'S BRIGADE, LOGAN'S DIVISION, McPHERSON'S CORPS, STORMING FORT HILL, AFTER THE EXPLOSION OF THE MINE, JUNE 26TH, 1863.

BATTLE OF CORINTH, MISS., OCTOBER 4TH, 1862—SCENE IN THE ROUNDABOUTS OF FORT ROBINETT AFTER THE REPULSE OF THE CONFEDERATES.

We present an exact copy of a photograph showing the scene which presented itself to the Federals at Fort Robinett. As our readers are aware, the battle of Corinth, which took place on the 3d and 4th of October, was one of the most sanguinary, in proportion to the numbers engaged, that occurred in the West, and it was contested on both sides with great valor and skill. The Federal troops were led by General Rosecrans, and those of the enemy by Van Dorn, Price and Villepigue. The Confederates lost two acting brigadier generals, Johnson and Rogers, who, by a singular coincidence, both fell at the same time and within a few feet of each other. In addition to those officers, they lost Colonels Ross, Morton and McLaine, and Major James. An officer of the Third Michigan Cavalry said: "Fort Robinett was garrisoned by the First United States Artillery, and here the greatest slaughter took place. In the roundabouts of the fort were found the remains of Generals Johnson and Rogers, and close to them were the bodies of fifty-six of their men, principally of the Second Texas and Fourth Mississippi Regiments. General Rogers was a brave man; he was killed while planting the Confederate flag upon the parapet of the fort, from which the enemy were finally repulsed with great slaughter."

346

SIEGE OF VICKSBURG—SHARPSHOOTERS IN THE RIFLE PITS CONSTRUCTED BY CAPTAIN HICKENLOOPER.

THE CAPTURE OF ARKANSAS POST, ARK.—GENERAL STEPHEN G. BURBRIDGE, ACCOMPANIED BY HIS STAFF, PLANTING
THE STARS AND STRIPES ON FORT HINDMAN, JANUARY 11TH, 1863.

No sooner was the fort surrendered than General Burbridge and his staff sprang across the ditch, mounted the parapet, and planted the flag of the republic upon its bloody battlements, thus making a fitting *finale* to one of the most glorious achievements of the war. The number of prisoners surrendered was 5,000, the Federal forces in action being 27,000. An immense quantity of quartermaster's, commissary and ordnance stores were also obtained, among which were 20 guns, 8,000 stands of small arms, and 100 army wagons, with herds of horses and mules.

THE ADVANCE UPON CHARLESTON, S. C.—ENTRANCE TO THE STONO RIVER.

FREDERICKSBURG, VA., AND THE CONFEDERATE BATTERIES AND PICKETS, AS SEEN FROM FALMOUTH HEIGHTS, HEADQUARTERS OF GENERAL BURNSIDE

THE CREW OF THE UNITED STATES GUNBOAT "MAHASKA," CAPTAIN FOXHALL A. PARKER, DESTROYING THE WATER BATTERY BUILT BY THE CONFEDERATES AT WEST POINT, YORK RIVER.

THE TOWN OF FALMOUTH, VA., ON THE RAPPAHANNOCK, OPPOSITE FREDERICKSBURG, HEADQUARTERS OF GENERAL BURNSIDE AND THE ARMY OF THE POTOMAC.

THE CONFEDERATE INVASION OF MARYLAND AND PENNSYLVANIA—THE CONFEDERATE CAVALRY CROSSING THE POTOMAC, JUNE 11TH, 1863.

When the Confederate cavalry force under General Jenkins crossed the Potomac, a movement happily portrayed by our artist, and hurried across Maryland, within the borders of the Keystone State all was confusion and alarm. As they advanced it was impossible to tell what point would be assailed. Pittsburg, with its machine shops and foundries; Harrisburg, the capital, with the State archives; Philadelphia with its great wealth, might any or all be reached. In this emergency the Governor exerted his full powers, the citizens to some extent rallying to his call.

BATTLE OF GETTYSBURG, THURSDAY EVENING, JULY 2D, 1863, AS SEEN FROM ROCKY HILL ON MEADE'S LEFT.

Our illustration shows the fight on Thursday evening, July 2d, 1863, and we almost may say on Friday evening, from Rocky Hill, on the left of General Meade's position, where the Fifth Corps was posted. The lines of the enemy can be seen coming over the hill and out of the woods, in their fierce onset on the Federal line in the rocky field. The fire that met the Confederates at the foot of the ridge was so hot that the entire line of the now fairly exhausted Confederates for a moment wavered and then recoiled. Seeing this, Meade ordered a general advance, in which the remainder of Doubleday's force participated. After another spirited contest it succeeded just before sunset in driving back the Confederates nearly up to their line of reserves, and in taking some of the guns that had been previously captured. Thus ended the engagement on the left centre. A new line was then formed with the divisions of Doubleday and Robinson, and by part of the Twelfth Corps, then under General Williams, who had taken Slocum's place when the latter assumed command of the entire right wing. Contrary to Lee's expectation, Ewell on the extreme left did not advance until quite awhile after Longstreet had attacked Birney's division. Johnson's force crossed Rock Creek, and with its extreme right moved against Wadsworth and Greene, the latter being the only brigade of Geary's division left at Culp's Hill. Geary's other brigades, under Colonel Charles Candy and George Cobham, had previously been ordered away by Meade toward Little Round Top.

351

NIGHT BURIAL OF COLONEL GARESCHE. CHIEF OF STAFF TO MAJOR GENERAL ROSECRANS, ON THE BATTLEFIELD OF STONE RIVER, TENN.

We publish a most striking sketch, the temporary burying of one of the fallen Federal heroes, Colonel Garesche, chief of staff to General Rosecrans, who was killed by the side of the general at the battle of Stone River. Our artist thus describes this most emphatic scene, which in its chief characteristic so closely resembles the burial of Sir John Moore: "In a small graveyard on the top of a ridge near the railroad track the body of Colonel Garesche rested for a time, while the fate of the battle was yet undecided. What a contrast does the inhuming of this gallant soldier present to what so many consider as the pomp and circumstance of glorious war! No procession of plumed officers, no rolling of muffled drums, no parting volley of rattling musketry, none of the rites and ceremonies of religion. Alas! the living comrades of the dead hero are too terribly in earnest. They cannot even turn aside to give a farewell glance at their departed friend. The fate of battle, possibly of the republic, hangs upon the swing of an arm, the glance of an eye. To-day is for action—to-morrow, for regret. 'Let the dead bury the dead' is the silent impulse of even his dearest friends. In front the sullen roar of cannon still proclaims the deadly conflict, and General Rosecrans and the friends of Garesche have their eyes strained upon the fight and dare not look back on the solemn group behind them. There stand some orderlies around the body of the fallen colonel. See how tenderly these rough and battle-scarred veterans perform their labor of love and sorrow. Their eyes, which gazed unblenched on the death-foaming cannon, are filled with tears, and not a word is spoken. There is no coffin, no shroud, no pall—it will be truly ashes to ashes and dust to dust. The grave is dug; beside it is the disfigured and headless corpse. Ah! there is a pause. A thought has come to one of them. From the trees around they gather green cedar branches; over the poor clay they carefully lay these protecting boughs; and then, beneath the light of our flaming torch and a dim lantern, the earth is gently laid over the gallant Garesche."

GENERAL ALBERT J. MYER.

General Myer, born in Newburg, N. Y., September 20th, 1827, died in Buffalo, N. Y., August 24th, 1880, was graduated at Hobart College in 1847, and at Buffalo Medical College in 1851. In September, 1854, he entered the United States Army as assistant surgeon, and was assigned to duty in Texas. While so engaged he devised a system of army signals with flags and torches for day and night, by means of which messages could be sent as fully and accurately as with the electric telegraph, though less rapidly. In 1858–'60 he held command of the Signal Corps and was engaged in perfecting his system. He was commissioned major in 1860, and made chief signal officer of the United States Army. At the beginning of the Civil War he was ordered to Washington and assigned to duty in the Army of the Potomac. Throughout the Peninsular campaign he served as chief signal officer to General McClellan, participating in all the battles from Bull Run to Antietam. He then returned to Washington, where he took charge of the United States Signal Office on March 3d, 1863, with the rank of colonel. In December he was relieved of his command by the Secretary of War on the ground that his appointment had not been confirmed, and his appointment of chief signal officer was revoked July 21st, 1864; but he was brevetted brigadier general March 13th, 1865. He was reappointed colonel and chief signal officer July 28th, 1866.

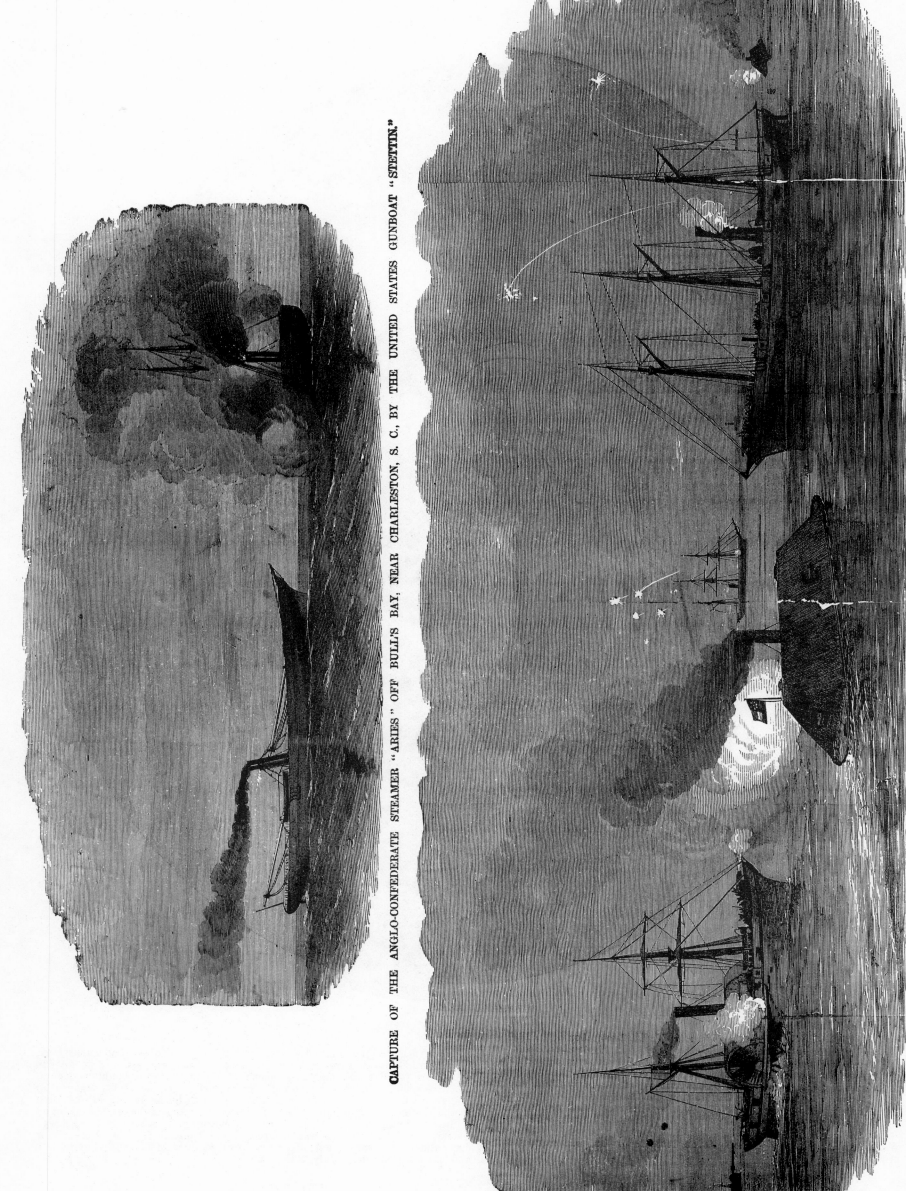

CAPTURE OF THE ANGLO-CONFEDERATE STEAMER "ARIES" OFF BULL'S BAY, NEAR CHARLESTON, S. C., BY THE UNITED STATES GUNBOAT "STETTIN."

CONFEDERATE RAMS FROM CHARLESTON HARBOR ATTACKING THE FEDERAL BLOCKADING SQUADRON. JANUARY 31st, 1863.

THE FEDERAL SIEGE WORKS ON BOGUE ISLAND, N. C., ERECTED FOR THE REDUCTION OF FORT MACON.

FORT ON FENWICK'S ISLAND, SOUTH EDISTO RIVER, S. C.

BATTLE OF CHICKAMAUGA—REPULSE OF THE CONFEDERATES AT CRAWFISH CREEK.

We present a most interesting sketch of the battle of Chickamauga, the repulse and check of the Confederate cavalry by the Twenty-fourth Illinois and Company K of the Nineteenth Illinois. They were separated from the Confederates by a stone fence and a small creek. Their daring and heroic resistance was never surpassed, some of them climbing the stone fence to meet the Confederates as they rushed madly down upon the gallant little band. They had the whole Confederate cavalry and four divisions of infantry and artillery to fight, but notwithstanding this vast odds they held their position until re-enforcements reached them. The Twenty-fourth Illinois was commanded by Colonel G. Michalotzy, who was slightly wounded in the right hand. They went into the battle with 330 men, and came out with but 163, less than half their number.

THE WAR IN VIRGINIA—CAPTURE OF THREE CONFEDERATE GUNS, NEAR CULPEPER, BY GENERAL CUSTER'S CAVALRY BRIGADE, SEPTEMBER 14TH, 1863.

General Pleasonton, on the 14th of September, 1863, drove the Confederates back on Culpeper, and General Custer with his brigade came up with Stewart's horse artillery, which he charged twice, himself at the head, and he second time took guns, limbers, horses and men. His horse was killed by a round shot, which wounded the general in the leg and killed a bugler behind him.

357

REAR ADMIRAL JAMES ALDEN.

Rear Admiral Alden, born in Portland, Me., March 31st, 1810, died in San Francisco, Cal., February 6th, 1877. He was appointed midshipman in 1828, and in that capacity accompanied the Wilkes Exploring Expedition around the world in 1838–'42. He was commissioned lieutenant in 1841, and served during the Mexican War, being present at the capture of Vera Cruz, Tuspan and Tabasco. In 1855–'56 he was actively engaged in the Indian war on Puget's Sound. At the outbreak of the Civil War he was in command of the steamer *South Carolina*, re-enforced Fort Pickens, Fla., and was in an engagement at Galveston, Tex. He commanded the sloop of war *Richmond* at the passage of Forts Jackson and St. Philip and the capture of New Orleans, April, 1862, and was also at Port Hudson. He was made captain in 1863, and commanded the *Brooklyn*, participating in the capture of Mobile Bay, August, and in the two attacks on Fort Fisher. He was commissioned commodore in 1866, and two years later was placed in charge of the navy yard at Mare Island, Cal. In 1869 he was appointed chief of the bureau of navigation and detail in the Navy Department. He was promoted to the rank of rear admiral in 1871 and assigned command of the European Squadron.

GENERAL J. H. HOBART WARD.

GENERAL EDWIN V. SUMNER.

General Ward, born in New York city, June 17th, 1823, was educated at Trinity Collegiate School; enlisted at the age of eighteen in the Seventh United States Infantry, and in four years rose through the several grades to that of sergeant major. In the Mexican War he participated in the siege of Fort Brown, received wounds at Monterey, and was at the capture of Vera Cruz. At the beginning of the Civil War he recruited the Thirty-eighth New York Volunteers, was appointed colonel of the regiment and led it at Bull Run and in all the battles of Peninsular campaign, and subsequently at the second Bull Run and Chantilly. Being promoted brigadier general of volunteers, October 4th, 1862, he commanded a brigade in the Third Corps at Fredericksburg, Chancellorsville, Gettysburg, the Wilderness and Spottsylvania. On the third day at Gettysburg, where he was wounded, as also at Kelly's Ford and Wapping Heights, he was in temporary command of the division. He was wounded at Spottsylvania, and was frequently commended for courage and capacity in official reports.

General Sumner, born in Boston Mass., January 30th, 1797, died in Syracuse, N. Y., March 21st, 1863, was educated at Milton (Mass.) Academy, and entered the army in 1819 as second lieutenant of infantry. In 1838 he was placed in command of the School of Cavalry Practice at Carlisle, Pa. He was promoted major in 1846, and in the Mexican War led the cavalry charge at Cerro Gordo in April, 1847. In March, 1861, he was appointed brigadier general in the regular army and sent to relieve General Albert Sidney Johnston, in command of the Department of the Pacific, but was recalled in the following year to the command of the First Corps of the Army of the Potomac. He served with gallantry at the siege of Yorktown and Fair Oaks. In the Seven Days' Battles he was wounded twice. In 1862 he was appointed major general of volunteers, led the Second Corps at the battle of Antietam, where he was wounded, and commanded one of the three grand divisions of Burnside's army at Fredericksburg.

RUSH'S LANCERS GUARDING THE ROADS, THE DAY AFTER THE BATTLE OF ANTIETAM, TO PREVENT THE PASSAGE OF CIVILIANS.

SIEGE OF VICKSBURG—GENERAL SHERMAN'S FIGHT WITH HAND GRENADES, JUNE 13TH, 1863.

On the 13th of June occurred in the siege of Vicksburg a scene hitherto unparalleled in the Civil War. By two o'clock in the morning General Sherman's corps had pushed up to the rifle pits, and to within twenty yards of one of the bastions. The Confederates threw lighted shells over the parapet on the Federal approach, and received in return twenty-three hand grenades, twenty of which exploded, driving the Confederates out. Cannon had now become useless to either party, and as musketry was of no avail, they had to resort to the old hand grenade.

BATTLE OF CHANCELLORSVILLE, SUNDAY, MAY 3

Early on May 3d Stuart renewed the attack upon Hooker's force, with the battle cry, "Charge, and remember Jackson!" and the advance
lost in crowning that eminence with all the heavy artillery obtainable, and as soon as this could be made to play upon the Federal lines a charge w
struggle the Confederates succeeded in capturing the high ground where the Federals had posted some more heavy artillery, and in turning the la
charge in order to capture the new positions, but unavailingly, and when re-enforcements arrived from Meade's corps they were forced to abandon

HOOKER REPULSING THE ATTACK OF THE ENEMY.

impetuosity that in a short time he was in possession of the crest from which the Eleventh Corps had been driven the preceding day. No time was upon the position held by Generals Berry and French, both of whom were supported by the divisions of Williams and Whipple. After a severe who soon had to fall back to their second and third line of intrenchments. The Confederates followed close upon them, and made charge after

DRURY'S BLUFF, A CONFEDERATE POSITION ON THE JAMES RIVER, NEAR RICHMOND, VA.

The principal Confederate defense of Richmond was Fort Darling, a heavy work on a high bank called Drury's Bluff, eight miles below Richmond. Here the river was closed with heavy piling and vessels loaded with stone sunk in the channel. The work was casemated and mounted with heavy guns. It will be remembered that the Federal ironclads, the *Galena* and the *Monitor*, were repulsed here during the progress of the Peninsular campaign. The *Monitor* was unable to elevate her guns sufficiently to reach the works, and the sides of the *Galena* were not thick enough to resist the plunging shot from the fort, which struck its sides at right angles. The *Naugatuck*, the only other vessel engaged in the assault, burst her single gun on the second discharge.

TOWING THE WOUNDED FEDERAL SOLDIERS DOWN THE BAYOU ON A RAFT, ON THE NIGHT OF JANUARY 14TH, 1863, AFTER THE BATTLE OF BAYOU TECHE, LA.

General Banks had arranged to stop the depredations which the Confederate steamer *J. A. Cotton* had been long committing along the Bayou Teche. He had advanced from Labadieville on January 11th with four gunboats, ten regiments of infantry and one of artillery, reaching Carney's Bridge, near Pattersonville, early on the 14th. Their progress here was stopped by several earthworks, under whose guns lay the *J. A. Cotton*. Early on the 15th Commander McKean Buchanan opened fire from the *Calhoun*, and was joined in it by the other gunboats, while the troops were advancing on shore to engage the Confederate vessels and batteries from the rear. The troops were not long in subjecting their enemy to a fierce enfilading musketry and artillery fire from the woods; and such was its destructive effect that the *J. A. Cotton* had finally to retire toward an upper battery at Butte La Rose, on the Atchafalaya. Early on the following morning the *J. A. Cotton* was seen floating down the bayou in a sheet of flame, having been set afire and abandoned by the Confederates. The troops, therefore, returned to Brashear City, the Federal wounded having been meanwhile placed on a raft and towed down the river.

WATERHOUSE'S BATTERY, SHERMAN'S CORPS, BEFORE VICKSBURG.

The interior view of Waterhouse's battery, in Tuttle's division, shows the guns in position and the huts in which the men are crowded. These were built of canes tied together and covered with branches, the soldiers resorting to the style of dwellings of the Indians who dwelt there two centuries ago.

A STREET IN FREDERICKSBURG, VA., SHOWING THE RESULT OF THE BOMBARDMENT—FEDERAL SOLDIERS GROUPED ABOUT.

Our correspondent wrote: "Considering the terrible nature of the bombardment, it is wonderful that not a single inhabitant was killed by it, although many families refused to avail themselves of the opportunity to leave before the firing commenced. These found shelter in the cellars of the houses, and thus escaped. The rest of the building, in many cases, was so shattered as to be perfectly uninhabitable. A fine old mansion in Main Street presented a melancholy spectacle, no less than thirty round shot having gone right through it, leaving the appearance of so many portholes. In the street the Federals bivouacked the night before the battle and the night after."

BOMBARDMENT OF FORT McALLISTER, OGEECHEE RIVER, GA., BY THE UNION IRONCLADS "PATAPSCO," "PASSAIC" AND "NAHANT," TUESDAY, MARCH 5TH, 1863.

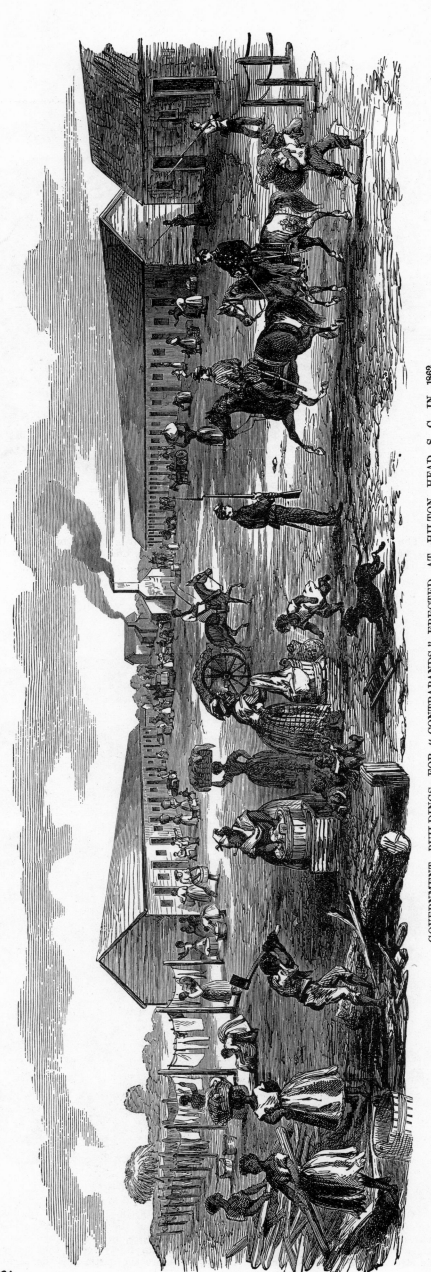

GOVERNMENT BUILDINGS FOR "CONTRABANDS," ERECTED AT HILTON HEAD, S. C. IN 1862.

SIEGE OF VICKSBURG—CANNON DISMOUNTED INSIDE THE CONFEDERATE WORKS—SKETCHED WITH A GLASS FROM THE RIFLE PITS.

THE ADVANCE UPON CHARLESTON, S. C.—PIONEER MOVEMENT—LANDING OF THE ONE HUNDREDTH NEW YORK VOLUNTEERS UPON COLE'S ISLAND, MARCH 28TH, 1862.

VIEW OF THE TOWN OF CENTREVILLE, VA., WITH THE BATTLEFIELD OF BULL RUN, BULL RUN MOUNTAINS, THOROUGHFARE GAP, AND THE BLUE RIDGE IN THE DISTANCE

An undying interest centres around the field of Bull Run, so often the scene of battle, *skirmish* and military operations. The ground dyed with the blood of so many thousand American soldiers, where some of the mightiest armies have met in deadly strife, will long show, in its broken outlines, in its ruined dwellings, in its grass-grown earthworks, and in its sadder graves and unburied remains of mortality, the traces of war. We give a view of Centreville, with a battery of the Third Connecticut Heavy Artillery in the foreground, their caissons and shelter tents beside the grassy mound that marks the intrenchments thrown up by the Confederates in the fall and winter of 1861. The village of Centreville lies to the right, the battle ground of Bull Run lies beyond the last two houses on the right, and still further in the background are the Bull Run Mountains, divided opposite the last house by Thoroughfare Gap, and in the remote distance looms up the Blue Ridge.

THE WAR IN VIRGINIA—OFFICERS AND MEN OF MEADE'S ARMY DISCOVERING UNBURIED FEDERAL DEAD ON THE OLD BATTLEFIELD OF BULL RUN.

Our sketch was taken on the ground where the Fifth Corps was repulsed on the second day of the battle of Groveton in 1862. The old railroad embankment and cut where the Confederates held their position, defying the efforts of the Federals, who lost so terribly in the attempt, appear on the right, while in front a group of officers and men are gazing on the unburied remains of gallant men, which claim a sepulchre soon given them. Our correspondent wrote: "In the long, luxuriant grass one strikes his foot against skulls and bones, mingled with the deadly missiles that brought them to the earth. Hollow skulls lie contiguous to the hemispheres of exploded shells. The shallow graves rise here and there above the grass, sometimes in rows, sometimes alone, or scattered at irregular intervals."

EPISCOPAL CHURCH.

Gen Stephen's Headquarters.

BAPTIST CHURCH.

JAIL and WORKS

Ancient Tomb

THE ARSENAL

Public Library & High School

Hon. J. G. Barnwell's House.

The Pos Office.

Sketches in Beaufort.

SKETCHES IN BEAUFORT, S. C., AND ITS VICINITY.

FIVE LOCOMOTIVES BUILT AT VICKSBURG, MISS., BY THE FEDERAL SOLDIERS, UNDER THE SUPERINTENDENCE OF COLONEL COOLBAUGH, OF GENERAL McPHERSON'S STAFF.

Our special artist transmitting this sketch wrote: "I herein inclose a sketch of five locomotives just completed here, being the result of the mechanical ingenuity displayed by the men in this department. General Grant, in one of his reports during the siege, remarked that there was no department of mechanical labor required to be performed but that men were always on hand well skilled in the business. The completion of these fine specimens of workmanship affords ample proof of the truth of his remark. On entering the city, last July, we found the *débris* of a machine shop and some scattered fragments of locomotives. Out of these our men have created a good workshop, with all the necessary machinery for casting car wheels, etc., and the result stands forth in these engines, of which our Rogers & Baldwins might well be proud."

369

FORT CALHOUN, ON THE RIPRAPS, SITUATED BETWEEN FORTRESS MONROE AND SEWELL'S POINT, IN HAMPTON ROADS, VA.

RECONNOISSANCE IN THE GREAT OGEECHEE RIVER, NEAR OSSABAW SOUND, GA., BY THE IRONCLAD MONITOR "MONTAUK," CAPTAIN WORDEN, AND OTHER FEDERAL GUNBOATS, JANUARY 27TH, 1863

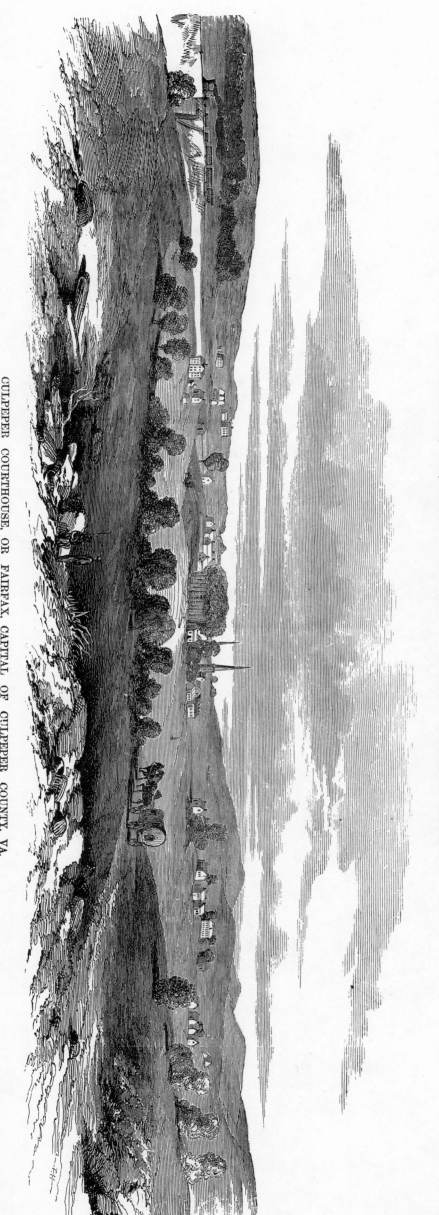

CULPEPER COURTHOUSE, OR FAIRFAX, CAPITAL OF CULPEPER COUNTY, VA.

TUSCUMBIA, ALA., ONE OF THE SCENES OF COLONEL GRIERSON'S EXPLOITS.

CUMBERLAND GAP AND HEIGHTS, TENN., FROM THE KENTUCKY SIDE.

Cumberland Gap was a place of such importance during the war as to be constantly the object of operations on both sides, who indeed alternately held it. Like Harper's Ferry, it was deemed a strategic point of great value; but the fact that no action took place, and that its evacuation was compelled by distinct movements, tend to modify this idea. It is a natural gap in a mountain, 80 miles long, or rather the only natural gap, although other points bear that name. Cumberland Gap is 150 miles southeast of Lexington, Ky. The mountain is here 1,200 feet high, but the notch is a cut nearly two-thirds of this, the road through the gap being only 400 feet high. On the southern or Tennessee side this mountain is abrupt, and in some places perpendicular, and the summit almost inaccessible, except through the gap. The northern or Kentucky side is more irregular, breaking off in a succession of smaller mountains and hills to the Valley of the Cumberland. Our sketch shows the Kentucky side.

VIEW FROM LOUDOUN HEIGHTS, VA., SHOWING HARPER'S FERRY, MARYLAND HEIGHTS, BOLIVAR, ETC.

Harper's Ferry, immortalized by the pen of Jefferson, became too often the scene of stirring events during the Civil War to require a long description, and we give a fine engraving of it to enable our readers to understand fully the operations that took place there. The view shows Maryland Heights, and on the other side Harper's Ferry, with the railroad and pontoon bridges. The place in the foreground is Bolivar, and the river runs in the gorge between it and Maryland Heights. This sketch was made by an artist who spent several days examining the neighborhood so as to give the best possible view of a point deemed so strategically important.

373

GENERAL EDWARD R. S. CANBY.

General Canby, born in Kentucky in 1819, killed in Siskiyou County, Cal., April 11th, 1873, was graduated from the United States Military Academy in 1839; commissioned second lieutenant and assigned to the Second Infantry. He served in the Florida and Mexican wars with distinction; was present at the siege of Vera Cruz, at Cerro Gordo, Contreras and Churubusco. He received the brevets of major and lieutenant colonel for his services in this campaign, and was promoted to the full rank of captain in June, 1851. In May, 1861, he was made colonel of the Nineteenth Regiment, United States Infantry, and was acting brigadier general of the forces in New Mexico. In 1862 he repelled the Confederate general Sibley in his daring attempt to acquire possession of that Territory, and had the satisfaction of seeing the invader retreat. He took command of the United States troops in New York city and harbor during the draft riots of July, 1863, and by his energetic measures assisted materially in the suppression of the rioters. At the opening of the campaign of 1864 General Canby received the rank of major general of volunteers, and was placed in command of the Military Division of West Mississippi, a place that he held until some months after the close of the war. He was killed by the Modoc Indians, April 11th, 1873.

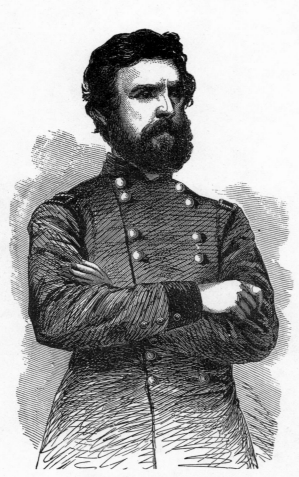

GENERAL RUFUS KING.

GENERAL DANIEL TYLER.

General King, born in New York city, January 26th, 1814, died there, October 13th, 1876, was graduated at the United States Military Academy in 1833, and appointed to the Engineer Corps. He resigned from the army, September 30th, 1836, and became assistant engineer of the New York and Erie Railroad. From 1839 till 1843 he was adjutant general of the State of New York. He was then associate editor of the Albany *Evening Journal*, and of the Albany *Advertiser* from 1841 till 1845, when he removed to Wisconsin, and was editor of the Milwaukee *Sentinel* until 1861. He was United States minister to Rome from March 22d till August 5th, 1861, but resigned, as he had offered his services in defense of the Union. He was made a brigadier general of volunteers, May 17th, 1861, and commanded a division at Fredericksburg, Groveton, Manassas, Yorktown and Fairfax, remaining in the army until 1863, when he was reappointed minister to Rome, where he resided until 1867.

General Tyler, born in Brooklyn, Windham County, Conn., January 7th, 1797, died in New York city, November 30th, 1882, was graduated from the United States Military Academy in 1819. He served as a lieutenant of artillery, was adjutant of the School of Practice at Fortress Monroe, 1824–'26; and while commanding the arsenal at Pikesville, Md., 1826–'27, translated "Manœuvres of Artillery" from the French. In 1828 he was sent abroad to observe the French improvements in artillery. This he did at Metz and elsewhere. In 1832 he was superintendent of the inspectors of arms furnished by contractors. Resigning in 1834, he became president of an iron and coal company. He was colonel of the First Connecticut Regiment in April, 1861; brigadier general of volunteers in March, 1862, and served in the Army of the Mississippi at the siege of Corinth in June. Served as one of the commission to investigate Buell's Kentucky campaign, and afterward in command at Harper's Ferry, in Baltimore and in Delaware. He withdrew from the

army in April, 1864.

THE OLD HARRISON MANSION, HARRISON'S LANDING, VA., THE BIRTHPLACE OF PRESIDENT WILLIAM HENRY HARRISON, USED
AS A HOSPITAL AND THE HEADQUARTERS OF THE SIGNAL CORPS.

This old-fashioned residence was situated at Berkeley, on the banks of the James River, only a few hundred yards from the water. It was constructed of brick and surrounded by a grove of poplar and other trees. Here, on February 9th, 1773, William Henry Harrison, ninth President of the United States, was born, and for this it remained famous till it became of still higher historical interest by being selected as the *point d'appui* of General McClellan's army, and the chief landing place of all its stores. It was at once chosen for hospital purposes, and upon its roof the Signal Corps erected a tower for the survey of the surrounding country.

RECRUITING IN PHILADELPHIA, PA., FOR THE BUCKTAIL PENNSYLVANIA REGIMENT, AUGUST, 1862.

This famous regiment suffered so much that recruiting became necessary. As it was a Pennsylvania pet regiment, Philadelphia was all alive with the resounding music of the horns, calling upon all who had killed a buck in fair combat to accept an invitation to their supper of glory. Our artist has, however, told more with a few dashes of his pencil than we can in a column. The Bucktails were a splendid set of fellows, and deserved the reputation they achieved. The fight at Dranesville, the Valley of the Shenandoah and the battle of Cross Keys have been consecrated by their valor. It will be remembered that when Colonel Sir Percy Wyndham of the First New Jersey Cavalry fell into an ambuscade the gallant Bucktails volunteered to his rescue, and were terribly cut up.

BATTLE OF CHAMPION HILLS, MAY 16TH, 1863—THE FORMIDABLE POSITION OF

On the morning of the 16th of May, General A. P. Hovey's division, occupying the right of McClernand's corps, encountered the Confederate p
force which Pemberton had brought together at Champion Hills. Two batteries which had been planted along a high ridge were doing considerable
hand-to-hand fight; but the arrival of fresh Confederate troops and the want of re-enforcements prevented their being held for any length of
Another advance was then ordered, and while Pemberton's right was thus engaged Logan's division attacked his left, and succeeded in flanking and
was so fierce that Stevenson's line became completely demoralized, yielded in turn, and by four o'clock the Confederates were in full retreat toward
until dark, and resulted in the capture of many prisoners and arms of all descriptions. The total loss in killed and wounded on both sides approxi

...TON CARRIED BY GENERALS HOVEY, LOGAN AND CROCKER, OF GRANT'S ARMY.

...ement took place until about eleven o'clock, when the Indiana troops, led by General McGinnis, made a deliberate attack upon the rapidly increasing ...s finally determined to assault them. They were both taken by the Eleventh and Forty-sixth Indiana and the Twenty-ninth Wisconsin, after a fierce ...s withdrew, and remained under cover of their artillery till joined by part of Quimby's late division, commanded by General Marcellus M. Crocker. ...n such manner as to completely isolate for awhile the whole of General Loring's brigade, which occupied the extreme Confederate right. The attack ... Just then the other division of McClernand's corps came upon the scene, and a pursuit was ordered by Generals Carr and Osterhaus. This lasted

RE-ENFORCEMENTS FOR GRANT'S ARMY LEAVING MEMPHIS, TENN.

Our sketch shows the *Alice Dean*, a crack Western steamer, leaving Memphis with re-enforcements, and with doctors, nurses, etc., for the wounded. She was in charge of the Cincinnati branch of the United States Sanitary Commission, and commanded by Mr. R. B. Moore, of Cincinnati. She was a very fast boat, having run up to Cincinnati from Memphis in 2 days, 23 hours and 5 minutes. The scene depicted was one of constant occurrence, as troops were pouring daily into Memphis from all parts.

THE BANKS EXPEDITION—SCENE ON THE LEVEE, BATON ROUGE, LA.—CONTRABANDS UNLOADING MILITARY STORES FROM THE UNITED STATES TRANSPORT "NORTH STAR," OVER THE MISSISSIPPI STEAMER "IBERVILLE."

The *Iberville* had quite a history in connection with the military operations on the Mississippi. She was taken possession of by the United States authorities on the surrender of New Orleans, and was engaged as a transport during the expedition. She several times ran the gantlet of Confederate batteries and guerrillas. On one occasion she sustained a running fire from a battery of six guns for at least twenty minutes, while passing Donaldsonville, having four men killed and four wounded, one of her engines disabled and her upper works riddled.

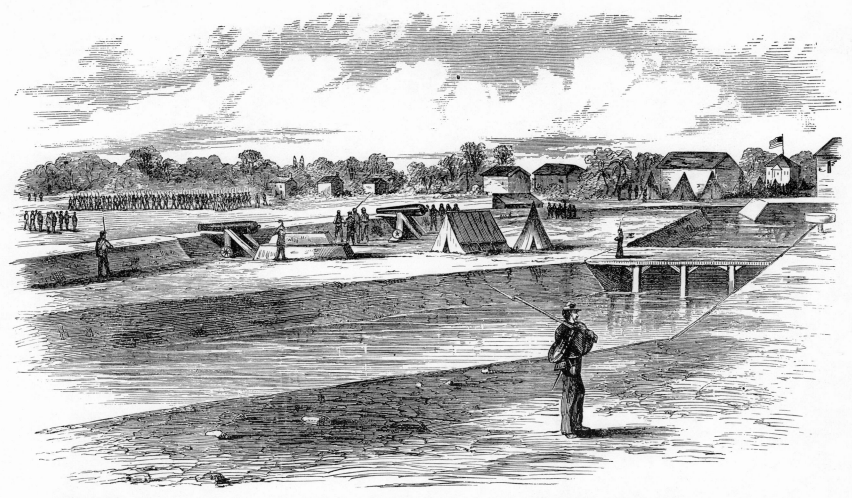

VIEW FROM THE INTERIOR OF FORT WALKER, HILTON HEAD, S. C., LOOKING INLAND, SHOWING THE DEFENSES
FROM THE LAND SIDE.

We have given so full a description of this fort that we have now merely to add that our view was taken inside the fortification, looking to the interior of Hilton Head Island. Fort Walker was nearly surrounded on its land side by the Federal camp, which had been strengthened by earthworks extending across the island. Camp Sherman was, therefore, protected by Scull's Creek on the west, Fort Welles (lately called Fort Walker) on the north, the Atlantic on the east, and by this intrenchment on the south.

THE ARMY OF THE CUMBERLAND—WILDER'S MOUNTED INFANTRY PASSING A BLOCKHOUSE ON THE NASHVILLE AND
CHATTANOOGA RAILROAD.

Among the strange anomalies of the war was the active corps of mounted infantry, of which the portion commanded by Colonel Wilder, and which appears in our engraving passing a blockhouse on the Nashville and Chattanooga Railroad, was the most important. The mounted infantry brigade consisted of Colonel Wilder's regiment, the Seventeenth Indiana, the Seventy-second and Seventy-fifth Indiana, and Ninety-eighth Illinois; they were mounted by Colonel Wilder in order to enable him to cope with Morgan and other Confederate guerrillas. But the step cost the government nothing, his horses and accoutrements being all captured from the enemy.

THE BANKS EXPEDITION—A CONFEDERATE SCHOONER RUNNING INTO THE UNITED STATES TRANSPORT "CHE-KIANG," OFF THE FLORIDA REEFS, ON THE NIGHT OF DECEMBER 11TH, 1862, WITH THE INTENTION OF SINKING HER.

On the night of December 11th, 1862, as the United States transport *Che-Kiang*, laden with troops, was off the Florida Reefs, a schooner, supposed to be a Confederate one, ran at full sail against the *Che-Kiang*. As the latter vessel was painted white and had no lights burning, there can be little doubt it was a daring and desperate attempt to wreck the transport, more especially as the schooner's crew, immediately after the collision, put off into a boat and rowed away with all expedition. After disengaging herself from the sinking schooner the *Che-Kiang* pursued her way, and reached Ship Island in such a leaky condition that the troops had to be landed.

DISABLING AND CAPTURE OF THE FEDERAL GUNBOATS "SACHEM" AND "CLIFTON," IN THE ATTACK ON SABINE PASS, TEX., SEPTEMBER 8TH 1863.

One of the objects of this expedition was to take Sabine City; and on September 8th Generals Franklin and Weitzel proceeded to the pass, and prepared to enter and land their troops as soon as the enemy's batteries were silenced. The strength and the position of these were known, the pass having been in Federal hands in 1862, yet the only preparation for attack was to send the *Clifton*, an old Staten Island ferryboat, and the *Sachem*, an inferior propeller, to attack the batteries, putting on them about one hundred sharpshooters. The vessels advanced firing, but without eliciting a reply till they were well in range, when the batteries opened. The *Sachem* was soon crippled and forced to strike, while a shell penetrated the boiler of the *Clifton*, causing an explosion that made her a perfect wreck. Many were killed in the action and by the explosion; some few escaped, but nearly all that survived were made prisoners.

Bombardment of Fort Moultrie.

SIEGE OF CHARLESTON, S. C.—1. BOMBARDMENT OF FORT MOULTRIE AND BATTERIES BEE AND BEAUREGARD BY THE MONITORS AND "IRONSIDES," SEPTEMBER 7TH-8TH, 1863.—2. INTERIOR OF BATTERY GREGG, LOOKING TOWARD WAGNER.

The bombardment of Fort Moultrie and the batteries on Sullivan's Island, on the 7th and 8th of September, was of the most determined and vigorous character, the *Ironsides* devoting herself to the fort, while the monitors paid their respects to Batteries Bee and Beauregard. Our artist gives a striking sketch as viewed from a favorable point. Moultrieville is seen on the extreme right, and next to it Moultrieville on fire, the dark smoke of the burning houses contrasting with the white puffs of smoke from the cannon thundering along the whole line. Behind the *Ironsides* is Fort Moultrie; the Confederate battery to the extreme left is Battery Bee; and nearly in front of it, the second in the line of monitors, is the stanch *Weehawken*, aground. A striking featu,e in this picture is the effect of the ricochet shot knocking up a series of *jets d'eau.*

CONFEDERATE CAVALRY ATTACKING A FEDERAL SUPPLY TRAIN, NEAR JASPER, TENN.

We give a sketch of the capture of a Federal supply train of several hundred wagons, loaded with ammunition and subsistence, by a large body of Wheeler's Confederate cavalry, near Jasper, Tenn., while on the way to Chattanooga. The guard made a stubborn resistance, but being few in number were soon overpowered by the Confederates, whose headlong attack and numerical superiority threw the whole train into confusion and prevented escape. The cavalry were supposed to have crossed the Cumberland at Kingston, above General Burnside, and come down in his rear. This daring act showed how materially a large force of cavalry was needed in the Army of the Cumberland.

GENERAL WALTER Q. GRESHAM.

General Walter Q. Gresham, Secretary of State, born near Lanesville, Harrison County, Ind., March 17th, 1833; died at Washington, D. C., May 28th, 1895. He was educated in country schools, and spent one year in the State University of Bloomington, Ind., but was not graduated. He then studied law in Corydon, Ind.; was admitted to the bar in 1853, and became a successful lawyer. He was elected to the Legislature in 1860, but resigned in August, 1861, to become lieutenant colonel of the Thirty-eighth Indiana Regiment. He was promoted to colonel of the Fifty-third Indiana in December, and on August 11th, 1863, after the fall of Vicksburg, was made brigadier general of volunteers. He commanded the Fourth Division of Blair's corps in the fighting before Atlanta, and received a severe wound that disabled him for a year and prevented him from seeing further service. On March 13th, 1865, he was brevetted major general of volunteers for his gallantry at Atlanta. General Gresham twice ran for Congress, and was defeated by Michael C. Kerr. He accepted President Grant's appointment as United States District Judge for Indiana in 1869, and during the twelve years that he held that district judgeship not one of his decisions was reversed. President Arthur called him from the bench to become a member of his cabinet in 1883, and since that time Mr. Gresham has been a conspicuous figure in national politics. He took the portfolio in President Arthur's cabinet left vacant by the death of Postmaster General Howe. Perhaps the most noticeable incident of his career as postmaster general was the exclusion of the Louisiana Lottery Company from the use of the mail. Near the close of President Arthur's term, on the death of Secretary Folger, Mr. Gresham was appointed Secretary of the Treasury. Mr. Gresham, however, longed for a return to the bench, and in the closing days of the Arthur Administration he was appointed Circuit Judge to succeed Judge Drummond for the Seventh Judicial District. This was an appointment for life. He was a candidate for the Republican nomination for President in 1884, and again in 1888. He received 111 votes on the first ballot in the convention in 1888. His vote rose to 123 on the third ballot, and then dwindled to 59 on the eighth and last. He refused, it is said, the nomination by the People's Party in 1892. Judge Gresham announced his intention of voting for Grover Cleveland in the last Presidential campaign. In his letter, dated October 27th, 1892, and addressed to Major Bluford Wilson, he announced that he thought a Republican could vote for Mr. Cleveland without joining the Democratic party. When Mr. Cleveland was elected he offered him the first place in the cabinet, and he became Secretary of State. Mr. Cleveland and Mr. Gresham were old friends, having met in the White House in 1885. His course as Secretary of State has been in accord with the policy of President Cleveland. Judge Gresham was married in 1858. His wife was a Kentuckian. They had two children—a son, Otto Gresham, and a daughter, now Mrs. Andrews. Judge Gresham's personal appearance was that of a handsome man. His bearing was soldierly and manly. He was broad and square-shouldered, with a figure that was athletic and symmetrical. His hair was thick and of a whitish gray, and he wore it combed back from his forehead. He was somewhat careless in his attire, and apparently paid very little attention to it.

GENERAL LAFAYETTE C. BAKER.

General Baker, Chief of the United States Secret Service, born in Stafford, Genesee County, N. Y., October 13th, 1826, died in Philadelphia, Pa., July 2d, 1868. In 1848 he went to New York and Philadelphia, and in 1853 to San Francisco, in each of these cities working as a mechanic. When the lawless element became dominant in San Francisco, in 1856, General Baker joined the Vigilance Committee and took an active part in the summary proceedings that restored order in the city. He went to New York on business in 1861, expecting to return at once, but the Civil War intervened, and he went to Washington and offered his services. At the suggestion of General Hiram Walbridge, of New York, he was introduced to General Scott, and as a result of the interview he started on foot for Richmond, where, in spite of arrest, imprisonment and several interviews with Jefferson Davis, while under suspension as a spy, he succeeded in collecting much information and returning to Washington after an absence of three weeks. This was but the first of a series of adventures involving high executive ability and a wonderful talent for tracing conspiracy and frustrating the designs of Confederate spies and agents. He was commissioned colonel, and subsequently brigadier general. His duties naturally made him enemies in influential quarters, and charges of a serious nature were several times preferred against him, but were never substantiated. When President Lincoln was assassinated General Baker organized the pursuit of the murderer, and was present at his capture and death.

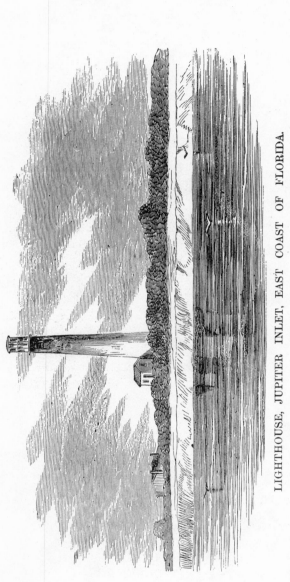

LIGHTHOUSE, JUPITER INLET, EAST COAST OF FLORIDA.

CUTTING THE LEVEES NEAR THE STATE LINE OF LOUISIANA AND ARKANSAS, TWENTY MILES ABOVE LAKE PROVIDENCE, BY ORDER OF GENERAL GRANT.

GRANT'S CAMPAIGN IN VIRGINIA—THE BATTLE OF COLD HARBOR, JUNE 1st, 1864.

LIGHTHOUSE, TAMPA BAY, WEST COAST OF FLORIDA.

FEDERAL CAVALRY COVERING THE ESCAPE OF FEDERAL PRISONERS FROM LIBBY PRISON, RICHMOND, VA.

The feeling of sympathy for the unfortunate Federal officers and men who so long suffered outrage at the hands of the Confederates gave way to a momentary feeling of joy as news came of the escape, at one time, of one hundred and nine officers and men. From time to time a few had escaped, and the narrative of their escapes had been among the most intensely exciting incidents of the war. But when more than a hundred contrived to get out of the Southern dungeon the interest knew no bounds. The method employed was as follows: Having managed to find access to the cellar, they commenced work, relieving one another as opportunity offered. Their instruments were case knives, pocket knives, chisels and files. After getting through the wall they disposed of the excavated soil by drawing it out in a spittoon, which they attached to a cord. This would be filled by the party at work in the tunnel, and pulled out into the cellar by their companions, who disposed of it by spreading it in shallow layers over the floor, concealing it beneath the straw. The tunnel, completed by fifty-one days of patient toil, was about sixty feet long, and opened into an old tobacco shed beyond the line of guards. In order to elude their pursuers, who they knew would soon be on their track, they scattered as much as possible. Many were the hardships and sufferings of the fugitives, and frequent were their narrow escapes from the Confederate cavalry, who the next morning were bushwhacking in every direction for them. The joy which Colonel Streight and

THE ENTHUSIASM OF THE NORTHERN ARMIES—RE-ENLISTMENT OF THE SEVENTEENTH ARMY CORPS.

While Alabama troops were shooting down Kentuckians who refused to re-enlist, the Federal Army almost unanimously re-enlisted. Hence the difference. There was no want of faith in the Federal cause, the government, or success. In some corps almost all the regiments re-enlisted: in the Seventeenth Army Corps thirty-nine took their stand as veterans. We give artistically a view of this army enthusiasm.

GENERAL JEREMIAH M. RUSK.

General Rusk, born in Morgan County, Ohio, June 17th, 1830; died in 1894. He divided his time between farm work and the acquisition of a common-school education till he attained his majority, and in 1853 removed to Wisconsin and engaged in agriculture in Vernon County. He entered the National Army in 1862, was commissioned major of the Twenty-fifth Wisconsin Regiment, rose to the rank of lieutenant colonel, and served with General William T. Sherman from the siege of Vicksburg till the close of the war. In 1865 he received the brevet of brigadier general of volunteers for meritorious services at the battle of Salkehatchie. Beginning with 1881, he was elected Governor of Wisconsin for three successive terms. During the threatened Milwaukee riots in May, 1886, he did good service by his prompt action in ordering the militia to fire on the dangerous mobs when they attempted to destroy life and property. In 1889 President Harrison appointed General Rusk Secretary of Agriculture.

GENERAL HENRY W. BENHAM.

GENERAL CUVIER GROVER.

General Benham, born in Connecticut in 1817, died in New York June 1st, 1884, was graduated from the United States Military Academy in 1837, and assigned to the Corps of Engineers. Served in the Mexican War, 1847–'8, and was brevetted captain for gallant and meritorious services in the battle of Buena Vista. At the beginning of the Civil War, in 1861, Captain Benham entered upon active service; was on General Morris's staff as engineer of the Department of the Ohio; was brevetted colonel for gallantry at the battle of Carrick's Ford, July 13th, 1861; in August was made brigadier general of volunteers, and was engaged in the Virginia campaigns. In 1862 he was present at the capture of Fort Pulaski and James Island; later in the year he superintended fortifications in Boston and Portsmouth harbors, and was in command of the Northern District of the Department of the South. He proved very efficient in throwing pontoon bridges across the Rappahannock, the Potomac and the James Rivers, and was in command of the Pontoon Department at Washington in 1864. In March, 1865, he was brevetted brigadier general and major general, United States Army, and major general, United States Volunteers, for gallant services during the Rebellion.

General Grover, born in Bethel, Me., July 24th, 1829, died in Atlantic City, N. J., June 6th, 1885, was graduated from the United States Military Academy in 1850, entered the First Artillery, and served on frontier duty till 1853. He was promoted to first lieutenant March 3d, 1855, and captain of the Tenth Infantry on September 17th, 1858, serving at various Western stations. He became brigadier general of volunteers April 14th. 1862, and was transferred to the Army of the Potomac, with which he took part in many battles, serving with distinction at the battles of Williamsburg, Fair Oaks and Bull Run. Being transferred to the Department of the Gulf, he took command of a division of the Nineteenth Corps from December 30th, 1862, till July, 1864; was in command of the right wing of the army besieging Port Hudson, La., in May, 1863; and commanded a division in the Shenandoah campaign from August to December, 1864. He was wounded at the battle of Cedar Creek, on October 19th, 1864, and brevetted major general of volunteers on the same day for gallantry at Winchester and Fisher's Hill. On March 13th, 1865, he was brevetted brigadier general, United States Army, and major general, United States Army. He was mustered out of the volunteer service August 24th, 1865.

LIEUTENANT J. H. RAYMOND CAPTURING THE CONFEDERATE FLAG FROM THE BURNING CONFEDERATE STEAMER "FANNY,"
AT THE ACTION OFF ELIZABETH CITY, N. C., FEBRUARY 11TH, 1862.

Our sketch represents Lieutenant Raymond rushing on board the Confederate steamer *Fanny* and carrying off, through flame and smoke, the Confederate flag which was still flying on board the vessel. This heroic act was performed in the battle before Elizabeth City.

BATTLE OF GRAND COTEAU, LA., NOVEMBER 3D, 1863—FURIOUS ATTACK ON THE SIXTIETH INDIANA, COLONEL OWEN.

On the 3d of November, 1863, the enemy, about six thousand strong, under General Green, attacked in force; but the Seventeenth Ohio Battery kept them at bay, supported by the Eighty-third Ohio, the Sixtieth Indiana watching the flank. A lull soon occurred, and the Sixtieth was sent to hold a bridge and small bayou on the skirt of the woods. This they did, and at last, by Burbridge's order, advanced till friend and foe were so mingled in strife that cannon could not be used; but finally the Sixtieth Indiana, with the Ninety-sixth Ohio and the Twenty-third Wisconsin, who came to its aid, fell back, the Twenty-third losing their brave colonel, Guppy. In this retrograde movement the enemy's mounted Texan infantry surrounded the Sixty-seventh Indiana. General Burbridge in vain endeavored to save them with a section of the Seventeenth Ohio Battery, but the Confederates closed around them so that he had to suspend his fire for fear of killing his own men, and Lieutenant Colonel Bushler, with two hundred men, surrendered to the enemy.

BATTLE OF CHICKAMAUGA, GA., SEPTEMBER

Our sketch of this most important battle shows General Thomas and his staff anxiously looking for re-enforcements as his gallant troops, from t
berland from destruction. After skirmishing on Thursday and Friday, September 17th and 18th, General Rosecrans on Saturday formed his line,
Crittenden's corps, consisting of Palmer's and Van Cleve's divisions, formed the centre, with part of McCook's on each side. The line generally follo
first attack, and in a few moments the whole division was forced back. Thomas then ordered his entire line to advance, and Longstreet was driven
with impetuosity on Crittenden, and after a fierce struggle routed him, and drove to the right, in similar disorder, Davis's division, of McCook's co
with Negley and Wood, from the right, rallying some of the routed centre, drove the enemy back. Before the deadly fire of this new line the Confed
Missionary Ridge, Van Cleve, Wood and Sheridan on the left, and Thomas more in the centre. The fight commenced on the extreme left, and the C
took place. At last General Reynolds began to give way, and Wood was sent to his relief. As Davis moved to fill Wood's place the Confederates t
gathered up the other portion of the army in a strong line on Missionary Ridge, and prepared to resist the last Confederate attack, made with all the
would tell whether the day's disaster must close in irreparable ruin or there was yet hope of repulsing the foe. It was General Granger with two fre
fell back, unmolested, to Rossville.

WEEN GENERALS ROSECRANS AND BRAGG.

work of logs and knapsacks, are repulsing the repeated assaults of the overpowering Confederate forces and saving the whole Army of the Cum-
as on the left, having under him Brannan, Baird and Reynolds; Negley and Wood held the extreme right at Owen's Ford and Gordon's Mill.
a, though on the left it took the course of the Lafayette Road. Between ten and eleven A. M. Cranston's brigade. of Brannan's division, met the
losing the ground and cannon he had gained, and his corps was fast melting under the blows of Thomas, when Polk and Hill threw their corps
gap in the line, and exposing Thomas to a heavy flank attack. Back then his victorious troops returned to meet the new enemy, and Thomas,
red, and before sunset Rosecrans's army held its old line. During the night Rosecrans fell back to a new line, resting Negley with his right on
a in the morning, attacked Negley with all their strength, and Longstreet again rolled his veterans on Thomas, and again a bitterly contested fight
nd routing them, severed Rosecrans's line, leaving him, with Sheridan, Davis and Wilder, cut off entirely from the mass of his army. Thomas
; but his men stood firm, and a cloud of dust to the left soon showed a line advancing on the Lafayette Road. Every eye was strained; a moment
esh for battle, now rushed on the enemy and drove them from a hill which they had gained: and thus aided, Thomas repulsed the enemy, and

THE INVASION OF MARYLAND—GENERAL KILPATRICK REPULSING THE CONFEDERATE STUART AT BOONSBOROUGH,
JULY 8TH, 1863.

The Civil War showed many affairs quite confusing old ideas. We had colonels commanding fleets and marines serving ashore, mounted infantry and dismounted cavalry. On the 8th of July, 1863, General Kilpatrick, who was endeavoring to cut off the Confederate trains from Gettysburg, was attacked by Stuart, and both these fine cavalry officers fought with their men dismounted, Kilpatrick repulsing his antagonist and subsequently capturing a large number of prisoners and wagons.

GENERAL McPHERSON ENTERING CLINTON, MISS.

To facilitate the movements of the Federal armies near Chattanooga and divert the Confederate forces from hastening to the relief of Bragg, General McPherson marched from Vicksburg on the 15th of October, 1863. On the 17th he came up with the enemy in a strong position on the Canton Road, ten miles beyond Brownsville, and after a short, sharp fight, routed them, the Federals charging gallantly over the bridge and through the tall grass and corn to the enemy's line. The next day he entered Clinton, on the Vicksburg and Jackson Railroad. His gallant troops broke the Sabbath stillness of the place as they marched in, and the Confederates scattered on all sides in flight. General McPherson then proceeded to Canton, and finally returned to Vicksburg after destroying Confederate mills and factories, and a arming all the neighboring stations.

GALLANT CHARGE OF THE SIXTH MICHIGAN CAVALRY OVER THE ENEMY'S BREASTWORKS, NEAR FALLING WATERS, MD.,
JULY 14TH, 1863.

The exploits of the Federal cavalry in Virginia, Maryland and Pennsylvania in 1863 would fill a volume in themselves. Among the many gallant charges there are few more brilliant than that of the Sixth Michigan at Falling Waters, where they rode, without drawing rein, right over the Confederate breastworks, scattering all before them. The cavalry were not more than sixty at most, but they charged up a steep hill in the face of a terrific fire; and though they lost in killed and wounded nearly two-thirds of their number, they captured almost the entire force of the enemy, with three regimental battle flags.

DESPERATE HAND-TO-HAND COMBAT BETWEEN FEDERAL CAVALRY, COMMANDED BY GENERAL AVERILL, AND STUART'S
CONFEDERATE TROOPS, AT KELLEY'S FORD, ON THE RAPPAHANNOCK, VA., MARCH 17TH, 1863.

The first stand-up cavalry fight on a large scale took place at Kelley's Ford, on the Rappahannock, on St. Patrick's Day, 1863. To the Federal general Averill and the daring Confederate general Fitzhugh Lee belong the chief honors of this brilliant affair. Once across the river, a regular cavalry and artillery fight took place between General Averill's command and the Confederate forces under the command of Generals Stuart and Fitzhugh Lee; and for once during the war there was a fair cavalry fight. The forces opposed to each other were about equal in numbers and similarly appointed and equipped. The Confederates, made desperate by the advance of Federal troops across the Rappahannock and upon soil which they had sworn to defend with the last drop of their blood, disputed every rood of ground. Again and again they charged on the Federal lines, formed *en échelon*, and as often were they repulsed in the most gallant manner. When the Federals charged upon the enemy's lines it was done with such impetuosity that successful resistance was impossible. Sword in hand they dashed upon the foe, who, after attempting to stand up against the first charges, doggedly retired before them. The object of the expedition having been accomplished, General Averill retired to the left bank of the river without molestation from the enemy.

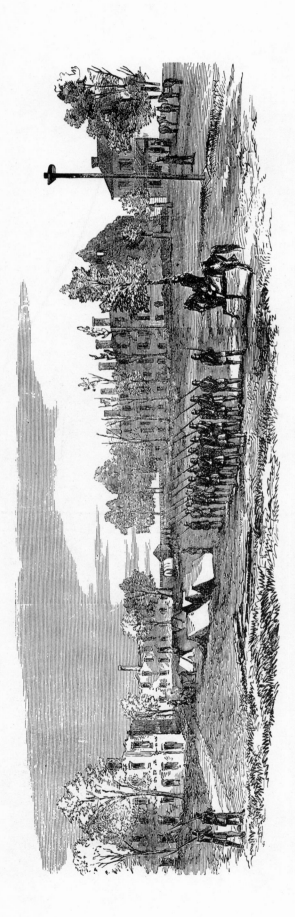

CARLISLE, PA., SHOWING GENERAL SMITH'S HEADQUARTERS, AND THE BARRACKS DESTROYED BY GENERAL W. H. F. LEE.

THE WAR IN VIRGINIA—BATTERY ON THE LEFT OF THE ENEMY'S LINE, IN FRONT OF PETERSBURG, CAPTURED BY THE EIGHTEENTH ARMY CORPS.

THE WAR IN VIRGINIA—BURNSIDE'S CORPS CHARGING THE CONFEDERATE POSITION ON THE RIGHT OF THE ENEMY'S LINE, IN FRONT OF PETERSBURG.

LEE'S ARMY CROSSING THE POTOMAC AT WILLIAMSPORT, IN SCOWS GUIDED BY WIRES, AFTER THE INVASION OF MARYLAND.

PRESENTATION OF COLORS TO THE TWENTIETH UNITED STATES COLORED INFANTRY, COLONEL BARTRAM, AT THE UNION LEAGUE CLUBHOUSE, NEW YORK, MARCH 5TH, 1864.

The Twentieth Regiment, United States Colored Troops, left Riker's Island at nine o'clock on the 5th of March, 1864, on board the steamer *John Romer*, and were conveyed to the foot of Twenty-first Street, East River, New York, where they were disembarked and formed in regimental line, and marched to Union Square, arriving in front of the Union League Clubhouse at one o'clock. A vast crowd of citizens, of every shade of color and every phase of social and political life, filled the square and streets, and every door, window, veranda, tree and housetop that commanded a view of the scene was peopled with spectators. Over the entrance of the clubhouse was a large platform, ornamented with flags and filled with ladies. In the street was another platform, tastefully decorated and occupied by prominent citizens. From the stand the colors were presented by President King of Columbia College, who addressed them with warmth and eloquence. After the presentation ceremony was over the men stacked arms and partook of a collation provided for them.

CAPTURE OF FORT DE RUSSY, LA., ON THE 14TH OF MARCH, 1864, BY THE FEDERAL FORCES UNDER GENERAL ANDREW JACKSON SMITH.

This fort was captured, March 14th, 1864, by the Federal forces under General A. J. Smith. The expedition left Vicksburg on March 10th, landed at Summerville, La., on the 13th, and marched to Bayou Glace, where General Scurri's Confederate brigade had been encamped, which fled on the approach of the transports, leaving considerable camp equipage and commissary stores. General Smith pushed forward to Yellow Bayou, where strong fortifications had been erected; but the Confederates again fled. As he came up the enemy was pressed, and some skirmishing occurred, resulting in the capture of several prisoners and a small wagon train. At daylight the entire command started for Fort de Russy, twenty-eight miles distant, hotly pursued by General Dick Taylor, who hoped to save the fort; but Smith had the lead, and at four o'clock in the afternoon the Third and Ninth Indiana Batteries opened on the fort, which replied vigorously with three of its heaviest guns. The cannonade continued an hour, when General Smith ordered the First and Second Illinois Regiments, Sixteenth Corps, under General Mower, to charge the enemy's rifle pits and storm the fort. The Eighty-ninth and One Hundred and Nineteenth Indiana and Twenty-fourth Missouri Regiments charged over deep ditches and a thick abatis in the face of a galling fire, and within twenty minutes after the order was given the color sergeant of the Fifty-eighth Illinois Volunteers planted the American flag upon the enemy's works.

HORSESHOEING IN THE ARMY.

Not like the country blacksmith, by the highroad upon the skirt of the village, with children peering around, and all men, from the squire to the poorly paid minister, stopping to get his services or to chat, does the army smith ply his labors. But even with his toils and risks he is better off than the toiling craftsman in the close lanes of the city, with filth and misery around, and a tavern visible wherever he turns his eye. The army blacksmith smacks of the army; if not a soldier he smacks of camps and battles, and though he sees the battle generally from afar, and does his needed labor under the shady tree or leafy roofing of a rustic shed in summer, and in the warmest nook he can find in winter, he will doubtless in other years recount to his wondering grandchildren the story of the great battles in Virginia, if he does not attribute the final success to his own handiwork. The regular army forge is a four-wheeled carriage, the front, or limber, bearing a box about four feet long by two in width, containing the anvil, tongs and other implements, with a limited supply of iron for immediate use; on the rear wheel is a box containing the bellows, worked by a lever. In front of this is a cast-iron ash pan for the fire, with a sheet-iron back. On the stock is a vise, and the back of the box is a receptacle for coal. The whole is very compact, and on the march takes up very little room, the men riding on the limber box.

THE WAR IN VIRGINIA—CONTRABANDS COMING INTO THE FEDERAL CAMP.

The negro furnishes, in his various phases of existence, wonderful studies for the artist and philosopher. Never, perhaps, has a race seen such a moment as during the Civil War, when the chains of bondage were breaking from the limbs of 4,000,000 of men. The distant roar of battle was to them a sound of deliverance. With all the uncouth, odd and queer manifestations of joy they prepared to reach the camp of the delivering Yanks. Yoking together most incongruous teams before the farm wagons of their fled masters, with ass and ox and horse, with household gear queerly assorted, with useless truck and little that could rarely serve them, they started for the Promised Land, and might often have been seen coming in as our artist, a most close student of nature, depicted them, with his usual felicity of portraiture.

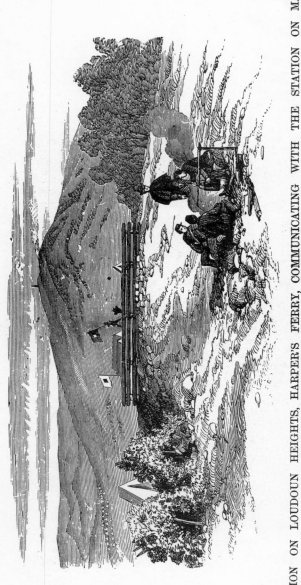

FEDERAL SIGNAL STATION ON LOUDOUN HEIGHTS, HARPER'S FERRY, COMMUNICATING WITH THE STATION ON MARYLAND HEIGHTS.

THE WAR ON THE RED RIVER—ADMIRAL PORTER'S FLEET PASSING THROUGH COLONEL BAILEY'S DAM, ABOVE ALEXANDRIA, MAY, 1864.

GRANT'S CAMPAIGN IN VIRGINIA—THE BATTLE OF BETHESDA CHURCH, BETWEEN CRAWFORD'S DIVISION, FIFTH CORPS, AND THE CONFEDERATES, MAY 30TH, 1864.

THE WAR IN VIRGINIA—CAISSONS AND HORSES ON THE FIELD AT BRISTOE STATION.

THE WAR IN VIRGINIA—SKETCH ON THE LINE OF THE SECOND CORPS AT THE BATTLE OF THE WILDERNESS, MAY 6TH, 1864—WAITING FOR THE ENEMY

On the night succeeding the passage of the Rapidan both armies camped near by each other, Grant unsuspicious of the close presence of the enemy. Next day Ewell attacked Warren as he moved by the flank through the wood roads. Grant and Meade, at Old Wilderness Tavern, supposed this to be the attack of a simple rear guard. Before Sedgwick could come up on Warren's right Ewell had inflicted a loss of 3,000 men upon the Fifth Corps. Grant being ready to accept battle here, Sedgwick was ordered to join Warren's right, and Hancock was summoned from Chancellorsville. On his arrival he promptly attacked Hill. Both Grant and Lee determined to attack on the morrow. Burnside was ordered up to take position between Warren and Hancock. Lee awaited the arrival of Longstreet, whom he wanted to place opposite Hancock's right. Grant ordered an attack along the whole line at 5 A. M. Lee determined to turn Grant's left and throw him back upon the river. Hancock fell upon Hill at five o'clock, and drove him back over a mile down the Plank Road, when he stopped to rearrange his troops. While thus pausing, Longstreet came upon the field and attacked him. Hancock, by the suddenness of this attack, was driven back to his old lines on the Brook Road. Here he rallied his men, and Longstreet being wounded, the violence of the Confederate attack subsided. In the afternoon Lee again attacked Hancock; night once more supervened; nothing had been decided. Grant lost 15,000 men; Lee's loss was less by several thousand. Our sketch was taken on the line of the Second Corps, on the 6th, showing the gallant men of that corps awaiting the enemy's attack.

THE WAR IN VIRGINIA—BATTLE OF SPOTTSYLVANIA COURTHOUSE—OPENING OF THE FIGHT AT ALSOP'S FARM, MAY 8TH, 1864.

The direct route to Spottsylvania Courthouse is by the Brock Road, via Todd's Tavern. On this road the Fifth Corps, under General Warren, was to take the advance, and by rapid march seize Spottsylvania Courthouse. Hancock's corps was to follow on the same line, while Sedgwick and Burnside were to move on an exterior route by way of Chancellorsville. The vital interest of this movement centred in the march of Warren to seize Spottsylvania Courthouse. Warren's corps advanced at 9 P. M. on the 7th. Reaching Todd's Tavern, he was delayed for an hour and a half by the cavalry escort of General Meade blocking the way. On the 8th he was again detained by the cavalry division of General Merritt, who had been engaged in fighting and driving Stuart's cavalry, whom Lee had sent to block the Brock Road, and who still barred further advance. Merritt, after two hours of ineffectual effort, gave way to Warren, who advanced to clear his own path. The advance brigades, under Robinson, were deployed in line of battle, while the remainder of the corps followed in column. At 8 A. M. of the 8th the column emerged from the woods into a clearing, known as Alsop's Farm, two miles north of Spottsylvania Courthouse. Anderson (Longstreet's corps) had in the meantime arrived at the same place, and a sharp engagement ensued, when the woods on both flanks of the Federals were cleared of the enemy. Warren waited for Sedgwick to come up. Before the latter arrived night had fallen. As a consequence of all those incidents, Lee had managed to place himself across Grant's path, and having drawn upon the Spottsylvania Ridge a bulwark of defense, he was able to hold the Army of the Potomac in check. Our illustration shows the opening of the battle of the 8th, as viewed from General Warren's headquarters.

GENERAL THOMAS J. (STONEWALL) JACKSON.

General Jackson, born in Clarksburg, W. Va., January 21st, 1824, died at Chancellorsville, Va., May 10th, 1863, was graduated from the United States Military Academy, in 1846. He was ordered to Mexico, became a lieutenant in Magruder's battery, and took part in General Scott's campaign from Vera Cruz to the city of Mexico. He was twice brevetted for good conduct at Churubusco and Chapultepec. He resigned from the army in 1851, on his election as professor of philosophy and artillery tactics in Virginia Military Institute. A few days after the secession of Virginia he took command of the troops that were collecting at Harper's Ferry, and when Virginia joined the Confederacy, a few weeks later, he was relieved by General Joseph E. Johnston, and then became commander of a brigade in Johnston's army, which rank he held at the battle of Bull Run. For his conduct on that occasion he was made major general, and in November, 1861, was assigned to the command of the district that included the Shenandoah Valley and the portion of Virginia northwest of it. In 1862 Jackson defeated Banks at Front Royal and Winchester, Fremont and McDowell at Cross Keys, Shields at Port Republic, Fitzjohn Porter at Gaines's Mill, Banks at Cedar Run and Pope at the second Bull Run. He invested and captured Harper's Ferry with 13,000 prisoners, and joined Lee at Antietam. He defeated Hooker at Chancellorsville, where he received his death wounds, accidentally, at the hands of his own men.

GENERAL JOHN H. MORGAN.

GENERAL RICHARD S. EWELL.

General Morgan, born in Huntsville, Ala., June 1st, 1826, died near Greeneville, Tenn., September 4th, 1864. He served in the War with Mexico as first lieutenant in a cavalry regiment. At the opening of the Civil War he entered the Confederate Army as captain of the Kentucky Volunteers, and joined General Simon B. Buckner at the head of the Lexington Rifles. During the winter of 1862–'3 he commanded a cavalry force in General Braxton Bragg's army, and greatly annoyed General Rosecrans's outposts and communications. He soon began a series of raids in Kentucky, which made it necessary to garrison every important town in the State. In 1862 he was appointed major general. In 1863 he headed a bold and extensive raid into Kentucky, Ohio and Indiana, but was captured and imprisoned in the Ohio Penitentiary. He escaped by digging his way out in November, 1863, and then undertook a raid in Tennessee. While at a farmhouse near Greeneville, Tenn., he was surrounded by Federal troops under General Gillem, and in attempting to escape was killed. **406**

General Ewell, born in Georgetown, D. C., February 8th, 1817, died in Springfield, Tenn., January 25th, 1872, was graduated at the United States Military Academy in 1840; served in the Mexican War, and was promoted captain, August 4th, 1849. When the Civil War began he resigned his commission, entered the Confederate Army, and was actively engaged throughout the war. He was promoted to the rank of major general, and fought at Blackburn's Ford, July 18th, and at Bull Run, July 21st, 1861. In the following year he distinguished himself under General Jackson. He lost a leg at Warrenton Turnpike, on August 28th, 1862. When Jackson was fatally wounded at Chancellorsville, Ewell, at the former's request, was promoted to lieutenant general and assigned to the command of the Second Corps. At the head of Jackson's veterans he fought valiantly at Winchester, at Gettysburg, and at the Wilderness on the Confederate left. He was captured, with his entire force, by Sheridan, at Sailor's Creek, April 6th, 1865. After the war he retired to private life.

BANKS'S EXPEDITION—BURNING OF THE STATE CAPITOL OF LOUISIANA, BATON ROUGE, TUESDAY NIGHT, DECEMBER 30TH, 1862.

THE WAR IN TENNESSEE—FEDERAL PICKETS APPROACHED BY CONFEDERATES IN CEDAR BUSHES NEAR CHATTANOOGA.

Our sketch shows the Confederate device for shooting down the Federal pickets. We have here not a whole wood marching, but single trees moving in the dusky twilight, continuously and stealthily, that their onward movement may be taken for the mere swaying of the trees in the wind. But the pickets in the third year of the war were keen of eye and quick of ear, and the hand on the trigger tells that some will fall in their cedar coffins to lie with no other cerements of the grave and molder away amid the crags and woods of that wild territory.

THE WAR IN TENNESSEE—HOOKER'S BATTLE ABOVE THE CLOUDS, AND CA

The wild mountains of Tennessee, where nature revels in producing the most fantastic forms, and piling rocks upon rocks, forms one of the
combatants, the flash and the roar of the guns appearing to the spectators in the plain below like the lightning and the thunder of heaven. By ei
hatchie. But here, filing his troops to the left, General Hooker began the difficult task of the ascent of the mountain. The head of the column, l
formed the front, with Greene's brigade of New York troops on the right. General Hooker then formed a second line of the two brigades of the
aid any part of the line which might need it. Thus arranged. the corps was ordered forward, with a heavy line of skirmishers thrown out, and mar
hend the situation Colonel Ireland's skirmishers had penetrated far toward the point of the mountain, and got in a heavy fire upon the enemy,
the Confederates on Lookout Mountain opened a heavy fire upon each other, and soon the whole mountain was hid from view in Chattanooga by th
behind jutting rocks and from trees. Holding Ireland's right well against the palisades, Geary threw Kennedy forward on the left, and he, after bei
mountain, at Craven's House. General Geary swung around until his line was parallel with that of the enemy, and again advanced. but being met by
they lacked numbers to man them, having lost severely. They were compelled to expose their right flank. Hooker then sent the Eighty-fourth and
centre. Geary turned their left, as Osterhaus did the enemy's right, and then, with one charge of the whole line, Hooker carried the position.

CONFEDERATE POSITION ON LOOKOUT MOUNTAIN, NOVEMBER 24TH, 1863.

he land, have been the scene of one of the most extraordinary battles in history. a battle fought with the mists and clouds rolling beneath the
y, November 24th, Hooker's column was moving up Lookout Valley. and, to the surprise of the enemy, disapppeared in the woods south of Wau-
lisades, went into line of battle facing to the north, and with the right resting against the palisades stretched down the mountain. Geary's division
ad been sent him, placing Whittaker on the right and Grose on the left. General Osterhaus formed a third line, and held himself in readiness to
of the ridge, soon came upon the rear of the enemy. who were taken completely by surprise. Before those at the foot of the hill could compre-
te escape up the hill, while the Federals assaulted them from above. At the same time the Federal batteries on Moccasin Point and those of
h rose above and around it. The enemy made but little organized resistance, yet their skirmishers for a long time kept up a heavy fire from
se, the enemy on the point of the mountain gradually gave way and fell back in some disorder to the line of breastworks on the east slope of the
irected resistance, for a time recoiled. The enemy were now in strong position, Craven's House being the centre of a line of heavy breastworks; but
to hold the road across the mountain, and advanced on the enemy, with Geary on the right, Osterhaus on the left, Whittaker and Grose in the

THE WAR IN LOUISIANA—THE ARMY OF GENERAL BANKS CROSSING VERMILION BAYOU, OCTOBER 10TH, 1863.

Our artist presents a view of the Federal army under General Banks crossing Vermilion Bayou on October 10th, 1863. He reached it on the 9th, and finding the bridge destroyed, shelled the shores, and meeting no response, ordered his engineers to lay the pontoon bridges, on which the forces crossed, as shown in our engraving.

THE WAR IN MISSISSIPPI—GENERAL McPHERSON'S ARMY CROSSING THE BIG BLACK AT MESSENGER'S FERRY, THURSDAY, OCTOBER 15TH, 1863.

When the Confederates began to concentrate all their available forces before Rosecrans at Chattanooga a diversion was made by General McPherson, who led an expedition into Mississippi as far as Canton, and compelled them to sacrifice much or change their plans. The alarm caused was beneficial. General McPherson, whom the Confederates learned to respect at Vicksburg, moved rapidly and struck severely. Our sketch represents the army crossing by bridge and ford the Big Black, at a place called Messenger's Ferry, on Thursday, October 15th.

THE INVASION OF PENNSYLVANIA—WORKING ON THE FORTIFICATIONS NEAR HARRISBURG, PA., JUNE 16TH, 1863.

Our artist gives a view of the citizens of Harrisburg laboring on the fortifications of that city, showing the tardy but ineffective preparations made. Meanwhile the New York regiments, all accustomed to military drill and evolution, some already tried by actual service, were hurrying to the scene of action; and on these men, till the War Department could assign regulars or volunteers, depended the safety of Pennsylvania.

THE WAR IN GEORGIA—STEVENSON, ALA., DEPOT FOR GENERAL ROSECRANS'S ARMY.

The campaign of General Rosecrans brought him to a district where it was not easy to remember the State in which places were. Chattanooga, the object of the struggle, was in Tennessee; but the battle of Chickamauga was fought in Georgia, and Rosecrans's depot of supplies was in Alabama. As a man may actually stand in three States, we may credit the assertion that from Lookout Mountain your eye can discern seven of the sovereignties of the New World. In the railroad line from Memphis, which at Cleveland branches to Lynchburg, Raleigh, Charleston, Savannah and Montgomery, Stevenson is an important point, as there a railroad from Nashville comes in.

THE WAR IN VIRGINIA—CONFEDERATE SIGNAL STATION NEAR BEVERLEY FORD.

THE WAR IN TEXAS—BROWNSVILLE. OCCUPIED BY THE ARMY UNDER MAJOR GENERAL N. P. BANKS, IN 1863.

THE WAR IN VIRGINIA—GENERAL MEADE RECROSSING THE RAPPAHANNOCK, OCTOBER, 1863, BEFORE LEE'S ADVANCE

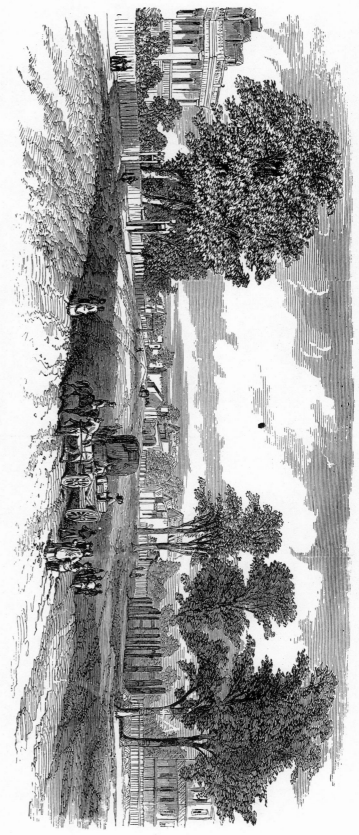

THE WAR IN LOUISIANA—NEW IBERIA.

THE OPERATIONS NEAR WASHINGTON—SCENE OF THE FIGHT IN FRONT OF FORT STEVENS, JULY 12TH–13TH, 1864.

When news of the Confederate invasion reached Grant he sent up to City Point the old Sixth Corps, that had so long battled under Sedgwick, whence they embarked for Washington. They went perhaps enjoying the scare of the Washington people, little suspecting that they were to have a brilliant little battle of their own under the eyes of the President. About six o'clock on the 12th the Confederates showed themselves coming down a declivity on both sides of Seventh Street road (Brookville Turnpike) into a little valley running across the road about a mile north of Fort Stevens. General Wright ordered a small brigade of infantry to clear out the enemy from his front. The dwellings on the hill opposite, shelter for sharpshooters, were preliminarily emptied by shells, which set them on fire—shells sent from Forts Massachusetts and Slocum. Then the Federal infantry rose, and, with a fanlike spreading to the right and left, dashed with hurrahs of delight at the two positions on each side of the Seventh Street road. The Confederates slid out of their rifle pits and leaped from behind their fences and trees, and raced. They did not stand a moment. A regiment of cavalry issued from a wood, seemingly Blair's, to the succor of their flying infantry and sharpshooters. The Federals halted to receive the troopers' charge, fired into them at close quarters, checked them, fired again, and kept firing. In three minutes neither Confederate cavalry nor infantry was in sight. The Federals double-quicked in line of battle over the crest of the heights, and disappeared in pursuit, with hurrahs and laughter, on the other side, driving Rodes's and Gordon's divisions of Ewell's corps in headlong flight before them.

THE WAR IN VIRGINIA—ROEMER'S BATTERY, THIRD DIVISION, NINTH ARMY CORPS, SHELLING PETERSBURG.

Our readers will be able to study the siege of Petersburg in our illustrations as they did that of Vicksburg. It is one of those cases where pictorial illustration has an advantage over mere verbal accounts. Here we see the Thirty-fourth New York Battery (Roemer's) and the Seventh Maine (Twitchell's), of Wilcox's Third Division of Burnside's Ninth Army Corps, shelling the city of Petersburg itself as it stands in full sight, and less than three miles off.

GENERAL BENJAMIN H. GRIERSON.

General Grierson was born in Pittsburg, Pa., July 8th, 1826. At an early age he removed to Trumbull County, O., and was subsequently engaged in the produce business at Jacksonville, Ill. At the beginning of the Civil War he became aid-de-camp to General Prentiss; was made major of the Sixth Illinois Cavalry, in August, 1861; became colonel, March 28th, 1862, and commander of a cavalry brigade in December. He was engaged in nearly all the cavalry skirmishes and raids in Western Tennessee and Northern Mississippi, and in April, 1863, made a successful cavalry raid from La Grange to Baton Rouge to facilitate General Grant's operations about Vicksburg. He became a brigadier general of volunteers on June 3d, 1863; major general, May 27th, 1865; colonel of the Tenth United States Cavalry, July 28th, 1866; and was brevetted brigadier and major general, United States Army, March 2d, 1867, for his expedition of December, 1864, against the Mobile and Ohio Railroad.

GENERAL BENJAMIN HARRISON.

General Benjamin Harrison, twenty-third President of the United States, was born at North Bend, Ohio, August 20th, 1833; was graduated at Miami University in Ohio in 1852; studied law in Cincinnati, and in 1854 removed to Indianapolis, Ind., where he has since resided. He was elected Reporter of the State Supreme Court in 1860, and in 1862 entered the army as a second lieutenant of Indiana Volunteers. After a short service he organized a company of the Seventieth Indiana Regiment, was commissioned colonel on the completion of the organization, and served through the war, receiving the brevet of brigadier general of volunteers on January 23d, 1865. He then returned to Indianapolis, and resumed his office of Supreme Court Reporter, to which he had been re-elected during his absence in 1864. In 1876 he was the Republican candidate for Governor of Indiana, but was defeated by a small plurality. President Hayes appointed him on the Mississippi River Commission in 1878, and in 1880 he was elected United States Senator, taking his seat on March 4th, 1881. He was Delegate at Large to the Republican National Convention in 1884. On June 19th, 1888, at Chicago, Ill., and on the eighth and final ballot, he had received 544 votes to 118 for John Sherman, 100 for Russell A. Alger, 59 for Walter Q. Gresham, 5 for James G. Blaine and 4 for William McKinley, as the candidate of that party for President. The nomination was made unanimous, and in November he was elected, receiving 233 votes in the Electoral College to 168 for Grover Cleveland. He was duly inaugurated, March 4th, 1889.

THE WAR IN LOUISIANA—GENERAL BANKS'S ARMY, IN THE ADVANCE ON SHREVEPORT, CROSSING CANE RIVER, MARCH 31ST, 1864.

We give a view of the Army of the Gulf, under General Franklin, crossing the Cane River by bridges and pontoons, on March 31st, 1864. The point sketched is about fifty-four miles from Alexandria.

'THE WAR IN VIRGINIA—GENERAL BUTLER'S LINES SOUTH OF THE JAMES, VA. WITH TROOPS IN POSITION NEAR THE FEDERAL CENTRE, AWAITING AN ATTACK PREVIOUS TO THE ARRIVAL OF GENERAL GRANT'S ARMY, JUNE 3d, 1864.

The sudden transfer of operations by General Grant from the old battle ground on the Chickahominy, historic from the bloody campaign of 1862, and laden with the deadly miasm of the Chickahominy swamps, to the point south of the James River occupied by General Butler, gave that comparatively fresh locality additional interest to the public. We lay before our readers a sketch of the fortifications between the James and the Appomattox. Our view is taken from within, showing the shelter tents inside the works, and the men manning the line, awaiting an attack of the enemy.

419

THE WAR IN VIRGINIA—A REGIMENT OF THE EIGHTEENTH CORPS CARRYING A PORTION OF BEAUREGARD'S LINE IN FRONT OF PETERSBURG.

The first line of Confederate works, on the right, was carried by Burnside's corps. Said an officer: "It was now about five o'clock P.M. We opened our battery at once and commenced shelling the Confederate fort. In five minutes we had three wounded. We kept on firing for about half an hour, when our infantry—Griffin's brigade—made a charge and captured the fort, taking five guns and about 200 prisoners. We had, we found, dismounted the Confederate guns by our shells." The works on the left were carried, after a desperate fight, by the Eighteenth Corps, of which we give a near view.

THE WAR IN GEORGIA—CAPTURE OF LOST MOUNTAIN BY GENERAL HOOKER, JUNE 16TH, 1864.

On June 14th General Hooker pushed forward, with Geary in the advance, and soon came up with the enemy. Having driven the Confederates from two hills, Geary, being without support upon his right, was forced to halt. Butterfield and Williams having arrived and formed in open fields on the right of Geary's position, about three o'clock P.M. General Hooker ordered an advance of the corps. The lines moved forward, driving the enemy's pickets rapidly before them, halting now and then a moment to dislodge some of the more stubborn of the Confederates, who maintained their fire until almost under the feet of the advancing troops. General Geary's division was the first to encounter the enemy in strong force, with whom one or two sharp volleys were exchanged, and they then fell back to their strongly intrenched lines, from which they opened a terrible fire. This was the commencement of a fierce struggle, which lasted until after dark. Under the cover of darkness the enemy threw out a strong line of skirmishers. The morning of the 15th opened with heavy firing, resulting in repelling an attack of the Confederates to break the picket lines of Geary's Second and Third Brigades. Artillery was placed along the lines, and took a prominent part in the struggle, which continued with varying intensity till after

421

SHERMAN'S CAMPAIGN IN GEORGIA.—THE ATTACK OF THE FOURTEENTH, SIXTEENTH AND TWENTIETH ARMY CORPS ON KENESAW MOUNTAIN, JUNE 22D, 1864.

Kenesaw Mountain, a second Lookout among its fellows, is about four miles in length and some four hundred feet high, difficult of ascent, with spurs on the flanks, and presenting a most dignified appearance. Sherman resolved to flank it, and on June 22d the corps of the right and left of his army advanced, the centre maintaining its position around and upon the base of the mountain in the teeth of a very heavy artillery fire from the Confederate batteries. The Twentieth and Twenty-third wheeled on the left to hem in the Confederates between the Federal line and the railroad. The Fourteenth Kentucky met the enemy first, who charged furiously to check the movement. Schofield and Hooker were, however, ready. Williams's division drove back the enemy with artillery alone, without the employment of a musket. Batteries I and M of the First New York had second position, which gave them a cross fire upon the Confederates as they advanced over an open field, and it proved entirely too hot for them. Again, about six o'clock, they made the same attempt, and were driven back still more rapidly by a combined fire of artillery and musketry, which must, from the openness of the ground, have proved very destructive. The Federal losses were slight. They did not exceed two hundred killed and wounded during the day, and one-quarter of this loss was suffered by the Fourteenth Kentucky.

THE SIEGE OF PETERSBURG, VA.—CHARGE OF THE SECOND DIVISION, NINTH ARMY CORPS, INTO THE CRATER, JULY 30TH, 1864.

The charge made finally by the Second Division of the Ninth Army Corps is shown from the hand of one who witnessed it near by. It was made bravely, but from faults which could not be explained valuable time had been lost, officers were absent, and the result was a sad slaughter of men which the country could not afford to lose. On arriving at the exploded fort the Federals found it a heterogeneous mass of loose earth, guns and gun carriages, dead and wounded gunners, etc. One of the charging officers, noticing the earth move near him as if a mole or gopher were at work under it, commenced digging, and finally extricated a Confederate lieutenant, who actually revived and conversed freely with the officer before being brought from the ground. Several others were exhumed from their living graves and restored to consciousness.

THE WAR IN VIRGINIA—SHERIDAN'S GREAT BATTLE WITH J. E. B. S

We give a sketch, which our readers cannot fail to admire, of the battle of Yellow Tavern, May 11th, 1864, where General J. E. B. Stuart, whose
composing the outer line of the Richmond defenses. The position was a strong one, being situated upon a hill, commanding our whole corps, with d
general ordered Custer to take his gallant brigade and carry the position. General Custer placed himself at the head of his command, and with dr
ammunition and horses, which he brought off in safety. It was, without exception, the most gallant charge of the raid, and when it became known
Gregg's brigade of the Second Division, under General Wilson, was hotly engaged with Stuart. General Wilson sent word to General Sheridan that
Gregg's brigade being re-enforced by a regiment from the First Brigade, charged the enemy and drove them nearly a mile. The day was now ours,
which in turn withdrew and also crossed, without being annoyed by the enemy." In a desperate charge at the head of a column the Confederate g

TAVERN, MAY 11TH, 1864—THE CONFEDERATE RAIDER'S LAST FIGHT.

cessful raid around McClellan, fell mortally wounded. Our correspondent wrote: "We found the enemy very strongly intrenched behind fortifications nded on our driving them out. General Sheridan was equal to the emergency. The enemy was already pursuing us closely in the rear. The ing cheers charged directly in the face of a withering fire, captured two pieces of artillery, upward of one hundred prisoners, together with caissons, er after cheer rent the air. The Confederates retreated behind the Chickahominy, destroying in their flight Meadow Bridge. In the rear, Colonel ng him slowly back. General Sheridan replied that he must hold the position at all hazards—that he could and must whip the enemy. Colonel ppeared from our front, and we succeeded in rebuilding the Meadow Bridge, and the First and Third Divisions crossed, covered by the Second Division, tally wounded.

THE SIEGE OF PETERSBURG—BATTLE OF REAM'S STATION.—THE ATTEMPT OF THE ENEMY TO REGAIN THE WELDON RAILROAD ON THE EVENING OF AUGUST 25TH, 1864.

The enemy having been repulsed, the Federal skirmishers followed, advancing nearly to the position they had formerly held, and capturing a number of prisoners. Shortly after the enemy again advanced, and were again driven back with heavy loss; and their third assault, made about four o'clock P. M., was attended with a like satisfactory result. In the first three charges the enemy used no artillery, but about five o'clock P. M. they opened a heavy, concentrated fire from a number of batteries, pouring a storm of shell and other missiles over the entire amphitheatre included within the Federal lines. After about twenty minutes of this artillery fire the enemy again made their appearance in front of General Miles's division, their assault being directed mainly against his centre. The Federal artillery and musketry greeted them, as before, with a rapid fire, but without checking their progress. On they came, with bayonets fixed and without firing a shot. They approached the Federal lines, gained the outside of their intrenchments, and at some points a hand-to-hand conflict ensued over the top of the breastworks, the Federals beating back the Confederates with their bayonets as they attempted to climb over. But soon it was found that the Federal line was broken near the centre, and the gap once made grew wider, until nearly the entire line was swept back, leaving the Federal breastworks and artillery in the hands of the enemy. General Miles, with great coolness, set to work to rally the men, and in a short time succeeded in forming a line with its right resting against the breastworks. At the same time General Hancock ordered the Second Division to be faced about, and cheering and urging the men forward, led them in person in a charge at double-quick. This charge, which was made under a heavy fire, was gallantly executed, and in conjunction with the line rallied by General Miles instantly checked the enemy and regained the intrenchments for some distance further toward the left. After the enemy had been checked in the centre and along that portion of the line against which they had chiefly directed their attack the greater part of the Second Division returned to their own intrenchments. By this time it was dark and the fighting ended. Our sketch shows the repulse of the last Confederate assault.

426

HOWLETT'S CONFEDERATE BATTERY ON THE JAMES RIVER, VA., SHELLING THE FEDERAL MONITORS AND LABORERS ON THE DUTCH GAP CANAL.

Our sketch, derived from a Confederate source, represents the battery which annoyed the Federal gunboats on the James River and retarded the labor on the Dutch Gap Canal. This Confederate work was situated on the upper side of the James, in almost a northerly direction from Dutch Gap. The illustration representing it is very spirited, and will enable our readers to comprehend at a glance both the character of the enterprise and the peril under which it was prosecuted. Our sketch represents the gunners at work. In the distance are seen the obstructions which defended the river at the end of Farrar's Island. Dutch Gap, which is more to the left, does not appear in the picture. Its position is, however, sufficiently indicated by the direction of the guns and shells.

VIEW OF SAVANNAH, GA., LOOKING EAST, TOWARD FORT JACKSON.

Savannah, the entry port of Georgia, is built on a sandy plain, forty feet above low-water mark. It is the centre of a very extensive system of railroads, which contribute greatly to its commercial importance. As a harbor f r blockade runners it was not of much importance after Fort Pulaski fell into the Federal hands. Savannah was founded by General Oglethorpe in 1732. The river is navigable for steamers up to Augusta, 230 miles from i s mouth, Savannah itself being 18 miles from the sea. Our view was taken from the cupola of the Exchange, looking east, with Fort Jackson on the left.

BLOWING OUT OF THE BULKHEAD OF THE DUTCH GAP CANAL, JAMES RIVER, VA., JANUARY 1ST, 1865.

At twelve minutes before four o'clock A. M. the mine was sprung, in the presence of General Butler and staff. A dense black smoke, at first immediately following the upheaval of the earth, was succeeded by a ponderous cloud of white smoke, which entirely filled the gap and concealed the result of the scheme. On rolling away it revealed the bank settled again into nearly its former position, but indented with a species of crater, into which the water ran slowly from the canal below. No connection between the canal and the river was immediately established, although, as we have intimated, the disturbance of the embankment disposed it suitably for the gradual action of the current, and lightened the subsequent labors of the gang.

VIEW OF RICHMOND, VA, FROM THE PRISON CAMP AT BELLE ISLE, JAMES RIVER.

Belle Island is situated in the James River, a little above the bridge which connects the Richmond and Petersburg Railroad. It is about an acre and a half, and in this small space there were on an average ten thousand Federal soldiers imprisoned and slowly tortured. The Confederate capital has been so often described that we shall confine ourselves to the special view before us. The prominent building is the Capitol; the five churches on the left are St. Paul's, First Baptist, St. James's, Second Baptist and Grace Street Methodist; the large building at the end of the bridge is Haxall's flouring mill, the largest one of the kind in the world, being thirteen stories high.

THE BATTLE OF BENTONVILLE, N. C.—MAJOR GENERAL MOWER, COMMANDING FIRST DIVISION, SEVENTEENTH CORPS, TURNING THE CONFEDERATE LEFT, HALF A MILE, FROM BENTONVILLE, MARCH 20TH, 1865.

This pretty and thriving little town, in Johnston County, N. C., was the scene of a desperate struggle between a portion of General Sherman's army on the 20th of March, 1865. Our artist has given a spirited sketch of a brilliant dash upon the Confederate forces by a division of the Seventeenth Corps, commanded by General Mower, and spoke with great admiration of the dogged valor of a Confederate captain who refused to surrender his gun. A sharp encounter ensued between him and one of the Federal soldiers, in which the unfortunate Confederate got his brains dashed out with the butt-end of a musket. The defeat of the Confederates was very much attributed to the brilliant charge made upon their lines by which their right was flanked. When the Federal troops entered, it was found that the retreating Confederates had fired a large

431

SHERMAN'S "BUMMERS" FORAGING IN SOUTH CAROLINA.

Our artist sent us with this sketch of "Bummers Foraging," a graphic account of their *modus operandi*. He wrote: "These active and unscrupulous fellows generally started out every morning mounted on very mean horseflesh, and, as a general rule, they always came back very well mounted, with the animals they rode in the morning laden, with all the good things of this world. In one place in South Carolina they came to a large plantation owned by a leading Confederate named Fitzgerald. Here the Federal soldiers found, buried in various out-of-the-way places, an immense quantity of gold and silver plate, of the aggregate value of over $70,000; here they also found a large quantity of the finest Madeira wine, which had been stowed away in the old gentleman's wine cellar for nearly thirty years. Indeed, as a general thing, it may be said that the

THE SIEGE OF ATLANTA, GA.—CONFEDERATE ATTACK ON GENERAL LOGAN'S CORPS, JULY 28TH, 1864.

SHERIDAN'S CAMPAIGN IN THE SHENANDOAH VALLEY—THE FEDERAL FORCES FALLING BACK THROUGH CHARLESTOWN, AUGUST 21ST, 1864.

RUINS OF CONFEDERATE FORT ON THE SOUTHEAST SIDE OF ATLANTA, WITH CHEVAUX-DE-FRISE AND ABATIS IN FRONT.

THE WAR IN VIRGINIA—EXPLOSION OF A TORPEDO UNDER THE "COMMODORE BARNEY," ON JAMES RIVER, AUGUST 4TH, 1863.

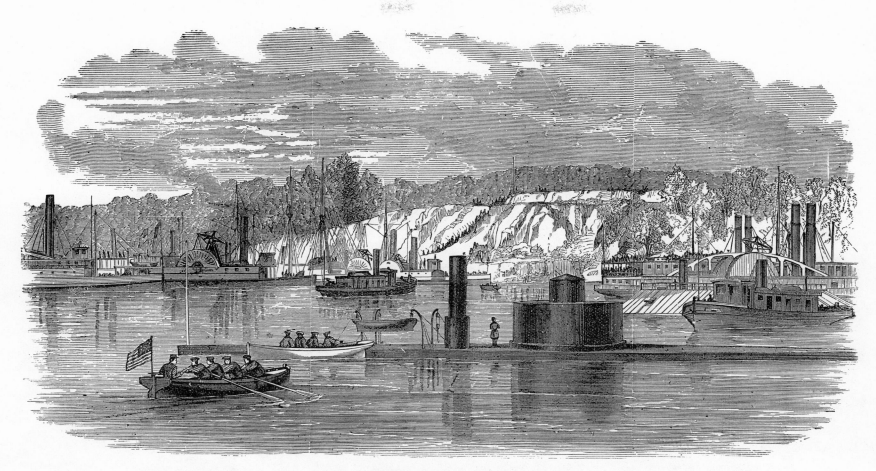

THE CAMPAIGN ON THE JAMES RIVER—GENERAL BUTLER LANDING AT FORT PAWHATAN.

FARRAGUT'S NAVAL VICTORY IN MOBILE HARBOR—THE "HARTFORD" ENGAGING THE CONFEDERATE RAM "TENNESSEE."

435

BATTLE OF RESACA, GA., MAY 14TH, 1864—GEARY'S SECOND BRIGADE CHARGING UP THE MOUNTAIN.

SHERMAN'S CAMPAIGN—THE CAPTURE OF BUZZARD'S ROOST AT HOVEY GAP, GA., MAY 8TH, 1864.

THE WAR IN VIRGINIA—THE EIGHTEENTH ARMY CORPS STORMING A FORT ON THE RIGHT OF THE CONFEDERATE LINE
BEFORE PETERSBURG, JUNE 15TH, 1864.

THE WAR IN VIRGINIA—THE TWENTY-SECOND COLORED REGIMENT, DUNCAN'S BRIGADE, CARRYING THE FIRST LINE
OF CONFEDERATE WORKS BEFORE PETERSBURG.

SHERMAN'S CAMPAIGN IN GEORGIA—THE BATTLE OF RESACA.

SIEGE OF PETERSBURG—THE COLORED INFANTRY BRINGING IN CAPTURED GUNS AMID CHEERS OF THE OHIO TROOPS.

SHERMAN'S SEVENTEENTH CORPS CROSSING THE SOUTH EDISTO RIVER, S. C., ON PONTOONS, AT BENNAKER'S BRIDGE, FEBRUARY 9TH, 1865.

THE CAMPAIGN IN GEORGIA—A BAGGAGE TRAIN CROSSING THE MOUNTAINS IN A STORM.

BOMBARDMENT OF PORT HU[DSON]

ASSAULT OF THE SECOND LOUISIANA COLORED REGI[MENT]

FARRAGUT'S FLEET.

CONFEDERATE WORKS AT PORT HUDSON, MAY 27TH, 1863.

SHERIDAN'S CAMPAIGN—BATTLE OF WINCHESTER—CHARGE OF CROOK'S EIGHTH CORPS—THE RIGHT.

SHERIDAN'S CAMPAIGN—BATTLE OF WINCHESTER—POSITION OF THE NINETEENTH CORPS GENERAL EMORY, SEPTEMBER 19th, 1864—THE CENTRE.

BATTLE OF MIDDLETOWN, ON THE AFTERNOON OF THE 19th OF OCTOBER, 1864—GREAT VICTORY WON BY MAJOR GENERAL SHERIDAN.

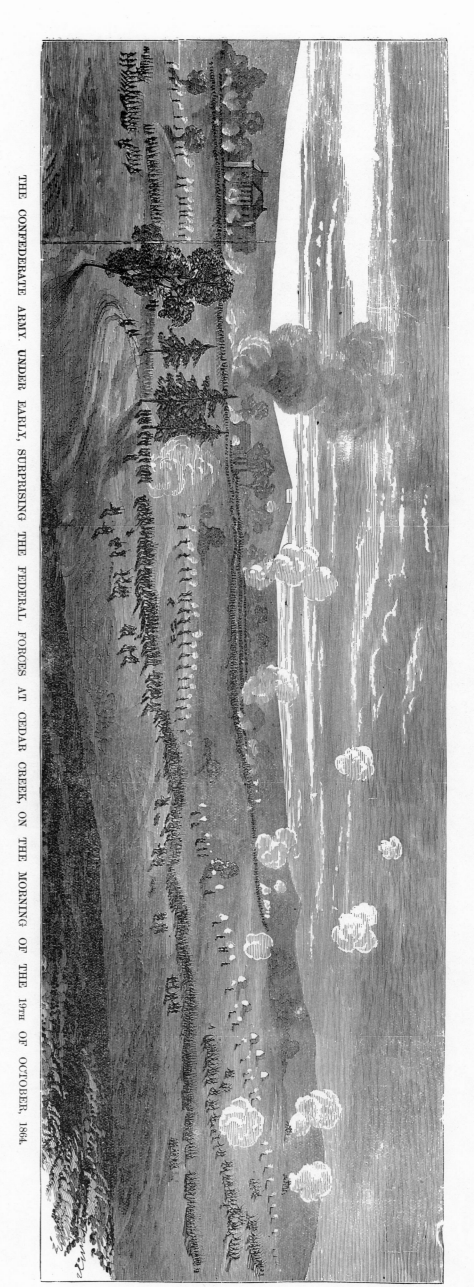

THE CONFEDERATE ARMY, UNDER EARLY, SURPRISING THE FEDERAL FORCES AT CEDAR CREEK, ON THE MORNING OF THE 19th OF OCTOBER, 1864.

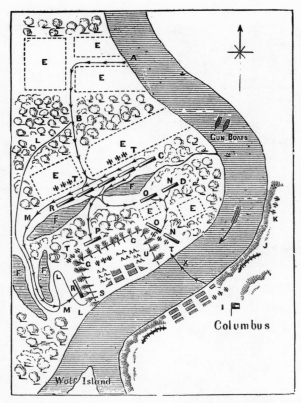

PLAN OF THE BATTLE OF BELMONT, MO., FOUGHT NOVEMBER 7TH, 1861.

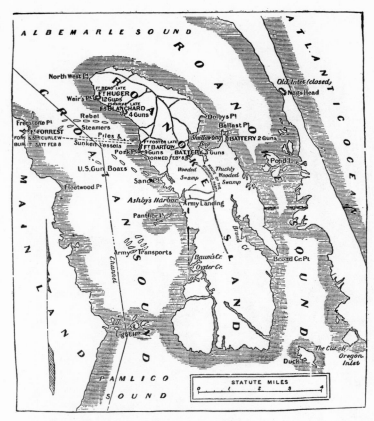

MAP OF ROANOKE ISLAND AND CROATAN AND ROANOKE SOUNDS.

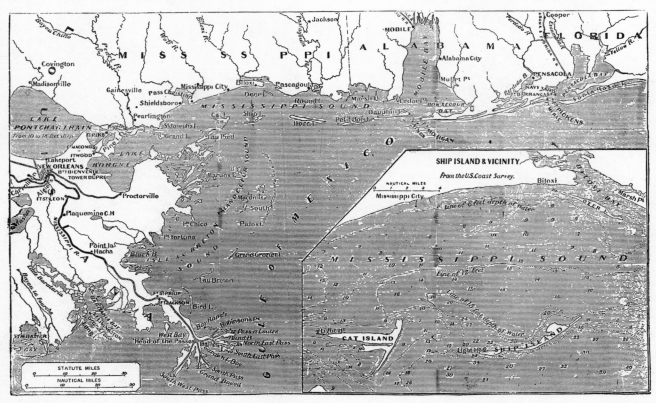

MAP OF THE SOUTHERN COAST OF THE UNITED STATES FROM PENSACOLA TO NEW ORLEANS, SHOWING THE STRATEGIC POSITION OF SHIP ISLAND, MISS.

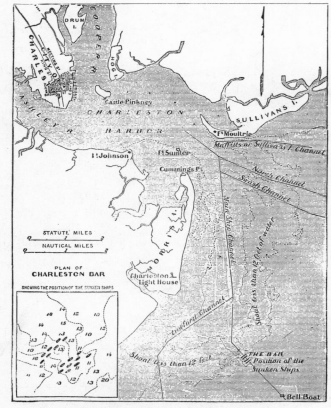

MAP OF THE HARBOR AND CITY OF CHARLESTON, S. C.

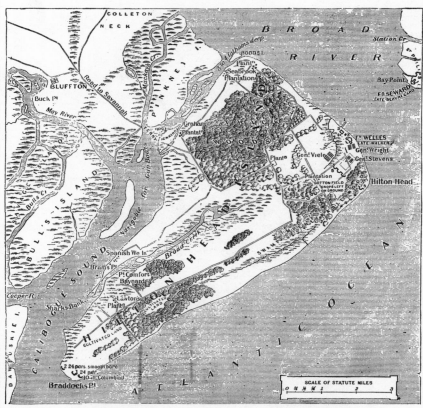

MAP OF HILTON HEAD ISLAND, SHOWING THE TOPOGRAPHY.

OFFICIAL MAPS AND PLANS OF BATTLES IN THE CIVIL WAR.—FURNISHED BY C. A. DANA, OF THE WAR DEPARTMENT.

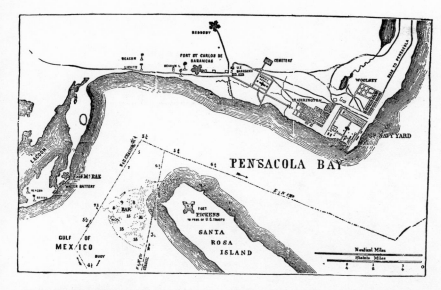

MAP OF PENSACOLA BAY, FLA., SHOWING THE SITUATION OF THE U. S. NAVY YARD,
FORT PICKENS, M'RAE, WATER BATTERY AND FORT SAN CARLOS DE BARRANCAS.

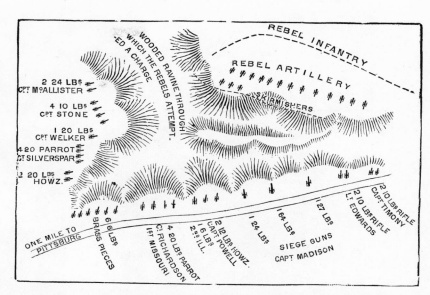

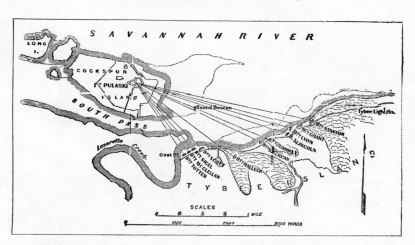

BATTLE OF PITTSBURG LANDING—PLAN SHOWING THE POSITIONS OF THE FORCES
DURING THE GREAT ARTILLERY FIGHT.

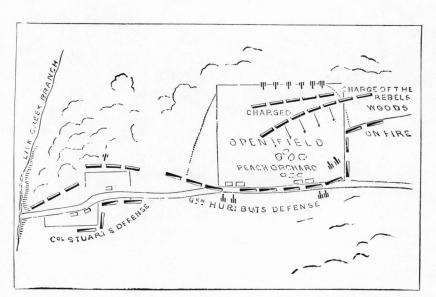

BATTLE OF PITTSBURG LANDING—PLAN OF THE DEFENSE AT THE PEACH ORCHARD.
LEFT WING.

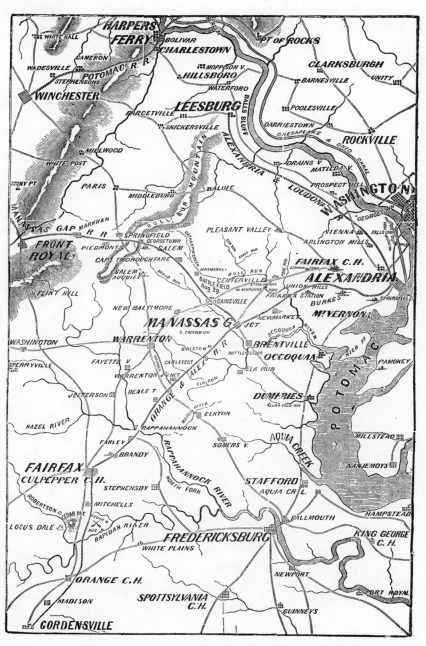

MAP OF FORT PULASKI, GA., WITH THE POSITIONS OF THE FEDERAL BATTERIES
ON TYBEE ISLAND.

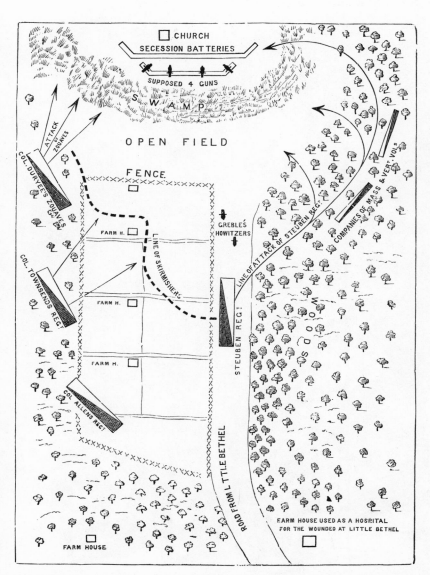

PLAN OF THE BATTLE OF GREAT BETHEL, SHOWING THE POSITION OF THE MASKED BATTERY
OF THE CONFEDERATES AND THE POSITION OF THE FEDERAL TROOPS.

SEAT OF WAR IN VIRGINIA, SHOWING THE OPERATIONS OF THE FEDERAL
AND CONFEDERATE ARMIES.

OFFICIAL MAPS AND PLANS OF BATTLES IN THE CIVIL WAR.—FURNISHED BY C. A. DANA, OF THE WAR DEPARTMENT.

SHERIDAN'S CAMPAIGN—AN INCIDENT AT THE BATTLE OF WINCHESTER—A FAITHFUL DOG WATCHING AND DEFENDING
THE DEAD BODY OF HIS CONFEDERATE MASTER.

VOLUNTARY DISPERSION OF KIRBY SMITH'S CONFEDERATE ARMY AT SHREVEPORT, LA., MAY 23D, 1865.

SHERMAN'S CAMPAIGN IN GEORGIA—FEDERAL FORCES AT JONESBOROUGH DESTROYING THE MACON RAILROAD.

THE WAR IN GEORGIA—WAGON TRAIN PASSING RESACA AT NIGHT.

SIGNALING WITH A PIECE OF LOOKING GLASS.

CUTTING COARSE FORAGE INTO CHAFF.

WATER SKIN AND MODE OF CARRYING.

HINTS TO SOLDIERS IN THE CAMP AND ON CAMPAIGN.

AN INCIDENT OF THE BATTLE OF THE WILDERNESS—LIEUTENANT GENERAL GRANT AND MAJOR GENERAL MEADE
IN CONSULTATION.

FRANK LESLIE'S
ILLUSTRATED HISTORY
OF THE
CIVIL WAR.

CHAPTER I.

EVENTS LEADING TO THE WAR — GROWING ANTAGONISM OF THE NORTH AND SOUTH—ELECTION OF BUCHANAN— THE "DRED SCOTT CASE" DECISION—SLAVERY CONSIDERED A NATIONAL INSTITUTION—PLOTTING FOR DISUNION—JOHN BROWN'S RAID—ELECTION OF LINCOLN—FORMATION OF THE CONFEDERACY.

ALTHOUGH the bombardment of Fort Sumter by the Confederates at Charleston marked the real opening of the Civil War and gave the signal for the beginning of active hostilities, the conflict between the two sections of the country had begun long before. For years previous to the firing of the first gun the North and South were arrayed against each other in a heated controversy on the question of slavery. Year after year the feeling between the two sections became more and more hostile, until at last a separation, or an attempted separation, seemed inevitable.

Then, in 1856, the question of whether slavery was to be allowed to grow and extend itself beyond the limits set for it by the Missouri Compromise Law was in a measure given to the people to decide through the Presidential election. A new party had arisen as a result of the anti-slavery sentiment in the North, and its platform declared against the extension of slavery. But the two branches of the Democratic party, one of them in favor of an anti-slavery policy and the other composed of friends and supporters of the slave system, were united against the new Republican party, and elected their candidate, James Buchanan.

In addition to this victory the slaveholders were aided by an important decision on the rights of the slave, rendered by the Supreme Court just after the inauguration of President Buchanan. In this decision, which was in answer to an appeal to the court in the famous "Dred Scott case," it was declared that a person who had been a slave, or was the descendant of a slave, had no right to citizenship. Then Chief Justice Taney went further, and in an extrajudicial opinion said that the framers of the Declaration of Independence did not include the negro race when it proclaimed "all men are created equal"; that the negroes had always been regarded as inferior beings, so much so that they had no rights which the white man was bound to respect, and that it was not unlawful to reduce the negro to slavery for the benefit of the white man. Then the Chief Justice took up the Missouri Compromise Act, and declared that law and all other laws for the restriction of slavery unconstitutional, and that neither Congress nor local legislatures had any authority for restricting the spread of the institu-

tion all over the Union. This decision, following on the election of a President who was not opposed to the slave system, was taken by many people as a settlement of the controversy—slavery was a national institution, and could exist in any part of the Union. But in the breasts of the lovers of freedom it stirred up indignation, and large numbers of the dominant party immediately enrolled themselves with the Republicans. The Legislature of the State of New York denounced the decision that descendants of slaves had no right to citizen-

GENERAL JOHN E. WOOL.

ship, and determined to sustain the statute in that State's code of laws which declared the immediate freedom of slaves brought involuntarily within its borders. Ohio, Maine, Massachusetts, Connecticut, Wisconsin and Michigan also declared strongly in favor of the freedom of slaves within its borders.

This movement on the part of the people of the free-labor States is just what the politicians of the South expected and hoped for. They had long looked for a good pretext to cause the feeling between the two sections of the country to become bitter and strong enough to bring about a disunion, and they noted with pleasure the indignation of the slaveholders over the action of the Northern States. Everything in their power was done by these politi-

cians to feed this indignation. For a time after this nothing particular occurred to disturb the condition of the country. Then suddenly, in the year 1859, the first blow at slavery was struck. John Brown, a native of Connecticut, with a handful of white followers and twelve slaves from Missouri, had secretly devised a plan for the freedom of the slaves. On the 16th of October Brown, with his little army, entered the village of Harper's Ferry, at the junction of the Shenandoah and Potomac Rivers, and seized the government armory and the railroad bridge. On their way the invaders entered the house of Colonel Washington, seized his arms and horses and liberated his slaves. The next morning Brown had full possession of the village and government buildings. His only purpose was a desire to free the slaves. He felt confident that if he made a stand for them they would all rise up in arms and flock to his standard, and he would at once be hailed as a great liberator. But his hopes were soon dashed to pieces. The Virginia militia, aided by a detachment of United States marines under Colonel Robert E. Lee, soon dislodged him and made him prisoner, but not before he had made a brave defense and lost two of his sons. Brown was immediately tried, found guilty of murder and treason, and sentenced to death. He was hanged at Charlestown, Va., December 3d, 1859.

The suspicion that Brown was an emissary of the Abolitionists, and that the leaders of the Republican party were in league with him in his scheme to liberate the slaves, turned out to be unfounded after an investigation by a committee of the United States Senate.

While John Brown's well-meaning effort at emancipation resulted in utter failure, as might have been expected, and had no immediate effect, it served to stir up the combatants on both sides of the question of slavery to such an extent that there was no rest until the matter was finally settled forever. It gained for the Republican party, whose platform was universal freedom, thousands of new followers, and thus helped to make possible the election of that party's candidate for President in 1860.

When the politicians of the South saw in the rapidly growing anti-slavery sentiment the probable overthrow of the domination of the friends of the slave system in the National Government they immediately laid plans to break up the Union and establish a new and separate government, whose corner stone would be slavery. To do this they saw that they must find some stronger cause for a contest between the two sections than any that had heretofore arisen. They decided that the success of the Republican candidate at the coming election would be of great help to them, as they could then at once raise the cry: "No sectional President! No Northern domination! Down with the Abolitionists!" This, they knew, would bring out a strong resentment among the people of the South, especially the slaveholding class, and produce a solid South in favor of breaking up the old republic. So they resolved to insure the election of a Republican by so hopelessly splitting the Democratic party that it would have no chance in the contest. In this determination they were eminently successful. The result was the election of Abraham Lincoln as President of the United States.

Immediately after this election South Carolina seceded from the Union by the holding of a State convention, at which it was resolved that "the union now subsisting between South Carolina and other States, under the name of the United States of America, is hereby dissolved." The other slaveholding States followed in quick succession, and on February 4th, 1861, a convention of delegates from six of the seceded States was held at Montgomery, Ala., to frame a constitution for the Confederacy and to form a provisional government. Jefferson Davis was elected President and A. H. Stephens, of Georgia, Vice President.

These, briefly outlined, were some of the most important events that took place just before the inauguration of President Lincoln, and which made way for the terrible struggle that shook this country from one end to the other.

CHAPTER II.

While preparations were being made in the South for the destruction of the Union the people of the North were preparing to preserve it. President Lincoln was inaugurated Chief Magistrate of the Republic at about the same time that Jefferson Davis took his office as President of the Confederacy. In his inaugural address Mr. Lincoln said: "We are not enemies, but friends. We must not be enemies. Though passion may have strained, it must not break our bonds of affection. The mystic chords of memory, stretching from every battlefield and patriot grave to every living heart and hearthstone all over this broad land, will yet swell the chorus of the Union, when again touched, as surely they will be, by the better angels of our nature." To the people of the slave-labor States he said: "I have no purpose, directly or indirectly, to interfere with the institution of slavery in the States where it exists. I believe I have no lawful right to do so, and I have no inclination to do so." Thus he tried to stem the tide that was rising against the Union.

President Lincoln found the resources of the government in a deplorable condition. The treasury was nearly empty, and both the army and the navy had been placed far beyond reach for immediate use. Most of the vessels in commission were in distant seas, and many of the naval and army officers, being natives of Southern States, had deserted the flag and joined the Confederates. This condition of affairs had been planned and arranged by the Secretaries of Navy and War under Buchanan, in the hopes of rendering powerless any design the new administration might have for preventing the secession.

At this time general attention was attracted to Fort Sumter, where Major Anderson had recently transferred his small body of men from Fort Moultrie because of the threatening aspect of Charleston. The question now came up as to the re-enforcement and maintenance of this fort. The President, not wishing to precipitate a war, considered the matter carefully for some time. Once before, during the administration of Buchanan, an attempt had been made to send supplies to Major Anderson, but the Confederates, learning of the attempt from Secretary Thompson, prevented the entry into the harbor of the *Star of the West*, containing the provisions

LOADING A 15-INCH GUN IN THE TURRET OF AN ERICSSON IRONCLAD DURING THE ATTACK ON FORT SUMTER.

and arms, by firing upon her from redoubts on Morris Island.

After due deliberation, and notwithstanding the result of this attempt, President Lincoln and his Cabinet decided that Fort Sumter must be maintained and re-enforced. For this purpose a squadron of eight vessels was sent from New York on the 9th of April. Only three of these ships reached Charleston harbor, and they could not enter at once because of a great storm that was then raging on the ocean in that region. It was while these vessels were rolling about in the tempest that the Confederate batteries in Charleston attacked Fort Sumter. Major Anderson had been compelled by his government to remain passive in his fort while preparations were being made all around him for an attack upon his position. He had orders to do nothing until he was fired upon. So while he saw the forts and batteries being rapidly erected on all sides of Fort Sumter, he was powerless to stop the work with his guns. As soon as the strength of the Confederate position in Charleston harbor was assured the leaders in the work of disunion became eager for the fray, and sought a pretext for the firing of the first gun. The

pretext was found when President Lincoln, on April 8th, telegraphed to Governor Pickens that he was sending relief to Fort Sumter. This message was communicated to L. Pope Walker, the Confederate Secretary of War, who immediately sent word to General Beauregard, who was in command of the army in Charleston, to demand the evacuation of the fort, and if this was refused to proceed in such manner as he might determine to reduce it. Early next morning the demand for the immediate surrender of Fort Sumter was made. Anderson saw that the supplies for his garrison were nearly exhausted, and accordingly replied: "I will evacuate the fort in five days if I do not receive controlling instructions from my government." But this would not satisfy the leaders in the movement against the Union, as they well knew that fresh supplies were then on their way to the fort. So, in reply, Beauregard sent word early in the morning of April 12th that within one hour the batteries, which formed a semicircle around Sumter, would open upon the fort.

Anderson calmly accepted this communication and awaited the beginning of hostilities. Promptly at the appointed time the first shot ushering in the great four years' war for the Union was fired. It was a large bombshell from a mortar on James Island, and exploded over the fort. It is said that the next shot, which struck the granite wall of the fort, was fired by an old Virginian by the name of Ruffin, who boasted of his deed all his life, and who shot himself in 1865 because, as he said, "I cannot survive the liberties of my country." Hundreds of shells and balls followed these shots, and a fearful contest began. Anderson replied with all the power he could muster, but he soon saw that his guns could not seriously injure the batteries opposed to him, while the walls and parapets of Fort Sumter were soon shattered, its barbette guns dismounted, and its barracks set on fire.

All day long and through the night the assault continued, and the next morning it was pushed with renewed energy. When the sun rose the little garrison was in a terrible condition. The provisions would not last much longer, almost all of the wooden structures in the fort were on fire, and the heat and smoke were so unbearable that the men were compelled to put wet cloths over their faces to breathe. The fierce bombardment continued until General Wigfall, who said he represented Beauregard, arrived at the fort in a small boat and said that Anderson's terms of evacuation would be acceded to. Then the gallant major raised the white flag, which immediately brought a deputation from Beauregard, who declared that Wigfall did not represent their chief in any way. This deception angered Anderson, and he ordered the white flag torn down at once. But upon the persuasion of the deputation the flag was left standing until a conference could be held with Beauregard. This conference resulted in a satisfactory arrangement for the evacuation of Fort Sumter, and on Sunday, April 14th, 1861, the brave defenders of the fort were conveyed to the steamship *Baltic*, that lay outside the bar, and in which they were taken to New York.

In a speech delivered to the people of Charleston just after the evacuation Governor Pickens said, among other things: "Thank God the war is open, and we will conquer or perish. We have humbled the flag of the United States. I can here say to you, it is the first time in the history of this country that the Stars and Stripes have been humbled. That proud flag was never lowered before to any nation on the earth. It has triumphed for seventy years. But to-day, the 13th of April, it has been humbled, and humbled before the glorious little State of South Carolina." The next day, Sunday, the fall of Sumter was commemorated by sermons and songs in the churches of Charleston. Everyone spoke exultingly of the result of the conflict.

The gallant defense of the fort by Major Anderson received due recognition in the

throughout every free-labor State. Flags went up everywhere, even on the spires of churches and cathedrals, and women and children wore red, white and blue dresses and ornaments. Cannons were fired, and enthusiastic meetings, addressed by eloquent orators, were held in every part of the North. The calls of the different Governors for troops in response to the President's proclamation brought forth five or six times the number of volunteers called for, and soldiers were soon on their way to Washington to protect it from a threatened invasion.

Immediately upon learning of President Lincoln's action the chief of the Southern Confederacy also issued a call for troops from the Southern States, and it was received with the same enthusiasm as was manifested over the Northern call.

It was at this time that Virginia, which had been wavering between the two sec-

Another assault by the Virginia troops was directed against the navy yard at Gosport, opposite Norfolk, on the Elizabeth River, and was more successful. It contained about two thousand pieces of heavy cannon, a large amount of munitions of war, naval stores, etc., and in the waters around it were several war ships. The post was in charge of Commodore Charles S. McCauley, who, for fear they would be seized, had the vessels in the river scuttled and sunk. Just as this had been accomplished, Captain Paulding, who had recently been appointed to McCauley's place, arrived on the scene, and ordered the further destruction of all the public property at the navy yard. But when the Confederates broke into the post they managed to save a vast number of heavy guns and some of the vessels. One of the latter, the *Merrimac*, they afterward converted into a powerful ironclad.

SCENE IN CAMP NEAR FALMOUTH, VA.—ARMY BLACKSMITH SHOEING A REFRACTORY MULE.

North. The loyal people of New York, Philadelphia and Taunton, Mass., showed their gratitude by substantial tokens, and the President of the United States at once commissioned the major a brigadier general in the army.

The roar of the cannon in Charleston harbor awoke the people of the North to a proper appreciation of the seriousness of the trouble that had come upon them. They forgot all minor differences and political animosities, and presented a solid front in their loyalty to the Union. The President, who at first hardly grasped the significance of the fact that several States, one after the other, had thrown off their allegiance to the republic and seized all the forts and arsenals within their borders, was aroused, and on the day after the evacuation of Sumter issued a proclamation in which he called for 75,000 troops to protect the Union. A loud shout of approval and enthusiasm greeted this call

tions, declared herself out of the Union. The people were summoned to arms, and preparations were at once made to capture the armory and arsenal of the United States at Harper's Ferry. Here were stored almost ninety thousand muskets. The commander of this post, Lieutenant Roger Jones, had learned of the impending danger and was fully prepared for it. As soon as he heard that about two thousand Virginia militia were on their way to seize the post and were but a mile away, he set fire to all the government buildings by means of a train of gunpowder that he had carefully laid, and escaped with his little garrison of forty men across a railroad bridge into Maryland, and thence to Carlisle Barracks in Pennsylvania. The Virginians were thus prevented from securing the large quantity of firearms they expected; but they took possession of Harper's Ferry and made it an important point for future operations.

This important post was recovered by the Federals early in May, the following year.

CHAPTER III.

PREPARATIONS FOR SEIZING THE CAPITAL — ANSWERING THE CALL FOR TROOPS—THE SIXTH MASSACHUSETTS REGIMENT ATTACKED BY A MOB — CRITICAL CONDITION OF WASHINGTON—ASSASSINATION OF COLONEL ELLSWORTH—BATTLE OF BIG BETHEL.

SOON after the call for troops had been made on both sides the leaders of the Confederacy began active preparations for the capture of the national capital. Alexander H. Stephens started the cry, "On to Washington!" and it was taken up and resounded throughout the slave-labor States. Troops were rapidly marshaled into service in Virginia, and the newspapers of the South urgently demanded the attack upon the city. One of the Richmond papers declared: "There never was half the unanimity among the people before, nor a tithe of the zeal upon any subject, that is now manifested to take Washington and drive from it every Black Republican who is a dweller there. From the mountain tops and valleys to the shores of the sea there is one wild shout of fierce resolve to capture Washington city, at all and every human hazard."

The preparations for the seizure of the capital were made in secret, and the people of the North knew nothing of the contemplated attack until the Confederates were almost ready to make it. But the call for troops had been issued, and a large body of armed men were soon on its way to protect the government and its rulers.

Massachusetts was the first to answer the President's call by sending one of its regiments, the Sixth, Colonel Jones, to Washington. Pennsylvania immediately followed, and on account of its closer proximity to Washington its regiment was the first to reach the capital. The Pennsylvanians met with a slight resistance on their arrival at Baltimore from a mob of Secessionists, who wished to make their State a barrier across the pathway of the troops from the North and East; but when the regiment from Massachusetts reached the city, and were marching from one railroad station to another, fully 10,000 persons had gathered in the streets, and assailed the soldiers with missiles of all kinds. A severe fight ensued, in which three of the troops were killed and nine of their assailants. Intense excitement was produced by this tragedy, as it was the first shedding of blood. Upon the arrival of the soldiers in Washington they found that all communication between that city and the North, by railroad and telegraph, was cut off through the orders of the Mayor and Chief of Police of Baltimore. The capital was in a critical condition, and intense anxiety was manifested throughout the free-labor States. For a time it seemed as if the city could not be saved. Then the "Union Defense Committee," a society of some of the leading citizens of New York city, held a conference with the Governor of the State (Morgan) and General John E. Wool, commander of the Eastern Department of the army, which included the whole country east of the Mississippi River. At this conference a plan of action for the relief of the capital was formed and put into operation. Troops and supplies were immediately sent forward, and in a short time the capital was put out of danger. General B. F. Butler, with a regiment of Massachusetts troops, opened communication with Washington by seizing the railroad between Annapolis and the capital and taking possession of the Relay House, nine miles from Baltimore.

It was now clearly perceived that the number of militia called out by the President's proclamation would not be adequate to cope with the force arrayed against the Union, and another proclamation was issued on May 3d, calling for 64,000 more volunteers for the army, and 18,000 for the navy, to "serve during the war." The capital soon became a vast citadel, as it was made the rendezvous for all troops raised eastward of the Alleghany Mountains. Thousands of soldiers poured into the city and were quartered in all the public buildings.

When Virginia resolved to enter the Confederacy Colonel Robert E. Lee, who was then an engineer officer in the National Army, resigned his commission and went to Richmond, where he was cordially welcomed and given the supreme command of the Confederate forces. Lee's first step was to arrange for the erection of a battery of heavy guns on Arlington Heights, which commanded a good view of the city of Washington. But before this work could be started the National troops took possession of Arlington Heights and Alexandria. Ellsworth's New York Fire Zouaves were among these troops, and crossed to Alexandria in two schooners. Another body was sent over the Long Bridge, and another the Aqueduct Bridge at Georgetown. These latter troops, under General Irwin McDowell, erected the first redoubts

REMAINS OF A CONFEDERATE CAMP AT MANASSAS.

constructed by the National troops in the Civil War. They were built on the spot where Lee proposed to erect a Confederate battery.

The Secessionists in Alexandria naturally did not relish the capture of their city by the Federals, and one of them, the proprietor of the Marshall House, showed his resentment by refusing to take down the Confederate flag flying on his roof. Seeing this, Colonel Ellsworth, with one or two of his zouaves, rushed up the stairs and pulled down the offending colors. As they descended with the flag in their hands the tavern keeper picked up a gun and shot the gallant young colonel dead, only to be immediately killed himself by one of the zouaves.

In the meantime Captain J. H. Ward had been sent to Hampton Roads, near Fortress Monroe, with a flotilla of armed vessels, to dislodge a Confederate battery on Sewells Point, at the mouth of the Elizabeth River. This was soon accomplished after a sharp engagement. Ward then sailed up the Potomac River, and at Aquia Creek, about sixty miles below Washington, he encountered some heavy batteries. A sharp fight took place, with no decisive result. A little later an attack was made on batteries at Mathias Point, and the flotilla was repulsed and Captain Ward was killed. For many months these batteries defied the National vessels, and the Potomac was effectively blockaded.

At this time, in June, 1861, the Confederate Government, in order to be nearer Washington, left Montgomery and made their headquarters at Richmond. Upon his arrival in the latter city their President, Jefferson Davis, addressed a multitude of people. He spoke some bitter words against the National Government, and after saying that there was "not one true son of the South who was not ready to shoulder his musket, to bleed, to die or to conquer in the cause of liberty here," he declared "We have now reached the point where, arguments being exhausted, it only remains for us to stand by our weapons. When the time and occasion serve, we shall smite the smiter with manly arms, as did our fathers before us and as becomes their sons. To the enemy we leave the base acts of the assassin and incendiary. To them we leave it to insult helpless women; to us belongs vengeance upon man."

The campaign in West Virginia opened briskly in May. A body of Confederates was badly routed at Philippi, and a little later they received another blow at Romney from an Indiana zouave regiment, led by Colonel Lewis Wallace. This regiment, one of the best disciplined in the field, had for some time been doing nothing in Southern Indiana, and upon Wallace's solicitation they were ordered to Cumberland, to report to General Robert Patterson, who was on his way to attack General Joseph E. Johnston, at Harper's Ferry. Wallace's regiment covered the ground between Indiana and Cumberland in three days. Then, resting a day, they started out to attack the Confederates at Romney. They reached the enemy's camp two days afterward, and at once attacked it. The result was a complete rout, the Confederates seeking shelter in the forests. These movements caused Johnston to leave Harper's Ferry and take up a position near Winchester.

While all this was going on in West Virginia there were stirring events near Fortress Monroe. The Confederates were planning to capture that post, and Colonel J. B. Magruder was sent down the Virginia Peninsula with a considerable force for that purpose; while General B. F. Butler, in command of the Department of Virginia and North Carolina, with headquarters at Fortress Monroe, was taking measures to oppose him. A detachment of troops, commanded by General E. W. Pearce, and consisting of Duryee's Fifth Zouave New York Regiment and Townsend's Third, was sent out from near Hampton to Little Bethel, where it was arranged they were to be joined by detachments from Colonel Phelps's com-

mand at Newport News, which was composed of battalions of Massachusetts and Vermont troops, the Steuben Rifle Regiment of New York, and a battery of two light field pieces in charge of Lieutenant John T. Greble, of the regular army.

As these two columns approached each other in the dead of night they unfortunately took one another for enemies and began firing. The mistake was soon discovered, but not before several men had been killed. The combined columns then marched on toward Big Bethel. The noise of the firing had put the Confederates on their guard. There was a short but sharp

day, July 4th, 1861. It was called to consider and take immediate action upon means for the salvation of the republic. The condition of the country demanded the prompt attention of its legislators. Civil war had begun in earnest. Both inside and outside the capital plans were being made to attack it. General Beauregard, with a large force of Confederates, was preparing to march upon the city, and in the halls of Congress and in the President's house secret emissaries were supposed to be prowling about, bent upon some deadly purpose. Several of the European governments were beginning to recognize the Southern

moment that they can grant that application and remain the friends of the United States. You may even assure them promptly, in that case, that if they determine to recognize they may at the same time prepare to enter into an alliance with the enemies of this republic. You alone will represent your country at London, and you will represent the whole of it there. When you are asked to divide that duty with others, diplomatic relations between the government of Great Britain and this government will be suspended, and will remain so until it shall be seen which of the two is most strongly intrenched in the

THE SIEGE OF VICKSBURG—GENERAL GRANT MEETING THE CONFEDERATE GENERAL PEMBERTON AT THE STONE HOUSE, INSIDE THE CONFEDERATE WORKS, ON THE MORNING OF JULY 4TH, 1863.

engagement, and the Nationals were repulsed. At this battle the first officer of the regular army to fall in the war was killed—Lieutenant Greble. This defeat of the Federal troops greatly alarmed the people of the North. It caused great excitement for a time, but other and more important events soon occurred to attract the attention of the nation.

CHAPTER IV.

EXTRAORDINARY SESSION OF CONGRESS—CONGRESS AUTHORIZES THE RAISING OF TROOPS AND MONEY—WOMEN'S WORK IN THE WAR—DOROTHEA L. DIX'S BENEVOLENCE—CAPTURE OF RICH MOUNTAIN—THE WAR IN WEST VIRGINIA—THE "PETREL'S" MISTAKE.

AN extraordinary session of Congress assembled at the National capital on Thurs-

Confederacy, and were preparing to give it moral and material aid. Among these governments was Great Britain, and that country's open recognition of the independence of the Confederacy was prevented only by the high position taken by Secretary of State Seward, who, in his instructions to the new representative at the Court of St. James, Mr. Charles Francis Adams, said : "You will in no case listen to any suggestions of compromise by this government, under foreign auspices, with its discontented citizens. If, as the President does not at all apprehend, you shall unhappily find her majesty's government tolerating the applications of the so-called Confederate States or wavering about it, you will not leave them to suppose for a

confidence of their respective nations and of mankind."

It was a critical time in the history of the republic, and the members of the National Legislature responded promptly to the call for an extra session. There were representatives of twenty-three States in the Senate and 154 Members of the House in their seats on the first day of the session, while ten slave-labor States were not represented.

In his message to this Congress President Lincoln recommended that at least four hundred thousand men and four hundred millions of dollars be placed at the control of the government, so as to make the contest in the preservation of the Union a short and decisive one. The

Secretary of War (Simon Cameron) recommended the enlistment of men for three years. The Secretary of the Treasury (Salmon P. Chase) asked $320,000,000 for war purposes and the current expenses of the government. He proposed to raise the money by an increase of taxes and the issue of interest-bearing Treasury notes or bonds.

These suggestions were all carried out. Congress at once authorized the raising of 500,000 troops, and made an appropriation of $500,000,000 to defray the expenses of the war. This prompt and energetic action on the part of Congress stirred up the people of the free-labor States, and enthusiasm was at fever heat.

This enthusiasm was not manifested by the men of the country alone. The women, too, were aroused, and demonstrated their patriotism by attending the sick, wounded and dying in the hospitals, and preparing lint and bandages. Associations of women were formed for this benevolent work. Miss Dorothea L. Dix was the leader in this movement, and gave her services to the government gratuitously, organizing at once a splendid system of providing comfort for the sick and wounded soldiers.

In accepting her services Secretary of War Cameron issued this card: "Be it known to all whom it may concern that the free services of Miss D. L. Dix are accepted by the War Department, and that she will give, at all times, all necessary aid in organizing military hospitals for the care of all the sick or wounded soldiers, aiding the chief surgeons by supplying nurses and substantial means for the comfort and relief of the suffering; also, that she is fully authorized to receive, control and disburse special supplies bestowed by individuals or associations for the comfort of their friends or the citizen soldiers from all parts of the United States." Without receiving any pecuniary reward this young woman labored day and night throughout the war for the relief of suffering soldiers. "She went from battlefield to battlefield when the carnage was over," says a historian of the war; "from camp to camp, and from hospital to hospital, superintending the operations of the nurses, and administering with her own hands physical comforts to the suffering, and soothing the troubled spirits of the invalid or dying soldier with a voice low, musical and attractive, and always burdened with words of heartfelt sympathy and religious consolation. . . . . Yet she was not the only Sister of Mercy engaged in this holy work. She had hundreds of devoted, earnest, self-sacrificing coworkers of the gentler sex all over the land, serving with equal zeal in the camps and hospitals of the National and the Confederate armies, and no greater heroism was displayed by soldiers in the field than was

exhibited by these American women everywhere."

While the Confederate troops, under Beauregard, were gathered at Manassas, awaiting an opportunity to march upon the capital, detachments were sent out along the line of the Upper Potomac from Georgetown to Leesburg on foraging expeditions. On June 17th one of these detachments came into contact with an Ohio regiment at Vienna. A sharp skirmish resulted. The Confederates were defeated, but soon returned and captured Vienna and Falls Church, at which latter village many stirring scenes afterward occurred.

In the early part of July General George B. McClellan, with 10,000 men, started out from Grafton, Va., to make an attack upon Laurel Hill, near Beverly, where General R. S. Garnett, in command of the Confederate forces in Western Virginia, had his headquarters. At the same time he sent 4,000 men, under General T. A. Morris, toward the same point by way of Philippi. Then still another detachment, under General Hill, proceeded to a point eastward of Philippi, to prevent the Confederates from joining Johnston at Winchester. Approaching Laurel Hill, McClellan learned that Colonel John Pegram, with a large body of Confederates, was strongly intrenched at Rich Mountain Gap, just in the rear of General Garnett's position. Wishing to dislodge this body before attacking Garnett, McClellan sent off Colonel W. S. Rosecrans, with a number of Ohio and Indiana soldiers and a troop of cavalry, for that purpose. They climbed a circuitous and perilous route up to the top of a ridge of Rich Mountain, above Pegram's camp. Here the Confederates caught sight of them, and Pegram, with 900 men, armed with muskets and cannon, attacked them vigorously. The battle was a hot one for some time, but Rosecrans at last succeeded in driving the enemy back and taking possession of its position. For his gallantry on this occasion Rosecrans was commissioned a brigadier general. Soon afterward, when McClellan was appointed to the command of the Army of the Potomac, Rosecrans succeeded him in Western Virginia.

Pegram soon got his troops together again, and being re-enforced, was about to attempt the recovery of Laurel Hill, when he heard of the approach of McClellan and disappeared in the night without waiting to be attacked. McClellan, however, caught up with him and compelled his surrender, with 600 followers. Being left unsupported, Garnett also withdrew in the darkness. He was pursued by General Morris and overtaken at Carricksford, on a branch of the Cheat River. Here he made a stand and bravely defended himself, but it resulted in his death and the dispersion of his forces. During this time ex-Governor Wise, with a considerable body of Confederates, was defeated and driven out of his position in the Great Kanawha region of West Virginia by a force of Ohio troops under General J. D. Cox. These triumphs of the Federals prompted McClellan to say, in a dispatch to the War Department: "We have completely annihilated the enemy in West Virginia. Our loss is about 13 killed and not more than 40 wounded, while the enemy's loss is not far from 200 killed, and the number of prisoners we have taken will amount to at least 1,000. We have captured seven of the guns of the enemy in all."

At the time Congress assembled on the 4th of July the Confederates had a good-sized navy of twenty armed vessels. The first of these vessels bore the name *Lady Davis.* They were all privateers fitted out to depredate upon the commerce of the United States. One of them, the *Petrel* by name, made a costly error in supposing the United States sailing frigate *St. Lawrence* was a richly laden merchantman. The mistake was soon seen by the crew of the *Petrel,* when, eagerly making toward the frigate to seize it, they were met by a flash and a bang that sent their vessel to the bottom in a twinkling.

CHAPTER V.

Battle of Bull Run—"Stonewall" Jackson—The War in Missouri—Engagement at Carthage—Battle of Wilson's Creek—Death of General Lyon—Fremont's Plan for Reaching New Orleans.

On the afternoon of July 16th, 1861, 50,000 of the troops that had been gathered at Washington started out against the Confederate hosts intrenched at Manassas Junction. The time had come to make an attempt to drive back the army preparing to seize the city. The soldiers, under General Irwin McDowell, moved in five divisions, commanded by Brigadier Generals Daniel Tyler and Theodore Runyon, and Colonels David Hunter, Samuel P. Heintzelman and Dixon S. Miles. Their opponents had strong positions along Bull Run, a tributary of the Occoquan, from Union Mills to the stone bridge on the Warrenton Turnpike, a distance of about eight miles, with reserves near Ma-

ARMY COOKHOUSE CONSTRUCTED IN AN OLD CHIMNEY OF AN OUTHOUSE OF THE LACY MANSION, ON THE RAPPAHANNOCK, FALMOUTH, VA.

...ssas. They were also stationed at **Centreville** and Fairfax Courthouse, ten **miles** from the main army, in the direction **of** Washington.

General McDowell first ordered **Tyler** to advance on Vienna, then took the **remainder** of the army in four columns **and** along different roads toward the enemy's camp. He hoped by a series of feints to throw the Confederates off their guard and surprise them in their rear, so as to compel the retreat of both Beauregard and Johnston from their strong positions near the seat of government. The columns met with but little opposition at first. They passed safely through Fairfax Courthouse,

his plan for gaining the rear of the Confederates was impracticable.

McDowell's troops were now massed at Centreville. After waiting a few days for needed supplies the army, at two o'clock on the morning of July 21st, moved from the village in three columns, to attack the left flank of the Confederates. General Tyler, with the brigades of Schenck and Sherman and the batteries of Ayres and Carlisle, started toward the stone bridge on the Warrenton Turnpike, in order to make a feigned attack near the bridge, so that the two columns of Hunter and Heintzelman could cross Bull Run at Sudley Church and fall upon the Confederate left.

The memorable battle of Bull Run then began by the firing of a shell by General Tyler into the ranks of the Confederates stationed near the stone bridge and commanded by Colonel Evans. Beauregard at once sent re-enforcements to Evans, and Johnston ordered an attack, led by General Ewell, upon McDowell's left wing at Blackburn's Ford. Colonel Evans soon saw that Tyler's attack was only a feint, and learning that a column was passing Bull Run at Sudley Church, he at once prepared to meet it. This column was Hunter's, composed of Rhode Island, Massachusetts and New Hampshire troops, with the batteries of Griffin and Ricketts,

SOLDIERS' GRAVEYARD, IN THE CAMP NEAR FALMOUTH, VA.

and the Confederates at Centreville fled at their approach. This had been arranged by Beauregard in order to lead the Federal army into a perilous position. They walked into the trap in high spirits, thinking they were driving everyone before them. Suddenly they were brought to a stop at Blackburn's Ford, on Bull Run, by General James Longstreet, with a strong force of men and concealed batteries. General Tyler, with his detachment of Michigan, Massachusetts and New York troops, and Ayres's battery, made a reconnoissance here, and a severe conflict was the result. The Nationals were defeated, and withdrew to Centreville. This satisfied McDowell that

The Confederates, meanwhile, were making active preparations for the coming battle. Johnston was ordered to hasten from Winchester and join the forces at Manassas with the Army of the Shenandoah. He managed to elude Patterson, who was stationed at Martinsburg to prevent this very movement, and arrived at Manassas at noon of the 20th with 6,000 infantry, the balance of his army to follow a little later. Beauregard's force now outnumbered McDowell's by 4,000 men, and he was in a much better position. Upon his arrival, Johnston, being the senior in rank, assumed chief command of the Confederate troops.

the whole led by Colonel Burnside. They soon appeared in the open field, and Evans, assisted by General Bee, who commanded the reserves, opened fire upon them. There was a terrible battle. After a time Evans's line began to waver, but new troops being advanced by General Bee, it recovered its losing strength, and Colonel Burnside was compelled to call for help. This came in the form of a battalion of regulars under Major Sykes. But even with this aid the Federals were fast becoming exhausted. More re-enforcements, however, soon arrived, in charge of Colonel Andrew Porter, and these were followed by Heintzelman's column and part

THE WAR IN TENNESSEE—CAPTURE OF MISSIONARY

SVILLE, BY GENERAL THOMAS, NOVEMBER 25TH, 1863.

of General Sherman's brigade, under Colonel Corcoran.

By a furious charge made just then by Colonel H. W. Slocum's New York regiment the Confederate line was broken, and the troops fled in confusion to a high plateau. Here their flight was checked by the appearance of General T. J. Jackson, who had arrived with reserves. Rushing up to Jackson, General Bee exclaimed: "They are beating us back!" "Well, sir," was the calm reply, "we will give them the bayonet!" Encouraged by this answer, Bee cried to the fugitives to halt, and shouted: "There stands General Jackson, like a stone wall!" It was thus that the calm officer became known as "Stonewall Jackson."

troops took a position to the left of the batteries.

Then a terrific struggle began. The Confederates poured such a murderous fire into the Federal ranks that the batteries were soon disabled. The slaughter on both sides was terrible. It would have been hard to say which army would be successful, although the National troops seemed to be gaining slightly, when suddenly the balance of Johnston's Shenandoah army, under General E. Kirby Smith, appeared on the scene, and the tide immediately turned. With these and other fresh troops Beauregard in a few moments drove McDowell's army from the plateau and sent it hurrying back to the turnpike in great confusion. As the regiments in

Booneville. There they made a stand. But being attacked and defeated by Lyon, they retreated toward the southwestern part of Missouri, and did not stop until they reached the Arkansas border, thus giving to the Union forces the important points of St. Louis, St. Joseph, Hannibal and Bird's Point on the Mississippi as bases of operations, with railroads and rivers for transportation. Knowing that General Jackson was gathering a large force in Southwestern Missouri, Lyon remained about a fortnight at Booneville preparing a vigorous campaign against him.

This was at the beginning of July, when there were at least 10,000 National troops in Missouri. At this time Colonel Franz Sigel was rapidly advancing on the Con-

HOW THE DAUGHTERS OF MARYLAND RECEIVED THE SONS OF THE NORTH AS THEY MARCHED AGAINST THE CONFEDERATE INVADERS—SCENE ON THE MARCH.

The National troops had gained possession of the Warrenton Turnpike, and they now turned their attention to driving the enemy from the plateau, to which Johnston and Beauregard had sent bodies of soldiers under Holmes, Early and Ewell, so that it held 10,000 men and 22 heavy guns. To capture this plateau five brigades, those of Porter, Howard, Franklin, Wilcox and Sherman, were detailed to turn the Confederate left, while Keyes was sent to annoy them on the right. Colonel Heintzelman's division began the attack. They pressed forward, and succeeded in gaining a portion of the plateau. With the support of Ellsworth's Fire Zouaves batteries were planted upon an elevation commanding the whole plateau. This done, New York, Massachusetts and Minnesota

front broke and fled the others were seized with panic, and the retreat at once became a disorderly rout. Three thousand of the Federals were killed, wounded or taken prisoners, while the Confederates lost over 2,000. A great exultant shout arose throughout the South over the victory, while a deep gloom settled upon the North. The depression of the people of the loyal States, however, did not last long; they arose quickly from despair to hope, and the gaps in the army were more than filled within a fortnight.

While the battle at Bull Run was being planned and fought the war was making great progress in the West, especially in Missouri. General Price, who led the Confederates in that State, was driven by General Lyon from Jefferson City to

federates stationed on the borders of Kansas and Arkansas. On reaching Carthage, July 5th, he encountered a large force under Jackson and Brigadier General Rains. A sharp fight took place, and, owing to superior numbers against him, Sigel was forced back and retreated in good order to Springfield. Lyon was then about eighty miles from that city, and learning of Sigel's peril, hastened to his relief, and took command of the combined forces. While this was being done Price was re-enforced by troops from Texas under Generals McCulloch, Rains, Pearce and McBride. This army, numbering about 20,000 men, and led by General Rains, then set out for Springfield. Although Lyon had not more than 6,000 men and 18 pieces of artillery, he bravely went out to meet the on-coming enemy. The opposing forces met at Dug Springs, about nineteen miles west from Springfield, and a desperate battle was fought. This was on August 2d. Lyon's cavalry, led by Captain Stanley, made a furious charge, and after a time the Confederates gave way and retreated to Wilson's Creek.

Early the next morning Lyon pushed on after the enemy to make another attack. The troops advanced in two columns, one led by Lyon to engage their front; the other, under Sigel, to attack the rear. The battle opened furiously. In the thickest of the fight was Lyon. Wherever needed he would dash in and give encouragement to his men by words and deeds. Although his horse was shot under him, and he was wounded in the head and leg, he was soon on another horse, and placing himself at the head of the Kansas troops, he swung his hat over his head, and dashed forward

the supplies of General Pillow and others in the vicinity of New Madrid, thus compelling their retreat, and allowing a flotilla of gunboats, then being built near St. Louis, to descend the Mississippi and assist in military operations against the batteries at Memphis; then push on toward the Gulf of Mexico with his army and take possession of New Orleans.

CHAPTER VI.

SIEGE OF LEXINGTON—BOMBARDMENT OF COLUMBUS—BATTLE OF BELMONT—CAMPAIGN IN WESTERN VIRGINIA—BATTLE AT CARNIFEX FERRY—McCLELLAN APPOINTED GENERAL IN CHIEF—THE "TRENT" AFFAIR—CAPTURE OF ROANOKE ISLAND.

ABOUT the middle of August General Price, with his force of Confederates, moved northward in the direction of Lexington, an important position in a curve of the Missouri River. It was garrisoned by about 3,000 troops under Colonel James A. Mul-

manded Fremont's orders for battle, and the disappointed army was sent back to St. Louis. Nine days after this General H. W. Halleck took command of the Department of Missouri. Fremont was afterward presented with a sword, on which was engraved: "To the Pathfinder, by the men of the West."

In response to an order from Fremont, just before he was deprived of his command, General Grant, then in charge of the district around Cairo, sent a co-operative force along the line of the Mississippi to attack Columbus, then in the hands of the Confederates. One column of about 3,000 Illinois volunteers, under General John A. McClernand, went from Cairo in transports and the wooden gunboats *Tyler* and *Lexington*, for the purpose of menacing Columbus by an attack on Belmont, opposite; and another column, under General C. F. Smith, marched from Paducah

THE CAMPAIGN IN GEORGIA—FEDERAL TROOPS FORAGING NEAR WARSAW SOUND.

with a determination to gain a victory. But a bullet in his heart stopped him, and he fell back dead. For two hours after this the battle raged; then the Confederates were forced to retreat. The loss on the Union side was between 1,200 and 1,300, and on the other about 3,000. The Union troops then went back to Springfield in order to protect a government train, valued at $1,500 000, from that city to Rolla, one hundred and twenty-five miles in the direction of St. Louis.

Just before the battle of Wilson's Creek General John C. Fremont was given the command of the Department of Missouri. He at once formed a plan for ridding Missouri and the whole Mississippi Valley of armed Secessionists, and for opening the navigation of the river, which was then obstructed by Confederate batteries at Memphis and elsewhere. It was a gigantic plan. He intended to capture or disperse the troops under General Price; seize Little Rock, the capital of Arkansas; cut off

ligan. Price reached its vicinity early in September, and immediately besieged it with 20,000 men. This was on the 11th, and although Mulligan was inadequately supplied with heavy guns and ammunition to sustain a siege he gallantly defended the post against overwhelming numbers until the morning of the 20th, when he was compelled to surrender. Fremont immediately sent an army of more than 20,000 men to retrieve this disaster by driving Price and his followers out of Missouri. The army moved in five columns, under Generals Hunter, Pope, Sigel, McKinstry and Asboth. It was accompanied by eighty-six heavy guns. As Fremont said in a report to his government, his plan was to go right through to New Orleans.

But Fremont's plan was upset. Just when he felt confident of his success and was about to attack Price he received orders, emanating from the jealousies of political enemies, to turn over his command to General Hunter. The latter counter-

to strike Columbus in the rear. While the gunboats fired on Columbus the troops landed near Belmont, and at once attacked that post. Although this place had been re-enforced by General Pillow, the National troops captured it after a severe contest; but, owing to a heavy fire of artillery from the bluff at Columbus, they were unable to hold it, and withdrew with captured men, horses and artillery. Polk, commanding Columbus, immediately opened his heaviest guns upon them and tried to cut off their retreat with a large body of fresh troops that he sent across the water. Although there was a severe struggle, Grant managed to fight his way back to his transports and escaped under cover of a fire from the gunboats. The loss in the engagement was about 500 Nationals and 600 Confederates.

The war in Western Virginia, which in the summer of 1861 seemed to have been crushed, was renewed in the autumn. General Robert E. Lee was then in charge of

THE IRONCLAD "WEEHAWKEN" RETURNING TO FIRE A PARTING SHOT AT FORT SUMTER, AFTER THE BOMBARDMENT,
APRIL 7TH, 1863.

the forces left by Garnett and Pegram. His headquarters were at Huntersville, in Pocahontas County. Plans were made by which General John B. Floyd (Secretary of War in Buchanan's administration), who had been given chief command in the region of the Gauley River, was to drive General Cox across the Ohio River, and Lee was to disperse the army under Rosecrans, successor of McClellan, at Clarksburg, on the Baltimore and Ohio Railroad, and in this way make possible an invasion of Confederates into Maryland, Pennsylvania and Ohio.

But these excellent plans failed. Rosecrans did not wait to be attacked, but started out to disperse Floyd's troops. After scaling the Gauley Mountains he came upon the object of his expedition at Carnifex Ferry on the Gauley River. A severe battle of three hours' duration was the result. Then Floyd, under cover of the darkness, stole away to Big Sewell Mountain, thirty miles distant. Meanwhile Lee had started out from Huntersville on the night of September 11th, with 9,000 men and a dozen pieces of artillery, for the purpose of attacking Elkwater and the outpost of Indiana troops on the summit of Cheat Mountain, and thus securing the pass and a free communication with the Shenandoah Valley at Staunton. But he was unsuccessful, suffering defeat at both places. He then joined Floyd at Big Sewell Mountain.

A few more vigorous movements on the part of the Union soldiers in West Virginia soon put an end to the war in that State.

Late in August an expedition, composed of eight transports and war ships, under Commodore S. H. Stringham, bearing about 900 land troops, commanded by General B. F. Butler, left Hampton Roads for Hatteras Inlet, at the entrance to which, off the North Carolina coast, the Confed-

erates had erected two forts. By an assault on these forts by land and water Stringham and Butler succeeded in capturing them. A portion of Colonel Hawkins's New York Zouaves, with their commander, was left to garrison the position, and the expedition returned to Hampton Roads.

Two months after this another expedition was sent out from Hampton Roads. This was composed of fifty war ships and transports, commanded by Admiral S. F. Dupont, and 15,000 land troops under General T. W. Sherman. After passing through a severe tempest off Cape Hatteras all of the vessels, with the exception of four transports that were wrecked, gathered at the entrance to Port Royal Sound, between Hilton Head and Philip's Island.

The entrance to this sound was guarded by two Confederate batteries, while within the sound was a small flotilla of armed vessels commanded by Commodore Tatnall, late of the United States Navy, who had espoused the Confederate cause. On the morning of November 7th Dupont silenced the two forts and drove Tatnall's fleet into shallow water. The National troops then took possession of Port Royal and the neighboring islands. At the close of 1861 the National authority was supreme over the coast islands from Warsaw Sound to the mouth of the North Edisto River.

General McClellan assumed command of the Army of the Potomac, as the forces around Washington were called after the battle of Bull Run, on July 27th. He at once became so popular in this position that when, a few months afterward (November 1st) General Scott resigned his place as general in chief of the armies, on account of old age and ill health, McClellan was appointed to that office. He immediately set to work to reorganize the army, which had been shattered by the terrible blow at Bull Run.

It was about this time that the country was stirred up over the capture of two Confederate ambassadors on their way to Europe. On October 12th, 1861, James Mason and John Slidell, who had been appointed to represent the Confederate Government in Great Britain and France, sailed from Charleston harbor for Havana, Cuba. There they embarked for St. Thomas in the British mail steamer *Trent*, intending to go to England in the regular packet from that port. Soon after the *Trent* sailed the American war ship *San Jacinto* stopped at Havana, and her captain, Wilkes, learned of the movements of the ambassadors. He at once set sail for the *Trent*, and overhauling her, demanded the delivery of the two men. They refused to leave the ship unless forced to do so. Marines were at once dispatched to the *Trent*, and compelled the ambassadors to surrender. They were taken on board the *San Jacinto* and conveyed to Boston, where they were placed in Fort Warren as prisoners of state.

While this act of Captain Wilkes was loudly applauded by loyal Americans the British Government called it an outrage, and followed up a peremptory demand for the release of the prisoners by preparing to enforce the demand by a war upon the United States. But their preparations came to naught, for, acting upon the principle that the flag of a neutral vessel is a protection to all beneath it, the United States disavowed the act of Wilkes and released the two men. The "*Trent* affair" caused a great deal of excitement in the country, but it soon subsided upon the peaceful settlement of the trouble.

The attention of the people was then directed to the fitting out of a third naval armament at Hampton Roads. This consisted of 100 war vessels and transports commanded by Commodore L. M. Goldsborough, and bearing 16,000 troops under General Ambrose E. Burnside, of Rhode Island. The fleet left the Roads, January 11th, 1862, for Roanoke Island and Pamlico Sound, on the coast of North Carolina. Roanoke Island was strongly fortified with Confederate batteries commanding the sounds on either side. They were in the hands of North Carolina troops under Colonel H. M. Shaw.

An attack was made upon these fortifications the first week in February. Goldsborough took a fleet of seventy vessels into Croatan Sound and opened on the batteries. These shots received a hearty response from the batteries and from a flotilla of small gunboats commanded by Lieutenant W. F. Lynch. The bombardment lasted all afternoon, and at midnight about 11,000 New England, New York and New Jersey troops were landed on the island. Early in the morning these troops, led by General J. G. Foster, attacked a line of intrenchments that crossed the island. The redoubts, one after the other, were captured, although the Confederates, far inferior in number, made a gallant defense. A particularly brave stand was made in the last redoubt, but through a furious charge by Hawkins's Zouaves they were compelled to beat a retreat and submit to capture after a short flight. Thus Roanoke Island passed into the hands of the National forces. Other portions of the North Carolina coast, including Elizabeth City, were speedily captured. These losses produced great depression throughout the South, as it opened a way by which Norfolk might be attacked in the rear.

CHAPTER VII.

PRICE DRIVEN INTO ARKANSAS — BATTLE OF PEA RIDGE — CAPTAIN McRAE'S BRAVERY — BATTLE OF MILL SPRINGS — BEAUREGARD TRANSFERRED TO THE WEST — SIEGE AND CAPTURE OF FORTS HENRY AND HEIMAN.

WHEN General Halleck assumed command of the Department of Missouri he placed General John Pope in charge of a considerable body of troops to oppose Price, who had gathered a large force of Confederates in Missouri. Pope did his work well, acting with great vigor and skill. By a few sharp, effective blows here and there he succeeded in preventing organized troops from joining Price, and compelled the latter to withdraw to the borders of Arkansas for supplies and safety. Price, however, soon moved back to Springfield with about 12,000 men, and was preparing to spend the winter there, when Halleck's troops, under General S. R. Curtis, assisted by Generals Sigel, Davis, Asboth and Prentiss, drove him away and forced him again into Arkansas. The Missouri campaign, from June, 1861, to late in February, 1862, had been very active, sixty battles and skirmishes having been fought. The loss on both sides during this campaign, in killed, wounded and prisoners, was about 12,000.

When General Curtis had driven the Confederates into Arkansas he encamped in a strong position in the vicinity of Pea Ridge, a spur of the Ozark Mountains. In the meantime Price had been joined by General Earl Van Dorn, who brought with him from Western Arkansas Generals McCulloch, Pike and McIntosh. General Van Dorn took command of the forces,

which numbered about 25,000 men, and immediately led them out to Curtis's encampment.

Curtis learned through his scouts of the approach of the Confederates, and at once concentrated his little army in the Sugar Creek Valley; so that when, on the morning of March 7th, 1862, Van Dorn had by a flank movement gained Curtis's rear, he found that general's troops in battle array. Generals Sigel and Asboth, commanding the First and Second Divisions, were on Curtis's left; General Davis, with the Third Division, was in the centre, and the Fourth, under Colonel Carr, formed the right. The line of battle extended about four miles. The contest opened toward noon, and continued throughout the remainder of the day, without either side gaining the advantage. The loss was great on both sides, among the killed being Generals McCulloch and McIntosh. At night both armies rested on their arms.

Early the next morning the conflict was renewed with great vigor. But the Nationals soon put a stop to the battle by pouring in such a strong, steady, destructive fire that the Confederates were unable to stand it, and fled in almost every direction in wild confusion. Van Dorn's army was really broken into fragments. Curtis lost 1,380 men, and the other side about the same number.

During this time the war was kindling in the Department of New Mexico, commanded by General Canby. Attempts were made to attach that Territory to the Confederacy. Colonel H. H. Sibley, a Louisianian, with 2,300 Texans, most of

KELLEY'S FORD, ON THE RAPPAHANNOCK, THE SCENE OF THE BATTLE OF THE 17TH OF MARCH, AND OF GENERAL STONEMAN'S RECONNOISSANCE OF THE 21ST OF APRIL, 1863.

them rough rangers, invaded the Territory in February, and called upon the inhabitants for allegiance to the Confederacy and support for his troops. He felt confident of success, and marched slowly toward Fort Craig, on the Rio Grande, to attack Canby. But, finding that general ready to meet him, and having only light field-pieces, he crossed the Rio Grande and took up a position out of reach of the guns of the fort. Then, by a series of skirmishes, he drew Canby out. The latter began advancing on the Confederates, when a body of Texans, horse and foot, armed with carbines, revolvers and bowie knives, suddenly burst from a thick wood and charged furiously on two of the National batteries, commanded respectively by Captains McRea and Hall. Although the

a provisional government, General Johnston had concentrated a large force at Bowling Green and strengthened the position of Polk at Columbus. Right across Kentucky were a series of fortified posts, the most important of which were Fort Donelson, on the Cumberland River, and Fort Henry, on the Tennessee River.

At the same time General Buell had a large force of Union troops at Louisville and vicinity, and had strengthened various advanced posts. He had altogether about 114,000 men under his command. They were arranged in four columns, commanded respectively by Brigadier Generals Alexander McDowell McCook, Ormsby M. Mitchel, George H. Thomas and Thomas L. Crittenden, and aided by twenty brigade commanders. They occupied an irregular

his troops defeated. They fled into Northeastern Tennessee.

This defeat was a great blow to the Confederates. It broke their line in Kentucky, and made possible a series of movements by which they were soon driven out of that State and also Tennessee. It also aroused them to the necessity of a bold, able commander in the West. They chose Beauregard, and transferred him from Manassas to Johnston's department, appointing General G. W. Smith to succeed him in the East.

After the important victory at Mill Springs an expedition against Fort Henry and Fort Donelson was arranged. Twelve gunboats, which had been constructed at St. Louis and Cairo, were armed with heavy guns and light artillery, and placed

CONFEDERATE PRISONERS BROUGHT IN AFTER THE BATTLE OF CHANCELLORSVILLE.

cavalry were driven back, the Confederate infantry bravely pressed forward through a murderous hail of grapeshot, and captured the battery of McRae. Its gallant commander defended his guns as long as he could, but was shot dead while sitting astride a cannon and fighting his assailants with a pistol. The Union soldiers soon broke and fled to the shelter of Fort Craig. Sibley did not follow up this victory, but hurried off to Santa Fé, which he captured but could not hold. He was soon afterward driven into Texas.

The region of Southern and Western Kentucky was at this time held by the Confederates under General A. S. Johnston, an able officer and veteran soldier. When the Secessionists of this State, in a convention held in November, 1861, declared for the Confederacy and organized

line across Kentucky, almost parallel with that of the Confederates.

On January 7th Colonel James A. Garfield, with a body of infantry and cavalry, went out and dispersed a large force of Confederates under Humphrey Marshall at Prestonburg, on the Big Sandy River, in Eastern Kentucky. For his gallantry on this occasion Garfield was commissioned a brigadier general. A few days later (January 19th) an important battle was fought at Beech Grove, near Mill Springs, on the borders of the Cumberland River. General Thomas was sent there to attack the strongly intrenched Confederate camp, then in charge of General Crittenden. The Confederates, led by General Zollicoffer, came out to meet him. The two forces met on the morning of January 19th, and a severe conflict ensued. Zollicoffer was killed and

under the command of Commodore A. H. Foote. A portion of this fleet gathered on the Tennessee River, February 3d, 1862, a few miles below Fort Henry, while a large force of troops, commanded by General U. S. Grant, assisted by General C. F. Smith, were landed from transports. The fort was armed with seventeen guns, and was in charge of General Tilghman.

Grant and Foote arranged to strike Fort Henry simultaneously. Part of the land troops were first sent up the opposite side of the river to capture Fort Heiman and prevent its assistance of Fort Henry, while the others proceeded to gain a point between Forts Henry and Donelson. Before these troops reached their destination, Foote, by a heavy bombardment from his gunboats, *Essex, St. Louis, Cincinnati* and *Carondelet,* compelled the surrender of

Fort Henry. The little garrison made a gallant defense, but were forced to give in at the end of an hour's time. Fort Heiman was also captured.

Upon learning of this important naval victory the Secretary of the Navy wrote to Foote : " The country appreciates your gallant deeds, and this department desires to convey to you and your brave associates its profound thanks for the service you have rendered."

CHAPTER VIII.

The Assault on Fort Donelson — Cowardly Flight of Floyd and Pillow — " Unconditional Surrender " — Fall of Donelson — Confederate Retreat from Bowling Green — Capture of Island No. 10 — Battle of Shiloh.

By their capture of Forts Henry and Heiman, on the Tennessee River, the Nationals gained formidable and important posts, and it gave them a strong hold upon the vicinity of Fort Donelson and a good

water batteries. They did little damage, while the gunboats received such a tremendous pounding in return that Foote was compelled to withdraw. He hastened to Cairo to have damages repaired and to bring up a larger naval force. In the meantime Grant resolved to wait.

That night the Confederates held a council of war. The fort was in command of ex-Secretary Floyd, assisted by Generals Pillow and Buckner. On the suggestion of Floyd it was decided, as the only way to save the garrison, to make a sortie the next morning, and rout or destroy the besieging army, or cut through it and escape in the direction of Nashville. So at five o'clock in the morning Generals Pillow and Buckner started out, the former to strike the Nationals on the right, McClernand's division, and the latter to engage Wallace in the centre. Pillow's attack was quick and vigorous, and in a short time the op-

ville. The two cowards were at once suspended from command by the Confederate Government.

At an early hour the next morning Buckner requested the appointment of commissioners to agree upon terms of surrender. Grant's reply was brief and to the point : " No terms other than unconditional and immediate surrender can be accepted. I propose to move immediately upon your works." The surrender speedily followed. Thirteen thousand five hundred men were captured, besides 3,000 horses, 48 field-pieces, 17 heavy guns, 20,000 muskets and a large quantity of military stores. The loss was estimated at 237 killed and 1,000 wounded on the Confederate side, and 446 killed and 755 wounded among the Federals.

When General A. S. Johnston heard of the fall of Fort Donelson he immediately ordered the evacuation of Bowling Green

ADMIRAL DUPONT'S MACHINE SHOP, STATION CREEK, S. C.

position in the rear of Columbus, on the Mississippi. They determined to at once follow up the advantage thus gained by an attack on Fort Donelson, on the left bank of the Cumberland River, near Dover, Tennessee.

Two divisions of General Grant's army, under McClernand and Smith, left Fort Henry for Fort Donelson on the morning of February 12th, 1862. Another division, in charge of General Lewis Wallace, was left to hold the vanquished forts. Grant and his two divisions arrived in the vicinity of the fort the same evening, and went into camp to await the arrival of the armored flotilla. Upon looking over the situation Grant decided to send for Wallace and his troops. They arrived at noon on the 14th, and Commodore Foote, with his gunboats, having arrived, the attack on Fort Donelson was begun at three o'clock that afternoon by the vessels *Carondelet, Pittsburg St. Louis* and *Louisville* firing upon the

posing line gave way excepting Colonel John A. Logan's Illinois regiment, on the extreme left. This gallant stand, with the assistance of the light batteries of Taylor, McAllister and Dresser, made the Confederate line recoil. But being re-enforced, it soon put the whole of McClernand's division in great peril. Wallace was then called upon for help, and he gave such a hearty response that after a hard struggle the combined forces of Pillow and Buckner were compelled to fall back to their trenches.

The strength of the Union forces led Floyd and Pillow to see that the fort would soon be obliged to surrender, and fearing the consequences to themselves if captured, they turned over the command to Buckner, and under cover of night cowardly deserted their companions in arms and fled. Floyd took a part of his Virginians with him up the river toward Nashville in a steamboat, while Pillow escaped to his home in Nash-

and Columbus. The troops in the former place retreated to Nashville, but being rapidly pursued by a part of Buell's Army of the Ohio, under General Mitchel, they soon left that city and moved quickly southward. Thus Nashville fell into the hands of the Federals, February 26th, 1862. Tennessee was now almost free of Confederate soldiers, and as the people displayed signs of loyalty to the Union, the National Government resolved to re-establish civil government there. Andrew Johnson, of East Tennessee, was made Provisional Governor, with the military rank of brigadier general, and he entered upon his duties at Nashville on March 4th.

Stirring events were now occurring on the Mississippi River. New Madrid and Island No. 10 were occupied by the Confederates who had evacuated Columbus. Those at New Madrid were commanded by General McCown, and Island No. 10 was in charge of General Beauregard, who, as we have seen, had been sent West. While Commodore Foote was at Cairo preparing for a siege of those two places, General Pope, dispatched from St. Louis by General Halleck, drove the Confederates from New Madrid, and as they sought refuge on Island No. 10, that became the chief object of attack by the Federals.

The island had been thoroughly fortified by Beauregard, so that when, on the morning of March 16th, Foote opened upon it

While awaiting assistance from Pope Foote determined to get a better position, so as to give his guns chance for more effective work. For this purpose an expedition composed of Illinois troops and seamen was sent on April 1st to capture one of the seven formidable redoubts on the Kentucky shore. This was successful, and on the night of the 3d they took another. Then one of Foote's gunboats (the *Carondelet*, Captain Walke,) sailed down, amid a tremendous cannonading from all the bat-

check the movement of Federal troops through Middle Tennessee toward Northern Alabama and Mississippi. The next day McCall attempted to escape from the island with his troops. They were stopped by Pope's forces under Generals Stanley, Hamilton and Paine, and Island No. 10, with the troops, batteries and supports on the main, fell into the hands of the Federals on April 8th. More than 7,000 men were surrendered prisoners of war, and among the spoils of victory were 123 can-

THE SOLDIER'S REST—THE FRIENDS OF THE SEVENTH AND EIGHTH REGIMENTS, NEW YORK VOLUNTEERS, WELCOMING THE RETURN OF THEIR HEROES TO NEW YORK, TUESDAY, APRIL 28TH, 1863.

with heavy guns and mortars no apparent effect was made for some time. While the siege was going on General Pope, at the suggestion of General Schuyler Hamilton, was having a canal cut from the bend of the Mississippi, near Island No. 8, across the neck of a swampy peninsula, to the vicinity of New Madrid, where Pope was encamped. This was made to open a passage for Pope's troops and some gunboats, so that they might flank Island No. 10 and insure its capture. The canal was twelve miles long, and was completed, after much hard labor, in nineteen days.

teries on the shore to the assistance of Pope. This daring feat was successfully accomplished, and the vessel was received with wild huzzas by the troops at New Madrid.

This passage of the *Carondelet* and the near completion of the canal showed Beauregard that the siege of the island must soon end in disaster. So he immediately turned over the command of the fortifications to General McCall, and the troops on the Kentucky and Tennessee shores to General McCown, and with a large number of his best soldiers departed for Corinth to

nons and mortars, 7,000 small arms, many hundred horses and mules, 4 steamboats, and a large amount of ammunition. The fall of this stronghold was a great blow to the Confederacy, and produced widespread alarm in the Southern States.

It now seemed probable that Fremont's plan would be successfully carried out. Curtis had broken the military power of the Confederacy west of the Mississippi at the battle of Pea Ridge; and then another Federal force had pushed its way up the Tennessee and gained an important victory on the left bank of that stream, not many miles from Corinth. After the battle of Pea Ridge, Curtis marched in a southeasterly direction and encamped at Batesville, the capital of Independence County, Ark., on the White River.

General Grant's army at the beginning of April was encamped between Pittsburg Landing, on the left bank of the Tennessee, and the Shiloh Meetinghouse, which stood back in the forest about two miles. Grant's objective point was Corinth, an important position on the line of the Charleston and Memphis Railroad. The seizure of this place would give the Federals control of the great railroad communication between the Mississippi and the East and the border slave-labor States and the Gulf of Mexico. It would also allow the troops to give material aid to Foote in the plan he was then making to capture Memphis.

While Grant was thus encamped a large force of about 40,000 Confederates, unknown to him, had crept up from Corinth to within a few miles of Shiloh Meetinghouse. This force was in command of General A. S. Johnston, assisted by Generals Beauregard, Polk, Hardee, Bragg and Breckinridge. They decided to await the arrival of Van Dorn and Price, who were approaching Memphis with a large force from Central Arkansas, before attacking the Federal camp; but, learning that General Buell's army was on its way to join Grant, and knowing that the latter was ignorant of the near presence of his enemy, it was resolved to strike before dawn the next day.

The Union camp was just awaking from its slumbers on the morning of April 6th, 1862, when it was startled by the wild cry of pickets rushing in with the intelligence of the enemy's approach. The assault was opened by an attack by Hardee's division on General W. T. Sherman's troops stationed in the woods near Shiloh Meetinghouse. The Confederates dashed into the camp, fighting desperately, and drove the half-dressed, half-armed troops before them. General Prentiss's division, which was planted across the road leading to Corinth, was next attacked. His column also gave way under the onslaught, and he and a large portion of his followers were made prisoners. A fierce general struggle then began. For ten hours the battle raged, with terrible slaughter on both sides, General W. H. L. Wallace, of the Federals, and General Johnston, of the Confederates, being killed. At length, when night set in, the Federals were pushed back to the Tennessee River, and the day was fairly won by the Confederates. Still the Federals held their position, and during the night were re-enforced by the arrival of a portion of Buell's army and a division under General Lewis Wallace.

On the morning of the 7th the fight was renewed by an attack by Wallace on the Confederate left, which was in charge of Beauregard himself. The others soon joined in, and although the Confederates fought bravely they were soon driven back, and at length fled toward Corinth to the heights of Monterey, nine miles away. They lost at least 10,000 men, while the Federals lost in killed, wounded and prisoners 13,000. Beauregard's army soon

afterward fell back to Corinth, and Grant would have pursued it, and, in its weak condition, probably captured it, had not General Halleck, his superior at that time, come up just then from St. Louis, and ordered the troops to rest for awhile. This gave the Confederates a chance to reorganize their forces and make themselves ready for another battle.

CHAPTER IX.

HALLECK TAKES CORINTH — A DARING RAID — CAPTURE OF MEMPHIS — FEDERAL VICTORY AT NEW BERNE — SIEGE AND FALL OF FORT PULASKI — BRILLIANT AND SUCCESSFUL PLAN FOR THE TAKING OF NEW ORLEANS — REWARD OFFERED FOR BUTLER'S CAPTURE.

IT was not until more than two weeks had elapsed after the battle of Shiloh that General Halleck put his army in motion to capture Corinth. He reached the vicinity of that place on May 3d, and at once started the work of erecting fortifications preparatory to a siege. These were com-

GENERAL WILLIAM B. FRANKLIN.

pleted by the 29th, and arrangements were made for an attack the next morning. But during that night the enemy fled. Beauregard felt that his army was hardly strong enough to cope with the Army of the Tennessee, and so, after destroying everything he could not carry away, he took his troops in haste to Tupelo, many miles southward of Corinth. Arriving there, he turned over his command to General Bragg and retired to some mineral springs in Alabama for his health. Halleck marched into Corinth and held it until, shortly afterward, he was appointed general in chief of all the armies, and left for Washington. General Thomas then took command in Corinth, and General Grant of his old army.

The fall of Corinth completed a series of events by which the Federals gained possession of all Kentucky, Western and Middle Tennessee, Northern Mississippi and Northern Alabama; for just before (April 11th) General Mitchel, with part of

Buell's army, had by rapid marches from Nashville and by a sudden charge on the city of Huntsville, Ala., secured control of the Charleston and Memphis Railroad from Tuscumbia on the west to Stevenson on the east, and also of the Tennessee River for about one hundred miles.

Mitchel was a daring and audacious general, and accomplished splendid work for the Union cause. It was he who set in motion one of the most remarkable enterprises undertaken during the war. This was an attempt to destroy railroad communication between Chattanooga and Atlanta. Under his orders J. J. Andrews, with twenty-two picked men, disguised as Confederate citizens, walked to Marietta and took a train for a station a short distance from the foot of the Great Kenesaw Mountain. There they took advantage of the absence of the engineer and conductor at breakfast by uncoupling the engine, tender and box car. With these they dashed up the road at full speed, and soon began the destruction of the track. But it was not long before a train was started in pursuit of them. An exciting chase ensued. Onward sped pursued and pursuer. For many miles the two engines flew at a terrific pace. But having to stop now and then to cut telegraph wires and tear up the track, Andrews and his men began to lose ground, and the pursuers rapidly gained upon them. At length the fuel of the fugitives gave out, and they were compelled to leave their engine about fifteen miles from Chattanooga. They fled to the shelter of the woods near Chickamauga Creek, and defied capture for some time. But the Confederates, with the aid of bloodhounds, at last ferreted them out, and the whole party was caught. Andrews and seven of his companions were hanged. This daring raid elicited the approval of the Secretary of War, and he presented each of the survivors a bronze medal.

After the capture of Island No. 10 Commodore Foote started down the Mississippi River with his armed vessels and transports containing Pope's army, in the hope of taking Memphis. He was stopped about eighty miles above that city by the appearance of a Confederate flotilla under Captain Hollins, and 3,000 troops under General Jeff. Thompson from Fort Pillow, on Chickasaw Bluffs, then in command of General Villepigue. Foote opened upon the enemy at once, but being unassisted by Pope's troops, who, after landing on the Arkansas shore, were prevented from advancing by the flooded condition of the country, was compelled to withdraw. Hollins then reorganized his flotilla, and on May 10th, with the assistance of the heavy guns on Fort Pillow, attacked Foote. He was, however, repulsed, and as Foote was unable to follow up this victory, the opposing fleets stood quiet for two weeks. Then the Confederates, learning of the loss of Corinth, hurried down to Memphis. Foote was now re-enforced by a "ram" squadron, prepared by Colonel Charles Ellet, Jr., and on June 6th he attacked the Confederate squadron in front of Memphis. This being disposed of, Federal troops under General Lewis Wallace took possession of the city.

A short time before the events just recorded General Burnside and Commodore Rowan set out to follow up the capture of Roanoke Island and vicinity by other important movements on the North Carolina coast. On March 12th, 1862, they reached the Neuse River, and the next morning 15,000 troops, under Generals Foster, Reno and Parke, were landed and marched against a strongly intrenched position of the Confederates, under General Branch, at New Berne. On the morning of the 14th the attack was made, and although the Confederates held out bravely and persistently, they were at length overcome by superior numbers and fled across the Trent. By burning the bridges behind them they managed to escape. The Federals then took possession of New Berne. This was followed on April 25th by the capture of Fort Macon, on a point of Bogue Island near the entrance to Beaufort harbor, and by the accession of other important places on the coast, among them Plymouth, Winton and Washington.

Early in 1862 General T. W. Sherman, in command of the Department of the South, began preparations for the bombardment of Fort Pulaski. Batteries of rifled guns and mortars were planted on Big Tybee Island southeast of Cockspur Island, on which the fort stood. Then the Savannah River, in the rear of the fort, was effectually closed by the erection of a heavy battery at Venus's Point, on Jones's Island, and a smaller one on Bird Island. Before the attack on Fort Pulaski was made General Sherman was succeeded by General David Hunter in the command of the Department of the South (8th of March, 1862).

The siege opened on April 10th by a heavy cannonading from Big Tybee Island, under the direction of Generals Gillmore and Viele. For two days the fort was well defended. Then the balls and shells had played such havoc with its walls that the garrison was obliged to surrender. The gain of this important position made it possible for the Federals to close the port of Savannah against the numerous blockade runners that were then making mischief all along the coast.

Meanwhile Commodore Dupont, then in command of the navy on the Southern coast, with the assistance of General Wright, had captured Fort Clinch, on Amelia Island, and compelled the Confederates to abandon their other forts along the coasts of Florida and Georgia. Jacksonville was captured, March 11th, by a flotilla of gunboats and a body of troops under Lieutenant T. H. Stevens, and St. Augustine was taken possession of by Commander C. R. P. Rodgers. This alarmed the Confederates, and they at once fled from Pensacola and all their fortifications on the main opposite Fort Pickens.

In order to gain possession of Mobile,

New Orleans, Baton Rouge and Galveston the National Government placed General Benjamin F. Butler in command of the Department of the Gulf, and directed him to co-operate with the navy there in an effort to capture those places. Just before leaving Washington General Butler said to the President: "Good-by. We shall take New Orleans or you will never see me again." And Secretary Stanton, who was standing near, replied: "The man who takes New Orleans is made a lieutenant general."

New Orleans being the chief object of the expedition, it was arranged to have all the land and naval forces gather at Ship Island, off the coast of Mississippi. So when Butler arrived at that place with about 14,000 troops from Fortress Monroe he found there General Phelps with Massachusetts and Connecticut troops, Admiral Farragut with a naval force, and a fleet of bomb vessels commanded by Commodore David D. Porter. He also found the passage to New Orleans well guarded. Two forts—Jackson and St. Philip—stood on a bend of the Mississippi River, seventy-six

THE MULE CORRAL AT PITTSBURG LANDING.

miles from the Gulf of Mexico, and a number of smaller fortifications were above these, and obstructions had been placed in the river below.

General Butler at once conferred with Farragut and Porter, and the three agreed upon a plan for the capture of New Orleans. It was arranged that first an attack would be made on the forts below by Porter's bomb vessels. If this failed Farragut was, if possible, to take his stronger vessels past the forts, cut off their supplies and supports, and attack the Confederate vessels up the river. General Butler was then to attempt the capture of Fort St. Philip by an assault in the rear with his troops. Then the land and naval forces could press on to New Orleans.

According to this plan the two fleets, in which there were forty-seven armed vessels and some transports bearing troops, proceeded up the river. Porter's mortar boats, which led the procession, managed to get a good position near the forts by assuming a disguise in the shape of mud on their hulls and branches of trees in their masts, yards and rigging. The obstructions in the Mississippi had been swept away by the swelling of the river.

A shot from Fort Jackson opened the

battle on the morning of April 18th, 1862. Porter's mortar boats, supported by the gunboats, responded, and there was a severe conflict for several days. But Farragut soon saw that he would not be able to silence the enemy, and he determined to run by the forts on the night of the 23d. The perilous voyage started at two o'clock in the morning, the mortar boats covering the movements of the gunboats. The flagship *Hartford*, with Farragut, and two other strong vessels, sailed up the right bank of the river to attack Fort Jackson, while eight gunboats, commanded by Captain Theodorus Bailey, kept the eastern bank to look after Fort St. Philip.

The dark night was soon lighted up by the rapid flashes from the forts and on the mortar boats, and from blazing fire rafts sent down by the Confederates. The scene was a grand one and the noise terrific. Twenty mortars and 260 great guns bellowed forth their thunder, and these, with the constant explosion of shells, made the earth fairly tremble. Farragut climbed into the fore rigging of the *Hartford* and by watching the combat through a night glass directed the movements of the boats as far as possible. The fleet passed the forts safely, only to be attacked by a large flotilla of "rams" and gunboats. These, however, were soon disposed of. The gunboat *Veruna*, Captain Boggs, especially distinguished herself here, rushing in among the Confederate vessels and firing broadsides right and left until she had driven three of them ashore. Nearly the whole of the Confederate flotilla was destroyed within the space of half an hour. This great victory cost the Federals the loss of but 30 men killed and 125 wounded. In the meantime Butler had landed his troops and gained the rear of Fort St. Philip, where he soon compelled the surrender of the garrison. A little later Porter captured Fort Jackson with nearly 1,000 men. Then Farragut, with a fleet of thirteen vessels, sailed up to New Orleans. The people there were panic-stricken. Men and women rushed through the streets crying, "Burn the city! Burn the city!" Thousands of dollars' worth of cotton was hurriedly carried to the levees to be burned; specie to the amount of $4,000,000 was sent out of the city by railroad, and a large number of citizens fled from the doomed town. As Farragut approached, on April 25th, General Lovell and his troops set fire to the cotton and quickly decamped. Farragut held the city until General Butler arrived with his troops and took formal possession. Butler made his headquarters at the St. Charles Hotel and at once proclaimed martial law. One of his first acts was to cause the arrest and immediate trial on a charge of treason of a man named Mumford for pulling down the national flag on the Mint. Mumford was convicted and quickly hanged.

Butler's rigorous rule of New Orleans excited a violent personal hatred of the general. Richard Yeadon, a prominent citizen of Charleston, offered a reward of $10,000 for his capture and delivery, dead or alive, to any Confederate authority. Jefferson Davis issued a proclamation in which he pronounced Butler to be a felon deserving of capital punishment, and "should not be treated as a public enemy of the Confederate States, but as an outlaw and common enemy of mankind;" and he ordered that, "in the event of his capture, the officer in command of the capturing force do cause him to be immediately executed by hanging." Then, in a letter to the Charleston *Courier*, a "Daughter of South Carolina" wrote: "I propose to spin the thread to make the cord to execute the order of our noble President Davis when old Butler is caught; and my daughter asks that she

February 22d. McClellan was then ordered to first march against Manassas. The general in chief, however, remonstrated against this, and proposed to take his army to Richmond by way of Fortress Monroe and the peninsula, between the York and James Rivers. The President did not agree to this, and it was decided to submit the matter to a council of officers, when McClellan's plan was accepted. The general, however, thought best to wait until the forces in the West had gained victories before starting for Richmond.

Then, learning that the Confederates had retreated from Manassas toward Richmond, McClellan took his whole army across the Potomac and advanced on abandoned Manassas, to give his soldiers, as he explained, a little active experience preparatory to the campaign! The army had

pending disaster. But relief came to them unexpectedly that night in the shape of the *Monitor*, a small but strong gunboat, with its deck almost level with the surface of the water, and having in its centre a round tower of heavy iron. This tower was made to revolve so that its two heavy guns within could be brought to bear upon any point without changing the position of the vessel. This little craft had been constructed by Captain John Ericsson at New York, and arrived at Hampton Roads just in the nick of time to show its usefulness.

Upon reporting to the flag officer in the Roads, Lieutenant John L. Worden, commander of the *Monitor*, learned the situation of affairs, and at once made preparations to meet the mischief maker from Norfolk. Early the next morning, March 9th, 1862, the *Merrimac* appeared coming out

THE ARMY OF THE POTOMAC—SCENE AT THE CROSSING OF KETTLE RUN.

may be allowed to adjust it around his neck."

CHAPTER X.

DISAGREEMENT OF THE PRESIDENT AND GENERAL MC-CLELLAN — THE "MONITOR" AND THE "MERRIMAC" — BATTLE OF WINCHESTER — OPENING THE CAMPAIGN ON THE VIRGINIA PENINSULA — ENGAGEMENT AT WILLIAMSBURG.

THE Grand Army of the Potomac, under General McClellan, lay idle for some time in the vicinity of Washington, awaiting orders to advance. It had, however, been disciplined and recruited from time to time, so that early in 1862 it comprised a strong force of 200,000 men.

The people had at last become impatient for these troops to do something to help crush the Confederacy. So the President, on January 27th, issued a general order directing a simultaneous movement of all the land and naval forces of the United States against the Confederates on

a pleasant little outing, and then moved back to Alexandria. This so disgusted the President that he at once relieved McClellan of his position as general in chief, and put him in command of only the Department of the Potomac.

At about this time a short, sharp and decisive battle between two small but powerful vessels occurred in Hampton Roads. The Confederates, as before noted, had raised the *Merrimac*, one of the ships sunk in the river at Norfolk, and converted her into an ironclad gunboat. On March 8th this vessel started on a trip of destruction among the ships at the mouth of the James River, and succeeded in sinking the wooden sailing frigates *Congress* and *Cumberland*. This spread alarm among the army and navy officers in Hampton Roads, as they feared other transports and war vessels would share the fate of the frigates. They could devise no means to prevent the im-

of the Elizabeth River, and the *Monitor* went down to stop it. There was a terrific conflict, both vessels hurling huge missiles with tremendous force against each other. No effect seemed to be produced on the iron sides of the *Monitor*, while the *Merrimac* suffered so much, she was soon obliged to give up the fray and fly to Norfolk. Both of the commanders were wounded, Lieutenant Worden being struck in the face by the sudden dislodgment of the cement around the peephole in the turret, caused by the striking of one of the shots on that point. The *Merrimac* never ventured out again.

When the Confederates evacuated Manassas Stonewall Jackson had taken up a position at Winchester, in the Shenandoah Valley. General N. P. Banks, then in command of the Federal troops near Harper's Ferry, wishing to secure control of the valley, dispatched General Shields to attack Jackson. The latter withdrew further up, and Shields, after pursuing him for some distance, encamped at Winchester. Jackson then, being re-enforced, came down the valley with a large body of troops, infantry and cavalry, and attacked Shields at Kernstown, just west of Winchester, on March 22d. After a sharp and severe engagement, in which Shields was badly wounded, the Confederates were defeated. They fled up the valley, with Banks's men close on their heels.

The Army of the Potomac began its campaign on the Virginia Peninsula early in April. All but about 73,000 of that army, which were left for the protection of Washington, had been transferred to Fortress Monroe by General McClellan. There were now about 121,000 men at that place, and these were moved in two columns up the peninsula; one column under General Heintzelman marching near the York River, and the other, under General Keyes, near the James River. A fortified line had been formed across the peninsula by a comparatively small Confederate force under General J. B. Magruder. Being deceived as to the number of the Confeder-

turned the flank of the enemy. This drove the Confederates into a precipitate retreat, leaving about 800 of their wounded behind them.

The Federals would have pressed on in pursuit of the fugitives, and probably captured or dispersed the whole army, but McClellan came on the battlefield just then and would not allow it. Instead he marched slowly forward, and when he reached the Chickahominy River Johnston was safe beyond it. In the battle of Williamsburg the Federal loss was 2,200 and the Confederate 1,000.

McClellan had moved only thirty-six miles toward Richmond during the month after his arrival at Fortress Monroe. The principal reason given for this slow progress was his fear that he had not troops enough to defeat the enemy. His army had been somewhat depleted by the withdrawal of Blenker's division of 10,000 men to strengthen Fremont, who was in command of the Mountain Department, beyond the Blue Ridge, and of McDowell's army corps, who were ordered to a position where they could be ready to assist in the defense of the capital or in an attack upon

structions in the river put a stop to the chase.

After Johnston had withdrawn his troops from Manassas, McDowell with 30,000 men took up a position at Fredericksburg, ready for any emergency. Banks was then, as we have seen, in the Shenandoah Valley. At the beginning of May General Ewell, who had just joined Stonewall Jackson near Harrisonburg, in the upper part of the valley, was ordered to hold Banks, while General Robert E. Lee should push across the Rappahannock and cut off all communication between Alexandria and Winchester.

While on the way to join the Federals in the valley one of Fremont's brigades, under General Milroy, fell in with Jackson's troops. The latter at once moved against Milroy, and at McDowell, west of Staunton, a severe battle of about five hours took place, May 8th. Although neither side could be said to have won, Jackson sent a note to Ewell the next morning, saying: "Yesterday God gave us the victory at McDowell." In this battle the Federals lost in killed and wounded 256 men, and the Confederates 461.

Some stirring events now occurred in the

THE INVASION OF PENNSYLVANIA—BATTLE OF GETTYSBURG, FRIDAY, JULY 3D, 1863.

ates, McClellan decided he could not get beyond Yorktown without re-enforcements, and while awaiting these remained nearly a month below that place. Then a regular siege of Yorktown was begun by General Fitzjohn Porter, although the Federals were ten times stronger in number than the Confederates. After an attempt to capture the intrenchments on the Warwick River by a division under General Smith, of Keyes's column, had failed, Magruder fell back to the stronger intrenchments in front of Williamsburg. He was pursued by General Sumner and the main body of the Federals, while McClellan remained at Yorktown and sent troops under General Franklin up the York River to strike the enemy on the left.

General Joseph E. Johnston now made his appearance and assumed chief command of the Confederates. He soon withdrew his main army and fell back toward Richmond, leaving the remainder to hold Williamsburg. On his retreat he was surprised by an attack, on May 5th, by Generals Hooker, Kearny and Hancock. A severe battle followed. Hooker led the assault, and kept it up for fully nine hours, when Kearny came to his aid and Hancock

Richmond. In addition to these withdrawals, General Wool, with his 10,000 men at Fortress Monroe, was made independent of McClellan's orders. As the latter felt that he could not absolutely depend on any of these troops for support, he kept hesitating and complaining of a want of men, although the President urged him to act at once before the enemy should gather in greater strength on his front.

General John E. Wool, feeling certain that the Confederates could easily be driven out of Norfolk, started from Fortress Monroe and made a personal reconnoissance. Then he crossed Hampton Roads and landed a few regiments for the purpose of striking the rear of the fortifications below that city; but upon reaching the place he found that General Huger, in command at Norfolk, had already retreated, and Wool gained the city without a fight, on May 9th. Before leaving Norfolk the Confederates set fire to the once powerful but now much-battered *Merrimac*. The Confederate vessels in the James River set off for Richmond, hotly pursued by Commodore Rodgers's flotilla of gunboats to within eight miles of Richmond, where a strong fort on Drewry's Bluff and ob-

Shenandoah Valley. Ewell pressed back Banks to Strasburg, and a little later (May 23d) the combined forces of Jackson and Ewell captured or dispersed the Federal troops at Front Royal, under Colonel J. R. Kenly, of Baltimore. Then Banks retreated quickly down the valley, pursued by 20,000 Confederates. Arriving at Winchester, he made a stand, with 7,000 men, against an attack by Ewell, on May 25th. After fighting gallantly for several hours Banks was compelled to retreat because of the approach of Jackson with an overwhelming force. The Federals were pursued as far as Martinsburg, and they encamped for the night on the Potomac, at Williamsport.

Learning of these movements, McDowell sent a force over the Blue Ridge to intercept the Confederates if they should retreat, and Fremont hurried on from the west, toward Strasburg, with the same object in view. At this Jackson moved with his whole force up the valley, and the Federals gave chase. Fremont overtook Ewell at Cross Keys, beyond Harrisonburg, on June 7th. The battle was sharp but undecisive. At the same time troops under Generals Carroll and Tyler were pressing

Jackson at Port Republic, beyond the Shenandoah River, so closely that he called upon Ewell for help. The latter set out at once to obey the call, and by burning the bridge over the Shenandoah, near Port Republic, stopped the pursuit of Fremont. Jackson then, with his large force, easily routed his enemies, and they fell back to Winchester.

By the middle of May General McClellan managed to get within nine miles of Richmond, making his headquarters at Cold Harbor, near the Chickahominy River, and toward the close of that month the two armies of McClellan and Johnston confronted each other upon opposite sides of the Chickahominy. Nothing was done for a time, as both generals were waiting for re-enforcements from the Shenandoah Valley.

The proximity of the Federals alarmed

erals took possession of the Richmond side of the Chickahominy. Seeing the result of this bold dash, McClellan the next day ordered an immediate advance on Richmond; but with his usual hesitancy he waited until it was too late to carry out the order, and nothing was done for several days except the sending of General Fitz-john Porter with a large force to Hanover Courthouse to keep the way open for McDowell to join the army, which McClellan persistently demanded. After some sharp skirmishes Porter succeeded in cutting all railroad communication with Richmond except one leading to Fredericksburg, and then rejoined the main army.

The apparent timidity of McClellan emboldened General Johnston to march out from his intrenchments and attack the Federals on the Richmond side of the river. General James Longstreet led the

more furiously, and continued until the early evening, when a bayonet charge by the Federals broke the Confederate line and stopped the fighting for the night. The next morning (June 1st) the contest was renewed, and lasted several hours, when the Confederates withdrew to Richmond. The losses on each side amounted to about 7,000. Among the wounded were General Johnston of the Confederates and General O. O. Howard of the Union side. The latter lost his right arm.

CHAPTER XI.

Stuart's Raid—Battle of Mechanicsville—Struggle at Gaines's Mill—McClellan Seeks a New Position—Conflict at Savage's Station—Battle of Glendale — Malvern Hill — Second Battle of Bull Run.

After the battle of Fair Oaks the Army of the Potomac lay quietly in its position

THE INVASION OF MARYLAND—CITIZENS OF BALTIMORE BARRICADING THE STREETS, MONDAY EVENING, JUNE 29TH, 1863.

the Confederate Government at Richmond, and preparations were made for a hasty flight into South Carolina if necessary. They even covered the railroad bridge leading out of the city with plank, so as to facilitate the flight of artillery, and held a train of cars in constant readiness for Davis and his Cabinet. These preparations called forth from the Virginia Legislature resolutions demanding the defense of Richmond at all hazards, and assuring the President "that whatever destruction or loss of property of the State or individual shall thereby result will be cheerfully submitted to."

On May 23d portions of the contending armies came together at New Bridge and had a sharp battle, and on the 24th they fought at Mechanicsville. There the Confederates were driven back and the Fed-

Confederate advance, and fell suddenly and vigorously upon General Silas Casey, who held a position on both sides of the Williamsburg Road, half a mile beyond Seven Pines. Casey made a brave stand, but he was soon driven back with one-third of his command disabled. Troops were at once sent to his aid by Keyes, but the opposing forces were so strong, the whole body gave way and retreated to Fair Oaks Station, on the Richmond and York Railroad. Here re-enforcements were received from Heintzelman and Kearny, but as the Confederates also gained fresh troops the Federals were as badly off as ever, and it looked like a victory for the former. Just then General Sumner, seeing the peril of his friends, hurried to the scene of action with the divisions of Generals Sedgwick and Richardson. The battle then raged

on the borders of the Chickahominy for nearly a month. The decisive move upon Richmond was put off from day to day. Meanwhile General Robert E. Lee, who succeeded the wounded Johnston in the command of the Confederate troops, had been joined by Jackson and Ewell from the Shenandoah Valley, and with this added strength he prepared to attempt the dispersion of the Federals. While these preparations were being made a body of 1,500 cavalrymen under General J. E. B. Stuart started out on a daring raid. They rode all around McClellan's army, seized and burned 14 wagons and 2 schooners laden with forage on the Pamunkey River, and captured and carried away 165 prisoners and 260 mules and horses. Stuart's raid set an example for many other similar exploits by both parties during the war.

General Lee completed his preparations by June 26th, 1862, when he sent Stonewall Jackson with a large force from Hanover Courthouse to turn the right wing of the Union army and fall upon their base of supplies at the "White House," so named because of its being the site of the old "White House" in which Washington passed the first months of his married life. Another and heavier force, under General Longstreet and others, crossed the Chickahominy near Mechanicsville, about the same time, and made an attack upon McClellan's right wing, commanded by General Fitzjohn Porter, at Ellison's Mill. The battle was a severe one, and resulted in the defeat of the Confederates with a loss of more than 3,000 men. Porter lost about 400.

Had this victory been immediately followed up by a movement on Richmond that city might then have been taken by the Federals; but McClellan feared that his army and stores were in peril, and so prepared to transfer both to the James River. This movement was begun on

Early on the morning of June 28th the Federal army started on a march to Turkey Bend of the James River. In the procession was a train of 5,000 wagons, laden with ammunition, stores and baggage, and a drove of 2,500 head of beef cattle. General Lee did not learn of this movement, so skillfully was it masked, until the army was far on its way toward a new position on the James River. He then determined to overtake and destroy, if possible, the retiring army.

McClellan's rear guard was composed of the divisions of Sedgwick, Richardson, Heintzelman and Smith, and these had just reached Savage's Station when Sedgwick was attacked by a Confederate force under Magruder, which had been sent out by Lee. In the battle that followed Magruder was repulsed by General Burns's brigade, supported by those of Brooke and Hancock. At night the Federals fell back to White Oak Swamp, leaving about 2,500 of their wounded at Savage's Station. The entire army passed the swamp the next morning.

erates moved from Glendale in a strong, steady line and charged furiously up the hill in an endeavor to carry it by storm. The Federals bravely met the fierce onslaught, and one of the most terrible battles of the war began. In the thickest of the fight were the troops of Porter, Couch and Kearny, until toward evening, when Richardson and Meagher brought fresh soldiers to their aid. The gunboats on the river did effective work with well-directed bombshells. At last, at nine o'clock in the evening, the Confederates were driven away and took shelter in the woods and swamps.

Again did McClellan's hesitation prevent the capture of Richmond. The victory on Malvern Hill was so decisive, the generals of his army felt sure he would pursue Lee's shattered forces in the morning and march into Richmond within twenty-four hours. But no; McClellan ordered the army to fall back to Harrison's Landing, the spot he had selected as a secure place for his soldiers and base of supplies. Thus ended a campaign which had been little but a series of failures. McClellan's retreat sat-

THE WAR IN VIRGINIA—RAILROAD BRIDGE OVER THE RAPPAHANNOCK, AT RAPPAHANNOCK STATION.

June 27th. The stores at the White House were to be removed under the protection of Porter's corps, which was also ordered to attend to carrying away the siege guns and covering the army in its march for the James River. When for this purpose the troops were arranged on the rising ground near Gaines's Mill, on the arc of a circle between Cold Harbor and the Chickahominy, they were attacked by a large force under Generals Longstreet and Hill. A severe conflict took place. Porter was soon so hard pressed, he had to send to McClellan, who was on the opposite side of the river, for help. Slocum's division, of Franklin's corps, was sent over, but was soon found to be insufficient, and the brigades of French and Meagher were hurried across the river. They arrived just in time to rally Porter's shattered column, which was fast falling back in disorder. The Confederates were then driven from the field. At this battle of Gaines's Mill the Federals lost about 8,000 and the Confederates 5,000. That night Porter withdrew to the right side of the Chickahominy, and destroyed the bridges behind him.

While General Franklin, with a rear guard, was protecting the passage of the main bridge in White Oak Swamp and covering the withdrawal of the wagon trains from that point, on June 30th, the Confederate pursuers came up and engaged him in a severe contest, lasting nearly all day. Franklin managed to keep the enemy back until night, when the Federals destroyed the bridge and withdrew. On the same morning the Federal troops were attacked by a column of Confederates under Longstreet and Hill at Glendale, near by. It was a sanguinary battle, and resulted in a victory for the Federals after fresh troops under Hooker, Meagher and Taylor had arrived. In the conflict General McCall, who led the Pennsylvania troops, was captured, and General Meade received a severe wound. The next day (July 1st) the whole Army of the Potomac had gained a strong position on Malvern Hill, within the reach of Federal gunboats on the James River.

Not being satisfied with this position, McClellan that day went down the river on the gunboat *Galena* to find another place. While he was gone his army was attacked on Malvern Hill. The Confed-

isfied the authorities at Richmond that no further attempts to take the city would be made at that time, so they ordered Lee to push on to Washington.

General John Pope was at this time in command of the Army of Virginia, which comprised the three corps of McDowell, Banks and Sigel. Pope's main army was near Culpeper Courthouse, when Stonewall Jackson, by Lee's orders, left Gordonsville, and crossing the Rapidan came upon General Banks at the foot of Cedar Mountain, a few miles west of the Courthouse. A terrible struggle, which at times was carried on hand to hand, took place. Banks, although ably assisted by Generals Crawford, Augur, Geary and others, was being rapidly pushed back, when the arrival of Ricketts's division, of McDowell's corps, saved the day. Each side lost about 2,000 men, killed and wounded. Jackson kept his position in the mountains until August 11th, when he fell back behind the Rapidan.

Lee had now concentrated his forces for the march on Washington. They pushed rapidly forward in heavy columns. Finding they could not force a passage of the Rappahannock, they took a circuitous route to flank the Federals. Jackson, leading this flanking force, crossed the river on August 25th. He quickly marched over the Bull Run Mountain at Thoroughfare Gap, and at daylight the next morning he reached Manassas Junction. There he was soon joined by Longstreet and his troops. General Pope, with his whole Army of Virginia excepting Banks's division, then gave battle to the combined Confederates at Groveton, not far from the Bull Run battle ground, on August 29th. After a loss of about 7,000 men on each side the contest ended without any decisive result. Pope prepared to renew the battle the next morning, expecting help from McClellan, who had, on orders from General Halleck, brought his Army of the Potomac to Alexandria. But McClellan refused support,

cations around Washington. Pope, on his own request, was now sent West, and the Army of Virginia became a part of the Army of the Potomac, with McClellan at the head of all the troops defending the capital.

Another call for volunteers to serve during the war was made by the President in July, 1862; and the next month he called for 300,000 more to serve for three months, adding that an equal number would be drafted from the citizens who were between eighteen and forty-five years of age if they did not appear among the volunteers. A hearty response was given to these calls. The Confederate Government saw that it must do something at once or its cause would be lost, so General Lee was ordered to make a strong effort without delay to capture Washington before the new army should be brought into the field.

Union flags were ordered to be hauled down. This order was obeyed by every-one except a patriotic old woman named Barbara Frietchie, and the national ensign was flying from her window when Stonewall Jackson, with the advance of Lee's army, approached. Jackson ordered his riflemen to shoot away the staff. As the flag fell the woman snatched it up and waved it defiantly. Admiring her pluck, Jackson's nobler nature, as Whittier says,

—"within him stirred
To life at that woman's deed and word:
'Who touches a hair of yon gray head
Dies like a dog! March on!' he said."

Upon Lee's evacuation of Frederick the Federals followed him in two columns over the South Mountain into the valley of the

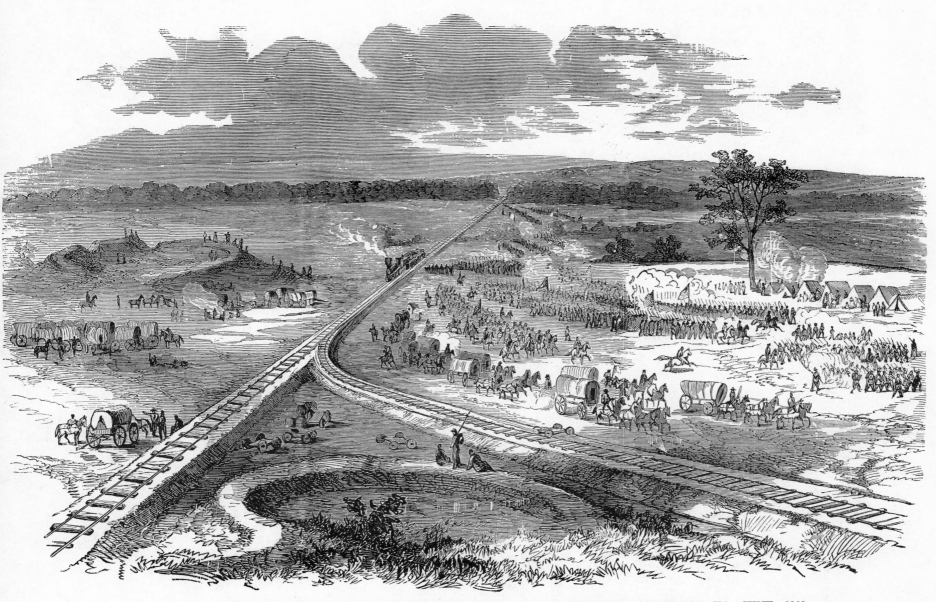

THE WAR IN VIRGINIA—GENERAL HOOKER'S ARMY MARCHING PAST MANASSAS, VA., JUNE, 1863.

and Pope had to go it alone. The Confederates skillfully drew the latter into an ambuscade on a part of the former battle ground of Bull Run, not far from Groveton, and a most sanguinary conflict was the result. The Federals were badly defeated and were sent flying across Bull Run to Centreville, where they were re-enforced by the troops of Franklin and Sumner.

There they made a stand, and Lee, not daring to attack them, sent Jackson on another flank movement. The latter came upon the Federals, under General Birney, at Chantilly, north of Fairfax Courthouse, and a battle was fought in a cold and drenching rain. It was a severe conflict, and in it Generals Philip Kearny and Isaac I. Stevens were killed. When the night fell the Federals still held the field, but they were broken and demoralized, and soon fled to the shelter of the fortifi-

Lee at once formed his plan of operations. He crossed the Potomac near the Point of Rocks into Maryland with almost his entire army, and encamped at Frederick, on the Monocacy, September 7th. His plan was to take possession of Harper's Ferry, so as to open communication with Richmond by way of the Shenandoah Valley, then march toward Pennsylvania, entice McClellan to pursue him, then turn suddenly, defeat the Federals, and march upon Washington.

Learning of Lee's invasion of Maryland, McClellan at once set out to drive him back. Leaving General Banks with some troops to defend the capital, he crossed the Potomac above Washington with about 90,000 men, and advanced cautiously toward Frederick. Lee did not wait to be attacked, but fled at his enemy's approach.

When Lee's army entered Frederick all

Antietam Creek. The right and centre moved by way of Turner's Gap, Burnside leading the advance; and the left, composed of Franklin's corps, by way of Crampton's Gap, on the same range, nearer Harper's Ferry. When Burnside reached Turner's Gap he found a large Confederate force awaiting him, and a desperate battle ensued on September 14th. It continued until dark, when the Confederates withdrew to join Lee's concentrated forces at Antietam Creek, near Sharpsburg. Burnside lost about 1,500 men, among the killed being the gallant General Reno. Franklin, meantime, had to fight his way at Crampton's Gap into Pleasant Valley. He succeeded in doing so, and on the evening of September 14th was within six miles of Harper's Ferry, where Colonel Miles, a Marylander, was in command of Federal troops. This place was in great

GRANT'S CAMPAIGN IN VIRGINIA—REPULSE OF LEE'S NIGH

...TH'S BRIGADE, HANCOCK'S CORPS, FRIDAY, JUNE 3D, 1864.

danger of capture by the Confederates, as they held strong positions on Maryland and Loudoun Heights, on each side of the Potomac. Franklin therefore immediately started to Miles's aid; but before reaching him the latter surrendered to Jackson, thus depriving the Federals of an advantage they might have easily had.

CHAPTER XII.

McClellan's Hesitation—Battle of Antietam Creek —General Burnside Made Commander of the Army of the Potomac—A Brave Drummer Boy— Battle of Fredericksburg — General Hooker Succeeds Burnside—The Guerrillas—Battles of Munfordville, Perryville, Iuka and Corinth.

Once again McClellan's chronic hesitancy asserted itself at a critical time and proved unfortunate for the Federals.

At dawn the next morning (September 17th) Hooker opened the battle of Antietam by an attack, with about 18,000 men, on the Confederate left under Jackson. Doubleday was on Hooker's right, Meade on his left and Ricketts in the centre. Until late in the afternoon the contest raged with varying fortunes. McClellan watched the progress of the battle from the opposite side of the Antietam. General Burnside, with the left wing of the Federals, especially distinguished himself in this battle, holding in check and fighting the enemy's right under Longstreet, until the latter was re-enforced by General A. P. Hill's division from Harper's Ferry. The desperate struggle lasted all day, and ended only because of darkness. Both armies suffered great losses, that of the

called for re-enforcements and supplies to enable him to pursue the fugitives. Then, instead of ordering a swift pursuit, he announced his intention of holding his troops there so as to be able to "attack the enemy should he attempt to cross into Maryland." Such an astounding declaration was almost too much for President Lincoln, and he hastened to McClellan's headquarters in person to see what it meant. Being satisfied that the army was in condition to make a successful pursuit, he ordered McClellan to start at once. But that general wasted another twenty days in raising objections to the carrying out of his orders, so that when he did deign to obey them Lee's army was thoroughly recruited.

McClellan had not advanced very far before he decided to disregard the instruc-

THE SIEGE OF CHARLESTON—ENGINEER DEPOT, MORRIS ISLAND, S. C.

When he followed the Confederates from South Mountain he did so cautiously, professing to believe them to have overwhelming numbers, although actually Lee's army then numbered only 60,000, while McClellan had 87,000. Then, when the Confederates posted themselves on the heights near Sharpsburg, on the western side of Antietam Creek, he hesitated to attack them until he was placed on the defensive by a sharp artillery assault. Then he sent Hooker across the Antietam with a part of his corps, commanded by Generals Ricketts, Meade and Doubleday; and they had a sharp conflict with the extreme right of the Confederates under General Hood. The Federals were successful, and at night they lay upon their arms. The divisions of Williams and Greene, of Mansfield's corps, passed over under cover of the darkness and encamped a mile in Hooker's rear.

Federals being 12,470, and the Confederates lost even a greater number. Lee's army, shattered and disorganized, retreated during the night. Had McClellan started a vigorous pursuit at once he might have made the whole Confederate force prisoners of war. But with his usual hesitation and indecision he refused to order a chase until thirty-six hours after the battle. As an excuse for this action he said in his report: "Virginia was lost, Washington was menaced, Maryland invaded—the National cause could afford no risks of defeat."

McClellan advanced on September 19th only to find Lee and his shattered army safe behind strong batteries on the Virginia side of the Potomac. He made a weak attempt at pursuit by sending two brigades across the river, but when they were driven back into Maryland and Lee had started up the Shenandoah Valley McClellan encamped at abandoned Harper's Ferry and

tions given him to go up the Shenandoah Valley, and instead prepared to move southward on the east side of the Blue Ridge. This was the last straw that broke the back of the patience of the government. He was promptly relieved from the command of the Army of the Potomac, and General Ambrose E. Burnside, of Rhode Island, was appointed in his place, November 5th.

Burnside immediately reorganized the Army of the Potomac, which at this time contained about 120,000 men. He decided to bring about the capture of Richmond as early as possible, rather than attempt the destruction of the Confederate army. Making Aquia Creek, on the Potomac, his base of supplies, he took measures to place his army at or near Fredericksburg, on the Rappahannock. Lee was at this time on the heights in the rear of Fredericksburg, with about 80,000 men and 300 cannon, so that when Burnside's army reached the Rappahannock during the second week in December the two opponents lay in parallel lines within cannon shot of each other, with a narrow river between them.

Lee had destroyed all of the bridges that spanned the river in that vicinity, so that there was no way for Burnside's troops to cross except on pontoons or floating bridges. Engineers were put to work on December 11th to construct five of these, but the men were driven away by sharpshooters concealed in buildings on the opposite shore. Efforts were made to quell this annoyance by opening a heavy fire upon the town from batteries placed on Stafford Heights, but although many buildings were set on fire by the shells the sharpshooters held their place. Then a party of volunteers crossed the river in

nearly five miles long and crowned with field artillery. After a sanguinary battle that lasted until night Burnside's forces, including the troops of Generals Franklin, Couch, Meade, Sumner, Hooker, Howard, Humphreys, Doubleday, Wilcox, French, Hancock, Sturgis and Getty were repulsed with a loss of more than 10,000. The Confederates lost about 4,000. On the night of the 15th, under cover of darkness, the Union army crossed the river.

Because of dissatisfaction at this defeat, although not the leader's fault, General Burnside, at his own request, was relieved of the command of the Army of the Potomac, January 26th, 1863, and General Joseph Hooker, "Fighting Joe," took his place. The army was then reorganized, and many changes and dismissals of officers were made to secure obedience and compe-

was moving in the same direction, on a parallel line, to foil them.

Part of Bragg's army, under General E. Kirby Smith, managed to get into Kentucky from East Tennessee, and, after routing a Federal force under General M. D. Manson, near Richmond, August 30th, pushed on rapidly through the State in the direction of the Ohio River, with the intention of capturing and plundering Cincinnati. But Smith's onward course came to a sudden stop when he reached the southern side of the river. There he found impassable fortifications and a large Union force under General Lewis Wallace, who had proclaimed martial law in Cincinnati, Covington and Newport. Smith turned back, and seizing Frankfort, the capital of the State, remained there to await the arrival of Bragg.

THE SIEGE OF CHARLESTON—ORDNANCE DEPOT, MORRIS ISLAND, S. C.

open boats in the midst of a terrific hail of bullets, landed on the other side, and effectually dislodged the sharpshooters.

When the party started a Michigan drummer boy named Hendershot, having been refused permission to go along, quietly slipped into the water, and clinging to the stern of one of the boats, was conveyed to the opposite shore. Although he saw several men in the boat shot down and his drum broken to pieces by a piece of shell, he was undaunted. Picking up the musket of one of the fallen soldiers, he fought gallantly with the rest.

The sharpshooters having been dispersed the pontoons were finished, and on the evening of the 12th the greater part of the Federal army crossed over and occupied Fredericksburg. The next morning the battle began with a series of assaults by the Federals upon the enemy's intrenched line,

tency. An important change was the consolidation of the cavalry force, which then numbered 12,000. It was also increased and drilled, and was soon in a condition of greater efficiency than it had ever been before.

After the Confederate armies had been driven out of Kentucky and Tennessee, and the Union forces withdrawn, several bands of daring guerrillas sprang up in those States, and hovered upon the rear and flanks of the Federal army, or roamed at will all over the country, plundering the Union inhabitants. One of these bands, led by John Morgan, a native of Alabama, raided through Kentucky and prepared the way for the advance of an invading army from Chattanooga under General Braxton Bragg. This army made its way toward Kentucky by a route eastward of Nashville at the same time that General Buell

Bragg entered Kentucky by crossing the Cumberland River, September 5th. General J. R. Chalmers, with 8,000 men, was leading the way when, upon his arrival at Munfordville, on the line of the Nashville and Louisville Railroad, he encountered a Union force under Colonel T. J. Wilder. The next morning (September 15th) the two forces clashed, and in a battle of five hours' duration the Confederates were defeated. Wilder's elation at his victory did not last long, for two days after another and stronger enemy appeared under General Polk, and fell upon him with such strength that he was compelled to fly from the field. Bragg then joined Smith at Frankfort and prepared to march on to Louisville. His army then numbered 65,000 men, while Buell, who was following him, had about 60,000. These two armies came together on October 8th near the lit-

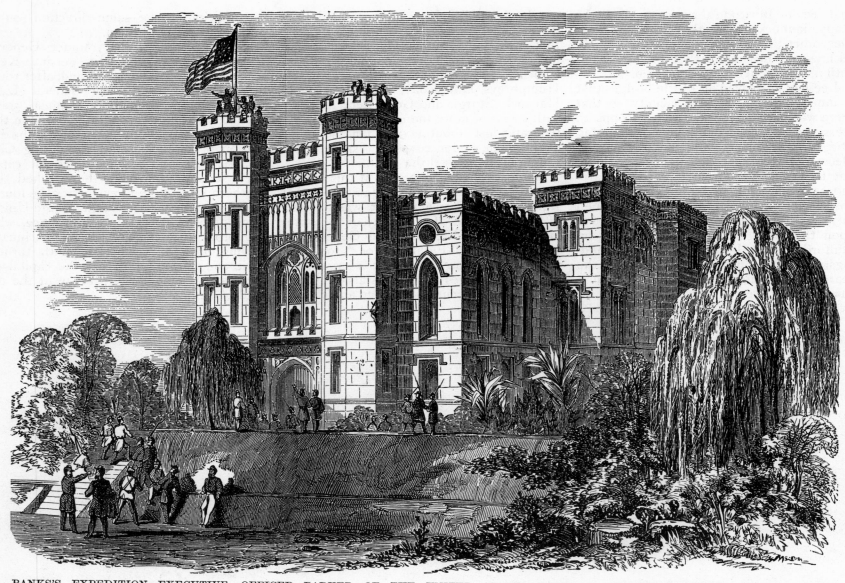

BANKS'S EXPEDITION—EXECUTIVE OFFICER PARKER, OF THE UNITED STATES GUNBOAT "ESSEX," HOISTING THE NATIONAL STANDARD ON THE STATE CAPITOL, BATON ROUGE, LA., ON ITS OCCUPATION BY THE FEDERAL FORCES COMMANDED BY GENERAL GROVER, WEDNESDAY, DECEMBER 17TH, 1863.

tle town of Perryville, Boyle County, and a severe battle was fought. All day it continued, and when night set in the Confederates had had enough of it, and fell back in haste to Harrodsburg, and thence out of the State. The Federals suffered in the fight to the extent of 4,350 men. The marauding bands that had come with the invaders had been so successful in their raids that when they retreated they had a wagon train of stolen property forty miles in length. A large portion of this had to be left behind.

At this time the Confederate army in Northern Mississippi, commanded by General Beauregard, had advanced toward Tennessee under Generals Van Dorn and Price. General Grant, hearing of this, sent word to General Rosecrans, then commanding the Army of the Mississippi, of the danger gathering west of him. Rosecrans at once moved toward Corinth, and as he did so Price went to meet him. When they met near the village of Iuka Springs, in Northern Mississippi, September 19th, Rosecrans with only 3,000 effective men successfully held the field against Price's 11,000. It was a fierce battle, and ended in the flight of the Confederates southward in great haste and confusion. A stirring incident of the conflict was a desperate hand-to-hand struggle for the possession of an Indiana battery which the Confederates had seized after the horses and 72 of its artillerymen had been killed. The Federal soldiers, although they fought hard, could not regain their battery, and it was dragged off the field with ropes. Rosecrans captured nearly 1,000 prisoners.

Grant had sent re-enforcements under General Ord to Rosecrans, but they did not reach him until the day was won. General Ord had stopped on his way at a place within four miles of Iuka, in order to follow out the instructions given him to wait there until he should hear Rosecrans's great guns. A high wind from the north prevented the sounds reaching him, and he knew nothing of the battle until it was over.

Rosecrans now gathered his troops at Corinth, knowing that Van Dorn and Price had united their forces and were preparing to attack him. The Confederates, 40,000 strong, moved up from Ripley and began the assault on Corinth, October 3d. For two days the battle raged with great fury. At length the Confederates were driven back and pursued to Ripley. They lost about 9,000 men, including prisoners, and the Federals about 2,300. General Ord, who was then at Hatchie River, attacked a part of Van Dorn's retreating army, and was severely wounded.

CHAPTER XIII.

EFFORTS TO TAKE VICKSBURG—BATTLE AT BATON ROUGE —THE CONFEDERATE RAM "ARKANSAS"—EVENTS IN MISSOURI—BATTLES AT PRAIRIE GROVE AND LABADIEVILLE—SURRENDER OF GALVESTON—BATTLE OF MURFREESBOROUGH.

IN the spring of 1862 Admiral Farragut was making active preparations for the capture of Vicksburg and Port Hudson, which were then the only obstructions to the free navigation of the Mississippi River. Vicksburg was a particularly important point, as it stood on high ground among the Walnut Hills, on the eastern bank of the Mississippi, and was strongly fortified by the Confederates. Until it could be taken the National Government could not hope to carry out its plans of gaining control of the great river. On May 7th the

Federal forces captured Baton Rouge. the capital of Louisiana, and thus made it possible for Farragut to go up the river close to Vicksburg, where, after consultation with the commanders of gunboats in the vicinity, he opened an attack upon the batteries. Then, in order to avoid the guns at the city, he had an effort made to cut a canal across a peninsula in front of Vicksburg; but, failing in this, he ceased his attack and withdrew his vessels down the river.

A little later, early in August, a Confederate force led by General J. C. Breckinridge attempted to regain possession of Baton Rouge, then in command of General Thomas Williams. A severe conflict was the result. During the battle the Twenty-first Indiana Regiment, which did splendid work, lost all of its field officers. When General Williams noticed this he dashed up to the regiment, and placing himself at its head, exclaimed: "Boys, your field officers are all gone; I will lead you!" A few minutes afterward he fell dead with a bullet in his breast. His soldiers then fell back, as did also the Confederates.

Just after this battle the Confederate ram *Arkansas*, intended for the destruction of all the Federal vessels in the Mississippi, appeared above Baton Rouge, ready to carry out its intentions. To prevent this Commodore Porter, with the gunboats *Essex*, *Cayuga* and *Sumter*, went to meet her. There was a short, sharp and decisive fight. The *Arkansas* soon became unmanageable and struck the shore, where, her magazine exploding, she was blown to pieces.

Missouri had become so overrun with guerrillas that in June, 1862, that State was made into a separate military district, with General J. M. Schofield as its commander. With a force of 30,000 men that active and vigilant leader soon dispersed the roaming bands and drove out the Confederate troops that came into Missouri over the southern border. These troops then gathered in Arkansas under General T. C. Hindman. But Schofield followed them with 8,000 troops under General J. G. Blunt. The latter came across a portion of Hindman's army at Fort Wayne, near Maysville, on October 22d, and attacking them fiercely, drove them into the Indian country. Another portion was found on the White River, eight miles from Fayetteville, and they were driven into the mountains by a cavalry force under General F. J. Herron. These successful movements resulted in General Blunt receiving the command of the Missouri District, when soon afterward Schofield retired on account of ill health.

Gathering about 20,000 men on the western borders of Arkansas, Hindman prepared to make a determined effort to recover Missouri. He started out against Blunt late in November. After attacking and defeating Hindman's advance, composed of Marmaduke's cavalry, on Boston Mountains, Blunt took up a position at Cane Hill. He then sent for Herron, who was just over the border in Missouri, and the two awaited the approach of Hindman. The latter soon came with 11,000 men, expecting to deal a crushing blow on Blunt's army ; but the combined Federal forces, in a battle at Prairie Grove, defeated him and drove his troops in confusion over the mountains.

Meanwhile vigorous efforts were being made to recover Texas from Confederate rule. Commander Eagle with a small squadron sailed up to Galveston in May, 1862, and demanded its surrender. Meeting with a prompt refusal, he withdrew, and nothing was done toward its capture until the following October, when the civil authorities of the city surrendered it to Commodore Renshaw. At this time General Godfrey Weitzel, leading an expedition sent out by Butler to gain control of La Fourche Parish, in Louisiana, had a severe engagement with a force of Confederates at Labadieville (October 27th). He was victorious, and soon afterward the eastern portions of the State, along the borders of the Mississippi, were brought under Federal control. Two months later General N. P. Banks succeeded Butler in the command of the Department of the Gulf.

Toward the close of the year 1862 General Rosecrans, with a greater part of the Army of the Cumberland, composed of troops under Generals Sheridan, McCook, Rousseau, Thomas, Crittenden, J. C. Davis, Palmer, Van Cleve, Wood, Matthews, Negley, Hazen and others, had moved southward, and on December 30th reached Stone River, near Murfreesborough. On the opposite side of the river, within cannonshot, was General Bragg's army with such good leaders as Generals Kirby Smith, Polk, Hardee, Breckinridge, Cleburne, Cheatham, Withers and Wharton. Bragg had come up from Kentucky by way of Chattanooga to invade Middle Tennessee, and had concentrated his forces at Murfreesborough, just south of Nashville.

The next morning, December 31st, a fearful battle began. Rosecrans advanced to fall upon the enemy's left, while the Confederates had massed and made a dash upon Rosecrans's right, held by General McCook. The latter was soon hard pressed by overwhelming numbers, and sent to Rosecrans for assistance. The reply was : "Tell him to contest every inch of ground. If he holds them we will swing into Murfreesborough with our left and cut them off." But the attack on McCook was too strong to withstand, and as his troops were slowly driven back Rosecrans saw that he must change his original plan and hasten to the assistance of his right. Meanwhile Sheridan was assailed. The Confederates advanced toward him in a compact mass across an open field. He at once opened three batteries upon them with telling effect. They kept bravely on, however, until within about fifty yards, when Sheridan's troops, who had been lying in the woods under cover, suddenly arose to their feet and poured such a murderous volley into their ranks that they broke and fled.

The Confederates at once sent another division against Sheridan, only to be again repulsed. Three more times he was attacked, but each time he stood his ground, and the enemy, with terrible loss, at length retired to its intrenchments. On the next day nothing but heavy skirmishing was done.

Then, on January 2d, the fight was renewed in terrible earnest. The losses soon became so great that it seemed for a time as if the battle would end only when there were no more troops to fight. At length the Nineteenth Illinois, the Seventy-eighth Pennsylvania, the Eleventh Michigan, the Thirty-seventh Indiana and the Eighteenth, Twenty-first and Seventy-fourth Ohio Regiments made a simultaneous charge on the Confederate line and broke and scattered

A SOUTHERN CARICATURE—"GENERALS WHEELER AND WHARTON FALLING SLOWLY BACK, CONTESTING EVERY FOOT OF THE WAY."

it in confusion. The next night Bragg took his badly smitten army southward to Tullahoma. The Federals lost at Murfreesborough, in killed and wounded, 8,778, and the Confederates more than 10,000 and about 1,500 prisoners. Great alarm and discouragement were produced among the leaders of the Confederacy and among the people of the South by this crushing blow. It marked the last of a series of failures the Confederates had made in every aggressive movement from Antietam to Murfreesborough.

CHAPTER XIV.

Proclamation of Emancipation—The Confederate Government Made a "Permanent" One—Its President and Cabinet—Capture of Fort Hindman—Running by the Vicksburg Batteries—Grant Takes Jackson—The Siege of Vicksburg.

When the war had been going on for almost two years President Lincoln saw that something must be done to abolish the slave system, as through it the Confederacy could call on every available man to fight against the government without the necessity of leaving some to till the ground and produce food for the army, the slaves being put to that work. So on September 22d, 1862, the President issued a proclamation in which he said that he would declare the emancipation of all slaves in the States wherein insurrection existed on January 1st, 1863, unless the offenders should lay down their arms.

This offer to protect the human property of the slaveholders, should they give up their war against the Union, was rejected; they would make no concessions of any kind. They hoped that the question of emancipation would divide the people of the free States, and thus enable them in the end to secure their much-desired separation from the Union. So their resistance to the National Government became stronger than ever. Accordingly, on the first day of January, 1863, the Proclamation of Emancipation prepared by the President and approved by his Cabinet was promulgated. Thus were declared to be free and independent more than three millions of slaves.

The Confederacy made its Provisional Government a permanent one early in 1862. Its Provisional Congress expired by limitation on February 18th, and a new "permanent" one began on the same day with representatives from all the slave-labor States excepting Maryland and Delaware. The next day Jefferson Davis was declared elected President of the Confederacy for six years. His Cabinet consisted of Judah P. Benjamin, of Louisiana, Secretary of State; George W. Randolph, of Virginia, Secretary of War; S. R. Mallory, of Florida, Secretary of the Navy; Charles G. Memminger, of South Carolina, Secretary of the Treasury, and Thomas H. Watts, of Alabama, Attorney General. Randolph resigned soon afterward, and James A. Seddon, of Richmond, was appointed to fill his place.

As we have seen, the chief object of the Federal forces at the beginning of 1863 was the capture of Vicksburg and Port Hudson, on the Mississippi River. For this purpose General Grant concentrated his army near the Tallahatchie River, in Northern Mississippi. He planned to get to the rear of Vicksburg by capturing Jackson, the capital of the State; then await the arrival of Sherman, who was to pass down the river from Memphis in transports guarded by Porter's gunboats, then up the Yazoo to a point where he could make a junction with Grant's forces. Grant moved first to Holly Springs, where he left a large quantity of supplies; then on to Oxford, after flanking the enemy drawn up for battle on the other side of the Tallahatchie. While there Grant learned that Van Dorn, with his cavalry, had surprised the regiment guarding the supplies at Holly Springs and effectually destroyed them. This compelled the Federals to fall back to Grand Junction.

Meanwhile Sherman, with 12,000 troops, left Memphis in transports, with siege guns, to beleaguer Vicksburg. At Friar's Point he was joined by Commodore Porter and his fleet of gunboats, and they all went up the Yazoo River. At attempt was made to capture some batteries which protected the rear of Vicksburg, but after a sharp battle at Chickasaw Bayou (December 28th) Sherman was repulsed and retired to Young's Point and Milliken's Bend, opposite the mouth of the Yazoo River, where the army was concentrated twelve miles above Vicksburg. Grant then took his forces from Memphis down the river to the same place, after convincing himself that the city could not be taken by direct assault.

While waiting for Grant, General John A. McClernand, who arrived at headquarters, near Vicksburg, and took temporary command, captured Fort Hindman, at Arkansas Post, fifty miles from the mouth of Arkansas River, January 11th. The troops were convoyed by Porter's gunboats and rams to within three miles of the fort, where they were landed. Porter then passed up to close range, and a sharp conflict was begun. The fort was soon surrendered with 5,000 prisoners.

The following month Porter ran by the batteries at Vicksburg with nearly his whole fleet and a number of transports, which were protected from shot by bales of cotton and hay. These transports were manned by volunteers, which led Grant to say, in one of his reports: "It is a striking feature of the volunteer army of the United States that there is nothing which men are called upon to do, mechanical or professional, that accomplished adepts cannot be found for the duty required, in almost every regiment."

When the gunboats and transports had successfully passed down, on the way attacking the batteries at Grand Gulf, they stopped at Bruensburg to ferry across the Mississippi Grant's army, which had marched down the west side of the river. This done, Grant pressed on to Port Gibson, which he captured after a short battle (May 1st).

Grant then waited five days for Sherman, who had been sent to attempt the capture of Haines's Bluff, on the Yazoo River.

THE WAR IN MISSISSIPPI—DEFEAT OF WIRT ADAMS'S CONFEDERATE CAVALRY BY THE SECOND WISCONSIN CAVALRY, MAJOR EASTMAN, NEAR RED BONE CHURCH, MISS.

Being unsuccessful in this, Sherman crossed the Mississippi and joined Grant on May 8th. The army then started for Jackson, the capital of Mississippi. On the way they found a large force of Confederates strongly posted in the woods, near the village of Raymond. They were driven out after a battle of three hours, and the Federals continued their march. Generals Sherman and McPherson were in the advance, and when they arrived within three miles of Jackson they came upon a Confederate force of 11,000 men, under General Joseph E. Johnston (May 14th). McPherson at once attacked the main body, while Sherman passed round, flanking the enemy and driving the riflemen from their pits. After a short engagement the Confederates fled northward, leaving 250 prisoners and 18

demoralized condition of the enemy, it might be taken that way. But he found it too strongly fortified, and the troops were withdrawn. After a rest of two days Grant decided to make another effort to carry the city by storm. So at ten o'clock on the morning of the 22d almost the whole army moved at an appointed signal and made a dash upon the Confederate works. A terrible scene took place. The frowning fortifications became almost a mass of flame as they poured forth a deadly fire upon the uncovered troops below. Bravely the army struggled, with terrible loss of life, to gain a foothold where they could stop the murderous guns. After a time General McClernand sent word to Grant that he had won some intrenchments and wanted help to hold them and enable him to push further

man lying across Stout's Bayou, and touching the bluffs on the river. Parke's corps and the divisions of Smith and Kimball were sent to Haines's Bluff.

For more than a month the siege of Vicksburg continued. Shot and shell followed each other in quick succession throughout every day. Batteries on land and water sent death-dealing messages into the very heart of the city, playing havoc with the buildings, and driving the inhabitants into the shelter of caves dug into the earth. While the iron hail was dropping on to the devoted citadel Grant's army dug its way nearer and nearer to the city, until it got close enough to undermine one of the principal forts in the line of the defenses on the land side. This was done, and the fort blew up with fearful effect. Meanwhile

THE WAR IN MISSISSIPPI—McPHERSON'S TROOPS FORAGING AT THE CONFEDERATE GENERAL WHITFIELD'S HEADQUARTERS.

guns. Grant then seized the capital. He left Sherman there to destroy the war material and public property, while he, with a large force, marched to Champion Hill, where General Pemberton, with 25,000 men, held a strong position. Upon his arrival there Grant decided to wait until McClernand, with the Thirteenth Corps, could come up, but the Confederates would not wait, and on the morning of May 16th began the battle. The struggle was short and decisive. Pemberton's troops were driven from the field and fell back to Black River railroad bridge. There they were followed and again defeated, and sent flying in disorder to Vicksburg.

The victorious army swept on and closely invested Vicksburg in the rear the next day (May 19th). An assault upon the city was soon ordered, Grant expecting that, in the

on. More troops were sent him, and new vigor was put into the assault. But it was a false hope. McClernand had not gained as much as he intimated, and after a little more slaughter the broken army was at length compelled to fall back and abandon the struggle. Grant, feeling that McClernand had made a grievous mistake in calling for aid, removed that general from command and put General Ord in his place.

Grant now saw that he could not take the city by storm, and so, with the co-operation of Porter's fleet, began a regular siege. He at once sent for re-enforcements, and when these came the investment of Vicksburg was complete. He arranged his forces by placing Sherman's corps on the extreme right, McPherson's next and extending to the railroad, and Ord's on the left, with the divisions of Herron and Lau-

famine stared in the face of the citizens of Vicksburg. The food was portioned out sparingly, and the people had to eat anything they could lay their hands on that was at all edible.

At last on July 3d, a flag of truce went up on the fortifications, and two officers appeared before Grant with a note from Pemberton, in which he suggested the appointment of three commissioners to settle upon terms of capitulation. Grant wrote in reply that, as he could not listen to anything but unconditional surrender, it would be useless to appoint commissioners, and if Pemberton wished the cessation of the siege he could have it by an agreement on those terms. Pemberton then asked for a personal interview, and the two generals met midway between the lines, under a gigantic oak. When Grant repeated that his terms were unconditional surrender Pemberton haughtily answered: "Never, so long as I have a man left me!" "Then," said Grant, "you can continue the defense; my army was never in a better condition to continue a siege." Not being able to agree, the interview ended with a promise from Grant to consult with his officers, and to let Pemberton know the result by messenger. The

Thus ended a short, stirring campaign, the result of which was, as Grant said in his report, "the defeat of the enemy in five battles outside of Vicksburg; the occupation of Jackson, the capital of Mississippi, and the capture of Vicksburg and its garrison and munitions of war—a loss to the enemy of 37,000 prisoners, among whom were 15 general officers, at least 10,000

capturing it." His own loss in killed, wounded and missing he estimated at 8,575.

In the meantime General Banks, after an active campaign, in which, as he reported, he managed to break the Confederate power in Northern and Central Louisiana, had invested Port Hudson, then in command of General Frank Gardner. With

THE WAR IN TENNESSEE—LOOKOUT MOUNTAIN AND ITS VICINITY, FROM THE POSITION OF THE ELEVENTH ARMY CORPS.

terms agreed upon were, that the entire place and garrison should be surrendered, but that the troops would be paroled and allowed to march out of the lines—the officers taking with them their regimental clothing, and the staff and field and cavalry officers a horse each. This proposal being accepted, the stronghold of Vicksburg, with 37,000 men and a vast amount of ordnance, was surrendered, July 4th, 1863.

killed and wounded, and among the killed Generals Tracy, Tilghman and Green, and hundreds and perhaps thousands of stragglers who can never be collected and reorganized. Arms and munitions of war for an army of 60,000 men have fallen into our hands, besides a large amount of other public property, consisting of railroads, locomotives, cars, steamboats, cotton, etc., and much was destroyed to prevent our

the assistance of Farragut's squadron, the *Hartford*, *Albatross*, *Monongahela*, *Richmond*, *Essex* and *Tennessee*, and some mortar boats, Banks began the siege of Port Hudson late in May. Like Grant at Vicksburg, he made two unsuccessful and disastrous attempts to take the place by storm. For forty days the siege continued. At length the want of ammunition and the fall of Vicksburg made it impossible to hold the post any longer, and on July 9th General Gardner surrendered to Banks. The Federals lost during the siege about 3,000 men, and the Confederates, exclusive of prisoners, about 800.

The capture of Vicksburg and Port Hudson sent a thrill of joy throughout the North, for in it the people of the loyal States could see signs of the early ending of the war. The loss of these important places would be a blow to the Confederacy from which it could never recover. Grant was hailed as a great general and took a high place in the regard of the people.

CHAPTER XV.

THE FIRST CAVALRY CONTEST—THE BATTLE OF CHANCELLORSVILLE—DEATH OF STONEWALL JACKSON—LEE AGAIN INVADES MARYLAND —GENERAL GEORGE G. MEADE SUCCEEDS GENERAL HOOKER.

AFTER the battle of Fredericksburg the Army of the Potomac, under General Joseph Hooker, remained in comparative quiet on the northern side of the Rappahannock River, near Fredericksburg, for nearly three months. The army numbered about 100,000 men, while General Lee's army, on the other side of the river, numbered but 60,000, as a large force under General Longstreet had been detailed to watch the movements of the Federals under General Peck, in the vicinity of Suffolk. During these three months nothing but a few cavalry movements disturbed the two armies. Early in February the Federal troops at Gloucester, opposite Yorktown, were attacked by a mounted force under General W. H. F. Lee, and March 8th the Federal forces at Fairfax Courthouse were surprised in the middle of the night by a band of guerrillas led by Colonel Mosby. They dashed into the village, and after taking some prisoners, among them the commander at that place, galloped away. A little later the first real cavalry contest of the war took place. It was between a body of Federal horsemen led by General Averill and some mounted Confederates under General Fitzhugh Lee. They met at Kelley's Ford, on the Rappahannock, and after a severe battle Averill's men were repulsed.

When the three months had almost gone with nothing accomplished Hooker determined to put his army in motion toward Richmond. So, after making an unsuccessful attempt with General Stoneman's cavalry to destroy the railroads in Lee's rear, Hooker sent 10,000 mounted troops to raid in the rear of the enemy. Then, while his left wing, under General Sedgwick, engaged Lee in front, Hooker took 60,000 troops of his own right wing across the Rappahannock, several miles above Fredericksburg, to Chancellorsville, a small village in a region known as the Wilderness. Hooker made his headquarters there and began to intrench himself. He placed Howard's corps on his extreme right, with Sickles next to him, Slocum in the centre, and Meade and Couch on the left.

Lee, instead of being frightened at these preparations and retreating toward Richmond, as Hooker expected, sent Stonewall Jackson, with a large force, early in the morning of May 1st, to strike the Federal army a heavy blow. Hooker's troops went out to meet him, but after a sharp engagement were driven back to their intrenchments.

The next morning, Saturday, May 2d, Lee sent Jackson, with the whole of the latter's command, about 25,000 men, to execute a grand flank movement on Hooker's extreme right, where Howard was stationed. Jackson cut his way through the tangled wilderness, which effectually covered his approach, and reaching Howard's position, suddenly burst from the woods upon him. Fierce and terrible was the on-

ADMIRAL SAMUEL F. DUPONT.

slaught, crushing the Federal column like an eggshell, and driving its broken pieces back upon the remainder of the line. In vain did the gallant Howard gallop furiously among his panic-stricken men and wave his empty sleeve as a banner to them. His column was wrecked, and he could not save it. Back it fell, and Jackson was about to gain the army's rear. But Hooker, taking in his peril at a glance, sent his old division, then Berry's, to the rescue. Presenting a solid front to the enemy, it enabled Sickles and Howard to rally their troops behind it, and Jackson's victorious course was checked. But, regardless of the terrific loads of canister that poured into their ranks from thirty pieces of artillery massed in front of Berry's position, the Confederates continued their attack until late in the evening.

Just after the conflict had ended for the day the Confederates lost one of their most brilliant leaders. In order to make observations toward arranging a plan of battle for the next day, General T. J. Jackson ("Stonewall") rode, with his staff, over the ground in front of the skirmishers. Then, as he was returning to the lines in the darkness, he was shot and mortally wounded by one of his own men, who mistook him and his staff for Federal cavalry.

At dawn the next morning (May 3d) the battle was renewed by an attack upon the troops of General Sickles. The Confederates were bravely met by the divisions of Birney and Berry, supported by forty pieces of artillery. For a time these made a stand against General Stuart, who had taken the place of the fallen Jackson; but the Confederates, undaunted by the heavy cannonading they received, dashed up at a furious pace and drove Sickles's corps gradually back, and after six hours' hard fighting they were pushed from the field to a strong position on the roads back of Chancellorsville.

While this battle was being fought General Sedgwick, with Hooker's right wing, had crossed the Rappahannock on Lee's front, and by a brilliant dash had captured the heights of Fredericksburg. Then, leaving a part of his force to hold these works, he took his main army toward Chancellorsville to join Hooker. Learning of this move, and having Hooker well in hand, Lee at once dispatched an overwhelming force to intercept him. There was a severe battle, and Sedgwick was compelled to retreat across the river at Banks's Ford. The troops left on the heights were also attacked and driven over the river. Hooker soon followed, with the rest of the Army of the Potomac, reaching the north side of the Rappahannock in safety on May 4th, while Lee resumed his former position on the heights of Fredericksburg. The loss on both sides was heavy, that of the Federals, in killed, wounded and prisoners, more than 17,000, and the Confederates, about 15,000.

Soon after the battle of Chancellorsville General Longstreet rejoined Lee. During his absence he had besieged General Peck in a strongly fortified position, near Suffolk, in Southeastern Virginia, in the hope of driving the Federals from that post, so as to enable him to seize Norfolk and its vicinity and attack Fortress Monroe. But failing in this, he abandoned the siege and went back to Lee.

With this addition to it, Lee's army was reorganized into three army corps, commanded respectively by Generals Longstreet, A. P. Hill and Ewell. Then Lee, made confident by his successes, resolved to invade Maryland again. With this purpose in view, he sent his left wing, in charge of General Ewell, toward the Potomac, through the Shenandoah Valley, by way of Chester Gap, while Longstreet, with another large force, moved along the eastern bases of the Blue Ridge. At Winchester the Confederates came upon General Milroy, with 7,000 Federal troops, and after a battle drove him across the Potomac to Harper's Ferry. Ewell then crossed the stream and marched rapidly up the Cumberland Valley to within a few miles of the Susquehanna, opposite Harrisburg, the capital of Pennsylvania. He was soon followed by the divisions of Early, Hill and Longstreet, and on June 25th, the whole of Lee's army was again in Maryland and Pennsylvania.

The Army of the Potomac, which had followed Lee on his right flank, took up a position at Frederick, Md., June 27th. There General in Chief Halleck and General Hooker had a decided disagreement over some proposed military movements, and the latter was forced to resign his command of the Army of the Potomac. He was succeeded by General George G. Meade, who kept the position until the close of the war. His forces then numbered 100,000 men.

Lee now determined to move upon Harrisburg and then push on to Philadelphia, but learning that Meade was well across the Potomac and was threatening his flank and rear, he decided to first concentrate his army at Gettysburg, and then deal such a demoralizing blow upon Meade that he could march on to Baltimore and Washington without trouble. Accordingly, Longstreet and Hill were ordered to march from Chambersburg to Gettysburg, and Ewell from Carlisle. As the advance of General Hill's corps approached their destination they were met by Buford's division of National cavalry, at Seminary Ridge, July 1st, and a sharp skirmish took place. General J. F. Reynolds, with the left wing of Meade's army, then came up and hastened to Buford's relief. Hardly had he reached the field before he was instantly killed. His place was taken by General Abner Doubleday and the battle went on. General O. O. Howard now arrived with his corps and took chief command. The Federals at once began to press the enemy back, and seemed to be winning the day, when Ewell's corps appeared on the scene, outflanking Howard's line of battle. This turned the tide, and Howard was driven off the field to a strong position on a range of hills near Gettysburg, of which Culp's Hill and Little Round Top were the two extremes of the line, and Cemetery Hill, at the village, was the apex. The Confederates pursued them fiercely, capturing about 2,500 prisoners, until they reached the ridge of hills, where they were met by such a deadly artillery fire that, struggle as they would, they had to fall back, and the conflict ended with the day.

Learning of Reynolds's death, Meade at once dispatched General Hancock to the field to find out and report to him the state of affairs. Hancock's information was such that Meade determined to give battle at the strong position Howard had selected. He immedi-

FLAG OF TRUCE FROM THE CONFEDERATES FOR A SUSPENSION OF FIRING, TO BURY THEIR DEAD, AT PORT ROYAL, S. C.

ately dispatched orders to the different corps to march with utmost speed to Gettysburg, and then started off himself, reaching the place a little after midnight. Lee also concentrated his forces that night and prepared for the great battle of the morning.

CHAPTER XVI.

BATTLE OF GETTYSBURG—A TERRIBLE CANNONADE—LEE'S RETREAT—A GALLANT CHARGE—CAPTURE OF RAPPAHANNOCK STATION—THE ARMY OF THE POTOMAC GOES INTO WINTER QUARTERS.

SOLEMNLY the morning of July 2d, 1863, opened around Gettysburg. Preparations were being made on all sides for a great battle. Troops were coming in from everywhere to swell the armies, soon to close in mortal combat. Promptly had the divisions of the Army of the Potomac responded to Meade's urgent call, and they were all in their appointed positions by two o'clock that afternoon.

The Federal line of battle extended for nearly five miles along both sides of the heights from Cemetery Hill, which overlooked Gettysburg and the field and woodland beyond. Howard, with the Eleventh Corps, occupied the centre; next to him, on the right, was Slocum and the Twelfth Corps, followed, across the road, on another hill, by the First Corps; on the left was the Second Corps, under Hancock, and Sickles's Third Corps. Hill held the centre of Lee's

army, with Longstreet on the right, and Ewell the left.

The battle began in the middle of the afternoon, when Longstreet made a fierce charge upon Meade's left, commanded by General Sickles. Amid the crash and thunder of artillery the Confederates dashed up savagely, but in splendid order, and dealt blow after blow, until the whole left wing of the Federals was shaken and gradually fell back. Just then the Fifth Corps, under Sykes, came up and re-enforced Sickles. But this did not arrest the onslaught of the enemy; instead, the terrible fire of the artillery that swept their ranks seemed to make them bolder and fiercer than ever, and they bravely continued to force the Federals back. They were at last arrested, but not driven away, by the arrival at the scene of Sedgwick's corps and part of the First. The struggle still continued, with fearful losses on both sides, for several hours. Meanwhile another mighty contest was going on between Ewell's corps and the Federal right and centre under Generals Slocum and Howard. This fight continued until ten o'clock in the evening, when the Confederates, driven back by Howard, had seized and held the works of Slocum on the extreme right of Culp's Hill.

The prospect was a very gloomy one for the Federals when the armies rested for the night. They had been pushed back on both the right and left wings; they had suffered great losses, and the soldiers were tired with hurried marches and the hard struggle of the day. But Meade knew that he had a strong position, and as a retreat would be disastrous, he resolved to fight it out right there.

At four o'clock the next morning the battle was renewed on the right. Ewell attempted to advance from the position he had captured the night before, and Slocum determined not only to prevent him doing so, but to recover his lost ground. For two hours there was a desperate struggle. Fearlessly the Confederates charged through the smoke and death-dealing balls of artillery. For a moment Slocum was pressed back, but Wheaton's brigade of the Sixth being hurried to his aid, he again advanced. More troops were brought up, and at last Ewell's brave followers were compelled to give up and fall back, defeated in their purpose.

Lee now looked for a more vulnerable point to attack, and fixing on the centre, he determined to make a desperate effort to crush it with his artillery. Bringing forward 145 heavy cannon, he opened a terrific fire upon Cemetery Hill and its vicinity. The Federal great guns, to the number of 100, responded, and one of the most fearful cannonades ever witnessed was begun. For two hours the country

CAVALRY SKIRMISHERS ADVANCING ON THE CONFEDERATE POSITION IN THE PASS OF THE BLUE RIDGE.

around shook with the reverberations. Then, at four o'clock, Lee ordered a grand charge. Gallantly his men obeyed the command. In splendid order they advanced rapidly in heavy columns. The steady hail of shot and shell had no terrors for them; on they hurried, and even when the Federals, reserving their fire, poured a volley into their ranks that annihilated their first line, they still kept on, and dashing over the rifle pits and up to the guns, bayoneted or drove the gunners away. But suddenly their triumphant charge was checked. The guns on the western slope of Cemetery Hill opened upon them with grape and canister with such awful effect that what was left of them fled in confusion. At sunset the battle of Gettysburg was over, the Confederates had been repulsed at every point. That night the field presented an awful sight, being

erates went up the Shenandoah Valley. After several skirmishes in the mountain passes, the Confederates managed to detain Meade at Manassas Gap in a heavy skirmish, while Lee hastened through Chester Gap, and crossing the Rappahannock, took a position between that stream and the Rapidan. When Meade followed Lee retreated and took up a strongly defensive position beyond the Rapidan.

Lee now determined to make another attempt to capture the national capital by turning Meade's right flank to gain his rear, and then going on rapidly to Washington. Lee partially succeeded in his flanking movement, and the two armies at once started northward, one with the hope of reaching Washington, the other with a determination to get a position where it could prevent the accomplishment of the other's purpose. After an exciting race,

were thus captured. Lee now fell back to a line of defenses on the bank of Mine Run, behind the Rapidan.

A few weeks afterward (November 26th) Meade decided to attempt the dislodgment of Lee's army. General Warren was sent ahead with a large force, and upon reaching the vicinity of the defenses he, with an escort, made a personal reconnoissance, in which twenty of his men were killed or wounded. Then, having made his plans, Warren resolved to make an attack the next morning; but, losing time in manœuvring in an unknown country, the day went by with nothing accomplished. Then Meade decided, after hearing Warren's report, to make a general assault on the fortifications at eight o'clock the next morning; but at daylight it was found that Lee had entirely changed his lines during the night, and was so strongly fortified as

THE WAR IN GEORGIA—THE SIXTEENTH ARMY CORPS FORDING THE CHATTAHOOCHEE AT ROSWELL'S FERRY, JULY 10TH, 1864.

covered with the dead, bodies of men and horses. The losses amounted to more than 23,000 men on the Federal side, and about 30,000, including 14,000 prisoners, on the Confederate.

So great was the importance of the battle of Gettysburg that the triumph of the Federal army moved the President of the United States to recommend the observance of August 15th as a day of thanksgiving therefor.

With the fragments of his shattered army Lee began a retreat toward Virginia on the evening of the day after the battle. He recrossed the Cumberland Mountains and pressed on to the Potomac, pursued by Sedgwick, with the Sixth Corps. Lee managed to hold the Federals at bay until he made ready to cross the river, which had been swollen by heavy rains, by pontoons and fording. Meade followed him three days later, and marched along the eastern base of the Blue Ridge, while the Confed-

during which there were many skirmishes, the Army of the Potomac reached Centreville Heights October 15th.

When Lee reached Bristoe Station Meade attacked him and drove him back to the Rappahannock; then, after repairing the railroad which Lee destroyed on his retreat, followed him to Rappahannock Station, where a sharp battle occurred. The place was protected by several strong forts. On the north side was a fort with two redoubts containing a force of 2,000 men. Toward these the Federals turned their attention, General Sedgwick directing an assault by the Fourteenth New York, Fifth Wisconsin and Sixth Maine Regiments. The troops gallantly charged into the rifle pits and forts in the face of a storm of grapeshot and bullets, and after a short hand-to-hand encounter drove back the defenders, whose retreat was cut off by the Federals sweeping around to their pontoon bridge. More than 1,600 men and 4 guns

to make the chances of success extremely doubtful. So Meade withdrew, and the Army of the Potomac went into winter quarters on the north side of the Rapidan.

CHAPTER XVII.

The Draft Riots in New York—Morgan's Raid—Brilliant Exploit of General Averill—Battle near Franklin, Tenn.—General Streight's Expedition—Bragg Evacuates Chattanooga.

In the summer of 1863, feeling the necessity for a larger force of troops, the National Congress authorized a draft, or conscription, to fill up the ranks of the army, and the President immediately put it into operation. This act met with the opposition of the party opposed to Mr. Lincoln's administration. The speeches of the leaders of this party and the utterances of the press in sympathy with them against the draft so inflamed some of the lower classes in New York city that they rose in a mob and entered upon a riot there on July 13th.

For three days they created a terrible disturbance. They destroyed the telegraph wires, paraded the streets with horrible cries against the draft, and plundered and murdered the colored people. Innocent men and women were clubbed to death or hanged on the lampposts, and a large orphan asylum for colored children was attacked and burned to the ground, while the fleeing inmates were pursued and many of them captured, to be cruelly beaten and maimed. Many colored people had to fly for their lives into the country. Finally the police, aided by armed citizens and soldiers from the forts in the harbor, suppressed the insurrection. Fully 200 persons were killed, and property to the amount of at least $2,000,000 was destroyed.

It was at this time that John Morgan, the guerrilla chief, made his famous raid through Kentucky, Southern Indiana and Ohio. He went swiftly from village to village, plundering, destroying and levying contributions. His purpose was to give the signal for the uprising of the Secessionists in those States. But he was unsuccessful, and was soon captured, with many of his

early in April, with about 9,000 troops, for the purpose of seizing that city, and thus be able to go on and capture Nashville. But in the battle that followed with the Federal forces under General Gordon Granger he was defeated, and he retired to Spring Hill.

Meanwhile Rosecrans was not idle. In the latter part of April he sent out an expedition to Georgia in the hope of taking Rome, where the Confederates had large iron works, and Atlanta, the centre of an important system of railroads. The expedition was led by Colonel A. D. Streight, and left Nashville in steamers for Fort Donelson, from whence the troops marched over to the Tennessee River and up that stream to Tuscumbia, where they were mounted on horses secured on the way. Then they moved eastward through Alabama into Georgia, in the rear of Bragg's army. They were getting well on the way to their destination when a body of cavalry, under Forrest and Roddy, set out in pursuit of them. A lively race ensued, and it was ended only by the giving out of Streight's horses and ammunition when he

and south and gain his antagonist's rear, when he could be cut off from his base of supplies and be compelled to retreat or give battle. With this plan in view, Rosecrans took the corps of Generals Thomas and McCook across the Tennessee, a few miles below Chattanooga, and went up the Lookout Valley and took possession of Lookout Mountain. Then the rest of the army, under Brigadier General Hazen, was left with orders to so arrange itself that the enemy would think the whole force was still on the north shore of the river. These orders were so well carried out that Bragg was thoroughly deceived and knew nothing of Rosecrans's movements until the latter was far to the south of him. Bragg immediately saw the danger of being cut off from his base of supplies, and at once broke up his camp and evacuated Chattanooga, passing through the gaps of Missionary Ridge to Chickamauga Creek, near Lafayette, in Northern Georgia.

When Rosecrans heard of Bragg's retreat his army was scattered. McCook's corps was forty-five miles away up the valley; Thomas was down the valley, thirteen

SIEGE OF CHARLESTON, S. C.— FEDERAL SHARPSHOOTERS APPROACHING FORT WAGNER BEFORE THE EVACUATION.

followers, in Southeastern Ohio, late in July. The remainder of his band were killed or dispersed.

A brilliant exploit was performed by a troop of Federal cavalry, led by General W. W. Averill, in December, 1863. They were sent to destroy the East Tennessee and Virginia Railroad in West Virginia, and so successfully did they conduct the raid that they almost entirely cleared that State of armed Confederates, and seriously interrupted railroad communication between Lee in Virginia and Bragg in Tennessee.

After the battle of Murfreesborough the two opposing armies of Rosecrans and Bragg remained within a few miles of one another until June, 1863. In the meantime the cavalry forces on both sides were busy. The Confederates, early in February, sent out 4,000 mounted men, under Generals Wharton and Forrest, to capture Fort Donelson. But they failed and were driven back. Then General Van Dorn, with a considerable force of cavalry, attempted to seize Rosecrans's supplies at Franklin, just below Nashville, in March, but was attacked and defeated by General Sheridan. Van Dorn went back to the army, and getting re-enforcements, reappeared near Franklin,

was within a few miles of Rome. The pursuers fell upon him on May 3d, and his condition compelled a surrender. Streight and his men were sent to Richmond and confined in Libby Prison, from which he and one hundred other officers afterward escaped by burrowing themselves out.

Rosecrans organized the Army of the Cumberland into three divisions, commanded respectively by Generals Thomas, McCook and Crittenden, with the intention of moving on to Chattanooga, in Northern Georgia. The march from Murfreesborough began late in June. Bragg left his intrenchments on the line of the Duck River at the same time, and fell back to Tullahoma; then, finding that Rosecrans was coming up and seriously menacing his flank, he quickly retreated from there toward Chattanooga, closely pursued. Passing over the Cumberland Mountains, Bragg crossed the Tennessee River at Bridgeport, destroying the bridge as he left it.

The Army of the Cumberland reached the Tennessee late in August, when Bragg was safe in Chattanooga. Rosecrans soon saw that the city was in too strong a position to be taken by a direct attack, so he made up his mind to flank it by the west

miles back; while Crittenden was on the river, only eight miles from Chattanooga. Rosecrans, supposing the enemy to be in full retreat toward Rome, ordered Crittenden to move up the Chickamauga Creek and take position at Gordon's Mill, where the road from Lafayette to Chattanooga crossed, so as to intercept the fleeing army. Just then Rosecrans learned that Bragg, instead of rapidly retreating, had turned about and was preparing to march back on Chattanooga.

To save Crittenden, if possible, from destruction by Bragg, Thomas was ordered to march with all haste over the mountain to his support. Bragg learned of this movement, and at once sent General Hindman to Stevens's Gap, through which Thomas would have to pass, so as to hold the latter and allow Polk to fall on Crittenden's isolated position. For some reason or other neither of these two movements was made, and so Thomas was able to cross the gap, after sending Negley to hold it, and push down the valley to Crittenden's side.

McCook was then ordered to join Thomas, and at midnight his columns were in motion. By taking an indirect route down Lookout Valley and across Stevens's

Gap he managed to elude a body of Confederates sent to intercept him. Rosecrans now concentrated his army as much as possible, and on the morning of September 19th it stretched along the Chickamauga Creek from Gordon's Mill toward the slope of Missionary Hill, with Thomas on the left, Crittenden in the centre and McCook on the right. Bragg's army was arranged on the opposite side of the creek.

CHAPTER XVIII.

BATTLE OF CHICKAMAUGA CREEK—ROSECRANS DRIVEN BACK TO CHATTANOOGA—THOMAS'S GALLANT STAND—"GIVE THEM THE COLD STEEL!"—LITTLE JOHN CLEM AND THE CONFEDERATE COLONEL.

THE battle of Chickamauga Creek opened on the morning of September 19th, 1863. General Croxton received the

bravely for a time they could not long resist the heavy human tide that swept down upon them. Forced back, they wheeled their batteries into new positions and hurled shot and shell into the ranks of their advancing foe. But all in vain. Steadily the Federals advanced, breaking the head of each column as it tried to stop them, and sweeping over everything, until the field was won and the Confederates had been driven back nearly a mile.

While the battle was raging on the left the Federal centre was assailed by Polk and Hill with such ardor that it was quickly forced back and was about to break in confusion when General J. C. Davis, who was on the right, came up and stemmed the current for a moment. But fresh Confederates immediately appeared and rushed

in great haste, charged furiously upon the Confederates. The two armies now stood face to face without either side having much of an advantage. But Bragg had been foiled in every attempt to break Rosecrans's line, and at nightfall he withdrew to prepare for another struggle on the morrow.

The Federal army rested uneasily that night. It had suffered great losses during the day and nothing had been gained. Although the troops were tired out by the struggle, and thirsty, because of having been driven from Chickamauga Creek to a place where there was no water, they knew they would have to fight out the battle in the morning. But they had the satisfaction of knowing that only their indomitable bravery had saved their army from total defeat.

SIEGE OF CHARLESTON—THE DOOMED CITY FIRED BY GILLMORE'S EXPLOSIVE SHELLS FROM FORT PUTNAM, JANUARY 3D, 1864.

first blow. He had been sent with his brigade from the Federal left toward the river to reconnoitre, when the Confederates opened the attack upon him. The divisions of Brannan and Baird were at once dispatched to the assistance of Croxton, but so severe was the assault that they soon fell back toward the centre, and Bragg seemed to be rapidly gaining his purpose to strike at the whole line from left to right to find the weak spot and break through, when Thomas came up, and, rallying the broken divisions of Brannan and Baird, hurled them upon the enemy. Then drawing all his columns into position again, Thomas ordered the whole line to advance. Presenting a solid, determined front, the troops marched out steadily and firmly, and although Longstreet's men stood their ground

into the fray so fiercely that the Federal line was parted in the middle, and the assailants pushed on into the gap thus made. For a moment it seemed as if they had gained the day; but Thomas came up just then, and while Hazen held the enemy in check, Wilder's brigade dashed up and drove the advancing columns back. But only for a brief spell; they soon rallied, and with re-enforcements again came on, forcing Wilder, in turn, to fall back. His retreat, however, was stopped by the arrival of Sheridan, who, with Bradley's brigade, turned the tide again in favor of the Federals. Then Bradley found himself giving way under an attack that, beginning at the extreme Federal left, had drifted rapidly down the line; but he was saved by Negley and Wood, who, coming down the stream

The Confederates, too, were unhappy over the result of their day's work. Their gallant struggles to get past the Federal line and recover Chattanooga had come to naught, and they must repeat their efforts the next morning. But the gloom that settled upon their camp was somewhat dispelled by the appearance in the night of General Longstreet, with the balance of his corps, that had been sent by Lee from Virginia to the assistance of Bragg, so that the latter's army was increased to 70,000 men, while Rosecrans had but 55,000.

The next morning, Sunday September 20th, the battle broke out again with a fierce attack upon Thomas's position. The Confederates made a gallant, determined charge, and although part of Thomas's line was protected by a rude breastwork, from which poured an incessant stream of bullets, they pushed on, rapidly filling the places of those who fell under the hot fire. As column after column melted away fresh troops sprang forward, their leaders being determined to put out the fire at any cost. Thomas was soon so hard pressed that Rosecrans sent Negley to his aid, filling the latter's place with Wood, of Crittenden's division. The Confederate generals then urged the men on to a last desperate assault. So well did they respond to the appeal that, reckless of death, they dashed up into the very mouths of guns and cannon and broke the solid columns in front of them and hurled them back. In vain did Thomas try to prop up the tottering columns with his presence and appeals; one by one they crumbled until the whole wing fell back in disorder. As they retreated Thomas hastily sought another position, and finding it, managed to rally the troops behind it, and another stand was made.

Rosecrans now ordered Wood to leave his position in the centre and join Reynolds, who was the hardest pressed in Thomas's line. To do this Wood had to pass around in the rear of Brannan, who stood between

the good position of Thomas and his well-directed, incessant fire were too much for even the bravest man, and the Confederate charge was checked. Falling back, they decided to assail the Federals on their flanks. In one dark mass they suddenly swung round on to Thomas's right and poured through the gorge in his rear. Thomas shuddered. All was up with him. In a few moments they would all be killed or captured, for he had no force to check the onslaught on the right and rear. But just at the critical moment General Granger, who had heard of the peril of Thomas and moved to his support from his position three miles away, arrived with the brigades of Mitchell and Whittaker, under the command of Steedman. Not a second too soon did they arrive; Hindman's troops were already shouting a victory, when Steedman, seizing the regimental colors, led the two brigades in a gallant charge against them. Like a cyclone they swept down upon the conquering foe and blew it from the ridge. Once more the Federals were secure in their position. Hindman's troops were rallied at once, and charged again upon the ridge, only to be driven back by the deadly

come separated from his companions, after taking part in the thickest of the fight, and was running to join them, with his musket on his shoulder, when a Confederate colonel saw him and shouted: "Stop, you little Yankee devil!" The boy came to a standstill and waited for the colonel to ride up. As he did so young Clem swiftly brought up his musket, and taking aim, shot the colonel dead. The boy escaped, and was rewarded for his achievement by promotion to a sergeancy.

CHAPTER XIX.

ROSECRANS'S SUPPLIES CUT OFF—GRANT IN COMMAND OF THE MILITARY DIVISION OF THE MISSISSIPPI—CAPTURE OF BROWN'S FERRY—KNOXVILLE BESIEGED—BATTLES OF LOOKOUT MOUNTAIN AND MISSIONARY RIDGE.

WHEN the Army of the Cumberland fell back to Chattanooga after the fierce battle of Chickamauga its position soon became precarious, for the Confederates by arranging themselves upon Missionary Ridge and Lookout Mountain, which commanded the Tennessee River, managed to effectually cut off all its supplies from that direction. Then by a raid they destroyed several hundred wagon loads coming from other

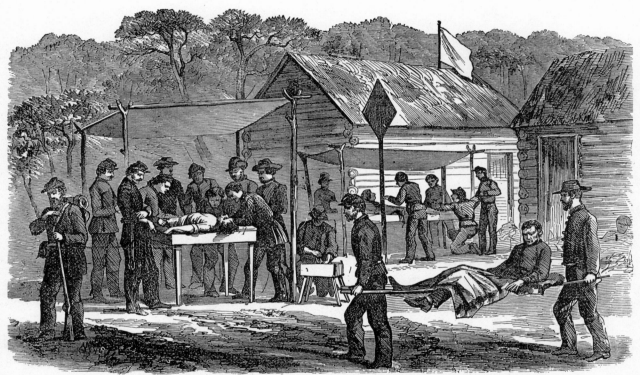

THE WAR IN VIRGINIA—HOSPITAL SCENE AFTER THE BATTLE OF BRISTOE STATION.

him and Reynolds. Always on the lookout for a weak spot in the Federal line, the Confederates, quick as a flash, saw the gap made by the departure of Wood, and without a moment's delay sprang into it. Davis, who moved quickly from the right to prevent this, was swept aside without ceremony, while those on the left of the gap shared the same fate. Sheridan, who had come from the right, rallied his troops and for awhile stood his ground obstinately against great odds. But the Confederates swept everything before them. Rosecrans himself and McCook and Crittenden were all borne backward, unable to breast the tide, and their troops fled to the shelter of Chattanooga.

Thomas's left wing was now left alone on the field, and he determined to make a stand and save the army if possible. Gathering his broken ranks on a semicircular ridge, he poured volley after volley from cannon and muskets into the masses of Confederates, who, flushed with their victory on other parts of the field, bore down upon him with great fury. Bravely the Federals stood their ground, and bravely their enemies rushed to the attack. But

fire. Again and again they returned to the attack. Then they tried an advance upon the left, but were routed by a bayonet charge led by Reynolds. The day was now fast closing, and the Confederates rallied for a decisive blow. Thomas's ammunition was exhausted, and he had nothing to stop this last assault except the bayonet. So when the foe came on and reached striking distance he shouted "Give them the cold steel!" Forgetting their weariness, his men sprang forward and charged so quickly and steadily that the Confederates turned and fled, and the left wing of Rosecrans's army was saved.

The next night Thomas withdrew from the field and joined the balance of the army, which had fallen back, defeated, to Chattanooga. The victory of the Confederates at Chickamauga cost them about 21,000 men, killed, wounded and taken prisoners. Rosecrans lost about 19,000, or nearly one-third of his splendid army. Besides this, he lost 36 guns, 20 caissons and 8,450 small arms.

One of the many incidents of the battle was the exploit of a little twelve-year-old volunteer named John Clem. He had be-

directions, and seriously damaged the railroad between Stevenson and Nashville, so that it seemed for a time as if all the communications of the Federal army would be destroyed and a retreat become inevitable. But the National Government determined to hold Chattanooga, and at once took measures to relieve the distress of the troops there. The Armies of the Cumberland and the Tennessee, constituting the Military Division of the Mississippi, were consolidated, and General Grant was made commander in chief. When he arrived at Chattanooga Grant made General Thomas the leader of the first-named army, and General Sherman of the latter; Rosecrans having been ordered to St. Louis.

In order to prepare the way for an attack upon the Confederates' position on Lookout Mountain it was found necessary to gain possession of Brown's Ferry, three miles below the mountain, and thus make possible a lodgment on the south side of the Tennessee River. After a reconnoissance by Grant and Thomas, the chief engineer, General W. F. Smith, was sent with 4,000 men to seize it. On the night of October 27th 1,500 of the men, specially picked out and led by General Hazen, were placed in pontoons and flatboats and pushed out into the stream, down which they drifted without the aid of oars, around Moccasin Point, in front of Lookout Mountain. They soon made a landing, and while the boats were rowed across the river to a point where stood the balance of the 4,000 troops, who had secretly marched thither by land, a strong position to resist the now alarmed enemy was secured. When the whole force had disembarked the Confederates retreated up the valley, and the Federals took the opportunity of building a pontoon bridge that soon spanned the river

was at once detached to charge the heights while the other kept on toward Geary. Another brigade, under Orlan Smith, from Steinwehr's division, which just then came up, was ordered to carry a hill in the rear of Schurz. They did so with the bayonet, after two desperate charges in the face of a fire from nearly 2,000 muskets and up a steep slope covered with underbrush and lined with gullies and ravines.

Geary had a severe struggle against overwhelming numbers, but being re-enforced, and the men being cheered by the presence of Hooker in the most critical places, the Confederates were at length driven away

self in that city. and at the middle of November was regularly besieged there by Longstreet. The siege continued until the close of the month, when the arrival of Generals Granger and Sherman, sent to Burnside's relief, drove Longstreet into a rapid retreat toward Virginia.

Grant now determined to take advantage of Longstreet's absence by an attack upon Bragg. So, ordering Hooker to attack Bragg's left, on Lookout Mountain, Sherman was directed to cross the Tennessee, above Chattanooga, and strike Bragg's right, on Missionary Ridge. Hooker moved rapidly on the morning of Novem-

THE WAR IN MISSISSIPPI—GENERAL McPHERSON DRIVING THE ENEMY FROM THEIR POSITION ON THE CANTON ROAD, NEAR BROWNSVILLE.

and opened a way for re-enforcement and supplies.

Hooker, who was at Bridgeport, was now ordered by Grant to advance to Lookout Valley and menace Bragg's flank and protect the passage of supplies up the Tennessee. He started off at once and took up a position at Wauhatchie, from which the Confederates attempted to dislodge him before daylight on the morning of October 29th. The attack opened against Geary's division, and he was soon so hard pressed by overwhelming numbers that Hooker ordered Schurz's division of Howard's corps to his aid. On the way this division was surprised by a sudden fire of musketry from the hills near by. A brigade under Tyndale

to the shelter of Lookout Mountain, after a three hours' battle in the darkness. During the contest about 200 mules, panic-stricken by the noise of the guns, dashed into the Confederate ranks, and the men, supposing it to be a charge of Hooker's cavalry, fell back in confusion for a moment.

Meanwhile General Burnside was making rapid progress in his efforts to expel the Confederates from the Valley of East Tennessee. He had taken possession of Knoxville, and was about to move on and join Rosecrans at Chattanooga, when, just after the battle of Chickamauga, Bragg sent Longstreet to the valley to recover Knoxville. Burnside then intrenched him-

ber 24th. With skill and celerity he fought his way up the steep, rugged sides of the mountain. For awhile he seemed to the on-lookers below to be above the clouds, as a thick mist concealed his men from view. "At this juncture," said an eyewitness, "the scene became one of most exciting interest. The thick fog, which had heretofore rested in dense folds upon the sides of the mountain, concealing the combatants from view, suddenly lifted to the summit of the lofty ridge, revealing to the anxious gaze of thousands, in the valley and on the plains below, a scene such as is witnessed but once in a century. General Geary's columns, flushed with victory, grappled with the foe upon the rocky ledges, and

SIEGE OF PETERSBURG—THE NINTH CORPS CHARGING ON

KS AFTER THE EXPLOSION OF THE MINE. JULY 30TH, 1864.

drove him back with slaughter from his works. While the result was uncertain the attention was breathless and painful; but when victory perched upon our standards shout upon shout rent the air. The whole army, with one accord, broke out into joyous acclamations. The enthusiasm of the scene beggars description. Men were frantic with joy, and even General Thomas himself, who seldom exhibits his emotions, said involuntarily, 'I did not think it possible for men to accomplish so much!'" The Confederates that night fled down the northern slopes to the Chattanooga Valley and joined their commander on Missionary Ridge.

Sherman, having crossed the Tennessee River, was now in a position on the northern end of the ridge, and soon after dawn on November 25th the attack on Bragg's concentrated forces began. Sherman's troops had to descend to a deep valley before climbing the hill upon which the enemy was perched. Corse, leading the advance, gained a foothold on the side of this hill, and others quickly followed amid a shout and a dash they sprang up and over into the deserted ditch beyond. Then up the ridge they climbed. Slowly, but steadily, they ascended the steep, rocky slope, while from above rocks and stones and shells with lighted fuses were rolled down upon them. Grant, from a commanding eminence in front of the ridge, known as Orchard Knob, which Thomas had captured and fortified two days before, watched his army rise slowly upward, and with intense anxiety saw the murderous work of shot and shell hurled against it. At last the brave soldiers reached the summit and dashed over the batteries, and with loud cheers drove Bragg and his army into hasty flight. They were pursued as far as Ringgold, when after a sharp engagement the Confederates fell back further, to Dalton. The Federals then returned to Chattanooga, and Sherman went to the relief of Burnside. The Federal loss in the battle of Missionary Ridge was about 4,000, while the Confederates lost about 3,100 in killed and wounded, and a little more than 6,000 prisoners.

Sumter and Charleston was planned. It was arranged that Fort Wagner, on Morris Island, should first be seized, then its guns used in silencing Fort Sumter and in destroying Charleston, if that city was not surrendered. As Dupont did not approve of this plan he was relieved early in July by Admiral John A. Dahlgren.

The expedition started July 10th. General Alfred H. Terry was first sent with a force to James Island to attract the attention of the Confederates, while Gillmore suddenly landed a large number of troops on Morris Island, and forced the Confederates there, with the aid of batteries on Folly Island, to the shelter of Fort Wagner. After doing this Gillmore planted batteries across the island. Then on July 11th his forces made an attack on the fort, but being repulsed, a simultaneous bombardment by sea and land was determined on. On the 18th a hundred great guns opened on the fort from Dahlgren's fleet and from the land batteries. At sunset the same day Gillmore's forces, which had been reenforced by General Terry joining him

THE WAR IN LOUISIANA—BATTLE OF MANSFIELD, BETWEEN GENERAL BANKS AND GENERAL DICK TAYLOR, APRIL 8TH, 1864.

terrific fire. Nobly they tried to reach the lofty heights above, and brigade after brigade was brought to their aid, but in vain. The deadly shot and shell kept them back, although they held stubbornly to their position. All morning the battle raged furiously at this place. Bragg, thinking, from Sherman's brave stand, that Grant intended to crush the Confederate right at any cost, withdrew his troops from the centre to use them in aiding the defense against Sherman. This movement Grant had expected and hoped for. Hooker, who had hurried down from Lookout Mountain after his victory there, was immediately dispatched, with three divisions under General Granger, to climb the declivities in front and attack Bragg's left. As they moved in steady columns toward the frowning heights the artillery all along the crest of the ridge opened and poured a decimating fire through the ranks. Still onward they marched without flinching. Reaching the mountain, they came face to face with a long line of rifle pits that sent forth a continuous shower of destructive bullets. But this did not stop them. With

CHAPTER XX.

ATTEMPTS TO TAKE FORT SUMTER—ASSAULT ON FORT WAGNER—DEATH OF GENERAL STRONG AND COLONELS SHAW AND PUTNAM—A MONSTER GUN—BOMBARDMENT AND DESTRUCTION OF FORT SUMTER—DESOLATION OF CHARLESTON.

IN the spring of 1863 the National Government determined to make a strong effort to gain possession of Charleston, S. C. The most formidable barrier to the accomplishment of this purpose was Fort Sumter, so on April 6th Admiral Dupont was sent with nine monitor vessels and five gunboats to attack that stronghold. At the same time General Truman Seymour was sent to co-operate with him with a force of 4,000 troops, who took a masked position on Folly Island. But the expedition came to naught, as the guns on Sumter and the adjacent batteries opened such a terrific concentrated fire upon Dupont's fleet that he was driven back to the ocean after losing one of his ironclads, the *Keokuk*.

When, two months later, General Quincy A. Gillmore succeeded General Hunter in the command of the Department of the South, another expedition against Fort

from James Island, moved in two columns to attack Fort Wagner. One column was led by General Strong, the other by Colonel H. L. Putnam, acting as brigadier. Strong's brigade, composed of the Fifty-fourth Massachusetts (colored) Regiment, under Colonel R. G. Shaw, the Sixth Connecticut, Forty-eighth New York, Third New Hampshire, the Seventy-sixth Pennsylvania and Ninth Maine, led the assault. Dashing forward on the double-quick, the troops passed through an awful storm of shot and shell from Sumter, Cummings Point and Wagner, on toward the fort, without flinching. They soon gained the ditch before it, and crossing this, they were mounting the parapet, when Colonel Shaw, waving to his men, fell dead. The fire from the garrison then became so hot that every commanding officer was killed or wounded, Strong being among the latter. So the brigade, torn to pieces, beat a hasty and disordered retreat.

Colonel Putnam's brigade now advanced and dashed into the same terrible storm of iron hail. They gained the ramparts, and in a fierce hand-to-hand encounter managed to get their feet into a portion of the fort;

but the brigade was shattered and exhausted, and when Putnam fell mortally wounded it broke and fled back to the intrenchments, leaving the beach strewn with the dead and dying. The Confederates, having a special hatred for Colonel Shaw because he commanded colored troops, pitched his body into a hole with a lot of his negro soldiers. General Strong was so badly wounded that he died shortly afterward in New York.

Gillmore now saw that he could not capture Fort Wagner by direct assault, and so began a regular siege. At the same time he decided to bombard Fort Sumter over the top of Wagner. For this purpose he had to construct a battery in a morass halfway between Morris and James Islands

and the platform put up six 200-pounder Parrott guns and one monster 300-pounder were mounted upon it. This latter gun was called the "Swamp Angel" and sent shells into Charleston, five miles away. One of these struck St. Michael's Church and destroyed a tablet containing the ten commandments, leaving only two of them visible, one of which was: "Thou shalt not kill."

On August 17th the bombardment began by an attack by the batteries and fleet upon Fort Sumter. All day long it was kept up, and so terrific was the fire directed against it that by night the walls began to crumble. In the meantime Gillmore's land troops pressed toward Fort Wagner, gradually moving their parallels nearer and nearer,

attempt the capture of Charleston, its importance as a commercial mart was destroyed. Here is a picture of the condition of the city at the time, given by a Southern paper: "Here and there, a pedestrian moves hurriedly along, and the rattle of a cart or a dray is alone heard for a whole square. The blinds are closed; vases of rare exotics droop and wither on the lonely window sill, because there is no tender hand to twine or nourish them. The walk glistens with fragments of glass, rattled thither by the concussion of exploding shells; here a cornice is knocked off; there, is a small round hole through the side of a building; beyond, a house in ruins, and at remote intervals the earth is torn where a shell exploded, and looks like the work of a giant

THE WAR IN TENNESSEE—CONFEDERATE MASSACRE OF FEDERAL TROOPS AFTER THE SURRENDER AT FORT PILLOW, APRIL 12TH, 1864.

by driving piles into deep mud and placing a platform upon it. When Gillmore ordered a lieutenant of engineers to attend to the construction of this battery the latter told him such a thing would be impossible. "There is no such word as impossible," said Gillmore. "Call for what you need." The lieutenant at once made a requisition on the quartermaster for "one hundred men eighteen feet high to wade in mud sixteen feet deep." But although this requisition could not be honored the redoubt was built by bringing timber for the piles from Folly Island, a distance of ten miles, in rafts. The rafts were floated to their places at night, and the piles driven into the mud under cover of the darkness, so as to keep the enemy in ignorance of the movement. For two weeks the work was carried on, and when it was completed

and digging their way, in spite of shot and shell, into the fort. When, at last, on September 6th, they were near enough to get within the ramparts by a single bound, and they were preparing for a sudden assault, the Confederates left it and fled to Fort Gregg, on the point opposite Sumter. The enemy was soon driven from there, and Morris Island was in the hands of the Federals. Its guns were now directed against Fort Sumter and it soon became silent. But when on the night of the 8th an armed force went from the ships in small boats to take possession of it the garrison suddenly arose from its silence and drove the assailants back with great loss. A little later (October) Gillmore concentrated his heaviest guns upon it and reduced it to a heap of ruins.

Although the Federals did not at once

in search of some hidden treasure; and little tufts of bright-green grass are springing up along the pave, once vocal with the myriad tongues of busy trade."

CHAPTER XXI.

MASSACRE AT LAWRENCE, KANS.—A HORRIBLE SCENE—CONFEDERATE ATTACK ON HELENA—GENERAL STEELE TAKES LITTLE ROCK—ATTEMPT TO CAPTURE SABINE PASS—GREAT BRITAIN IGNORES THE CONFEDERACY—GRANT MADE LIEUTENANT GENERAL.

DURING a part of the year 1863 the Confederates, having reoccupied Texas, carried on a sort of guerrilla warfare in Arkansas and Missouri. In January Marmaduke fell upon Springfield, Mo., but being repulsed with a loss of 200 men, went back to Arkansas. Then at Little Rock he got together 8,000 men and invaded Missouri again for the purpose of seizing the Federal stores at

Cape Girardeau, on the Mississippi. His raid, however, was checked by General McNeil, who attacked him at the Cape on April 20th and drove him out of the State. Other similar bands roamed over the western borders of Arkansas. On July 17th there was a sharp battle at Honey Springs, in Indian Territory, between a large force of Confederates, led by General Cooper, and Federal troops under General Blunt. Cooper was defeated and part of his force fled into Northern Texas. Guerrilla bands made much trouble in Blunt's rear. One of them, led by a brute named Quantrell, committed a horrible atrocity at Lawrence, Kans.

With a band of about 350 mounted men Quantrell dashed into the defenseless town on August 13th and began a scene of pillage and violence equaled only by the worst Indian atrocities. Houses were broken into and set on fire and the citizens cruelly murdered. Germans and negroes especially suffered, they being shot on sight. The people were taken prisoners and hurried toward the river to be killed. One man who was captured and whose

the dead bodies pieces of roasted flesh would remain in our hands. Soon our strength failed us in this horrible and sickening work. Many could not help crying like children. Women and little children were all over town, hunting for their husbands and fathers, and sad indeed was the scene when they did finally find them among the corpses laid out for recognition. I cannot describe the horrors; language fails me, and the recollection of the scenes I witnessed makes me sick when I am compelled to repeat them."

Quantrell soon afterward (October 4th) attacked General Blunt near Baxter's Springs, on the Cherokee Reservation, while the latter was on his way, with an escort of 100 cavalry, from Kansas to Fort Smith, which he had taken possession of and garrisoned the previous month. In the conflict that ensued nearly all of Blunt's little force were killed, as those who were only wounded at first were set upon and murdered. Blunt managed to escape with about a dozen of his men to Little Fort Blair.

A few months before this General Price,

and a premature attack by the gunboats, two of the latter—the *Clifton* and the *Sachem*—were disabled and captured with all on board, so that the expedition was a failure. Banks then concentrated his land forces on the Atchafalaya, in the hope of being able to enter Texas from the east by way of Shreveport, on the Red River; but he soon afterward concluded instead to try to obtain possession of the coast harbor of that State. Sending a large body of troops, under General C. C. Washburne, across Louisiana toward Alexandria, as a feint, Banks dispatched General Dana with 6,000 more troops and some war vessels up to the Rio Grande These soldiers landed, and after driving a body of Confederate cavalry up that river, pressed on to Brownsville, opposite Matamoras, where they encamped, November 6th. When the year closed the Federals were in possession of all the strong positions on the coast of Texas excepting Galveston Island and a fort near the mouth of the Brazos, and all the State west of the Colorado River had been freed of Confederates.

The third year of the Civil War, 1864,

THE WAR IN LOUISIANA—BATTLE OF GRAND COTEAU—CAPTURE OF THE SIXTY-SEVENTH INDIANA BY THE TEXAS MOUNTED INFANTRY, NOVEMBER 3D, 1863.

house was burned was told that if he would give the fiends his money he would not be killed; but when he procured his savings of years from the burning house and handed them over he was shot dead from behind. In another place a man was found protected by his wife and daughter, who threw their arms around him and begged for his life; but one of the ruffians deliberately pushed his revolver between the two women and fired a fatal shot.

The massacre was terrible. One hundred and forty unarmed men were killed and twenty-four wounded, while one hundred and eighty-five buildings were laid in ashes before the fiends left and made their escape. The horrible scene after Quantrell's departure is thus described by one of the citizens: "I have read of outrages committed in the so-called dark ages, and, horrible as they appeared to me, they sink into insignificance in comparison with what I was then compelled to witness. Well-known citizens were lying, completely roasted, in front of the spot where their stores and residences had been. The bodies were crisp and nearly black. We thought at first they were all negroes, till we recognized some of them. In handling

with 8,000 Confederates, made an attempt to capture the strongly fortified post of Helena, on the Mississippi, in Eastern Arkansas, then in command of General Steele. Price attacked the place on July 3d, 1863, but after a sharp battle was repulsed with heavy loss. As the Confederates then abandoned that section of Arkansas, General Steele, on August 10th, started out with 12,000 troops and 40 pieces of cannon to attempt the capture of Little Rock. He reached the vicinity of that city early in September, and arranging his forces in two columns, they moved up on each side of the Arkansas River. The Confederates fled at their approach to Arkadelphia, on the Ouachita River.

General Banks, who was now at New Orleans, determined at the beginning of September to make an effort to recover Texas. He sent General Franklin, with 4,000 troops, to seize the Confederate post at Sabine Pass, on the boundary line between Louisiana and Texas. At the same time four gunboats, commanded by Lieutenant Crocker, were detached from Commodore Bell's Gulf Squadron and sent to co-operate with Franklin; but, owing to the strength of the batteries at Sabine Pass

opened encouragingly for the believers in the Union. There were many signs pointing to the early downfall of the Confederacy. More than 50,000 square miles of territory had been recovered by the Federals, and there were about 800,000 Federal troops in the field against only half that number of Confederates. The people in the Southern States were no longer willing to volunteer for the military service, and the authorities at Richmond were getting desperate. They passed a law declaring every white man in the Confederacy liable to bear arms to be in the military service, and that upon his failure to report for duty at a military station within a certain time he was liable to the penalty of death as a deserter!

Another cause of satisfaction to the defenders of the republic at this time was the action of Lord John Russell, the British Foreign Secretary, in decidedly ignoring the existence of the Confederate States by issuing a notice to the effect that no more vessels should be fitted out in Great Britain for depredating on the commerce of the United States by persons employed by the "so-called Confederate States." ·

The National authorities determined to

push the war against the enemies of the government with vigor during the year 1864. For this purpose they selected their most vigorous military leader, Ulysses S. Grant, and creating anew for him the office of lieutenant general, placed him in command of all the armies of the republic. With a determination to crush the Confederacy as soon as possible, Grant at once planned a sharp and decisive campaign. He arranged for the capture of Richmond by the Army of the Potomac under General Meade, and for the seizure of the great railroad centre, Atlanta, in Georgia, by General Sherman and his forces.

enforcements he expected in the shape of General W. S. Smith with a considerable force of cavalry did not materialize, and he was compelled to give up his plan. After waiting a week for Smith he set fire to Meridian and started for Vicksburg with 400 prisoners and 5,000 liberated slaves. Alarmed by this raid, General Joseph E. Johnston, in command of Bragg's army in Northern Georgia, had sent re-enforcements to Polk, then in charge of the Confederates in that region, but soon afterward had to recall them to help in defending his own army against a force under General Palmer, which had been sent down from

throwing shells with marked effect into the Confederate ranks. Forrest soon found that he could not carry the place by assault; so, instead of sitting down to a regular siege of it, he sent under a flag of truce a demand for the surrender of the fort, and at the same time took advantage of the cessation of hostilities to move his men up to a position where they could with almost a single bound gain the inside of the works. Bradford's reply being a refusal to surrender, Forrest's men made a sudden rush, and with the cry, "No quarter!" sprang over the ramparts. The scene then enacted was so cruel and horrible that

SKETCHES OF ARMY LIFE—WEIGHING OUT RATIONS.

CHAPTER XXII.

SHERMAN'S RAID—MASSACRE AT FORT PILLOW—"NO QUARTER!"—BANKS'S ATTEMPT TO RECOVER TEXAS—GENERAL E. R. S. CANBY SUCCEEDS GENERAL BANKS—PRICE INVADES MISSOURI.

IN February, 1864, General Sherman at the head of 20,000 troops started on a destructive raid through Mississippi from Jackson to the intersection of important railroads at Meridian. Everything in the way of public property was destroyed. Railroad tracks were torn up, the ties set on fire, and all the stations and cars met on the line of march burned.

Sherman's purpose was to push on to Montgomery, Ala., and then, if circumstances favored it, to go southward and attack Mobile. But at Meridian the re-

Chattanooga. These two forces met between Ringgold and Dalton, in February, 1864, and it resulted in Palmer being driven back to Chattanooga.

A few weeks later General Forrest, with a band of inhuman Confederates, made an attack upon Fort Pillow, situated on a high bluff on the banks of the Mississippi, above Memphis. It was garrisoned with 557 men, 262 of whom were colored troops. The attack began on the morning of April 13th. It was vigorously pressed up to three o'clock without success, although the Confederates managed to kill the commander of the fort, Major Booth, whose place was at once taken by Major Bradford. The gunboat *New Era*, Captain Marshall, did good service in the defense of the fort by

a committee from the Joint Committee on the Conduct and Expenditures of the War was appointed to investigate the affair. They vividly described the events that took place after the surrender in their report, which in part was as follows:

"Then followed a scene of cruelty and murder without a parallel in civilized warfare, which needed but the tomahawk and scalping knife to exceed the worst atrocities ever committed by savages. The rebels commenced an indiscriminate slaughter, sparing neither age nor sex, white nor black, soldier nor civilian. The officers and men seemed to vie with each other in the devilish work; men, women and even children, wherever found, were deliberately shot down, beaten and hacked with sabres;

some of the children, not more than ten years old, were forced to stand up and face the murderers while being shot; the sick and the wounded were butchered without mercy, the rebels even entering the hospital building and dragging them out to be shot, or killing them as they lay there unable to offer the least resistance. * * * No cruelty which the most fiendish malignity could devise was omitted by these murderers. One white soldier, who was wounded in the leg so as to be unable to walk, was made to stand up while his tormentors shot him; others who were wounded and unable to stand were held up and again shot. * * * One man was deliberately fastened down to the floor of a tent, face upward, by means of nails driven through his clothing and into the boards under him, so that he could not possibly escape, and then the tent set on fire; another was nailed to the side of a building outside of the fort and then the building set on fire and burned. * * * These deeds of murder and cruelty ceased when night came on, only to be renewed the next morning, when the demons carefully sought among the dead lying about in all directions for any of the wounded yet

early in 1864. This was to be done by an invasion by way of the Red River and Shreveport. The expedition was to have the co-operation of Admiral Porter, with a fleet of gunboats, on the Red River, General Steele, at Little Rock, Ark., and a detachment from Sherman's army.

Sherman's troops, led by General A. J. Smith, went up the Red River in transports, followed by Porter's gunboats. They captured Fort de Russy, and on March 16th Smith took possession of Alexandria, where he was joined on the 26th by Banks's column, led by General Franklin, which had moved from Brashear by way of Opelousas.

Banks now took his whole force up the river to Natchitoches, where he met Porter's vessels. Then he pushed on toward Shreveport, while the lighter gunboats went up the river with a body of troops under T. Kilby Smith. The Confederates were driven as far as Sabine Crossroads, where they made a stand, April 8th, under Generals Taylor, Price and Green. The advance of Banks's army tried to drive them from this place, but the Confederates stood their ground so well and fought so desperately, that, even when Franklin's

the Red River at Alexandria had become so shallow that to get the fleet past them the river above had to be dammed and the vessels floated down over the rocks on the bosom of the flood that was suddenly set free through sluices. This was done with great skill and industry under the direction of Lieutenant Colonel Joseph Bailey, of a Wisconsin regiment. Upon its accomplishment the whole expedition pushed toward the Mississippi. Banks now returned to New Orleans, and General E. R. S. Canby took his place on the field. Steele was prevented from co-operating with the expedition by a Confederate force at Jenkinson's Ferry, on the Sabine River, where after a severe battle he was defeated and compelled to return to Little Rock.

The failure of this expedition and the expulsion of Steele from the region below the Arkansas River led Price early in the autumn to plan another invasion of Missouri. Secret societies had been formed in this and neighboring States to aid the Confederate cause and to assist the Democratic party in the election of its candidate for President of the United States—General McClellan. From these societies Price expected he would gain a large number of

THE WAR IN LOUISIANA—GENERAL FRANKLIN'S ARMY CROSSING THE PRAIRIE IN LAFAYETTE PARISH, NOVEMBER 16th, 1863.

alive, and those they found were deliberately shot."

The report was full of other instances of barbarity, but these will suffice to show to some extent the horrible cruelty of Forrest and his men. As to the fate of Major Bradford, the commander of Fort Pillow when it was captured, the evidence given before the committee showed that he was made a prisoner, and while being taken to Jackson, Tenn., was led out into an open space by five of Forrest's men and shot to death.

Forrest at once beat a retreat, and troops were sent out from Memphis by General Smith to intercept him. This force came up with him on June 10th, at Guntown, on the Mobile and Ohio Railroad, but after a severe battle the Federals were driven back with great loss. Then General A. J. Smith set out with 12,000 men to hunt him up and capture or drive him away. They found him near Tupelo, June 14th, and defeated him, after which they retreated to Memphis. Then, soon afterward, when Smith was in Mississippi with 10,000 men, Forrest flanked him, dashed into Memphis and escaped into Mississippi.

General Banks organized another expedition to attempt the recovery of Texas

troops came up and aided in the attack against them, they soon defeated the Federals with great loss, who fled in confusion. Their retreat was covered for awhile by a division under General Emory at Pleasant Grove, three miles from the battlefield. Emory, after a battle, fell back with the Federals, who continued their retreat fifteen miles further; but being pursued, another battle was fought, April 9th, at Pleasant Hill. Banks was victorious, and wished to renew the march for Texas, but on the advice of his associates he fell back to Grand Ecore, on the Red River, where Porter's larger vessels, unable to proceed higher up, were anchored. To that place the troops under T. Kilby Smith also returned, after some sharp fighting up the river.

As food and water could be procured only with great difficulty in that region, it was now determined to continue the retreat to Alexandria. As the river was falling rapidly the fleet had difficulty in passing the bar at Grand Ecore, but succeeded in doing so April 17th. Then the army started off on the 21st, and reached Alexandria on the 27th. The expedition against Shreveport was abandoned, and the land and naval forces prepared to return to the Mississippi River. The water in the rapids of

recruits upon his entering Missouri. But in this he was disappointed. Upon reaching the State in September, 1864, he found the Secessionists had been frightened and quieted by Rosecrans, then commanding the Department of the Missouri. Price, with General Shelby and 20,000 men, got as far as Pilot Knob, halfway to St. Louis, where, after a severe battle, he was badly beaten by a brigade of Federals under General Ewing. Price was soon afterward driven in disorder westward toward Kansas by troops under Generals A. J. Smith and Mower; and late in November he sought shelter in Western Kansas with a very much shattered army.

CHAPTER XXIII.

Kilpatrick's Raid—Death of Colonel Dahlgren—Movement of the Army of the Potomac—Battle of the Wilderness—Conflict at Spottsylvania—Death of General Sedgwick—Terrible Loss of Life.

A few months before Grant started the Army of the Potomac against Richmond General B. F. Butler, in command of the Department of Virginia and North Carolina, sent out an expedition toward that city for the purpose of liberating the Union soldiers confined in Libby Prison and on Belle Isle in the James River. The expedition consisted of 1,500 troops, foot and horse, under General Wistar, and 5,000 cavalry, led by General Kilpatrick, who came from the Army of the Potomac.

Kilpatrick started on his great raid on the last day of February. Capturing the entire picket stationed at Ely's Ford, on the Rapidan, without giving the alarm, he dashed on to Spottsylvania Courthouse, which he reached at daylight; then on to the first line of the defenses around Richmond, which he took, and opened an artillery attack upon the city. The sound of this attack was arranged to act as a signal for Colonel Dahlgren to advance to his aid. The latter, with Colonel Cook and 500 men, had been sent across the James River to go down its south bank and release the prisoners at Belle Isle, and then join Kilpatrick in the city. But Dahlgren failed to appear. Lacking this co-operation and finding the defenses stronger

manded by Hancock; the Fifth, by Warren; and the Sixth, by Sedgwick. The army safely crossed the Rapidan, and then started on a march through the dense wood known as the Wilderness, Sheridan commanding the cavalry, leading the advance and protecting the immense train of more than 4,000 wagons. The Wilderness extended from Chancellorsville to Mine Run, where Lee's army was intrenched. Lee decided to attack the army while it was on the march through this wooded country.

Before the battle opened Warren had reached the Old Wilderness Tavern, ten miles south of where he forded the Rapidan, and Sedgwick was on his right with his line extending down to the river. Grant, learning that a battle was to be forced upon him in this unfavorable spot, directed Hancock, who had crossed five or six miles down the river, to hasten forward to Warren and form the left wing. Lee at once attempted

Federal line, extending for seven miles through the forest, the battle raged. Hancock's attack was a furious one, and he steadily drove the enemy back for more than a mile. In this struggle General Wadsworth was especially distinguishing himself by leading the charge when he was killed by a ball in the head.

Hancock soon lost the ground he had gained. The Confederates rallied, and falling fiercely upon his exhausted troops, forced them steadily back to their original position. Then General Longstreet arrived on the scene from a forced march of twenty-five miles, and Lee decided to make a strong effort to turn the Federal left. In four lines the Confederates marched up and threw themselves so desperately on Hancock's position that they broke through, and for a moment it seemed as if they would win the day. But Gibbon's division immediately rushed up to

THE SIEGE OF PETERSBURG—THE FIFTH CORPS AWAITING THE ORDER TO ADVANCE, JULY 30TH, 1864.

than he supposed, and the Confederates in alarm concentrating quickly, Kilpatrick was compelled to retreat. He swung around Richmond to the Chickahominy, and crossing it, went into camp on the other side. There he was attacked by a heavy force. But he succeeded in repulsing it, and then encamped at Old Church to await the arrival of the scattered detachments. These all came in during the day except Dahlgren's command. That officer had been misled by a negro guide, and after a time became separated with about 100 men from his main force. They fought their way to within three miles of King and Queen Courthouse, where they were led into an ambuscade. Dahlgren was shot down, and all but 17 of his party killed or taken prisoners. The gallant officer was a son of Admiral Dahlgren.

The Army of the Potomac began its grand movement on May 4th. It was arranged in three corps—the Second, commanded by Hancock; the Fifth, by Warren;

to get into the gap between Warren and Hancock, and thus divide the army. But Grant prevented this by sending Mott's division, the advance of Hancock's corps, which just then came up, and the division of Getty, to hold the enemy until the balance of Hancock's corps could arrive. This was successfully done, and the line was closed on the left.

Then began the battle of the Wilderness, May 5th. It was a strange, hard-fought conflict. The ground was so thickly covered with pines, cedars, shrub oaks and tangled underbrush and vines that artillery was almost entirely useless, and although nearly 200,000 men were engaged not a thousand could be seen at one time. The contest raged with great fury until darkness put an end to it for that day.

The next morning at five o'clock Sedgwick attacked the Confederates under Ewell, and Hancock, on the left, fell upon those nearest him. Then all along the

the break and managed by hard fighting to keep the assailants in check. Longstreet being determined to effectually turn the Federal left, and Hancock being just as determined not to let him, the two battled with terrible ferocity for nearly an hour. All through the Wilderness the struggle went on until darkness again put a stop to it.

That night the field presented a dreary, desolate sight. The dead and wounded lay everywhere along the low ridges and slopes and in front of the hastily thrown up intrenchments. Grant spent the night in getting the troops into a new and stronger position, so as to be ready for the enemy if the battle should be renewed in the morning. But the Confederates did not make another attack the next day, and Grant decided they were preparing to retreat. In order to intercept them and cut off Lee's communications with Richmond, Grant ordered a rapid night march to

Spottsylvania. The advance started out at ten o'clock that night.

Hearing of this movement, Lee dispatched Longstreet to the same place, and a race between the two opposing columns took place. Longstreet, knowing the country well took the most direct route, and reached Spottsylvania first.

Upon the arrival of Warren's corps, which was in the Federal advance, Bartlett's brigade, of Griffin's division, was ordered to charge upon the place, as it was not known that Longstreet had already reached there. The result was the almost complete destruction of the brigade, one regiment, the First Michigan, losing three-fourths of its number. The troops were falling back in wild disorder when Warren came up. Dashing forward on his horse, he seized a division flag and gallantly rallied the men, and with them he held the Confederates in check until the other portions of his corps arrived. Then, with the assistance of the divisions of Crawford and Getty, an attack was made upon the Confederates' position, and after heavy loss the first line of breastworks was carried. By the next morning the Federal line had advanced to within three miles of Spottsylvania Courthouse.

On May 9th General Sedgwick, leader of the Sixth Corps, went forward to superintend the placing of some batteries. While doing so a bullet whistled past him. He laughed and called out to the nearest enemy in sight : "Pooh, man, you can't hit an elephant at that distance !" The next moment a bullet from a sharpshooter hidden in a near-by tree entered his brain, and one of the best of generals fell dead.

Nothing much but sharp skirmishing was done by either side that day. While the

THE OLD FLAG AGAIN ON SUMTER—RAISED (ON A TEMPORARY STAFF FORMED OF AN OAR AND BOATHOOK) BY CAPTAIN H. M. BRAGG, OF GENERAL GILLMORE'S STAFF, FEBRUARY 18TH, 1865.

armies were preparing for another battle Sheridan took his cavalry on a raid to sever Lee's communications with Richmond. He managed to get into the rear of the Confederates, and at once moved on, spreading destruction in his path, tearing up railroads, etc., until he reached the first line of works around the capital. Not being able to get any further, he then returned.

The next day, after pouring shot and shell into the Confederate position from daylight to about six o'clock in the afternoon, Grant ordered a grand assault. With cheers and shouts the columns advanced through a fire that swept their ranks at every step. It was a gallant charge, although useless. The fire was so destructive that it was soon found that the works could not be taken, and when night fell the Federals had suffered a fearful loss without having gained anything.

The next morning Grant, with a determination to make his campaign thoroughly decisive at whatever cost, telegraphed to Washington: "I propose to fight it out on this line if it takes all summer."

Having taken advantage of the darkness and changed his position in the night, Hancock on the morning of the 12th was on the enemy's right flank. About five o'clock his troops suddenly burst upon an angle of the Confederates' works held by Johnson, and without firing a shot swept over the ramparts and captured nearly all of Johnson's division. Hancock then drove the enemy before him nearly a mile, where they rallied and charged back upon him, and a terrible fight ensued. Other corps were brought up to the slaughter on both sides, and the struggle continued for hours. Bravely the Federals tried to follow up the advantage they had gained, and gallantly the Confederates resisted them and attempted to recover their ground. It was, however, but a useless waste of life. The positions were not changed at midnight when Lee withdrew behind a second line of intrenchments.

Since crossing the Rapidan the Army of the Potomac lost, within the brief space of a fortnight, nearly 40,000 men, killed, wounded and prisoners, while Lee's Army of Northern Virginia lost about 30,000.

CHAPTER XXIV.

Butler at Bermuda Hundred—General Kautz's Raid—Battle of Cold Harbor—Grant's Army before Petersburg—General Early's Invasion of Maryland—A Destructive Raid—Sheridan's Ride.

JUST before the terrible battles of the Wilderness occurred Grant ordered General Butler to move his army from Fortress Monroe up toward Richmond, to co-operate with the Army of the Potomac.

Butler started, May 4th, with about 25,000 men, up the James River in armed transports. He landed at City Point, at the mouth of the Appomattox River, fifteen miles below the Confederate capital, and planted his army on the narrow strip of land known as Bermuda Hundred. A line of intrenchments was at once cast up across the peninsula from the Appomattox to the James.

While this was being done General A. V. Kautz went up from Suffolk with 3,000 cavalry to attempt the destruction of the railroads south and west from Petersburg; but he found that city strongly defended by Beauregard, who had been summoned from Charleston to Richmond. The latter being greatly re-enforced, now massed some of his troops in front of Butler's forces, and on May 16th he attempted to turn Butler's right flank. A sharp conflict was the result, and Butler's forces were driven to their intrenchments.

A few days afterward Butler was requested to send a large part of his troops to the north side of the James River to assist the army against Lee in the vicinity of the Chickahominy. The compliance with this order deprived Butler of the power to make further offensive movements.

General Kautz started out on another raid from Bermuda Hundred, May 12th. Passing near Fort Darling, on Drewry's

GENERAL ISAAC P. RODMAN.

Bluff, he swept around by Chesterfield Courthouse and struck the Richmond and Danville Railroad, eleven miles west of the Confederate capital. Then striking it at other points, he went eastward, destroying the Southside Railroad and the Weldon Road, far toward North Carolina, and then returned to City Point with 150 prisoners.

Grant now decided to move on toward Richmond. His army started on May 21st, and reached the passage of the North Anna River on the 23d. Here it was found that Lee had already moved in that direction and reached there first. After a severe battle Lee was dislodged and Grant pressed steadily forward, and by May 28th, was south of the Pamunkey River. Lee, however, had followed, and taking a shorter road, was now in front, occupying a strong position on the Chickahominy River, which commanded a turnpike and two railroads leading to Richmond.

Grant saw at once that it would be necessary to drive Lee from his position before he could continue his march to Richmond. After a reconnoissance Grant decided to make a flanking movement and cross the Chickahominy at Cold Harbor. That place was seized and the army re-enforced by the arrival of the troops, under General W. F. Smith, sent by Butler.

For three days, June 1st, 2d and 3d, the two armies fiercely struggled on the ground where Lee and McClellan had fought two years before. The battle on the 3d was particularly sanguinary, thousands of men falling in the brief space of twenty minutes. At its conclusion the Federals held the ground, but they had failed in their attempt to force the Chickahominy. The strength of Lee's position showed Grant that Richmond could not be taken in that direction. So, after sending Sheridan with his cavalry to Gordonsville to destroy the railroad between Richmond and the Shenandoah Valley and Lynchburg, Grant decided to transfer his army to the south side of the James River, and attempt the capture of the Confederate capital in that way.

On the night of June 12th the army silently withdrew, and crossing the Chickahominy at Long Bridge, was well on its way before Lee knew of its departure. It moved below White Oak Swamp and on through Charles City Courthouse to the James, which it crossed in boats and on pontoon bridges. Grant hurried on to Burmuda Hundred while the crossing was being made and ordered Butler to send a portion of his troops to attempt the capture of Petersburg before Lee could re-enforce Beauregard. But this was unsuccessful, and on the evening of June 16th the Army of the Potomac took up a position near a strong line of intrenchments that Beauregard had cast up around the city.

At this time a formidable raid was made by General Early, with about 15,000 Confederate troops, for the purpose of drawing a large force away from Grant. He hurried down the Shenandoah Valley, and crossing the Potomac at Williamsport, moved through Maryland to Hagerstown and Frederick. Near the latter place, on the Monocacy River, he was confronted by a few troops which General Lewis Wallace. then in command of the Middle Department, had hastily collected at Baltimore, and a portion of Ricketts's division from the advance of the Sixth Corps, which Grant had dispatched to the protection of Washington. For eight hours, on July 9th, this little band battled with Early's large force, and although it was defeated with heavy loss, its gallant stand saved the national capital, as it allowed time for the Sixth and Nineteenth Corps to reach the city and secure it. Early, learning of this on his way to Washington, rapidly crossed the Potomac with his spoils. General Wright, who took Sedgwick's place in the Sixth Corps, pursued him to the Shenandoah Valley through Snicker's Gap, when, after a battle, in which the invaders were driven up the valley, Wright returned to Washington.

Early remained in the valley for some

time. After a contest with General Averill near Winchester, on July 20th, in which Early's troops were defeated, and a battle with General Crook, in which the latter was forced back toward the Potomac, Early sent a cavalry force of 3,000 men, under Generals McCausland, Bradley and Johnson, on a plundering tour in Maryland and Pennsylvania. They reached Chambersburg, Pa., on July 30th, and after demanding a tribute of $200,000 in gold to insure the town against destruction, which they did not receive, two-thirds of the village was laid in ashes. General Averill, who was ten miles away, heard of this, and at once moved against the raiders, driving them back into Virginia. To prevent a repetition of this raid the Sixth Corps, under General Wright, and the Nineteenth, under General Emory, were sent into the Shenandoah Valley, and the chief command of all the Federal forces there was given to General Sheridan, early in August.

Sheridan immediately took measures to drive Early from the valley. He attacked and defeated him at Winchester, September 19th, and followed him to a strong position on Fisher's Hill, near Strasburg, from which the Confederates were driven on the 22d and chased to Port Republic. From there the Federal cavalry followed Early to Staunton and compelled him to take refuge in the ranges of the Blue Ridge. The Federals then fell back behind Cedar Creek, and Sheridan went to Washington on the supposition that the valley would not be troubled again by the Confederates. But Early, being re-enforced, came back a month later and attacked General Wright at Cedar Creek so fiercely that he was compelled to fall back to Middletown and beyond.

General Sheridan was at Winchester when the attack began, and hearing the sound of the guns, sprang upon his black charger and dashed toward Cedar Creek. Meeting on the way portions of his army in confused retreat, he galloped up to them, and waving his hat shouted: "Face the other way, boys—face the other way! We are going back to our camp to lick them out of their boots!" Instantly the tide was turned, and following their commander, the troops hurriedly retraced their steps toward the lost battle ground. Regiments were at once re-formed, and cheered and encouraged by Sheridan, the men charged to victory and drove the Confederates in flight up the valley to Fisher's Hill. Early's force was almost annihilated and an end put to hostilities in the Shenandoah Valley.

While the Army of the Potomac lay near Petersburg Lee withdrew a large force from that city to defend Richmond from troops sent by Butler over a pontoon bridge across the James River. Grant took advantage of this, and made several attempts to penetrate the Confederate lines before Peters-

burg. He succeeded in undermining one of the principal forts, and on the morning of July 30th the whole fort, with 300 men, was blown high into the air. Then a heavy cannonade was opened upon the remainder of the works with great effect. But the assault was a failure, owing to slowness of motion of some of the assailants.

Soon after this the Army of the Potomac was massed on the right of the Confederates, south of the James, and made an attack upon Lee's works on Hatcher's Run. But after a severe contest they were repulsed, and on October 29th withdrew to their intrenchments in front of Petersburg. Very little of importance was done after that by the Army of the Potomac until the opening of the campaign of 1865.

CHAPTER XXV.

Sherman Moves Toward Atlanta—Capture of Allatoona Pass—Death of Bishop Polk—Johnston Succeeded by General J. B. Hood—Death of General James B. McPherson—Atlanta Taken—Sherman's March to the Sea—Destruction of the "Albemarle."

GENERAL SHERMAN started on his campaign against Atlanta on May 6th, 1864.

THE INVASION OF MARYLAND—GENERAL MEADE'S ARMY CROSSING THE ANTIETAM IN PURSUIT OF LEE, JULY 12TH, 1863.

He had a force of about 100,000 men, distributed in the Army of the Cumberland, led by General G. H. Thomas; the Army of the Tennessee, led by General J. B. McPherson, and the Army of the Ohio, commanded by General J. M. Schofield. Moving southward from Chattanooga, Sherman came upon a Confederate force of 55,000 strongly posted at Dalton, lying at the junction of the roads leading into East and West Tennessee. This force was commanded by General Joseph E. Johnston, and was arranged in three corps, under Generals Hardee, Hood and Polk. As the position of this force was too strong to warrant an attack in front, Sherman menaced its flanks by seeking a passage through Snake Hill Gap, on the left. This was successful, and the Confederates retreated to a point near Resaca Station, at the Oostenaula River, on the line of the railroad between Chattanooga and Atlanta.

Johnston was driven across the river after a sharp fight on May 15th, and being pursued by Thomas, McPherson and Schofield, he fled through to Allatoona Pass, where he took up a position on the other side of the Etowah River. The opposing

armies then rested for a short time on opposite banks of the stream.

Sherman now attempted to flank the Confederates out of their strong position by concentrating his forces west of them, at Dallas. This movement led to a battle near that place. Neither side gained a victory, and when darkness stopped the fight Johnston strongly intrenched himself through a broken, wooded country from Dallas to Marietta. After much severe fighting between these two towns Johnston was compelled to leave Allatoona Pass, June 1st, 1864. Sherman then took possession of the position, garrisoned it, and rebuilt the bridges that Johnston had burned during his flight. The gaps made in Sherman's ranks by the losses in the numerous engagements were here filled up by the arrival, on the 8th, of troops under General Frank Blair.

Sherman then pushed on with his strengthened army, and although Johnston contested his onward march at every point at which he could make a stand, the Confederates were driven, after a month of desperate fighting, from the Kenesaw Mountains, and from Lost and Pine Mountains, down toward the Chattahoochee River, in the direction of Atlanta. In these struggles the Confederates lost heavily; among the killed on Pine Mountain being Bishop Polk, one of their corps commanders.

When Johnston reached the Chattahoochee Sherman rode into Marietta, and at once planned to strike a severe blow on his antagonist while he was crossing that river. But Johnston was too quick and skillful to allow this, and he safely passed the stream and made a stand along the line of it. He was soon forced from this position and retreated to a new line that covered Atlanta, his left resting on the Chattahoochee and his right on Peachtree Creek. While there, on July 10th, Johnston was succeeded by General J. B. Hood, of Texas.

After a short rest the Federals, toward the end of July, began advancing again, and after detroying railroads and taking part in some heavy skirmishes, they were attacked by the Confederates on the 20th. Hood himself led the attack, which was particularly directed against the corps of Howard, Hooker and Palmer. The battle was a fierce one and both sides suffered greatly, but the assailants were repulsed.

Sherman then moved rapidly toward Atlanta. On the way he encountered some strong intrenchments, and while attacking a part of Hood's army behind them he was struck a severe blow in the rear by the main body of that army led by General Hardee, who had, by a long night march, passed around him. The blow was a crushing one, but after a most sanguinary battle, lasting many hours, the Federals were victorious and succeeded in driving the Confederates back to their works. While reconnoitring in a wood that day (July 22d), General McPherson was shot dead by a Confederate sharpshooter. He was succeeded in the command of the Army of the Tennessee by General Logan.

A few days later, July 28th, the Confederates again made a fierce attack, and were again sent back to their lines after a heavy loss. This put a stop to active hostilities for a few weeks. Then on August 31st the decisive battle that gave the Federals possession of Atlanta was fought. The forces of Howard and Hardee met on that day at Jonesborough, twenty miles below the city, when, the Confederates being defeated, Hood blew up his magazine at Atlanta, and forming a junction with Hardee, recrossed the Chattahoochee with his whole army. Sherman then entered Atlanta on September 2d.

The two armies now rested for a time, with only the river between them, and most of September was given up to reorganization on both sides. Then, hearing that Hood contemplated the seizure of Tennes-

tion by Hardee of Savannah, which Sherman entered the next day.

Early in 1864 General Truman Seymour was sent by General Gillmore to assist the citizens of Florida in driving out the Confederate troops under General Finnegan, so that that State might re-enter the Union. Seymour went up the St. John's River with 6,000 men and drove Finnegan from Jacksonville into the interior. After a hot pursuit Seymour came upon the Confederates strongly posted in the heart of a cypress swamp at Olustee Station. He made an attack, February 20th, but was defeated, and fell back to Jacksonville after destroying the enemy's stores to the value of $1,000,000.

On April 17th General Hoke, assisted by the Confederate ram *Albemarle*, made a successful assault upon Plymouth, on the North Carolina coast, near the mouth of the Roanoke River, then held by General Wessels with 1,600 troops. The *Albemarle* was a powerful vessel, and for several months kept that part of the coast free from

nessee. Late in October he crossed the Tennessee River near Florence, and pushed vigorously on toward Nashville with 50,000 troops. At Franklin he came to the intrenchments of General Schofield, who was trying to impede the invaders so that he could get himself and train to Nashville before they did. Hood reached Franklin on the afternoon of November 30th, and at once charged on Schofield so desperately that his troops were driven from their works. But they quickly rallied, and by a gallant dash recovered their lost ground and captured 300 prisoners. Schofield then went on to Nashville, quickly followed by Hood, who took up a position in front of that city early in December.

General Thomas was then in charge of the Federal troops in Nashville. On December 15th he sent out General T. J. Wood, with the Fourth Corps, to drive the Confederates away. Wood made a vigorous attack, and soon compelled Hood to retreat to the foot of the Harpeth Hills. There he was again assailed by the same

SHERIDAN'S CAMPAIGN IN THE VALLEY OF THE SHENANDOAH—BATTLE OF SUMMIT POINT, SUNDAY, AUGUST 21st, 1864.

see, Sherman sent Thomas to Nashville to organize and concentrate a new force of troops there. Hood in the meantime descended upon Allatoona Pass and attempted to capture the stores. He failed, and Sherman pursued him into Northern Alabama.

Sherman now planned his march from Atlanta to the sea. He turned over the command of a large portion of his troops to General Thomas, and then started out on the morning of November 14th. General Kilpatrick, with 5,000 cavalry, led the way, followed by Sherman and 65,000 men, arranged in two columns, commanded respectively by Generals Howard and Slocum. They marched for more than a month through the heart of Georgia, living entirely upon what they picked up on the way. Moving as they did in two columns, with wings extending sixty miles, the Confederates were bewildered, and offered but very little opposition. Upon reaching the Ogeechee River Sherman attacked and captured Fort McAllister, and a week later (December 20th) he compelled the evacua-

Federal gunboats. Its destruction, accordingly, was very much desired by the National authorities, and this was accomplished with great skill and bravery by Lieutenant Cushing. He, with thirteen men, on the night of October 27th, took a torpedo up into Plymouth harbor, and reaching the anchorage of the ram, succeeded in thrusting it under her hull and blowing her up with fatal effect. All the time during the placing of the torpedo, after they had reached within twenty yards of the ram, the brave men on the launch were subjected to a terrific hail of bullets fired from the shore by the alarmed Confederates, who, although they could see nothing in the darkness, heard the movements of their foe and directed their shots in the direction of the sound. Cushing and one of his men, after the work was done, escaped to a cutter that accompanied the torpedo boat, while the others of the fearless band were killed.

General Hood, after his unsuccessful attempt to seize the stores at Allatoona Pass, prepared for his invasion of Ten-

corps and other troops the following day. The result was that the Confederates were sent flying southward in great confusion. They were closely pursued, and at the close of the month Hood, with the remnants of his army, escaped across the Tennessee. During Thomas's four months' stay in Tennessee he captured 11,500 prisoners and 72 pieces of artillery, and inflicted a loss to the Confederates of more than 20,000 men. His own loss was about 10,000.

CHAPTER XXVI.

THE "KEARSARGE" AND THE "ALABAMA"—CAPTURE OF FORTS MORGAN AND GAINES—ADMIRAL FARRAGUT'S BRAVERY—CHARLESTON TAKEN—BATTLE AT BENTONVILLE—FALL OF MOBILE—STONEMAN'S RAID.

CONFEDERATE cruisers made great havoc among the merchant ships of the United States during the war, especially in the first two years. At the beginning of 1864 they had captured 193 vessels, whose aggregate cargoes were valued at $13,400,000. The most formidable of these plunderers was the *Alabama*, which was built, armed, manned and provisioned in England. She was under command of Captain Raphael Semmes, of Maryland. For two years she sailed along the paths of American merchantmen on the Atlantic, plundering and burning them, and always eluding the government vessels sent out in search of her.

At length Captain John A. Winslow, of the *Kearsarge*, who had sought her high and low, heard that the *Alabama* had put into the port of Cherbourg, France. He immediately took his vessel to that place and lying off outside the harbor, awaited her reappearance on the ocean. When she came out the *Kearsarge* moved beyond the jurisdiction of France, and then gave battle. The two vessels fought desperately for an hour, pouring broadside after broadside into each other. Then the *Alabama* began to sink, and in twenty minutes went to the bottom. Semmes and his officers and some of his crew were picked up by an English yacht, which had hovered near to be ready in case of such an emergency, and taken in safety to England, where Semmes was feted and presented with a sword as a token of sympathy and esteem.

Winslow's victory stirred up the author-

gan was captured, and the port of Mobile effectually closed.

The closing of the port of Wilmington was not attempted until December, 1864. Then an expedition was sent against Fort Fisher. It was composed of Admiral Porter's fleet, and land troops from Butler's department, under General Godfrey Weitzel. The expedition was a failure, and another attempt was made the following February with the same fleet, and land troops led by General A. H. Terry. This was a complete success, the fort was surrendered on the 15th, and the Federal army entered Wilmington on the 22d.

About a month after the capture of Savannah Sherman started on a rapid march through South Carolina, and pressed on almost unopposed until he reached Columbia, the capital of the State, which he captured, February 17th, 1865. Upon learning of this Hardee at once left Charleston, to which he had retreated after his evacuation of Savannah, and fled into North Carolina to join the forces of General Johnston. Sherman's forces then took possession of Charleston, and a few weeks afterward Major Anderson celebrated the

Point, on the James River, to consult the President and General Grant in regard to future operations.

The port of Mobile having been closed, plans were laid in March, 1865, for the capture of that city and the rest of Alabama. General Canby, who commanded the Department of the Gulf, started out against Mobile with 25,000 troops, at the same time that Thomas sent from his army 13,000 horsemen and about 2,000 foot soldiers, under General Wilson, to co-operate with him. While Canby was attempting the reduction of Mobile, Wilson swept down from the Tennessee and raided 650 miles through Alabama and Georgia, capturing cities and towns and destroying an immense amount of public property. He also succeeded in keeping Forrest's cavalry from assisting the besieged Confederates at Mobile. Canby managed to capture the city on April 11th, when General Maury, in command there, fled up the Alabama River with 9,000 troops. With the city were surrendered 5,000 prisoners and 150 cannon. The war in the Gulf region was now at an end.

Although the Armies of the Potomac

SHERIDAN'S CAMPAIGN IN THE VALLEY OF THE SHENANDOAH—FIGHT OF DUFFIE'S CAVALRY, NEAR HUNTER'S HOUSE, CHARLESTOWN, VA.—COVERING THE RETREAT OF THE FEDERAL FORCES.

ities of the National Government to a determination to close the two ports then open for blockade runners—Wilmington and Mobile. To close the latter port General Canby sent a force of 5,000 troops, under General Gordon Granger, from New Orleans to co-operate with Admiral Farragut's fleet of 18 vessels, which appeared off the entrance to Mobile on August 5th. These vessels, four of which were ironclads, then sailed in between Fort Morgan and Fort Gaines amid the terrific fire from their great guns. Farragut gave his orders through a tube from the maintop of his flagship (the *Hartford*), where he was lashed to the rigging to keep him from being dislodged by the shock of battle. He remained in that perilous position during the entire voyage past the forts. He made the passage safely, although one of his gunboats, the *Tecumseh*, was destroyed by a torpedo. He was then attacked by a fleet of Confederate gunboats, but after a severe fight they were defeated.

A simultaneous assault was now made by Farragut and Granger on Fort Gaines, and it was surrendered, August 7th. A little more than two weeks later Fort Mor-

anniversary of his evacuation of Fort Sumter four years before by raising over the ruins of that fortress the same flag which he had been compelled to haul down then, and which he had carried away with him.

Sherman soon passed on into North Carolina, reaching Fayetteville, March 12th. There he rested until the 15th, when he moved eastward toward Goldsborough. On the way he met a force of 20,000 Confederates, under General Hardee, at Averysborough. Defeating them, he continued his march. Two days afterward (March 18th), when near Bentonville, he was surprised by the whole of Johnston's army, which suddenly attacked a part of his force under General Slocum. There was a terrible battle. Six times did the combined forces of Hoke, Hardee and Cheatham fall fiercely upon the Federals, and nothing but the most desperate efforts saved Sherman's army from destruction. His troops made a brave stand, and at length succeeded in gaining the victory, the Confederates retreating to Raleigh, the capital of North Carolina. Sherman now went on to Goldsborough, where he was joined by Schofield and Terry, after which he hastened to City

and of the James remained in comparative quiet in front of Petersburg and Richmond through the winter of 1864–'65, they effectually prevented by their position a junction of the two forces of Lee and Johnston. Grant at length determined to make a general and vigorous movement against the Confederate capital. Late in February he ordered General Sheridan, then in the Shenandoah Valley, to move up and destroy all communications with Richmond north of the James River, and, if possible, capture Lynchburg, where a large number of Confederate supplies were stored.

With Generals Merritt and Custer and 10,000 men, horse and foot, Sheridan left Winchester on the 27th, and going up the valley, met Early's forces at Waynesborough. After a battle there he scattered his enemies, and then crossed the Blue Ridge and destroyed the railroad as far as Charlottesville. Finding Lynchburg too strong for him, he divided his force, one party going to break up the railroad toward that city, and the other to disable the James River Canal, by which the Confederate capital received a large portion of its supplies. Sheridan then rejoined the

Army of the Potomac by passing around Lee's left.

Lee now saw that it was absolutely necessary for him to form a junction with Johnston in North Carolina if he wished to save his army; and so, concentrating his forces near Grant's centre, in front of Petersburg, he, on March 25th, made a fierce assault on Fort Steadman, hoping by the capture of that point in the Federal lines to be able to break through. But he was unsuccessful, Grant being prepared for him and defeating him with heavy loss.

Early in February General Stoneman was ordered to take his cavalry on a raid into South Carolina for the purpose of assisting Sherman; but finding the latter in no need of help, Stoneman moved eastward and destroyed the Virginia and Tennessee Railroad for some distance toward Lynchburg, after which he turned southward and

fast being hemmed in. Many efforts had been made to bring about peace without the conquering of the armies of the Confederacy, but they had failed. President Lincoln would listen to no conditions except absolute submission, everywhere within the bounds of the republic, to the National authority, and the entire abolition of slavery. When Jefferson Davis, in answer to an appeal from Francis P. Blair, of Maryland, near the close of the year 1864, said that he would be willing to "enter into a conference with a view to secure peace to the *two countries*," President Lincoln expressed his willingness to confer if it was with a view "to secure peace for the people of our *common country*." Although Davis did not like the latter expression, he appointed as commissioners Alexander H. Stephens, John A. Campbell and R. M. T. Hunter. The conference was fruitless, as

the advance, fell back in confusion on Crawford's troops, which in turn were driven back on to the division under Griffin. There the enemy's onslaught was checked, and a division of the Second Corps being sent to Warren's support, he at once re-formed his ranks, and with a sudden dash regained the lost ground and captured the White Oak Road. Sheridan also was driven from Five Forks for a time, but with the aid of the Fifth Corps again advanced to that place, where, on April 1st, a sanguinary battle was fought. The Confederates were driven from their strong line of works and completely routed; the Fifth Corps doubling up their left flank in confusion, and the cavalry of General Merritt dashing on to the White Oak Road, capturing their artillery and turning it upon them. They soon took to flight in disorder, leaving behind them about 5,000 of

THE WAR ON THE UPPER POTOMAC—WILSON'S CAVALRY FORAGING AT THE SELDEN ESTATE, CLARKE COUNTY, VA.

struck the railroad between Danville and Greensborough. Some of his troops went as far as Salisbury, in the hope of releasing a large number of Union soldiers imprisoned there. But the prisoners were removed before Stoneman's men arrived, and although the raiders destroyed a vast amount of public property they did not accomplish their object. Then, while Stoneman and his main body pushed into East Tennessee, a part of his force, on April 19th, destroyed the magnificent bridge of the South Carolina Railroad which extended 1,100 feet across the Catawba River. This raid resulted in the capture of 6,000 prisoners, 31 pieces of artillery and a large number of small arms.

CHAPTER XXVII.

Efforts to Secure Peace—Davis's Declaration—Battle of Five Forks—Fall of Petersburg—Richmond Captured—Correspondence between Grant and Lee—Surrender of Lee's Army—Terms of Surrender.

THE Civil War was now coming to an end. The enemies of the republic were

Lincoln would not recede from the position he had taken.

Indignant at this result, Davis declared at a public meeting held at Richmond, February 5th, that "sooner than we should be united again I would be willing to yield up everything I have on earth, and, if it were possible, would sacrifice my life a thousand times before I would succumb." Then a few days later at another meeting it was resolved that the Confederates would never lay down their arms until their independence was won.

Upon Sheridan's return from his great raid at the close of March, Grant started the Army of the Potomac on a grand movement against the Confederate right. On the morning of March 31st, Sheridan, with his cavalry and a corps of infantry, moved forward and took possession of Five Forks, while Warren advanced toward the White Oak Road. The latter drove the Confederates before him for a short distance, but they quickly rallied, and attacked him so vigorously that Ayres's division, which had

their troops as prisoners of war. The fugitives were pursued westward about six miles by the cavalry of Merritt and McKenzie.

Grant heard of this victory in his position before Petersburg, and at once ordered a bombardment along his whole line against the city, to be kept up all night.

At dawn the next morning the works of the enemy were vigorously attacked. Wright with his corps managed to break through the lines, and, pushing on, drove the Confederates before him, captured a large number of guns and several thousand prisoners, and effectually crushed Lee's right. Parke with the Ninth Corps had meanwhile carried the main line in the enemy's front, but was checked at the second line; while a part of Gibbon's corps by a gallant charge captured two strong works south of Petersburg. The battle now raged furiously from right to left, the Confederates bravely fighting to hold their intrenchments. Especially determined were they to retain possession of Fort Mahone, which was defended by Hill's corps. In the gallant stand he made there Hill was killed. Sheridan now came up rapidly from the west, and sweeping down upon the Confederates' flank and rear, forced them to give up the contest and fly in confusion.

That day, Sunday, April 2d, Davis was attending church in Richmond, when an orderly hurried up the aisle and handed him a message from Lee. With a glance he saw that all was over. He must seek safety in flight, as Richmond would soon be taken. At eight o'clock that evening he abandoned the capital and fled to Danville, to which city his wife had gone a few days before. The Confederate Congress and the Virginia Legislature also took flight. Early the next morning General Weitzel, in command of the forces on the north side of the James, marched into Richmond with bands playing and colors flying. His army, composed in part of colored troops, was immediately set to work to put out the fires kindled by drunken incendiaries just after the evacuation, and which had destroyed all of the business

pushed for the Danville Road, followed by Meade with the Second and Sixth Corps, while Ord hastened along the Southside Railroad toward Burkeville, where that and the Danville Road intersect, a distance of fifty-three miles from Petersburg. Lee was also making for that place, so as to be able to join Davis at Danville. The Federals, having the inside track, reached there first. Sheridan gained a position above Burkeville, and thus cut off Lee's avenue of escape, while Ord stopped below.

Lee's position now became desperate. He was at Amelia Courthouse, and seeing that he could not advance by the railroad, he swung around to the west and struck the road again at Farmville. Here the head of his columns was met by two regiments of infantry and some cavalry, under General Theodore Read, who had been hurried forward to hold the Confederates until Ord could come up with the rest of his corps. Read accomplished this at the expense of his life. When Ord arrived Lee intrenched himself.

Grant now reached Farmville, and on the 7th wrote a note to Lee in which he

Grant then proposed a meeting to arrange definite terms for the surrender of the Army of Northern Virginia. Lee wrote back that he had not intended to propose the surrender of his army. "To be frank," he went on, "I do not think the emergency has arisen to call for the surrender of this army; but as the restoration of peace should be the sole object of all, I desired to know whether your proposals would lead to that end. I cannot, therefore, meet you with a view to surrender the Army of Northern Virginia; but as far as your proposal may affect the Confederate States forces under my command, and tend to the restoration of peace, I should be pleased to meet you at 10 A. M. to-morrow, on the old stage road to Richmond, between the picket lines of the two armies."

Grant would not listen to an interview on this basis, as, having no authority to treat on the topic of peace, he saw that such a meeting would be useless. "The terms upon which peace can be had," he wrote, "are well understood. By the South laying down their arms they will hasten that most desirable event, save thousands of human

SHERIDAN'S CAMPAIGN IN THE VALLEY OF THE SHENANDOAH—VIEW OF THE FRONT FROM THE FEDERAL LINES ON JACKSON HILL, VA.

part of Main Street. Weitzel found that the Confederates had abandoned 5,000 of their sick and wounded in the hospitals, and had left as trophies for the victors 500 pieces of artillery, 5,000 small arms, many locomotives and cars, and a large amount of other public property, together with a part of the archives of the Confederate Government. When Weitzel reached the Virginia Statehouse one of his staff, Lieutenant Johnston Livingston de Peyster, ascended to the roof and unfurled the National flag, and Richmond was once more in the hands of the Federal authorities.

The news of the capture of Richmond produced great joy throughout the loyal States, for it told of the downfall of the Confederate Government. In Washington the public offices were closed; the people of New York showed their pleasure in public meetings and in the ringing of bells in the tower of Trinity Church.

Finding that he could no longer hold Petersburg, Lee sent the message which Davis received in church, and then silently withdrew from his position on the evening of April 2d. At dawn the next morning the Federals learned of his retreat, and at once set out to intercept him. Sheridan

said: "The result of the last week must convince you of the hopelessness of further resistance on the part of the Army of Northern Virginia in this struggle. I feel that it is so, and regard it as my duty to shift from myself the responsibility of any further effusion of blood by asking of you the surrender of that portion of the Confederate States Army known as the Army of Northern Virginia." In his reply to this Lee said that, although he did not believe further resistance on the part of his army hopeless, he reciprocated the desire to avoid useless effusion of blood; "and therefore," he added, "before considering your proposition I ask the terms you will offer on condition of its surrender." Without waiting for Grant's answer Lee stole away in the night toward Lynchburg, hoping to escape to the shelter of the mountains beyond that city. Early the next morning the Federals set out in pursuit.

While on the move westward Lee received Grant's answer, in which he said: "There is but one condition I would insist on, namely, that the men and officers surrendered should be disqualified for taking up arms against the Government of the United States until properly exchanged."

lives and hundreds of millions of property not yet destroyed."

General Sheridan had by this time reached a position across Lee's path, near Appomattox Courthouse, so that there was no way for the latter to escape except by cutting through Sheridan's line. He made a brave, desperate effort to do this on the morning of April 9th. But with the aid of General Ord's command and the Fifth Corps, which just then came up, Sheridan repulsed the Confederates, and Lee was compelled to give in. He wrote to Grant: "I received your note this morning on the picket line, whither I had come to meet you, and ascertain definitely what terms were embraced in your proposal of yesterday, with reference to the surrender of this army. I now ask an interview, in accordance with the offer contained in your letter of yesterday for that purpose."

Arrangements were at once made for the interview. The dwelling of Wilmer McLean, at Appomattox Courthouse, was selected for the purpose, and in the parlor of that house, on Palm Sunday, April 9th, 1865, the two generals met and discussed the terms of surrender. It was agreed that Lee and his officers should give their parole of honor not to take arms against the Government of the United States until properly exchanged; that the officers were to be allowed to keep their side arms, baggage and private horses, and that the officers and men would not be disturbed by United States authorities so long as they should observe their parole and the laws in force where they should reside. On Wednesday, April 12th, the Confederates laid down their arms and departed for their homes. The number paroled was about 25,000. With the men were surrendered about 16,000 small arms, 150 pieces of artillery, 71 stand of colors, about 1,100 wagons and caissons, and 4,000 horses and mules.

That same day, April 12th, the War Department issued an order directing the suspension of all drafting and recruiting for the National Army, and of the purchasing of munitions of war and supplies.

the 17th a suspension of hostilities was agreed upon pending the ratification or rejection by the National Government of a basis of peace arranged by the two generals. The President and Cabinet refused to accept the agreement, whereupon Johnston surrendered to Sherman on the same generous terms as those granted to Lee. With him were surrendered and paroled about 25,000 men. One hundred and eight pieces of artillery and about 15,000 small arms fell into the hands of the Federals. A few days later, May 4th, General Taylor surrendered the Confederate forces in Alabama to General Canby, at Citronville; and the Confederate Navy in the Tombigbee River was surrendered to Admiral Farragut at the same time. Hostilities ended with a battle at Brazos Santiago, Tex., on May 13th.

When Davis heard of the surrender of Johnston's army he immediately left

tions. Mistaking each other for enemies, both opened fire, and thus aroused the sleepers. Davis tried to make his escape disguised in a woman's waterproof cloak and a shawl thrown over his head by Miss Howell, but he was detected and captured by Pritchard and his men. Davis was taken to Fortress Monroe and there imprisoned under an indictment for treason, for some time, when he was released on bail. He was never tried, enjoying his liberty until his death, in 1889.

While the people of the North were rejoicing over the capture of Richmond and the surrender of Lee their joy was suddenly turned into sorrow by the news of the assassination of the President. Mr. Lincoln was seated in a box in a Washington theatre, with his wife and friends, when John Wilkes Booth entered behind him and shot him in the back of the head. Then shouting, "Sic semper tyrannus!"—so may it

GRANT'S MOVEMENTS SOUTH OF THE JAMES—BATTLE OF POPLAR SPRING CHURCH—GALLANT CHARGE OF A PART OF THE FIFTH CORPS ON THE CONFEDERATE FORT, SEPTEMBER 30TH, 1864.

CHAPTER XXVIII.

JOHNSTON SURRENDERS TO SHERMAN—HOSTILITIES ENDED —FLIGHT OF DAVIS AND HIS CABINET—DAVIS CAPTURED—ASSASSINATION OF PRESIDENT LINCOLN—THE NAVY IN THE WAR.

WHILE the surrender of General Lee at Appomattox virtually ended the war, there were still Johnston's army in North Carolina, and smaller bodies elsewhere to be conquered. Sherman was preparing to march toward the Roanoke on April 10th, when he heard of the fall of Petersburg and Richmond. This changed his plans, and he at once turned his columns toward Raleigh and marched on Johnston, who retreated through Raleigh along the course of the railroad westward toward Greensborough, whither Davis and his Cabinet had fled after making Danville the seat of the Confederate Government for a few days.

Sherman pursued Johnston as far as Raleigh, where on the 15th the latter, having heard of the overthrow of Lee, requested an interview with Sherman for the purpose of making terms of surrender. This was granted, and after a meeting on

Greensborough, with his Cabinet and an escort of 2,000 cavalry, and fled toward the Gulf of Mexico. His wife and children and Miss Howell, Mrs. Davis's sister, made for the same place in wagons, but along a different route. Upon reaching Washington, Ga., Davis learned that some Confederate soldiers, supposing the treasure that he had taken from Richmond was with his wife's party, had formed a plot to hold up her train and seize the valuable property. He immediately set out, with a few followers, to protect his family. After a ride of eighteen miles he joined his wife at Irwinsville, nearly due south from Macon, Ga.

General Wilson, who was then at Macon, heard of Davis's flight to the Gulf, and sent out two bodies of cavalry, one under Lieutenant Colonel Pritchard, and the other led by Lieutenant Colonel Hardin, to intercept him. As a reward of $100,000 had been offered by the government for the capture of Davis, these two forces left no stone unturned to find him. They soon discovered his whereabouts, and at early dawn the two parties approached the camp where he was resting for the night, from opposite direc-

always be with tyrants—the assassin leaped out of the box on the stage, dashed through a back door, and fled on a horse that was in readiness for him. He was pursued and overtaken in a barn below Fredericksburg, Va., and shot dead by a sergeant named Boston Corbett.

President Lincoln died the next morning, April 15th, 1865. His body was taken to his home in Springfield, Ill., and there buried, May 4th. Andrew Johnson, by virtue of his office as Vice President and in accordance with the law, was sworn in as President of the United States a few hours after the death of Mr. Lincoln.

On the same night that the President was shot Secretary of State Seward was stabbed and badly wounded by an accomplice of Booth, which gave rise to a belief that a plot had been arranged for the murder of the President, all the members of the Cabinet, General Grant and others. A number of persons were arrested on suspicion of being implicated in this plot, and their trial resulted in the conviction and execution by hanging of David E. Harrold. Lewis Payne, Mrs. Mary E. Surratt and

MAJOR GENERAL SHERIDAN RIDING ALONG THE LIN

BATTLE OF FISHER'S HILL, VA., SEPTEMBER 22D, 1864.

George A. Atzeroth, while Samuel A. Mudd, Michael O'Loughlin and Samuel Arnold were sentenced to imprisonment for life.

The surrender of the two great armies of the Confederacy and the capture of its President effectually crushed that temporary government forever, and settled the question of slavery in the United States. The Civil War in America, which was more extended in area and more destructive of life and property than any other recorded in history, was over. The number of Union soldiers engaged on the field during the war was 2,666,999. According to a statement prepared by the Adjutant General's Office, the number of casualties in the volunteer and regular armies of the United States during the four years was as follows: Killed in battle, 67,058; died of wounds, 43,012; died of disease, 199,720;

city public receptions were held in honor of their noble work. A beautiful close to the terrible struggle they had passed through was the grand review in Washington of the two armies that had conquered Lee and Johnston. The troops were marched to the vicinity of the National capital, and then on May 22d and 23d they moved through the city in long procession, reviewed by the President and his Cabinet and the foreign Ministers.

The work of disbanding the armies was then begun, and in a remarkably brief space of time the habiliments of war were cast off, and the soldiers, now respected citizens, were back in their places in offices, stores, countingrooms and on farms. From the first of June to the middle of November 800,000 of the 1,000,000 soldiers whose names were on the rolls May 1st were mustered out of service.

in all time to come. In obedience to your country's call you left your homes and families, and volunteered in her defense. Victory has crowned your valor and secured the purpose of your patriotic hearts; and with the gratitude of your countrymen, and the highest honors a great and free nation can accord, you will soon be permitted to return to your homes and families, conscious of having discharged the highest duty of American citizens. To achieve these glorious triumphs, and secure to yourselves, your fellow countrymen and posterity the blessings of free institutions, tens of thousands of your gallant comrades have fallen, and sealed the priceless legacy with their blood. The graves of these a grateful nation bedews with tears. It honors their memories, and will ever cherish and support their stricken families."

Although it attracted less attention than

GRANT'S MOVEMENTS SOUTH OF THE JAMES—BATTLE OF POPLAR SPRING CHURCH—THE NINTH CORPS PASSING POPLAR SPRING CHURCH AND CONFEDERATE PRISONERS COMING IN, FRIDAY AFTERNOON, SEPTEMBER 30TH, 1864.

other causes, such as accidents, murder, Confederate prisons, etc., 40,154; total died, 349,944; total deserted, 199,105. Number of soldiers in the Confederate service who died of wounds or disease (partial statement), 133,821. Partial statement of deserted, 104,428. Number of United States troops captured during the war, 212,608; Confederate troops captured, 476,169. Number of United States troops paroled on the field, 16,431; Confederate troops paroled on the field, 248,599. Number of United States troops who died while prisoners, 30,156; of Confederate troops, 30,152.

A grand, imposing spectacle was presented when the brave soldiers who had endured hardships and risked their lives for the preservation of the Union returned from the field of battle to go back to their peaceful avocations. Everywhere they were received with expressions of gratitude and affection, and in almost every village and

Just before the disbandment of the soldiers took place General in Chief Grant issued, on June 2d, the following address to them:

"Soldiers of the Armies of the United States: By your patriotic devotion to your country in the hour of danger and alarm, and your magnificent fighting, bravery and endurance, you have maintained the supremacy of the Union and the Constitution, overthrown all armed opposition to the enforcement of the laws and of the proclamation forever abolishing slavery—the cause and pretext of the rebellion—and opened the way to the rightful authorities to restore order and inaugurate peace on a permanent and enduring basis on every foot of American soil. Your marches, sieges and battles, in distance, duration, resolution and brilliancy of results, dim the lustre of the world's past military achievements, and will be the patriot's precedent in defense of liberty and right

the Army, the National Navy was of inestimable value during the war. It did excellent work in the blockade service and in co-operation with the Army along the rivers and seacoasts. When the war broke out the Navy was composed of but 7,600 men, but before it ended that number had increased to 51,000. During the four years 208 war vessels were constructed and fitted out, and 414 vessels were purchased and converted into war ships. Three hundred and thirteen of these were steamers, and many of them were ironclads. They cost the government about $19,000,000.

The National vessels captured or destroyed more than 1,500 blockade runners, which had been fitted out by British merchants and furnished with every kind of supplies for the Confederates. The capture and destruction of these vessels meant an aggregate loss to their owners, taking the value of the ships and their cargoes into consideration, of close upon

$30,000,000; but this was probably balanced by the immense profits that were made on the cargoes of the vessels that successfully "ran the blockade," although this violation of the law could hardly have been a paying transaction.

CHAPTER XXIX.

Care of the Sick and Wounded—Two Noble Organizations—Liberal Contributions of the People for Benevolent Work on the Battlefield—The Negro in the War.

THE sick and wounded during the war were well cared for by the government authorities. They were very liberal in supplying a sufficient number of hospitals and in furnishing them with every necessity, and in the employment of a large

body was founded by Henry W. Bellows, and was organized under the sanction of the President and Secretary of War. The founder was made president of the board of managers of the commission, and Frederick Law Olmstead was chosen general manager of its affairs.

The commission at once appealed to the people for money and supplies to carry out its object, which was to help the wounded and sick soldiers with delicacies, ice, stimulants, fruits, etc., and with trained nurses, and to do other work to relieve suffering on the battlefield. The response was remarkably liberal. Money and supplies flowed in at once. Men, women and children worked for it and contributed to it. Fairs were held in all the large cities in aid

cared for, and tents and trained nurses were always on hand.

The United States Christian Commission was founded by Vincent Colyer, an artist of New York, and was organized at a National Convention of the Young Men's Christian Associations on November 14th, 1861. Its work was conducted on the same general plan of the other commission. It distributed a vast amount of food, hospital stores, delicacies and clothing, and at the same time looked after the moral and religious welfare of the soldiers. Bibles and other good books, newspapers, pamphlets, etc., were well circulated among the men in hospitals, camps and ships, while chapels for religious labors and public worship were erected at every permanent camp.

THE ARMY OF THE POTOMAC—BATTLE OF HATCHER'S CREEK, VA., OCTOBER 27TH, 1864—THE SECOND CORPS, UNDER MAJOR GENERAL HANCOCK, FLANKING THE CONFEDERATE WORKS AT ARMSTRONG'S MILL.

number of skillful surgeons. When the war was closed there were 204 general hospitals fully equipped, with a capacity of nearly 137,000 beds. Besides these, many temporary and flying hospitals were erected in camps and on vessels and on battlefields. In the report of Surgeon General Joseph K. Barnes, at the end of the war, it was shown that during the four years there had been treated in the general hospitals alone 1,057,423 cases, among whom the average rate of mortality was only eight per cent., which was smaller than had ever before been known in any army.

One of the chief causes for this low rate of mortality in the Union Army was the beneficent work done by two grand organizations, known as the United States Sanitary Commission and the United States Christian Commission. The first-named

of it, and they were well patronized, one fair in New York city taking in $1,181,500, while one held at Poughkeepsie, on the Hudson, netted in profit as much as an average of one dollar to each inhabitant. So generous was the response to the commission's appeal that when the war closed it was found that the people had contributed to it to the value of $5,000,000!

The commission nobly lived up to the high appreciation the people showed for it. It was untiring in its work of relieving distress. Everywhere the armies went it followed closely, and was always ready to afford instant aid to those who needed it. With ambulances, army wagons and steamboats, which it employed specially for the purpose, the sick and wounded were carefully and tenderly transported as soon as possible to places where they could be

The money and supplies contributed by the people to this commission amounted in value to $6,000,000.

Through these two great organizations and the various other associations formed everywhere for the same purpose, and by private contributions, the loyal people of the land spent many millions of dollars.

The employment of colored troops in the Union Army was for some time a much-debated question. When a number of colored men got together in New York city, and began to drill, in answer to the President's call for troops in April, 1861, the sympathizers with the Confederates became so indignant that they threatened the negroes with violence, and the superintendent of police was compelled, in order to preserve the public peace, to order them to cease drilling.

SCENE IN CAMP LIFE—CHIMNEY ARCHITECTURE—THE FEDERAL SOLDIERS AT THEIR CAMP FIRES

A year later the action of General Hunter, then in command of the Department of the South, in ordering the organization of negro regiments in his department, aroused the indignation of Southern sympathizers in the National Congress. Wickliffe, of Kentucky, made a motion to ask the Secretary of War whether General Hunter had organized a regiment of fugitive slaves, and whether the government had authorized the act. When Hunter was asked for an answer to the first question he said: "No regiment of fugitive slaves has been or is being organized in this department. There is, however, a fine regiment of persons whose late masters are fugitive rebels—men who everywhere fly before the appearance of the National flag, leaving their servants behind them to shift for themselves as best they can."

A few weeks afterward Secretary Stanton issued a special order directing General Rufus Saxton, military governor of the seacoast islands, to "arm, uniform, equip and receive into the service of the United States such number of volunteers of African descent, not exceeding five thousand," as would be useful.

In the summer of 1862 crowds of colored people flocked to the camp of General G. W. Phelps, in command above New Orleans, and volunteered their services. Phelps asked permission of General Butler to arm and equip these men and form them into negro regiments. Butler, not having authority to give this permission, suggested that the colored men be employed in servile work on fortifications. To this Phelps replied: "I am not willing to become the mere slave driver you propose, having no qualifications that way."

He then threw up his commission and returned to his home in Vermont. It was not very long after this that Butler had full regiments formed of negro volunteers

from the free colored men in New Orleans.

The prejudice against the arming of negroes did not abate a particle until another year had passed by. Then, in the summer of 1863, Congress authorized the President to accept colored volunteers, and regiments of them were formed in many places. In a very short time there were nearly 200,000 negro troops in the field, fighting for their freedom. The Confederates, naturally, did not arm their slaves. They used them in menial work about their camps and forts.

CHAPTER XXX.

EXCHANGE OF PRISONERS—PECULIAR POSITION OF THE GOVERNMENT—TREATMENT OF UNION SOLDIERS IN CONFEDERATE PRISONS—AN UNFAIR EXCHANGE—THE SOUTHERN PEOPLE.

A HISTORY of the Civil War would not be complete without some mention of the arrangements for the exchange of prisoners and of the treatment of Federal soldiers confined in Confederate prisons. It was a long time before any plan of exchange was adopted, because the National Government, considering the Confederates as rebels against its authority, would not at first consent to enter into any negotiations with them as equals, which it would have to do to arrange any plan for the exchange of prisoners. The government felt that the Confederates had no right to take or hold prisoners, and to treat with them would be an admission that they had, which would be worse than acknowledging them as belligerents. Still, the government could not treat the prisoners it took as rebels and hang them, for the enemy would at once retaliate, and the war would thus become mere butchery. The first prisoners captured by the Federals were privateers, and they were condemned as pirates and placed in felons' cells. Immediately the Confederates con-

fined in like manner the officers captured at Bull Run and reserved them for the same fate that should be meted out to the imprisoned privateers. Then the prisoners taken on both sides soon numbered among the thousands, and something had to be done.

At length the Federal authorities, after trying several devices to escape it, were compelled to open negotiations with the Confederate Government, and a plan of exchange was arranged. It is interesting to note the scale of equivalents that was agreed upon in this plan. When there was no officer of equal rank to be exchanged for a captive officer it was arranged that sixty privates or common seamen were to be given for a general in chief or an admiral; forty for a flag officer or major general; twenty for a commodore, carrying a broad pennant, or a brigadier general; fifteen for a captain of the navy or a colonel; ten for a lieutenant colonel or a commander in the navy; eight for a lieutenant commander or a major; six for a lieutenant or a master in the navy, or a captain in the army or marines; four for master mates in the navy or lieutenants and ensigns in the army; three for midshipmen and warrant officers in the navy, masters of merchant vessels and commanders of privateers; two for second captains, lieutenants, or mates of merchant vessels or privateers, and all petty officers in the navy, and all non-commissioned officers in the army or marines. Privates and common seamen were exchanged for each other, man for man.

This plan had been in operation but a short time, however, when Jefferson Davis, by his anger at the employment of colored troops in the Federal Army, interrupted it in January, 1863. On the 12th of that month he issued a proclamation ordering the delivery of all officers of the Federal Army, commanding negro soldiers, that might be captured after that date, to the respective State authorities, to be hanged, and directing that those soldiers be treated as rebels against their masters. Davis then instructed the Confederate Commissioner of Exchange to refuse to consider captive colored troops as prisoners of war. When, in August, 1863, the Federal Commissioner demanded the revoking of these instructions, the Confederate Commissioner wrote: "We will die in the last ditch before giving up the right to send slaves back into slavery."

Recognizing the just claim of its negro defenders to an equal right of exchange with other Federal soldiers, the National Government caused a cessation of the exchange of prisoners until the colored troops should be treated simply as prisoners of war. The result of this action was a large increase in the number and sufferings of the Union prisoners confined at Richmond, Salisbury, Charleston, Millen and Andersonville.

Stories of cruelty toward these prisoners soon became current, and before long it seemed as if Davis's purpose was to so obstruct exchanges that the Federal prisoners, by long and acute suffering, would be rendered unfit for active service against him. To investigate these stories of cruelty a committee was appointed by the United States Sanitary Commission, with Dr. Valentine Mott as chairman. After several weeks' investigation this committee rendered a report in which it said: "It is the same story everywhere; prisoners of war treated worse than convicts; shut up either in suffocating buildings or in outdoor inclosures without even the shelter that is provided for the beasts of the field; unsupplied with sufficient food; supplied with food and water injurious and even poisonous; compelled to live on floors often covered with human filth, or on ground satu

rated with it; compelled to breathe an air oppressed with an intolerable stench; hemmed in by a fatal dead line, and in hourly danger of being shot by unrestrained and brutal guards; despondent even to madness, idiocy and suicide; sick, of disease (so congruous in character as to appear and spread like the plague) caused by the torrid sun, by decaying food, by filth, by vermin, by malaria and by cold; removed at the last moment, and by hundreds at a time, to hospitals corrupt as a sepulchre, there, with a few remedies, little care and no sympathy, to die in wretchedness and despair, not only among strangers, but among enemies too resentful either to have pity or to show mercy. These are positive facts. Tens of thousands of helpless men have been, and are now being, disabled and destroyed by a process as certain as poison, and as cruel as the torture or burning at the stake, because nearly as agonizing and more prolonged. This spectacle is daily beheld and allowed by the Rebel Government. No supposition of negligence, or indifference, or accident, or inefficiency, or destitution, or necessity, can account for all this. So many and such positive forms of abuse and wrong cannot come from negative causes. The conclusion is unavoidable, therefore, that these privations and sufferings have been designedly inflicted by the military and other authorities of the Rebel Government, and cannot have been due to causes which such authorities could not control."

The man in charge of the prisoners at Richmond for some time, and who was responsible for much of the cruelty there, was Brigadier General John H. Winder, who was among the leaders of the mob that attacked the Massachusetts troops in Baltimore. His reputation for inhuman treatment of prisoners was so great, that when he was transferred to the prison at

Andersonville, in Georgia, the Richmond *Examiner* exclaimed: "Thank God, Richmond has at last got rid of old Winder! God have mercy upon those to whom he has been sent!"

The Confederates themselves furnished testimony corroborative of statements made by the prisoners. In a report made in September, 1862, by Augustus R. Wright, chairman of a committee of the Confederate House of Representatives upon the prisons at Richmond in which Union soldiers were confined, he said that the state of things was "terrible beyond description"; that "the committee could not stay in the room over a few seconds"; and that "the committee makes the report to the Secretary of War, and not to the House, because in the latter case it would be printed, and, for the honor of the nation, such things must be kept secret"!

When a committee of the United States Christian Commission appeared before the lines of Lee's army and asked permission to be allowed to visit the Union prisoners at Richmond and on Belle Isle for the purpose of affording them relief, with the understanding that similar committees on like missions would be granted the same privileges in Federal prisons, it was refused, because, as Confederate witnesses testified, the authorities at Richmond did not dare face an exposure of their methods.

During the cessation of the exchange of prisoners nearly 40,000 Union soldiers went through the starving process and were reduced to mere skeletons, so that they had hardly strength enough to walk. Having got them to this pass the Confederate authorities made a proposition for the resumption of exchanges. For the sake of humanity the National Government agreed to it, and the poor fellows in Confederate prisons were liberated. It could hardly be called a fair exchange that took

SEACOAST OPERATIONS AGAINST CHARLESTON—BRILLIANT DASH AND CAPTURE OF CONFEDERATE RIFLE PITS AND PRISONERS BY THE FEDERAL TROOPS ON JAMES ISLAND, S. C., FEBRUARY 9TH, 1865.

place then, for the soldiers confined at the North were well fed, and otherwise comfortably provided for. This was recognized by the Confederate Commissioner of Exchange, who, in a letter to General Winder, from City Point, when exchanges had been resumed, said : "The arrangement I have made works largely in our favor. We get rid of a set of miserable wretches, and receive some of the best material I ever saw."

If his own statements are to be believed General Lee was not one of the Confederate authorities who knew of the existence of a plan to starve the Union prisoners. In February, 1866, he testified before the National "Committee on Reconstruction" that he knew nothing of the alleged cruelties about which complaints had been made ; that no reports about them had ever been submitted to him ; and that he

who, by their selfish and sordid methods, brought the war upon the country. Had the people of the South been allowed to have a voice in the councils of the seceding States it is not unlikely that there never would have been a civil war, with its terrible loss of life and destruction of property. They would probably have found some other means more humane than war for settling the differences that arose between the two sections of the country.

CHAPTER XXXI.

Reorganization—President Johnson and Congress— The Reconstruction Committee—Slavery Abolished by Congress—Amendments to the Constitution—Return of the Seceded States to the Union —Conclusion.

It was a long time before the country recovered from the effects of the war that had been thrust upon it. So many differ-

sink into insignificance." Although such and even more severe language was used by the President when speaking of the leading Confederates, he soon showed by his actions that he not only did not mean to do what he said he would, but was in warm sympathy with the friends of the late Confederacy. In every way he could he seemed to try to retard Congress in its efforts at reorganizatition of the Union. He also seemed to do all he could to thwart any measures looking to the betterment of the condition of the people just made free by the proclamation of emancipation and by act of Congress. With the idea of deceiving the people as to his real purpose in regard to the colored race, he proposed to the Governor of Mississippi to give the franchise to such of the freedmen as could read the Constitution and possessed property worth $250, well knowing that the

BATTLE NEAR KINSTON, N. C., MARCH 8TH, 1865.

did not even know at the time who was in command at Andersonville, Salisbury and other places where Union soldiers were confined.

But whoever knew of these cruelties to Union soldiers, or whoever was responsible for them, it is only just to say that the great body of Southern people were entirely ignorant of them and in no way responsible for their existence. Had they known of the terrible suffering that was going on in their prisons they would have been just as indignant as were the people of the North, and if they had the power to do so would have corrected the abuses at once. The great majority of the people in the Southern States were, as they are now, kindhearted, loving, humane, hospitable, and would never for a moment have tolerated such a state of things in their part of the country if they had known about it and could have helped it. They were purposely kept in ignorance by the scheming politicians who were responsible for it, and

ences of opinion were entertained as to the best and most satisfactory methods of bringing about a thorough reorganization and reconstruction that it took several years to gather the different parts of the Union into one united nation again. The country was unfortunate in having at this time a weak President, and one who did not hesitate to usurp the powers of Congress whenever he could by so doing carry out his own ideas and further his own interests. For a long time there was a war between the Executive and Legislative branches of the government.

President Johnson had declared in his inaugural address his intention to punish the leading enemies of the government, and to a delegation from New Hampshire who waited upon him soon after his inauguration he said : "Treason is a crime, and must be punished as a crime. It must not be regarded as a mere difference of opinion. It must not be excused as an unsuccessful rebellion, to be overlooked and forgiven. It is a crime before which all other crimes

laws of Mississippi made it a punishable offense to teach a colored person to read, and that in the condition of slavery not one could hold property.

The first step toward the reorganization of the Union was taken by President Johnson in proclaiming the removal of restrictions upon commercial intercourse between the States, which he did on April 29th, 1865. Soon afterward the President appointed provisional governors for seven of those States which had formed the original Confederate States of America. He gave them authority to call conventions of the citizens, who would have power to reorganize State governments and elect representatives to Congress. These conventions met and acted according to the President's instructions ; but when Congress assembled, on December 4th, it virtually condemned the President's action, as a usurpation of power, by passing a joint resolution to appoint a joint committee to be composed of nine members of the House of Representatives and six of the Senate, to "inquire into the condition of the States which formed the so-called Confederate States of America, and report whether they, or any of them, are entitled to be represented in either House of Congress, with leave to report at any time, by bill or otherwise; and until such report shall have been made and finally acted upon by Congress no member shall be received in either House from any of the so-called Confederate States; and all papers relating to the representatives of the said States shall be referred

United States, or any place subject to their jurisdiction.

"Section 2. Congress shall have power to enforce this article by appropriate legislation."

After the appointment of the "Reconstruction Committee" Congress proceeded to the consideration of bills tending to the full and permanent restoration of the Union on a basis of equal and exact justice. In February, 1866, it passed an act for enlarging the operations of the Freedman's Bureau, which had been established for the

Still another bill of a similar kind, in which the elective franchise was granted to the people of the District of Columbia "without any distinction on account of color or race," had to be re-enacted over the President's veto, in January, 1867.

Despite the interference of President Johnson by vetoes and otherwise the work of reorganizing the Union was steadily pushed at different sessions of Congress. On June 13th, 1866, another amendment to the Constitution was adopted, and it was ratified by a sufficient number of States to

PRESIDENT LINCOLN RIDING THROUGH RICHMOND, VA., APRIL 4TH, 1865, AMID THE ENTHUSIASTIC CHEERS OF
THE INHABITANTS.

to the said committee." This body was known as the "Reconstruction Committee."

At this time (December, 1865,) the slavery amendment to the Constitution, which had been adopted at the previous session of Congress, early in the year, became part of the law of the land, by the ratification of the several State Legislatures. This amendment, the XIIIth, reads as follows:

"Section 1. Neither slavery nor involuntary servitude, except as a punishment for crime, whereof the party shall have been **duly convicted**, shall exist within the

relief of emancipated slaves and poor white men who had been rendered destitute by the war. This act was vetoed by President Johnson, who, although he had announced himself as a "Moses to lead the colored people to freedom," showed by various actions that he was not willing to give them any civil rights. The bill, however, was promptly passed over his veto. In March he vetoed without effect another law in behalf of the negro. This was the Civil Rights Law, which gave to *all* citizens, without regard to color or previous condition of slavery, equal civil rights in the republic.

make it a law in July, 1868. By this amendment "all persons born or naturalized in the United States, and subject to the jurisdiction thereof," were given the rights of citizenship; the privilege of being a Senator or Representative in Congress, or Elector of President and Vice President, or of holding any office, civil or military, under the United States, or under any State, was denied to everyone who had taken part in the war against the government after having, as member of Congress, or any State Legislature, or as an executive or judicial officer of any State, sworn to support the Constitution of the United States; the National debt was declared valid, and the payment of debts incurred in aid of the Confederacy was forbidden, and the obligations declared illegal and void.

Just before this amendment was formally adopted President Johnson, in order to forestall a portion of it, issued a proclamation, July 4th, 1868, declaring general and unconditional pardon and amnesty for all who had been engaged in acts of rebellion,

December, 1868. After several weeks' debate the following, as a Fifteenth Amendment, was adopted, February 26th, 1869:

"Section 1. The right of citizens of the United States to vote shall not be denied or abridged by the United States, or by any State, on account of race, color, or previous condition of servitude.

"Section 2. Congress shall have power to enforce this article by appropriate legislation."

and Texas, were allowed places, through Senators and Representatives, in the National Congress. There were three States still out of the Union, and they remained so until the year 1872. On May 22d of that year Congress passed an Amnesty Bill, in which it was resolved that the denial of the privilege of holding office imposed by the third section of the Fourteenth Amendment of the Constitution be removed from all persons excepting mem-

THE GRAND REVIEW AT WASHINGTON, D. C., MAY 24TH, 1865—PRESIDENT JOHNSON, LIEUTENANT GENERAL GRANT AND OTHERS INSPECTING SHERMAN'S ARMY—SHERMAN SALUTING AT THE HEAD OF HIS STAFF.

excepting a few who were under presentment or indictment for the offense. Then on Christmas Day of the same year he followed that proclamation by another, in which he granted, in direct defiance of the Fourteenth Amendment, unconditional and unreserved pardon to all and every person who had participated in the late rebellion.

Another amendment to the Constitution, one securing the enfranchisement of the freedman, was proposed in Congress, in

This amendment, being ratified by the Legislatures of the requisite number of States, became a part of the Constitution.

Having approved of the amendments by ratification, and having adopted State Constitutions approved by Congress, elected National Senators and Representatives, and complied with other requirements of Congress, seven of the late Confederate States, namely, North Carolina, South Carolina, Georgia, Alabama, Mississippi, Louisiana

bers of the Thirty-sixth Congress, heads of departments, members of diplomatic corps and officers of the army and navy who had given their services to the Confederacy. The day after this bill was passed the three remaining States were taken back into the Union. The reorganization of the country was now complete. All the seceded States had returned to their allegiance, and the United States again became one great nation.   THE END.